MODERN IRAQI ARABIC WITH MP3 FILES

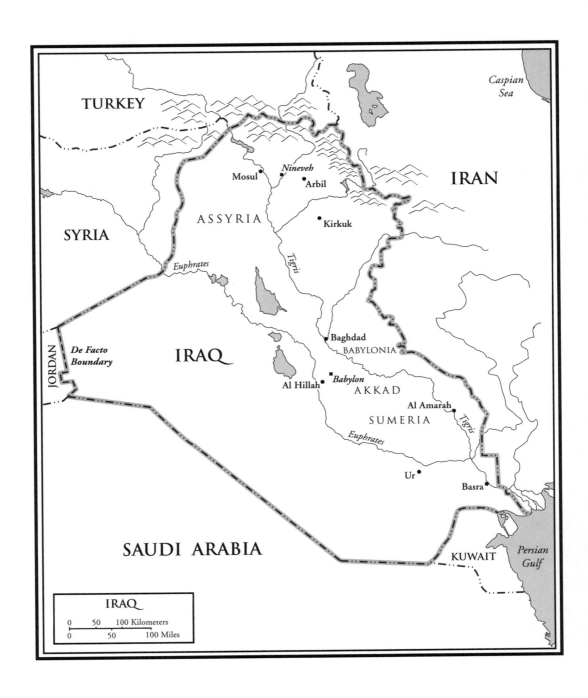

TURKEY

SYRIA

IRAQ

De Facto Boundary

JORDAN

SAUDI ARABIA

ASSYRIA

Mosul

Nineveh

Arbil

Kirkuk

Euphrates

Tigris

Baghdad

BABYLONIA

Al Hillah

Babylon

AKKAD

SUMERIA

Al Amarah

Euphrates

Tigris

Ur

Basra

KUWAIT

IRAN

Caspian Sea

Persian Gulf

IRAQ

0   50   100 Kilometers

0   50   100 Miles

Modern Iraqi Arabic
with MP3 Files

A Textbook

Second Edition

Yasin M. Alkalesi

GEORGETOWN UNIVERSITY PRESS
WASHINGTON, D.C.

to the PEOPLE *of* IRAQ
and to the memory of my FATHER

As of January 1, 2007, 13-digit ISBN numbers will replace the current
10-digit system.

Paperback: 978-1-58901-130-4

Georgetown University Press, Washington, D.C.

Al-Khalesi, Yasin M.
   Modern Iraqi Arabic with MP3 files / 2d edition / Yasin M. Alkalesi.
     p.   cm.
  ISBN 1-58901-130-9 (alk. paper)
  1. Arabic language—Dialects—Iraq—Grammar.   2. Arabic language—
Textbooks for foreign speakers—English.   I. Title.
  PJ6823.A42   2006
  492.709567—dc22   2006043984

13 12 11 10 09 08 07 06   9 8 7 6 5 4 3 2

First printing

Printed in the United States of America

CONTENTS

PREFACE

Since the publication of a series of valuable books on Iraqi Arabic by Georgetown University's School of Language and Linguistics more than three decades ago, very little has been written on the spoken Arabic of Iraq. Iraqi Arabic constitutes an extremely important linguistic and socioeconomic region of the Arab world. Hence, there is an urgent need for publications on this dialect that are more current and easy to read, such as the one I present here. The urgency of such works has increased tenfold because of the current political and economic events in Iraq.

This book sums up more than thirty years of experience in teaching Arabic at Yale University; University of California, Los Angeles; California State University, Fullerton; and at the Berlitz Language Centers, and in teaching business people working with Arab countries. During those years, I have been fortunate to have the opportunity of sharing with my students, colleagues, and laymen the knowledge and beauty of Arabic.

This book is designed for people who have no previous knowledge of Arabic or who have already studied Arabic but wish to learn the Iraqi dialect. It is organized in a method suitable for either classroom use or self-study with the help of the audio. The dialect that is offered in the book is spoken by the average, middle-class Baghdadi. The first edition of the book consisted of sixteen lessons, then four more lessons and Arabic script were added to this second edition. The lessons are based on everyday situation and arranged in a story-like format that follows a woman's activities as she travels from the United States of America to Iraq.

ACKNOWLEDGMENTS

My thanks go first to several hundred students over the years, whose curiosity, enthusiasm, and dedication to learning Arabic were a great motivation in writing this book. Special thanks go to my student John Spillman Jones for reading the first draft of the text and this revised edition. My deep appreciation goes to Professor Robert Biggs of the Oriental Institute at the University of Chicago for his valuable comments. Special thanks and gratitude are owed to Dr. Kristen Brustad of the University of Texas, Austin, for reading the manuscript and for her insightful suggestions. I am indeed grateful to my friend Thamir Aladhami (London) and delighted that he thoroughly read the manuscript and made important corrections. To Laila Darwish (Frankfurt) who made the drawings for the book, I am indebted and thankful.

For this revised edition I owe special thanks to Michael Cooperson, Professor of Arabic at the University of California, Los Angeles, for his great effort in reading this text and for his helpful comments. To Dr. Richard Brown, director, and Gail Grella, associate director, and to the entire staff of Georgetown University Press, I would like to express my appreciation for their help and enthusiasm.

INTRODUCTION

The Arabic language is characterized by the so-called "diglossia." This means the existence of two forms of the language, classical and colloquial, side-by-side with varying levels of differences. Several European and non-European languages share such characteristics.

Classical Arabic, the language of reading and writing, is also called "literary," "written," "formal," and "Modern Standard Arabic" (MSA). It is the same language in all Arab countries. It is used in formal situations: newspapers, magazines, books, schools and universities, radio and TV, conference discussions, lectures, and in most written materials. Arabs have to go to school to learn the MSA form, and, therefore, not every Arab can read and write.

Colloquial Arabic, on the other hand, is the spoken language of everyday activities at home, at work, on the street, and in social occasions. It varies not only from one Arab country to another but also within the same country depending on education, socioeconomic level, and religion. However, there is in each Arab country one standard and predominant colloquial vernacular based on the dialect spoken in the capital city or a major commercial city.

The differences between MSA and colloquial Arabic are basically phonological and morphological, whereas the differences between the dialects are in pronunciation, everyday expressions, and idiomatic phrases. The problem of the Arabic "diglossia" has always raised the question of which forms of Arabic—modern standard, colloquial, or which dialect of the colloquial—is to be learned or to be taught by educational institutions. It is not an easy choice, but there are criteria and ways that help the learner of Arabic to make that choice. We advise the beginning student and traveler to concentrate on studying and stick with a single form or dialect until it is learned fairly well. The learner will then be able to use that knowledge of Arabic in adapting himself or herself (tongue and ears) to another dialect. It is safe to state here that an average person with firm control of one dialect should be able to communicate with another person who speaks a different dialect. The communication level would be the same between a person speaking American English and another speaking British English.

There are three major geographical groups of dialects in modern Iraq that can be identified in general terms as northern, southern, and central. The northern dialect is centered around the city of Mosul (the largest city in the north), and the southern dialect is centered around the city of Basra (the largest city in the south). The central dialect is spoken in the capital city of Baghdad and its surroundings.

Although this book is titled *Modern Iraqi Arabic,* the text presented is the dialect spoken by Iraqis who live in Baghdad. Baghdad, as a great capital and metropolitan center, offers a dialect that is the most widely used and understood throughout Iraq. The modern Iraqi Arabic introduced in this book is spoken by an average, middle-class Baghdadi.

This text is written to serve the communication needs of students, travelers, and business people whose objective is to speak rather than read or write the language. To achieve that objective, a transliteration system of phonetic writing is used to express the sounds of Iraqi Arabic. The selection of the transcription symbols is based on the system used in the *Encyclopedia of Islam*, p. 7, by C. Glasse. The learner should master these transcriptions before proceeding to learn the structure of the language.

In this revised edition Arabic script has been added, so those who can read and write Arabic may be able to learn the dialect of Iraq without abandoning the Arabic writing. Those who are familiar with the writing convention of Modern Standard Arabic will notice certain modifications to the script made for the purpose of expressing certain sounds or combinations of sounds that are found only in colloquial Arabic.

Lesson 1 offers the reader a detailed discussion of consonants, vowels, and other characteristics of Iraqi phonetics, including a comprehensive list of pronunciation exercises on the audio. Make sure to listen to the audio frequently and practice by repeating the sounds.

The text is designed for people who have no previous knowledge of Arabic as well as those who have already studied some Arabic but wish to learn the Iraqi dialect. It is organized in a method suitable either for use in the classroom or for self-study with the help of the audio. The best way to learn a spoken language is to hear it spoken and to practice speaking it. The essential factors of learning spoken Arabic are repetition, mechanical exercises, and memorization, in addition to practicing with a partner.

This book contains twenty lessons based on everyday situations. The lessons are arranged in a story-like format that follows a woman named Basma traveling from the United States to Iraq and her activities within the country. Beginning with lesson 2, each lesson is divided into the following main parts:
- Basic Dialogue
- Vocabulary
- Additional Expressions (as needed)
- Grammar and Remarks
- Idioms and Common Phrases
- Drills
- Creative Dialogues

Basic Dialogue

The basic dialogue is preceded by a very brief description explaining the lesson subject matter, which always involves a female (Basma), a male, and sometimes more people. The basic dialogue is a conversation module usually between two people (male and female) about day-to-day matters. The dialogue is designed to be simple and practical, introducing the subject matter of the lesson and its grammatical structure. The student should memorize the vocabulary and the expressions in the dialogue. The same or similar sentences and expressions will recur in subsequent dialogues and drills to reinforce the learning process.

Vocabulary

This section contains the new words that occur in the lesson listed in the order in which they appear in the basic dialogue. Some vocabulary items may be listed in more than one lesson because of their importance to the learning reinforcement process. In addition to the meaning of the vocabulary, other forms of the words (with variation based on gender, number, and types of verb stems) are also included with a cultural explanation whenever it is appropriate. Cross-references are also made to the relevant discussions or expressions.

Additional Expressions

This is a list of additional vocabulary or expressions related to the subject of the lesson. Most of the vocabulary items will recur in subsequent drills and lessons.

Grammar and Remarks

The explanations of new grammatical structures are given in a simple and systematic way. The structure points are always illustrated with examples from the present lesson or the previous ones. The student needs only to grasp the basic knowledge of the structure. His or her effort will more wisely be spent on memorizing new vocabulary and drill examples. An attempt has been made to include no more than two main grammatical structures in each lesson.

Idioms and Common Phrases

Arabic is rich in idiomatic phrases, proverbs, sayings, and religious and cultural expressions. They constitute an important element of everyday spoken Arabic. There are two to three idioms in each lesson with cultural explanations and relevant drills. These idiomatic phrases and their drills will recur in later lessons. The learner should memorize the idioms and their drills, thus enriching his or her communication skills.

Drills

The purpose of the drills is to help the student develop a facility for recombining the vocabulary items he learned in the dialogue as well as to reinforce the grammatical structures of each lesson. All the drills, with the exception of the translation, are in Arabic in order to make the student use Arabic more often and to learn to think in the language. The most frequently used drills are replying, substitution, transformation, changing, repeating, translation, and formation of sentences with certain wordings. Most of the drill compositions are taken with little changes from the basic dialogues or the grammar sections. There are also many more formed by combining new and previous vocabulary items.

Creative Dialogues

These are open-ended creative activities that students can do with a partner. The objectives are to invite learners to be creative within a given lesson, to introduce new vocabulary, new sentences, and to enforce oral memorization.

Glossary

Much effort and attention have been given to this list of Arabic–English and English–Arabic vocabulary and other items that occur in this book in order to help the user maximize its use and obtain good results. For more information on the arrangement and the use of the glossary, please refer to the glossary.

Audio

The audio material included with the book is closely integrated with the text. The student should use the audio together with the book in order to get full use of them. It is also important to the process of learning to read the relevant explanations that accompany each segment on the audio. The recorded segments are designated as "Audio" or "Examples, Audio." Each word, idiom, and sentence is recorded twice. The student is asked to repeat each time in a loud voice. However, the student should play the audio as many times as he or she feels necessary to memorize the sentences and their meanings. A person learning on his or her own can conduct a recording test to see if the pronunciation is correct by comparing it with the audio.

adj.	adjective
adv.	adverb
col.	collective
D	dual
DV	double verb
F	feminine
FP	feminine plural
HV	hollow verb
imp.	imperative
lit.	literally
M	masculine
MP	masculine plural
MS	masculine singular
N	noun
P	plural
part.	participle
prep.	preposition
RV	regular verb
S	singular
V	verb
WV	weak verb
>	derived from

Iraqi popular handicrafts

Arabic Alphabet and Vowels
الألــفباء وحُروف الـكُعِلّة العربية

The Iraqi Alphabet   الألــفــباء العِراقية

Iraqi Arabic has thirty-one consonant sounds. About fifteen of them have equivalent sounds in English. The other sounds will require more attention and practice by students from the beginning. Students of Arabic in general must keep in mind that their ability to communicate with Iraqis will depend entirely on the ability to produce those sounds or to write them.

The best way to learn any foreign language is to hear it spoken by a native and imitate it as closely as possible. It is important for the student to imitate very closely the pronunciation of his/her instructor, or the audio when a native speaker is not available. Since this book is designed to teach students how to speak Iraqi Arabic, the transcription system is used in addition to the Arabic script. The following list of Iraqi Arabic alphabet sounds and their equivalents in English, and in some cases other languages, are approximate. The emphasis should, therefore, be on imitating the pronunciation of the instructor and the audio.

The Iraqi Alphabet (Audio)

Script	Name	Transcription	Example	Equivalent
ء	hamza	ᵓ	laᵓlaᵓ	uh-oh! (a glottal stop sound)
ب	bee	b	beet	boy
پ	pa	p	parda	pencil (used only in borrowed words)
ت	tee	t	tiin	take
ث	thee	th	thalij	third

The Iraqi Alphabet (continued)

Script	Name	Transcription	Example	Equivalent
ج	jiim	j	jaab	job
چ	cha	ch	cham	chair
ح	hee	h	haal	/ (strongly whispered deep in the throat, similar to the sound produced by someone who has just burned his mouth on hot coffee)
خ	khee	kh	khaaf	auch (German)
د	daal	d	dall	dip
ذ	dhaal	dh	dhill	this
ر	ree	r	naar	hurry (approx.)
ز	zee	z	zeet	zinc
س	siin	s	samm	sit
ش	shiin	sh	shaal	ship
ص	saad	s	saff	/ (emphatic "s," similar to the "s" in "sum" with the central part of tongue depressed and the back part slightly raised)
ض	daad	d	daaf	/ (this sound is not produced in Iraqi Arabic; the sound z ظ is used instead, see below)
ط	ta	t	batt	/ (sound is made with the front part of the tongue touching the upper palate behind the teeth)
ظ	za	z	zill	/ (sound is produced with the tip of the tongue slightly touching the back of the teeth)
ع	9een	9	9aali	/ (almost silent "ah," pronounced deep in the back of the throat)
غ	gheen	gh	ghaali	Parisian (French) (similar to the sound of gargling and as deep)
گ	ga	g	gaal	go
ف	fee	f	fariid	fit
ق	qaaf	q	qaas	/ (like the "c" in "cool" but made further back in the throat)
ك	kaaf	k	kilma	kitchen
ل	laam	l	leela	like
ل	laam	l	walla	bell (emphatic "l" appears mostly with certain emphatic consonants or words that invoke the name of "alla, God")

The Iraqi Alphabet *(continued)*

Script	Name	Transcription	Example	Equivalent
م	miim	m	maal	mother
ن	nuun	n	nahar	never
هـ	hee	h	hilaal	hot
و	waa	w	walad	well
ي	yee	y	yoom	yet

Notes on the Iraqi Arabic Consonants

1. The **hamza** هَـمْزة (ʾ), glottal stop, is a consonant and as such it appears in the beginning (initial), middle (medial), or end (final) of the word. However, in this textbook, the **hamza** is not rendered in the initial position. This is done for two reasons: to make the transcription writing system more practical, and also because English words beginning with vowels are pronounced with glottal stop, although it is not written. In Arabic, there is no word that begins with a vowel. The reader, therefore, must always assume that there is a **hamza** with every initial vowel. Words with initial vowels are listed under the heading (ʾ) in the glossary.

2. The consonant "**p**, پ" is a sound particular to Iraqi Arabic. It seems to occur mostly in loanwords "**soopa, poskaart**" (*heating stove* and *post card*, respectively).

3. The consonants "**ch**, چ" and "**k**, ك": The sound "**ch**" is a nonclassical–Arabic consonant. In many examples this sound replaces the sound "**k**" as in **chibiir** for **kabiir** (*big*), and **chalib** for **kalb** (*dog*). See these two headings in the glossary.

4. The consonants "**g**, گ" and "**q**, ق": The classical sound "**q**" is often used in Iraqi Arabic, although it is usually replaced by the sound "**g**," such as **giriib** for **qariib** (*close*), and **gaal** for **qaal** (*to say*). The "**g**" also occurs in some loanwords as **geemar** (*cream*) and **glaas** (*glass*).

5. The consonants "**d̲**, ض" and "**z̲**, ظ": The classical sound "**d̲**" has almost completely disappeared and has fallen together with the sound "**z̲**" in Iraqi Arabic, **abyaz̲** for **abyad̲** (*white*), and **khazz** for **khadd** (*to shake*). However, we have retained the consonant "**d̲**" in the book for practical reasons connected with the Arabic script.

6. The emphatic "**l̲**, ل": This sound is limited in number and use mainly in the words that invoke the name of God, "**al̲l̲a**." It also occurs in examples that contain some neighboring emphatic consonants such as **t̲**, **s̲**, and **z̲**, (**s̲ul̲t̲aan, t̲al̲l̲, z̲al̲l̲**) (see exercise 12).

The Iraqi Vowels ﺣُـﺮﻭﻑ الْـعِـلَّـة الْـعِـراقـيـة

Arabic vowels are of two types, long and short. The Iraqi dialect has five long vowels "**aa**," "**ee**," "**ii**," "**oo**," and "**uu**," and four short vowels "**a**," "**i**," "**o**," and "**u**." In the examples given below the English equivalents are only approximate.

The long vowels are simply the lengthened counterpart of the short vowels. For example, the long vowel "**aa**" is pronounced as in the word "had" and not as in the word "bat." In other words, the vowel "**aa**" is longer in duration than the vowel "**a**."

The pronunciation length of the Arabic vowels is very important because there are many words of quite different meanings that are distinguished only by the length of their vowels, as in the words **9alam** (*flag*) and **9aalam** (*world*); **shimal** (*to include*) and **shimaal** (*north*) (see exercise 14). Another difference between the two types in Arabic script is that the long vowels are written within the body of the script, whereas the short vowels appear as symbols above or below the consonants (see below).

1. The Long Vowels (Audio)

	Vowel	Equivalent	Example		
ا	aa	ham	naam	(*to sleep*)	نـام
ي	ee	bait	beet	(*house*)	بـيـت
ي	ii	beet	jiib	(*bring*)	جـيـب
و	oo	dog	zooj	(*husband*)	زوج
و	uu	root	kuub	(*cup*)	كـوب

2. The Short Vowels (Audio)

	Vowel	Equivalent	Example		
ـَ	a	bet	jamal	(*camel*)	جَـمَـل
ـِ	i	hit	sinn	(*tooth*)	سِـن
ـُ	u	put	kunt	(*I was*)	كُـنت
و	o	radio	raadyo	(*radio*)	راديو

Notes on the Vowels

1. The sound quality of the short vowels are affected by the surrounding emphatic consonants such as "**s**," "**t**," "**z**," and "**l**" (see exercises 1, 3, 4, 6, 8, and 12). They have more sound variations than those of the long vowels, depending on the surrounding consonants and their position in the word. They also have less sonority than the long vowels.

2. The short vowel "**a**" has a range of sound qualities depending on the surrounding consonants (whether emphatic or simple). For example, in the middle of the word it may have the sound "**e**" as in "get," "**a**" as in "car," or "**u**" as in "but." However, its precise quality rarely affects the meaning of the word.

3. The vowels "**i**" and "**u**" at the end of the word have a sound like that of their long vowel counterparts "**ii**" and "**uu**" as in **shuufi** (*look*, F) and **shuufu** (*look*, P). Thus, in Arabic script the final vowels "**i**" and "**u**" are written with their long vowel counterparts "**ii**, ي" and "**uu**, و."

4. The vowel "**o**" sounds like the long vowel "**oo**" but shorter. The vowel seems to appear mostly in loanwords at the end of the words, as in **raadyo, byaano,** and **maayo** (*radio,*

piano, and *bathing suit*, respectively). But it also occurs in the medial position as in **paasbort** and **poskaart** (*passport* and *postcard*, respectively). Although "o" is a short vowel it is traditionally written with "و" in Arabic script (MSA), since it appears mostly in the end of loanwords, such as "**maayo** مايو."

5. The long vowels "**ee**" and "**oo**" are, in most cases, regarded as reflexes of the classical Arabic diphthongs "**ay**" and "**aw**" as in **zooj** for **zawj** (*husband*) and **heel** for **hayl** (*strength*). They appear also in loanwords: **sooda** (*soda*), **maatoor** (*motor*), **meez** (*table*), and **heel** (*cardamom*). The long vowel "**oo**" occurs in some types of the weak verb as in **yoogaf** (*to stand*) and **yoosal** (*to arrive*).

6. The two vowels "**ee**" and "**ii**" are both expressed in Arabic script by the vowel "ي." Similarly, the two vowels "**uu**" and "**oo**" are written with the vowel "و." This is because the "**ee**" and "**oo**" are vowels peculiar to the colloquial Arabic only. To differentiate between sounds of "**ee**" and "**ii**," and sounds "**uu**" and "**oo**," readers are advised to consult the phonetic transcription.

Phonetics of Iraqi Arabic: Pronunciation Exercises (Audio)

أصْوات الـلَـهْجَـة الـعِـراقية: تَـمارين صَـوْتِـيَّـة

The following are a comprehensive list of exercises intended to cover certain sounds of Iraqi Arabic, especially those sounds that are new for nonnative speakers of Arabic. The words in the exercises are arranged in pairs based on the similarity of sounds with the exception of one different sound, either a consonant or a vowel. But notice the different meanings of those otherwise close sounds. The reader needs only to notice the different meanings of the horizontally paired words without memorizing them. The exercises are for the reader to practice aloud with the help of the audio. The instructor may find it useful to go over them in the classroom in repetition technique, especially using the new sounds.

On the audio we shall read horizontally each word of these exercises twice. Please repeat after the voice.

1. Contrast between h ﻫ and ḥ ح:

hamal	هـمـل	*to neglect*	ḥamal	حـمـل	*to carry*
hajar	هـجـر	*to abandon*	ḥajar	حـجـر	*stone*
halhal	هـلـهـل	*to rejoice*	ḥalḥal	حـلـحـل	*to loosen*
habb	هـبّ	*to blow*	ḥabb	حـبّ	*to like*
hanna	هَـنّـه	*to congratulate*	ḥanna	حَـنّـه	*to dye with henna*
nahar	نهـر	*river*	naḥar	نـحـر	*to slaughter*
laham	لهـم	*to swallow up*	laḥam	لحـم	*meat*
haram	هرم	*pyramid*	ḥaram	حرم	*forbidden*
shabah	شـبـه	*resemblance*	shabaḥ	شـبـح	*ghost*
hoosh	هوش	*cattle*	ḥoosh	حوش	*house*

2. Contrast between kh خ and gh غ:

khaali	خالي	*empty*	ghaali	غالي	*expensive*
khaab	خاب	*to fail*	ghaab	غاب	*absent*
kheema	خيمة	*tent*	gheema	غيمة	*cloud*
kheer	خير	*goodness*	gheer	غير	*other*
khalat	خلط	*to mix*	ghalat	غلط	*wrong*
khilaaf	خلاف	*difference*	ghilaaf	غلاف	*cover*
shakhar	شخر	*to snore*	shaghar	شغر	*to be vacant*

3. Contrast between s س and s ص:

saad	سـاد	*to dominate*	saad	صاد	*to hunt*
saar	سـار	*to walk*	saar	صار	*to become*
saam	سـام	*poisonous*	saam	صام	*to fast*
sabb	سبّ	*to curse*	sabb	صبّ	*to pour*
khass	خسّ	*lettuce*	khass	خصّ	*to specify*
seef	سـيف	*sword*	seef	صيف	*summer*
nasiib	نسـيب	*relative-in-law*	nasiib	نصيب	*lot*
si9ad	سـعد	*to be happy*	si9ad	صعد	*to go up*

4. Contrast between t ت and t ط:

batt	بتّ	*to decide*	batt	بطّ	*geese*
tall	تلّ	*hill*	tall	طلّ	*to look*
taab	تاب	*to repent*	taab	طاب	*to become good*
tiin	تين	*figs*	tiin	طين	*clay*
tuub	توب	*repent*	tuub	طوب	*bricks*
tamur	تمر	*palm dates*	tamur	طمر	*to cover with earth*
tooba	توبة	*repentance*	tooba	طوبة	*ball*
rutab	رتب	*ranks*	rutab	رطب	*fresh dates*
fatar	فتر	*to abate*	fatar	فطر	*to break fasting*

5. Contrast between ° ء and 9 ع:

sa°al	سـأل	*to ask*	sa9al	سعل	*to cough*
su°aal	سـؤال	*question*	su9aal	سـعال	*coughing*
la°la°	لألأ	*to shine*	la9la9	لعلع	*to roar*
naba°	نبأ	*news*	naba9	نبع	*to flow*
°amm	أم	*or*	9amm	عـمّ	*uncle*
baa°id	بائد	*perished*	baa9id	باعد	*to cause separation*
°imaara	إمارة	*emirate*	9imaara	عمارة	*multistory building*
°alam	ألم	*pain*	9alam	علم	*flag*
°ayyad	أيّد	*to support*	9ayyad	عيّد	*to celebrate*

maaʾ	ماء	water	maa9	ماع	to melt
shaaʾ	شاء	to want	shaa9	شاع	to spread
ʾaali	آلي	mechanical	9aali	عالي	high

6. Contrast between k ك and q ق:

kaas	كاس	cup	qaas	قاس	to measure
kaad	كاد	to work hard	qaad	قاد	to lead
kiis	كيس	bag	qiis	قيس	measure
shakk	شكّ	doubt	shaqq	شقّ	cut
salak	سلك	to follow	salaq	سلق	to cook in water
nakar	نكر	to deny	naqar	نقر	to dig
falak	فـلك	orbit	falaq	فـلق	to split
takriir	تكرير	repetition	taqriir	تقرير	report

7. Contrast between d د and d̲ ض:

9add	عـدّ	to count	9add̲	عض	to bite
khadd	خدّ	cheek	khad̲d̲	خض	to shake
darb	درب	road	d̲arb	ضرب	hitting
daar	دار	house	d̲aar	ضار	harmful
hadam	هدم	to destroy	had̲am	هضم	to digest
faad	فـاد	to benefit	faad̲	فاض	to overflow
marduud	مردود	rejected	mard̲uud	مرضوض	bruised
ridaaʾ	رداء	dress	rid̲aaʾ	رضاء	satisfaction

8. Contrast between dh ذ and z̲ ظ:

dhall	ذلّ	to humiliate	z̲all	ظلّ	to get lost
madhalla	مذلّة	humiliation	maz̲alla	مظلّة	umbrella
nadhar	نذر	to dedicate	naz̲ar	نظر	to see
ladhiidh	لذيذ	delicious	laz̲iiz̲	لظيظ	burning
afdhaadh	افذاذ	alone	afz̲aaz̲	افظاظ	rude
dhaliil	ذليل	lowly	z̲aliil	ظليل	shaded
mudhaakara	مذاكرة	memorizing	muz̲aahara	مظاهرة	demonstration

9. Contrast between gh غ and g گ:

ghuul	غول	demon	guul	گول	say
ghass	غصّ	to choke	gass	گصّ	to cut
ghashsh	غشّ	to cheat	gashsh	گشّ	to sweep
ghidar	غدر	to deceive	gidar	گـدر	to be able
yilghi	يلغي	to cancel	yilgi	يلگي	to find
daghdagh	دغدغ	to tickle	dagdag	دگدگ	to pound

gharram	غرّم	*to fine*	garram	گرّم	*to cripple*
ghisab	غصب	*to force*	gisab	گصب	*reeds*

10. Contrast between j ج and ch چ:

Jammal	جَمـّل	*make beautiful*	chammal	چَمـّل	*to add*
jaara	جارة	*neighbor*	chaara	چارة	*remedy*
jaarak	جارك	*your neighbor*	chaarak	چارك	*one-fourth*
jaal	جال	*to tour*	chaal	چال	*to measure*
juub	جوب	*travel*	chuub	چوب	*rubber tube*
jaay	جاي	*coming*	chaay	چاي	*tea*
jiis	جيس	*touch*	chiis	چيس	*bag*
fajj	فـجّ	*way*	fachch	فـچّ	*jaw*
rija	رجه	*to request*	richa	رچه	*to support*

11. Contrast between h ح and kh خ:

hoosh	حوش	*house*	khoosh	خوش	*good*
haal	حال	*condition*	khaal	خال	*uncle*
heel	حيل	*strength*	kheel	خيل	*horses*
hatt	حط	*to put*	khatt	خط	*line*
tahat	تحت	*under*	takhat	تخت	*bed*
hirza	حرزة	*amulet*	khirza	خرزة	*bead*
himad	حمد	*to thank*	khimad	خمد	*to subdue*
hall	حلّ	*solution*	khall	خلّ	*vinegar*
rahiim	رحيم	*kind*	rakhiim	رخيم	*soft (voice)*
saahir	ساحر	*magician*	saakhir	ساخر	*mocker*
buhuur	بحور	*seas*	bukhuur	بخور	*incense*

12. Contrast between l ل and l ل:

walla	ولّه	*to leave*	walla	والله	*by God*
galla	گـلّـه	*to tell*	galla	گـلّـه	*to fry*
balla	بـلّـه	*to make wet*	balla	بـلّـه	*by God*
illa	إلّا	*except*	alla	الله	*God*
khaali	خالي	*empty*	khaali	خالي	*my uncle*
dakhla	دخلة	*entering*	dakhla	دخلة	*wedding*
dakhal	دخل	*to enter*	dakhal	دخل	*income*
khalli	خلّـي	*leave*	khalli	خلّـي	*my vinegar*
			gilab	گـلب	*to turn over*
			galub	گـلب	*heart*
			inshaalla	إنشاالله	*God willing*

13. Contrast between single and double consonants:

9alam	علم	*flag*	9allam	علّم	*to teach*
jama9	جمع	*to add*	jamma9	جمّع	*to collect*
sharaf	شرف	*honor*	sharraf	شرّف	*to honor*
daras	درس	*to study*	darras	درّس	*to teach*
khabar	خبر	*news*	khabbar	خبّر	*to tell*
jamal	جمل	*camel*	jammal	جمّل	*to decorate*
9araf	عرف	*to know*	9arraf	عرّف	*to introduce*
salam	سلم	*to be safe*	sallam	سلّم	*to greet*
bana	بنه	*to build*	banna	بنّه	*builder*
mathal	مثل	*proverb*	maththal	مَثّل	*to act*

14. Contrast between short and long vowels:

khabar	خبر	*news*	khaabar	خابر	*to telephone*
9alam	علم	*flag*	9aalam	عالم	*world*
katab	كتب	*to write*	kaatab	كاتب	*to correspond*
nafas	نفس	*breath*	naafas	نافس	*to compete*
9id	عِد	*count*	9iid	عيد	*festival*
jidd	جِدّ	*grandfather*	jiid	جيد	*neck*
sadd	سَدّ	*to shut*	saad	ساد	*to dominate*
shaahid	شاهد	*witness*	shahiid	شهيد	*martyr*
nabil	نبِل	*arrows*	nabiil	نبيل	*noble*
jurr	جُرّ	*pull*	juur	جور	*oppression*
jarr	جَرّ	*to pull*	jaar	جار	*neighbor*

Drills   tamaariin   تَمارين

1. Listen to the audio and identify the different consonants.
2. Listen to the audio and identify the short and the long vowels.
3. Listen to the audio and identify the single and double consonants.

Sheik's guest house built of reeds in the marshes of southern Iraq

DARIS ITHNEEN   دَرِس ثُنـيــن

Greetings and Courtesy Expressions
taḥiyyaat wa mujaamalaat   تَحِـيّـات و مُجامَلات

Basma, an American-born Iraqi woman, meets Kamaal (a man), and exchanges the following greetings. Notice that in context of a greeting one can almost always use the same expression in reply.

Basic Dialogue (Audio)

1. Basma: marḥaba.
   Hello.

   مَرْحَبة.

2. Kamaal: marḥaba.
   Hello.

   مَرْحَبة.

3. Basma: shloonak?
   How are you?

   شُلونـك؟

4. Kamaal: aani zeen, ilḥamdu lillaah.
   w-inti shloonich?
   I am well, praise God. And how are you?

   آني زين. إلحَمدُ لله. وانْتي شُلونـچ؟

5. Basma: aani zeena, ilḥamdu lillaah.
   tfaḍḍal istariiḥ.
   I am well, praise God. Please sit down.

   آني زينة. إلحَمدُ لله. تُفَـضَّل إسْتَـريح.

6. Kamaal: shukran.
   Thank you.

   شُـكْـرا.

7. Basma: allaa bil-kheer.
   God bless (idiom).

   الله بالـخير.

8. Kamaal: allaa bil-kheer.
   God bless (in reply).

   الله بالْخير.

9. Basma: shloon l-ahal?
   How is the family?

   شْـلون الأَهَل؟

10. Kamaal: zeeniin, ilhamdu lillaah. shloon wildich?
    Well, praise God. How are your children?

    زينين. إلْحمد للّه. شْـلون ولْـدِچ؟

11. Basma: b-kheer, nushkur alla.
    Well, thank God.

    بُخير نُشْـكُر الله.

12. Kamaal: 9an idhnich.
    Excuse me.

    عَن إذنِـچ.

13. Basma: tfaddal.
    Please (in this context meaning: you are excused).

    تْفَـضَّل.

14. Kamaal: ma9a s-salaama.
    Goodbye.

    مَعَ السّـلامة.

15. Basma: ma9a s-salaama.
    Goodbye.

    مَعَ السّـلامة.

Additional Expressions (Audio)
Feminine Form

shloonich?	*How are you?*	شْـلونِـچ؟
inti shloonich?	*How are you yourself?*	إنتي شْلونِـچ؟
tfaddali stariihi.	*Please sit down.*	تفَـضَّلي سْتَـريحي.

Plural Form

shloonkum?	*How are you?*	شْـلونْـكُـم؟
intu shloonkum?	*How are you yourselves?*	إنتو شْـلونْـكُـم؟
tfaddalu stariihu.	*Please sit down.*	تْـفَـضَّلو سْتَـريحو.
shloon wilidkum?	*How are your children?*	شْـلون ولِـدْكُـم؟
9an idhinkum.	*Excuse me.*	عَن إذنْـكُـم؟
tfaddalu	*Please (P)*	تْـفَـضَّلو.

Some Basic Greetings (Audio)

marhaba	*Hello (informal, used any time of the day).*	مرحبة
marhaba (in reply)	*Hello.*	مرحبة
as-salaamu 9alaykum.	*Peace be upon you.*	السّلام عَـلَـيْـكُـم
wa 9alaykum is-salaam (reply)	*And peace be upon you (formal, used any time of the day).*	وعليكم السّلام

sabaah il-kheer	*Good morning.*	صباح الخير
sabaah in-nuur (reply)	*Good morning.*	صباح النّور
masaaʾ il-kheer.	*Good afternoon/evening.*	مساء الخير
masaaʾ in-nuur (reply)	*Good afternoon/evening.*	مساء النّور
ma9a s-salaama	*Goodbye.*	مَعَ السّلامة
ma9a s-salaama (reply)	*Goodbye.*	مَعَ السّلامة
tisbah 9ala kheer	*Goodnight (to a man).*	تِصْبح على خير
tisbah 9ala kheer (reply)	*Goodnight.*	تِصْبح على خير
tisbahiin 9ala kheer	*Goodnight (to a woman).*	تِصْبَحين على خير
tisbahiin 9ala kheer (reply)	*Goodnight.*	تِصْبَحين على خير
tisbahuun 9ala kheer	*Goodnight (to a group).*	تِصْبَحون على خير
tisbahuun 9ala kheer (reply)	*Goodnight.*	تِصْبَحون على خير
ahlan wa sahlan	*Welcome.*	اهلاً وسهلاً
ahlan wa sahlan (reply)	*Welcome.*	اهلاً وسهلاً
allaa bil-kheer	*God bless (see below).*	الله بالخير
allaa bil-kheer (reply)	*God bless.*	الله بالخير
tsharrafna	*Pleased to meet you.*	تْشَرَّفْنا
w-ilna sh-sharaf (reply)	*Pleased to meet you.*	وِلْنا الشَّرَف

Vocabulary (Audio)

tahiyya / tahiyyaat (S/P)	*greeting/s*	تَحِيّة / تَحِيّات
marhaba	*Hello.*	مَرْحَبَة
shloon?	*how?*	شْلون؟
shloonak / shloonich / shloonkum?(M/F/P)	*How are you?*	شْلونك؟ شْلونِج؟ شْلونْكم؟
zeen / zeena / zeeniin (M/F/P)	*well, fine, good* (adj.)	زين / زينة / زينين
ilhamdu lillaah	*praise be to God* (invariable standard expression to a question about how one is doing, see lesson 5).	إلْحَـمْـدُ لله
w/wa	*and*	و
aani	*I* (M and F)	آني
inta / inti / intu (M/F/P)	*you*	إنت / إنتي / إنتو
tfaddal / tfaddali / tfaddalu (M/F/P)	*Please* (used when someone offers something to another, varies depending on the context).	تْفَـضَّل / تفَـضَّلي / تفَـضّلو
stariih / stariihi / stariihu (M/F/P)	*Sit down* (imp. verb).	سْتَريح / سْتَريحي / سْتَريحو

shukran	*thanks, thank you* *(invariable).*	شـكـراً
a<u>ll</u>aa bil-<u>kh</u>eer	*God bless (idiom, see* *below).*	الله بالـخـير
ahal / l-ahal	*family/the family*	أَهَل /الأهل
walad / wilid (S/P)	*child/children, boy/s.*	وَلَـد / ولِـد
b-<u>kh</u>eer	*well, good, fine.*	بْخـير
nu<u>sh</u>kur alla	*Thank God.*	نُشْـكُر الله
9an idhnak / 9an i<u>dh</u>nich / 9an i<u>dh</u>inkum (M/F/P)	*Excuse me, with your* *permission.*	عَـن إذنَـك / عَـن إذنِـچ / عَـن إذنْـكُـم
ma9a	*with (prep.)*	مَعَ
salaama	*safety*	سَلامة
ma9a s-salaama	*goodbye*	مَعَ السَّلامة
tamriin / tamaariin (S/P)	*drill/s, exercise/s*	تَمُرين / تَـمارين
ta9baan / ta9baana / ta9baaniin (M/F/P)	*tired (adj.)*	تَعْـبان / تَعْـبانة / تَعْـبانين

Grammar and Remarks

Independent Pronouns (Audio)

English	Arabic	Examples	Meaning		
I	aani (M/F)	aani zeen (M)	*I am well.*	آني زين	آني
		aani zeena (F)	*I am well.*	آني زينة	
you	inta (M)	inta zeen	*You are well.*	إنت زين	إنت
you	inti (F)	inti zeena	*You are well.*	إنتي زينة	إنتي
he	huwwa	huwwa zeen	*He is well.*	هو زين	هو
she	hiyya	hiyya zeena	*She is well.*	هي زينة	هي
we	i<u>h</u>na (M/F)	i<u>h</u>na zeeniin (M)	We are well.	إحْـنا زينـين	إحْـنا
		i<u>h</u>na zeenaat (F)	*We are well.*	إحْـنا زينات	
you	intu (M/F)	intu zeeniin (M)	*You are well.*	إنْتـو زينـين	إنْتـو
		intu zeenaat (F)	*You are well*	إنْتـو زينات	
they	humma (M/F)	humma zeeniin (M)	*They are well.*	هُمَّـه زينـين	هُمَّـه
		humma zeenaat (F)	*They are well.*	هُمَّـه زينات	

There is no pronoun corresponding to the English pronoun "it" in the Arabic language. The pronoun "it" is expressed in Arabic by the pronoun for "he, **huwwa**," or "she, **hiyya**," depending on whether the "it" is referring to something feminine or masculine. "hiyya" can also be used to refer to groups of things (see below). The Iraqi independent pronouns are used much less often than their counterparts in English. They are used in sentences without verbs. They are mainly used with adjectives and adverbs, to add emphasis, or when changing the direction of the speech. The independent pronoun is always the subject of the sentence or the statement.

The chair (M) *is new; it is new.*	il-kursi jidiid; huwwa jidiid	إلكرسي جِـديد؛ هـو جِـديد
The newspaper (F) *is new; it is new.*	ij-jariida jidiida; hiyya jidiida	إلجّريدة جِـديدة؛ هـي جِـديدة
The newspapers (P) *are new; they are new.*	ij-jaraayid jidiida; humma jidiida	إلجّرايد جِـديدة؛ هـي جِـديدة

Note: Arabic statements have no words equivalent to the verb "to be" in English (am, is, are). Words for "was," " were," "will," and "shall" will be discussed in lesson 13.

aani zeen	*I am well.* (lit., *I well.*)	آني زين
ihna zeeniin	*We are well.* (lit., *We well.*)	إحنا زينين
humma juu9aaniin	*They are hungry.* (lit., *They hungry.*)	هُـمَّه جوعانين

Word Stress: Stress Syllable

Arabic words have one stress sound that stands out above the others, whether the words have one or more syllables. We call this a "stress syllable." The stress syllable is automatic and predictable according to certain rules. There are exceptions, however. The Arabic stress syllable is the syllable that contains a long vowel followed by a consonant (VVC) as, in the word "**raah**," or a short vowel followed by two consonants or more (VCC) as in the word "**sadd**." In words with two stress syllables, the stress is on the second syllable toward the end of the word; in words with three stress syllables, the stress is on the third syllable, and so on. Listen for the shift in the stress and emphasis in the following words on the audio.

mirtaah	mirtaahiin	مِرْتاحين	مِرْتاح
zeen	zeeniin	زيـنـين	زين
raayih	raayhiin	رايْـحين	رايِـح
juu9aan	juu9aaniin	جوعانين	جوعان

If there is no stress syllable of the types mentioned above, the stress falls on the first syllable in the word, as in kitab, inta, ihna كِتَب، إنِت، إحنا.

Idioms and Common Phrases (Audio)

1. allaa bil-kheer   الله بالـكـخيـر   *God bless* (lit., *God has brought goodness.*)

It is one of the most common idiomatic expressions used by Iraqis. Iraqis use it when someone (male, female, or a group) comes in. As soon as the person sits down, he is greeted with **allaa bil-kheer**. The reply is the same, **allaa bil-kheer**. This is an invariable idiom.

2. shaku maaku? شَكو ماكو؟ *What's happening? What's going on? What's new?*
(lit., *What's there and what's not there?*)

This is a very common idiomatic expression used among friends.

Basma: shaku maaku il-yoom?	*Basma: What's new today?*	بسمة: شَكو ماكو إليوم؟
Kamaal: maaku shii l-yoom.	*Kamaal: Nothing's new today.*	كمال: ماكو شِي إليوم
shaku maaku 9ar-raadyo?	*What is the news on the radio?*	شكو ماكو عَ الرّاديو؟
shaku maaku bis-suug?	*What is happening in the market?*	شكو ماكو بالسّوگ؟

Drills tamaariin تَمارين

1. Give appropriate oral replies to the following expressions:

marhaba	مَرحبة	9an idhinkum	عَن إذِنكم
shloonak il-yoom?	شْلونك إليوم؟	intu shloonkum?	إنتو شْلونكم؟
tfaddal istariih	تفضّل سْتَريح	shloon wildich?	شْلون ولْدِج؟
allaa bil-kheer	الله بالكْير	9an idhnak	عَن إذنَك
ma9a s-salaama	مَع السّلامة	shloon l-ahal?	شْلون الأهل؟

2. Change orally the following masculine forms to feminine and plural forms:

shloonak il-yoom?	شْلونك إليوم؟
tfaddal istariih	تْفَضّل سْتَريح
aani zeen, ilhamdu lillaah	آني زين، الحَمد لله
inta juu9aan	إنت جوعان
min fadlak	مِن فَضُلك
inta zeen	إنت زين
huwwa ta9baan	هو تَعُبان
shloon wildak?	شْلون ولْدَك؟

3. Decline orally the independent pronouns with the following adjectives or participles:

Example: aani zeen, aani zeena, inta zeen, inti zeena, huwwa zeen, hiyya zeena, ihna zeeniin (MP), ihna zeenaat (FP), intu zeeniin (MP), intu zeenaat (FP), humma zeeniin (MP), humma zeenaat (FP).

mirtaah	content, fine	مِرتاح	farhaan	happy	فَرُحان
juu9aan	hungry	جوعان	ta9baan	tired	تَعُبان
9at shaan	thirsty	عَطُشان	kaslaan	lazy	كَسُلان
msaafir	traveling	مُسافِر	raayih	going	رايِح

4. Read the following statements aloud:

<u>sh</u>loon ahal Basma il-yoom?	شْـلـون أَهَـل بسـمة إليوم؟
<u>sh</u>loon ahal Kamaal il-yoom?	شْـلـون أَهَـل كـمال إليوم؟
<u>sh</u>loon ahal Samiir il-yoom?	شْـلـون أَهَـل سـمير إليوم؟
<u>sh</u>loon ahal Jamiila il-yoom?	شْـلـون أَهَـل جميلة إليوم؟
<u>sh</u>loon ahal Ma<u>h</u>muud il-yoom?	شْـلـون أَهَـل محمود إليوم؟
<u>sh</u>loon ahlak il-yoom?	شْـلـون أُهْـلـك إليوم؟
<u>sh</u>loon ahli<u>ch</u> il-yoom?	شْـلـون أُهْـلِـج إليوم؟
<u>sh</u>loon ahalkum il-yoom?	شْـلـون أُهَـلْـئكم إليوم؟

5. Complete and read aloud:

a. Kamaal ta9baan il-yoom

كمال تعبان إليوم

Samiir juu9aan il-yoom

سمير جوعان إليوم

Basma _____	بسـمة	Basma _____	بسـمة
hiyya _____	هـي	hiyya _____	هـي
humma (M) _____	هُـمّـه	huwwa _____	هو
inta _____	إنت	humma (F) _____	هُـمّـه
inti _____	إنتي	inta _____	إنت
intu _____	إنتو	intu _____	إنتو
ihna _____	إحنا	ihna _____	إحنا
Basma wa Kamaal _____	بسـمة وكمـال	Ma<u>h</u>muud wa Samiir ___.	محمـود وسمـيـر
Basma wa Layla _____	بسـمة وليلى	Jamiila wa Samiira _____	جميلة وسمـيرة

b. allaa bil-<u>kh</u>eer Basma

الله بالخير بسمة

_____ Kaamil	_____ كامل
_____ Mahmuud	محمـود _____
_____ Jamiila	جميلة _____
_____ Jamiil	جميل _____

_____ Samiir   سمير _____

_____ Samiira   سميرة _____

c.   <u>sh</u>aku maaku il-yoom?   شكو ماكو إليوم؟

_____ 9ar-raadyo?   عَ الرّاديو؟ _____

_____ bis-suug?   بِالسّوگ؟ _____

_____ bil-9iraaq?   بِالعِراق؟ _____

_____ b-Baghdaad?   بُ بغداد؟ _____

_____ bil-beet?   بِالبيت؟ _____

_____ bish-shaari9?   بِالشّارع؟ _____

Creative Dialogues

Student 1:	masaaʾ il-kheer Jamiila	مَساء الخير جميلة
Student 2:	masaaʾ in-nuur Kamaal	مَساء الخير كمال
Student 1:	<u>sh</u>loona Mahmuud?	شلونَه محمود؟
Student 2:	huwwa zeen, il-<u>h</u>amdu lilaah	هو زين، الحمد لله
Student 1:	wi-<u>sh</u>loonha Basma?	وِشْلونْها بسمة؟
Student 2:	hiyya ta9baana	هي تعبانة
Student 1:	ween hiyya?	وين هي؟
Student 2:	hiyya bil-beet	هي بِالْبيت
Student 1:	ma9a s-salaama	مع السّلامة
Student 2:	ma9a s-salaama	مع السّلامة

A holy shrine in Baghdad

Asking for Directions

ittijaahaat   إتِّجاهات

Basma is looking for some places. She meets Samiir (a man) and asks him for directions.

Basic Dialogue: (Audio)

1. Basma: sabaah il-kheer.
   Good morning.

   بسـمة: صباح الخير.

2. Samiir: sabaah in-nuur.
   Good morning.

   سـمير: صباح النّور.

3. Basma: min fadlak, ween is-safaara
   l-Amriikiyya?
   Please, where is the American Embassy?

   بسـمة: مِن فَـضُّلك. وين السّـفارة الامريكية؟

4. Samiir: hiyya bil-Karrada.
   It is in Karrada.

   سـمير: هي بالكَرّادة.

5. Basma: min fadlak, ween il-bariid?
   Please, where is the post office?

   بسـمة: مِن فَـضُّلك. وين البريد؟

6. Samiir: il-bariid qariib mnis-suug.
   The post office is near the market.

   سـمير: إلبريد قريب مُن السّـوگ.

7. Basma: tu9ruf ween findiq ir-Rashiid?
   Do you know where is the Rashid Hotel?

   بسـمة: تعرف وين فِـندق إلرّشـيد؟

8. Samiir: na9am, findiq ir-Rashiid yamm
   il-bariid.
   Yes, the Rashid Hotel is near the post office.

   سـمير: نـعم. فِـندق إلرّشـيد يَـمّ إلبَـريد.

9. Basma: shukran.
   Thanks.

   بسمة: شُكراً.

10. Samiir: 9afwan.
    Welcome.

    سمير: عَـفواً.

11. Basma: ween suug is-Safaafiir?
    Where is the Safaafiir market?

    بسمة: وين سـوﮒ الصّفافـير؟

12. Samiir: fii shaari9 ir-Rashiid.
    On Rashid Street.

    سمير: في شارع إلرّشـيد.

13. Basma: bi9iid loo qariib?
    Is it far or near?

    بسمة: بِـعيد لو قَريب؟

14. Samiir: laa, muu bi9iid. mneen
    hadirtich?
    No, it is not far. Where are you from?

    سمير: لا. مو بعيد. مُنـين حَـضِرْتـِج؟

15. Basma: aani min Los Angeles.
    I am from Los Angeles.

    بسمة: آني من لوس اﻧﺠلوس.

16. Samiir: ahlan wa sahlan fii Baghdad
    Welcome to Baghdad.

    سمير: أهْلاً وسَـهْلاً في بـغداد.

17. Basma: shukran. ma9a s-salaama.
    Thank you. Goodbye.

    بسمة: شكراً. مَع السّلامة.

18. Samiir: ma9a s-salaama.
    Goodbye.

    سمير: مَع السّلامة.

Vocabulary (Audio)

sabaah	*morning*	صباح
il-kheer	*the good*	إلـْخير
sabaah il-kheer.	*good morning*	صباح إلخير
in-nuur	*the light*	إلنّور
sabaah in-nuur.	*good morning* (in reply)	صباح إلنّور
min	*from* (prep.)	من
min fadlak / min fadlich (M/F)	*please* (expression used to direct a request toward a male and female, respectively)	مِن فَـضْلك / مِن فَـضْلِج
ween?	*where?*	وين؟
is-safaara	*the embassy*	إلسّفـارة
l-Amriikiyya	*the American* (adj.)	إلأمريكية
Karraada	*an affluent district in Baghdad*	إلـْكَـرّادة
il-bariid	*the post office*	إلـْبريد

qariib, giriib	*near, close by*	قَـريب، گِـريب
bi9iid	*far*	بِـعـيـد
loo	*or*	لـو
is-suug	*the market*	إلـسّـوگ
suug i<u>s</u>-<u>S</u>afaafiir	*one of the oldest markets in Baghdad for metal craftsmanship*	سوگ إلصَّـفـافـيـر
tu9ruf / tu9urfiin / tu9urfuun (M/F/P)	*you know*	تُـعُـرف / تُـعُـرْفين / تُـعُـرفون
findiq	*hotel, motel*	فِـنْـدِق
na9am	*yes*	نَـعَـم
yamm	*next to, adjacent to, near*	يَـمّ
9afwan (invariable)	*welcome, don't mention it, sorry*	عَـفـوا
mneen, immeen?	*where from?* (see lesson 15)	مُـنـيـن، إمّـيـن؟
min ween?	*from where?*	مِن وين؟
<u>h</u>adra	*presence*	حَـضْـرة
<u>h</u>adirtak / <u>h</u>adirtich / <u>h</u>adratkum (M/F/P)	*your presence* (a polite way of addressing someone)	حَـضِـرْتَـك / حَـضِـرْتِـج / حَـضْـرَتْـكُـم
<u>sh</u>unu?	*what?*	شِـنُـو
<u>sh</u>ukran (invariable)	*thanks, thank you*	شكـراً
ahlan wa sahlan	*welcome*	أهلاً وسهلاً
isim	*name*	إسِـم
ismi	*my name* (see attached pronouns below)	إسْـمـي
t<u>sh</u>arrafna (invariable)	*Pleased to meet you* (lit. *we are honored*, always plural form).	تْـشَـرَّفْـنـا
w-ilna <u>sh</u>-<u>sh</u>araf (in reply to above)	*Pleased to meet you too* (lit. *the honor is ours*).	ولْـنـا إلشَّـرَف

Grammar and Remarks
Attached Pronouns (Pronoun Suffixes)
1. Pronouns Attached to Nouns: ktaab كْـتاب *book* (Audio)

-i*	*my* (M/F)	ktaab**i**	*my book*	كْـتابي	ــ ي
-na	*our* (M/F)	ktaab**na**	*our book*	كْـتابنا	ــ نا
-ak	*your* (M)	ktaab**ak**	*your book*	كْـتابَـك	ــَ ك
-i<u>ch</u>	*your* (F)	ktaab**ich**	*your book*	كْـتابِـچ	ــِ چ
-kum	*your* (P)	ktaab**kum**	*your book*	كْـتابْـكُـم	ــ كُـم

-a	*his*	ktaab**a**	*his book*	كْـتابْـَه	ـَ ه
-ha	*her*	ktaab**ha**	*her book*	كْـتابْـها	ها
-hum	*their* (M/F)	ktaab**hum**	*their book*	كْـتابْـهُـم	ـ هُـم

*With nouns only.

2. Pronouns Attached to Verbs: ygaabul يْـگـابُـل *he meets* (Audio)

-ni*	*me* (M/F)	ygaabul**ni**	*he meets me*	يْـگابُـلْـني	ـ ني
-na	*us* (M/F)	ygaabul**na**	*he meets us*	يْـگابُـلْـنا	ـ نا
-ak	*you* (M)	ygaabl**ak**	*he meets you*	يْـگابْـلَـك	ـَ ك
-<u>ich</u>	*you* (F)	ygaabl**ich**	*he meets you*	يْـگابْـلِـج	ـ ج
-kum	*you* (P)	ygaabul**kum**	*he meets you*	يْـگابُـلْـكُـم	ـ كُـم
-a	*him*	ygaabl**a**	*he meets him*	يْـگابْـلَـه	ـَ ه
-ha	*her*	ygaabul**ha**	*he meets her*	يْـگابُـلْـها	ـ ها
-hum	*them* (M/F)	ygaabul**hum**	*he meets them*	يْـگابُـلْـهُـم	ـ هُـم

*With verbs only.

Iraqi Arabic has a set of attached pronouns (also called pronoun suffixes) that appear as suffixes at the end of nouns, verbs, and some other words such as prepositions and interrogatives. When they are attached to nouns they have the meaning of possession (see group 1, above). When they are attached to verbs, they are the objects of the verbs (see group 2, above). Notice the differences in the meaning between the two groups. Also notice that the verb of the first person singular takes the pronoun "**ni**" instead of "**i**" as is the case with the noun.

Pronouns attached to prepositions and interrogative words are the subjects (I, you, he, etc.). Attached pronouns occur much more often than the independent pronouns.

minnak	مِنّـَك	minni<u>ch</u>	مِنّـِج	minnkum	مِنْـكُـم	*from you* (M/F/P)
9aleek	عَـليك	9alee<u>ch</u>	عَـلـيـج	9aleekum	عَـليكُـم	*on you* (M/F/P)
<u>sh</u>loonak?	شُـلونـَك؟	<u>sh</u>looni<u>ch</u>?	شُـلونِـج؟	<u>sh</u>loonkum?	شُـلونْـكُـم؟	*how are you?* (M/F/P)

The Article il- ـ إلْ *the*

The definite article "the" in English is expressed in Iraqi Arabic by the prefix "**il-**." This invariable prefix is used with nouns and adjectives. A word preceded by the article "**il-**" is definite and that is how you make definite words in Arabic, by adding this prefix. (Audio)

walad	*a boy*	وَلَد	il-walad	*the boy*	الـوَلد
baab	*a door*	باب	il-baab	*the door*	الـبْاب
beet	*a house*	بيت	il-beet	*the house*	الـبْيت
qalam	*a pen/pencil*	قَلَم	il-qalam	*the pen/pencil*	الـقْلَم

Proper nouns and nouns with attached pronouns are also definite, as in

beetak	*your house*	بيتَك
beethum	*their house*	بيتْهُم
qalamha	*her pen*	قَلَمُها

If the prefix "il-" is used in a word that begins with one of the consonants, the so-called sun letters: "t," "ṭ," "th," "j," "ch," "d," "dh," "ḍ," "r," "z," "s," "sh," "ṣ," and "n," the "l" of the article is assimilated, resulting in double consonants in the beginning of the word. (Audio)

taalib	*a student*	طالب	[il-taalib]	>	it-taalib	*the student*	الطّالب
nuur	*a light*	نور	[il-nuur]	>	in-nuur	*the light*	الـنّور
saa9a	*a watch*	ساعة	[il-saa9a]	>	is-saa9a	*the watch*	السّاعة
jariida	*a newspaper*	جريدة	[il-jariida]	>	ij-jariida	*the newspaper*	الجْريدة
daar	*a house*	دار	[il-daar]	>	id-daar	*the house*	الـدّار

If a word begins with a cluster of any two consonants, then the "il-" becomes "li-." This is done for easier pronunciation. (Audio)

fluus	*money*	فْلوس	[il-fluus]	>	li-fluus	*the money*	لِـفْلوس
hmaar	*a donkey*	حْمار	[il-hmaar]	>	li-hmaar	*the donkey*	لِـحْمار
ktaab	*a book*	كْتاب	[il-ktaab]	>	li-ktaab	*the book*	لِـكْتاب
stiikaan	*a tea glass*	سْتيكان	[is-stiikaan]	>	li-stiikaan	*the tea glass*	لِـسْتيكان
qmaash	*textile*	قْماش	[il-qmaash]	>	li-qmaash	*the textile*	لِـقْماش

When the prefix "il-" occurs in a word proceeded by a word ending in a vowel, the vowel "i" of the prefix drops out. (Audio)

ma9a il-bint	>	ma9a l-bint	*with the girl*	مَعَ الـبْنت
wara il-baab	>	wara l-baab	*behind the door*	وَرَى الـبْاب
haadha il-qalam	>	haadha l-qalam	*this pen/pencil*	هاذا الـقْلَم
haadhi is-sayyaara	>	haadhi s-sayyaara	*this car*	هاذي السّيارة

Idioms and Common Phrases (Audio)

1. 9ala keef + attached pronoun + على كيف *as someone likes; take it easy with, be careful with, slow down*

9ala keefi	*as I like*	على كيفي
9ala keefna	*as we like*	على كيفنا
9ala keefa	*as he likes*	على كيفه
9ala keefha	*as she likes*	على كيفها
9ala keefhum	*as they like*	على كيفهُم
9ala keefak	*as you* (M) *like*	على كيفك
9ala keefich	*as you* (F) *like*	على كيفِج
9ala keefkum	*as you* (P) *like*	على كيفكُم
9ala keefak bis-siyaaqa.	*Take it* (you, M) *easy with the driving (be careful).*	على كيفك بالسّيارة
9ala keefkum bil-akil.	*Take it* (you, P) *easy with the food (don't eat too much).*	على كيفك بِالأُكِل

Also:

9ala keef Basma	*as Basma likes*	على كيف بسمة
9ala keef Samiir	*as Samiir likes*	على كيف سمير

2. haay ween + pronoun? ؟ + هاي وين *Where have (you) been?*

haay ween inta / haay weenak?	*Where have you* (M) *been?*	هاي وين إنت / هاي وينـك؟
haay ween inti / haay weenich?	*Where have you* (F) *been?*	هاي وين إنتي / هاي وينِـج؟
haay ween intu / haay weenkum?	*Where have you* (P) *been?*	هاي وين إنتو / هاي وينـكم؟
haay ween huwwa / haay weena?	*Where has he been?*	هاي وين هو / هاي وينـه؟
haay ween hiyya / haay weenha?	*Where has she been?*	هاي وين هي / هاي وينـها؟
haay ween humma / haay weenhum?	*Where have they been?*	اي وين هُمّه / هاي وينـهم؟
Also:		
haay weenha Basma?	*Where has Basma been?*	هاي وينـها بسمة؟
haay weena Kamaal?	*Where has Kamaal been?*	هاي وينـه كمال؟
haay weena Samiir?	*Where has Samiir been?*	هاي وينـه سمير؟
haay weenha Jamiila?	*Where has Jamiila been?*	هاي وينـها جميلة؟

Drills   tamaariin   تَـمارين

1. Give appropriate oral replies to the following expressions:

sabaah il-kheer	صُباح إلخير
shunu isim hadirtich?	شْـنـو إسـم حَـضِرْتـج؟
tu9urfiin ween il-bariid?	تُعُرفـين وين إلبريد؟
ween is-safaara l-Amriikiyya?	وين إلسّـفـارة الامـريكية؟
ween is-suug?	وين إلسّـوگ؟
ahlan wa sahlan	اهلا وسـهلا
allaa bil-kheer	الله بالخير
min ween Basma?	من وين بسـمة؟
mneen hadratkum?	مُنـين حَـضُـرَتـْكـم؟
suug is-Safaafiir bi9iid loo qariib	سـوگ إلصّـفـافيربـِعيد لـو قَـريب؟
shaku maaku 9ar-raadyo?	شـكـو ماكـو عَ الرّادْيو؟
shaku maaku il-yoom?	شـكـو ماكـو الـْيـوم؟
ma9a s-salaama	مع السّـلامة
shukran	شـكـراً

2. Change orally the following masculine form to feminine and plural forms:

min fadlak	مِن فَـضْلك	tfaddal lis-tiikaan	تْـفَـضّـل لِسْـتـيكان
mneen hadirtak?	مُنـين حَـضِرْتك	min ween huwwa?	مِن وين هـو؟
min ween inta?	مِن وين انت؟	haay ween inta?	هـاي وين انت؟
tfaddal istariih	تْـفَـضّـل سْـتـريح	9ala keefa	عـلى كـيفَـه
9ala keefak	عـلى كـيفَـك	huwwa bi9iid loo qariib?	هـو بِـعيد لـو قريب؟

3. Complete and read the following aloud:

aani Basma min Amriika	آنـي بسـمة من أمريكا	haay weenak?	هـاي وينك؟
huwwa Kamaal _____	هـو كـمـال	haay _____ (you F)?	هـاي _____؟
inti Jamiila _____	إنتي جميلة	haay _____ (you P)?	هـاي _____؟
inta Waliid _____	إنت وليد	haay _____ (he)?	هـاي _____؟
hiyya Layla _____	هـي ليلى	haay _____ (she)?	هـاي _____؟
humma _____	همـّه	haay _____ (they)?	هـاي _____؟

4. Make the following nouns definite with the article il-:

baab _____ باب	taalib _____ طالب
saa9a _____ ساعة	sayyaara _____ سيّارة
walad _____ وَلَد	wilid _____ وِلِـد
binit _____ بنت	fluus _____ فلوس
hmaar _____ حُمار	ktaab _____ كْتاب
suug _____ سوگ	bariid _____ بريد
tamriin _____ تمرين	safaara _____ سفارة
jariida _____ جريدة	tayyaara _____ طيّارة
daris _____ درس	tamaariin _____ تمارين

5. Conjugate orally the following nouns with the attached pronouns:

qalam	قلم	beet	بيت	stikaan	سْتيكان
ktaab	كتاب	suug	سوگ	hmaar	حُمار
bariid	بريد	fluus	فلوس	nuur	نـور

6. Complete and read the following aloud:

a. tu9ruf ween il-barrid? تعرف وين البـريد؟
   tu9urfiin ween il-bariid? تعرفين وين البـريد؟

   _____ ween is-safaara? وين إلسّـفارة؟ _____

   _____ ween beet Samiir? وين بيت سـميـر؟ _____

   _____ ween is-suug? وين إلسّـوگ؟ _____

   _____ ween beet Laylaa? وين بيت ليلـى؟ _____

   _____ ween Basma? وين بسـمة؟ _____

   _____ ween Kamaal? وين كمـال؟ _____

b.   9ala keefak bis-siyaaqa   على كيفك بالسّيارة

9ala keefich _____   _____ على كيفِج

9ala keefkum _____   _____ على كيفْكُم

9ala keefa _____   _____ على كيفَـه

9ala keefha _____   _____ على كيفْها

9ala keefhum _____   _____ على كيفْـهُم

9ala keefi _____   على كيفي_____

9ala keefna _____   _____ على كيفْـنا

haay weena il-yoom?   هاي وينَـه اليوم؟

haay weenha _____?   ؟_____ هاي وينْـها

haay weenhum _____?   ؟_____ هاي وينْـهُم

haay weenak _____?   ؟_____هاي وينَـك

haay wee<u>ni</u>ch _____?   ؟_____ هاي وينِـج

haay weenkum _____?   ؟_____ هاي وينْـكُم

7. Translate the following into Arabic:

Good morning. _____

Good morning (in reply). _____

Thanks. _____

Hello. _____

Goodbye Samiir. _____

As he likes. _____

Where is the post office? _____

How is the family? _____

How are you (P) today? _____

Please, sit down (P). _____

Where have they been? _____

Where have you (M) been? _____

Welcome to Baghdad. _____

Please sit (P) down. _____

Take it easy with the driving. _____

What is happening today? _____

Creative Dialogues

a. taalib 1: aani min Baghdaad. mneen inti?

طالب 1:   آني من بغداد. مُنين إنتي؟

    taaliba 2: aani min Los Angeles

طالبة 2:   آني من لوس انجلوس

    taalib 1: shunu ismich?

طالب 1:   شـنو إسْمِـجِ؟

    taaliba 2: ismi Kariima, shunu ismak?

طالبة 2:   إسمـي كريمة. شُـنو إسْمك؟

    taalib 1: ismi Kariim.

طالب 1:   إسْمـي كريم

    taaliba 2: tsharrafna.

طالبة 2:   تْشَـرَّفْـنـا

    taalib 1: w-ilna sh-sharaf

طالب 1:   ولْـنـا الشـَّـرَف

b. taalib 1: haadha ktaabich loo ktaabi?

طالب 1:   هاذا كتابِـجِ لو كْتابي؟

    taaliba 2: haadha ktaabi.

طالبة 2:   هاذا كْتـابي

    taalib 1: ween ktaabi?

طالب 1:   وين كْتابي؟

    taaliba 2: ktaabak bil-beet.

طالبة 2:   كْتـابك بـالْـبِيت

    taalib 1: il-beet bi9iid loo qariib?

طالب 1:   إلْـبِيت بِـعـيد لو قَـريب؟

    taaliba 2: il-beet bi9iid.

طالبة 2:   إلْـبِيت بِـعـيد

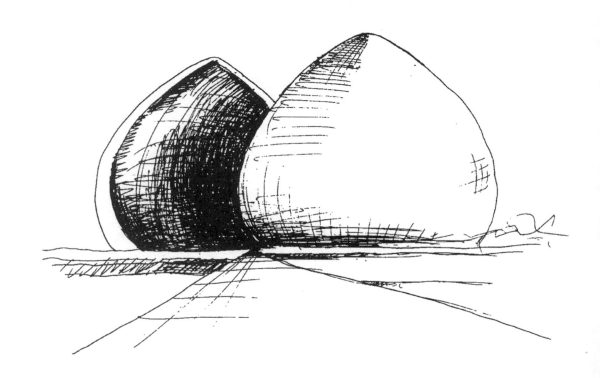

The Unknown Soldier monument, Baghdad

Arrival at Baghdad Airport, Part I

b-maṭaar Baghdaad   بُ مَطار بَـغْـداد

Basma just landed at Baghdad Airport and must go through the passport official (muwazzaf)
and customs inspector (mufattish).

Basic Dialogue (Audio)

1. Basma: masaaʾ il-kheer.
   Good afternoon.

   بسـمة: مسـاء إلخير.

2. muwazzaf: masaaʾ in-nuur. mneen
   hadirtich?
   Good afternoon. Where are you from?

   مُوَظَّـف: مساء إلنّـور. مُنين حَضِرْتـِـج؟

3. Basma: aani Amriikiyya jaayya min Los
   Angeles.
   *I am an American coming from Los
   Angeles.*

   بسـمة: آني أمريكية من لوس الجـلوس

4. muwazzaf: il-baasbort, min fadlich.
   The passport, please.

   مُوَظَّـف: إلبـاسْبورْت مِن فَـضْلِـج.

5. Basma: tfaddal haadha il-bassbort.
   Here is the passport.

   بسـمة: تَـفضّل البـاسْبورت.

6. muwazzaf: shukran. shgadd baaqya
   hnaa?
   Thanks. How long are you staying here?

   مُوَظَّـف: شُـكـراً. شُـگَـد باقْـيَة هُـنا؟

7. Basma: usbuu9een, inshaalla
   Two weeks, God willing.

   بسـمة: اُسْـبـوعين، إنْشـاللّه.

8. muwazzaf: shunu sabab iz-ziyaara?
   What is the reason for the visit?

   مُوَظّـف: شُـنو سَـبَـب الـزِّيارة؟

9. Basma: li-ziyaarat il-aathaar.
   To visit antiquities.

   بسـمة: لِزيارة الآثـار.

10. muwazzaf: tayyib, tfaddali l-baasport.
    Fine, here is the passport.

    مُوَظّـف: طَـيِّـب. تفَضّـلي الباسْـبـورت.

11. Basma: shukran, fiimaanilla.
    Thanks, goodbye.

    بسـمة: شـكرا، فيمانـيلّـا.

12. muwazzaf: safra sa9iida.
    (Have) a good trip.

    مُوَظّـف: سَـفْـرة سَـعيدة.

(Airport customs inspection continues in lesson 5.)

Vocabulary (Audio)

muwazzaf / muwazzafa / muwazzafiin (M/F/P)	*official/s, employee/s*	موظّـف / موظّـفة / موظّـفين
masaaɔ	*afternoon, evening*	مَساء
masaaɔ il-kheer	*Good afternoon/evening.*	مَساء الـْخير
masaaɔ in-nuur	*Good afternoon/evening (in reply).*	مساء الـنّـور
mneen?	*Where? Where from?*	مُـنـين؟
Amriiki /Amriikiyya / Amriikaan (M/F/P)	*American/s*	أمْريكي/ أمْريكية / أمْريكان
baasbort, paasbort	*passport*	باسْـبـورْت
jaay / jaayya / jaayyiin (M/F/P)	*coming (participle)*	جاي/ جايّـة / جايّـيـن
haadha / haadhi / hadhoola (M/F/P)	*this, that/these (see lesson 14)*	هاذا / هاذي / هَـذولـَه
shgadd?	*How long? how much? (depending on context)*	شْـگَـد
baaqi / baaqya / baaqiin (M/F/P)	*staying (part.)*	باقـي/ باقْـيَة / باقـيـن
hnaa	*here*	هْـنا
usbuu9 / usbuu9een / asaabii9 (S/D/P)	*week/two weeks/weeks*	أسْـبـوع /أسْـبـوعين/ أسابـيـع
sabab / asbaab (S/P)	*reason/s*	سَـبَـب / أسْـباب
ziyaara / ziyaaraat (S/P)	*visit/s*	زيارة / زِيارات
li-	*to, for, in order to (see lesson 14)*	لِـ

li-ziyaarat	*to visit*	لِـزيارة
athar / aathaar (S/P)	*antiquity/antiquities, ruins*	أثَر / آثـار
tayyib	*okay, all right, good, delicious* (depending on context)	طَـيّـب
fiimaanillaa	*goodbye* (lit., in God's safety, see lesson 5)	فيمانيـﻜلا
safra / safraat (S/P)	*trip/s*	سـَفـْرة / سَـفـْرات
sa9iida	*happy* (adj.)	سَـعـيـد
safra sa9iida	*(Have) a good trip*	سَـفـْرة سَـعـيدة

Grammar and Remarks

The Helping Vowels: i, u ُ ِ

The helping vowel in the Iraqi Arabic is the short vowel "**i**" and in some rare cases the vowel "**u**." The vowel "**i**" appears within one word or across words to help pronounce a sequence of three or more consonants. Within one word the presence of the helping vowel "**i**" is completely predictable. In a cluster of three consonants in a row, the helping vowel "**i**" is added automatically between the first and the second consonants and in between the second and the third of a cluster of four consonants. (Audio)

min fadlkum	> min fadilkum	مِن فَـضلـﻜكم
isim hadrtak?	> isim hadirtak?	إسِـمّ حَـضرْتَك؟
ariid stiikaan	> ariid istiikaan	أريد إسْـتيكان
shgadd saarlkum?	> shgadd saarilkum?	شگـد صارلـﻜكم؟
qariib min il-bariid	> qariib mnil-bariid	قريب مُن البـَريد

The helping vowel "**i**" may also occur in utterance of a word that has initial two consonants, as in:

hnaa	هـْنا	or	ihnaa	إهـْنا	*here*
hwaaya	هـْواية	or	ihwaaya	إهـْواية	*much*
mneen?	مـْنين؟	or	imneen?	إمـْنين؟	*where from?*

The presence and the absence of the initial helping vowel "**i**" with two consonants is random and has no effect on the meaning. It is a matter of a speaker's habit. We prefer to leave it to the students to decide for themselves the easier way of pronouncing such forms. In this book, the helping vowel "**i**" will not be indicated in transcription with the two-consonant cluster, with the exception of some very common examples.

The Negation

There are four basic negation words in Iraqi Arabic. They are usually more stressed than the words they negate. They are the following:

1. muu مُو *not*

The negative word **muu** is used to negate adjectives and adverbs only. (Audio)

inta muu 9iraaqi	*You are not an Iraqi.*	إنت مُو عراقي
hiyya muu hnaa	*She is not here.*	هي مُو هْنا
il-bariid muu yamm	*The post office is not near the*	إلبريد مُو يَـمّ إلسّفارة
is-safaara	*embassy.*	
aani muu juu9aan	*I am not hungry.*	آني مُو جوعان

2. maa / ma- مَ / ما *not*

The word **maa** and its short form **ma-** are used to negate verbs (except imperative verbs) and a few verb-like words. It more occurs as a prefix, **ma-**, than as an independent **maa**.

With Verbs (Audio)

ma-yu9ruf	*He does not know.*	مَ يُعْرُف
ma-tu9ruf	*She does not know.*	مَ تُعْرُف
ma-yriid	*He does not want.*	مَ يْـريد
ma-triid	*She does not want.*	مَ تْريد

With Verb-Like Words (indicating the meaning of possession or there is/are) (Audio)

9indi	*I have*	عِندي	maa 9indi	*I don't have*	ما عِندي
aku	*there is/are*	أكو	ma-aku	*there isn't/aren't*	ماكو
ma9ak	*with you* (M)	معك	maa ma9ak	*not with you*	ما معك

3. laa / la- لَ / لا *no, not*

The negative word **laa** and its short form **la-** are used in three contexts:

a. It precedes imperative verbs in the form of the prefix **la-** expressing the meaning "not" (see lesson 7). (Audio)

saafir	*Travel!* (M)	سافِر	la-tsaafir	*Do not travel!*	لَتْسافِر
saafri	*Travel!* (F)	سافْري	la-tsaafriin	*Do not travel!*	لَتْسافْرين
saafru	*Travel!* (P)	سافْرو	la-tsaafruun	*Do not travel!*	لَتْسافْرون

b. It is used with a question that requires a "yes" or "no" answer, and it conveys the meaning "no." (Audio)

triid <u>ch</u>aay?	*Do you* (M) *want tea?*	تريد چاي؟
laa, <u>sh</u>ukran	*No, thank you.*	لا. شكرا
zeena, in<u>sh</u>aalla?	*Well, God willing?*	زين. إنشاالله؟
laa, ta9baana <u>sh</u>wayya	*No, a little tired.*	لا. تعبان شْـوَيّة

c. It is used with the negative word "**wala**" (see below).

4. wala ولا *and not, nor, or*

The negative word **wala** consists of two elements: **wa** (*and*) and **la** (*not*). Therefore, it literally means "and not." The word **wala** does not appear by itself, but with one of the above-mentioned negative words when two or more items are to be negated. The first item is negated by one of the proceeding negatives (**maa, muu, laa**) and the second and any subsequent items may be negated by **wala**. The English equivalent of such a construction may be "neither . . . nor," "not . . . and not," or "not . . . or." (Audio)

maa aji wala aruuh	*I do not come or go.*	ما أجي ولا أروح
muu zeen wala mirtaah	*I am neither well nor content.*	مو زين ولا مِرْتاح
laa ahmar wala asfar wala aswad	*not red, yellow, or black*	لا أحْمَر ولا أصْفر ولا أسْوَد
laa ghaali wala rikhiis	*neither expensive nor cheap*	لا غالي ولا رخيص
laa juu9aan wala 9at shaan	*neither hungry nor thirsty*	لا جوعان ولا عَطشان

Idioms and Common Phrases (Audio)

1. laa ghaali wala rikhiis لا غـالي ولا رخيـص *neither expensive nor cheap*

il-mat9am laa ghaali wala rikhiis	*The restaurant is neither expensive nor cheap.*	إلمَطعم لا غالي ولا رخيص
is-sayyaara laa ghaalya wala rikhiisa	*The car is neither expensive nor cheap.*	إلسّيارة لا غالية ولا رخيصة
il-beet laa ghaali wala rikhiis	*The house is neither expensive nor cheap.*	إلبيت لا غالي ولا رخيص
il-akil laa ghaali wala rikhiis	*The food is neither expensive nor cheap.*	إلأكل لا غالي ولا رخيص

2. laa shiish wala kabaab لا شيش ولا كباب *not bad, okay, so-so* (lit., *neither the skewer nor the meat*, referring to the shish kebab food)

il-akil laa shiish wala kabaab	*The food is okay.*	إلأكل لا شيش ولا كباب
il-mat9am laa shiish wala kabaab	*The restaurant is not bad.*	إلمَطعم لا شيش ولا كباب
ish-shughul laa shiish wala kabaab	*The work is okay.*	إلشُّغـل لا شيش ولا كباب
id-dinya laa shiish wala kabaab	*Life is so-so.*	إلدّنـيا لا شيش ولا كباب

3. shmadrii + attached pronoun? شـمَـدُري +؟ *How does (he) know?*

shmadriik aani juu9aan?	*How do you (M) know that I am hungry?*	شـمَـدُريك آني جوعان؟
shmadriich huwwa 9iraaqi?	*How do you (F) know that he is an Iraqi?*	شـمَـدُريچ هو عراقـي؟

shmadriikum il-mat9am ghaali?	*How do you (P) know that the restaurant is expensive?*	شْـمَـدُريكم إلمطعم غالي؟
shmadriihum inta msaafir?	*How do they know that you are traveling?*	شْـمَـدُريهم إنت مُسافر؟
shmadriini intu Amriikaan?	*How do I know that you are Americans?*	شْـمَـدُريني إنتو امريكان؟
shmadrii il-akil tayyib?	*How does he know the food is good?*	شْـمَـدُري الأكل طَـيّـب؟

Drills   tamaariin   تَـمارين

1. Give appropriate oral replies to the following expressions:

masaaʾ il-kheer	مساء الخير
tfaddali il-baasbort	تفضّلي الباسبورت
fiimaanillaa	فيمانيـئـلا
mneen hadirtak?	مُنين حَضِرْتك؟
shloon il-akil bil-mat9am?	شْـلون الاكل بالمطعم؟
shunu sabab iz-ziyaara?	شنو سبب الزّيارة؟
shloon ish-shughul?	شْـلون الشّـغُـل؟
inta Amriiki loo 9iraaqi?	إنت أمريكي لو عراقي؟
shunu ismak?	شنو إسْمك؟
ween is-safaara l-Amriikiyya?	وين السّفارة الأمريكية؟

2. Negate orally the following expressions using the correct negative word:

aani Amriiki	آني امريكي
inti 9iraaqiyya	إنتي عراقية
il-bariid yamm is-suug	إلبريد يمّ السّوگ
aku safaara Amriikiyya	أكو سفارة أمريكية
intu juu9aaniin	انتو جوعانين
tu9ruf findiq 9ishtaar	تعرف فندق عِـشتار
hiyya zeena, ilhamdu lillaah	هي زينة، إلحمد للّه
humma min Baghdaad	هُمّه من بغداد
huwwa taalib	هو طالب
il-mat9am ghaali loo rikhiis?	إلمطعم غالي لو رخيص؟

3. Decline orally the following words by adding the attached pronouns:

isim	إسـم	hadra	حضرة	hmaar	خُـمار
ktaab	كتاب	baab	باب	wilid	ولِـد
saa9a	ساعة	tayyaara	طَـيّارة	mataar	مطار
qalam	قلـم	sayyaara	سَـيّارة	findiq	فِـنْـدِق
safaara	سفارة	baasbort	باسبورت	stiikaan	إسْـتيكان

4. Make the words between the parentheses plural:

(huwwa baaqi) usbuu9	(هو باقي) اُسبوع
(muwazzaf) bil-mataar	(موظّف) بالمطار
(anni) muu (juu9aan)	(آني) مو (جوعان)
(inti) muu (9iraaqiyya)	(إنتي) مو (عراقية)
mneen (hadirtich)?	منين (حضرتـچ)؟
mneen (huwwa)?	منين (هو)؟
ween (is-sayyaara)?	وين (إلسّيارة)؟
hiyya (jaayya) mnil-beet	هي (جايّة) مُن البيت
(tu9ruf) ween is-suug?	(تعرف) وين إلسّوگ؟
(tfaddal istariih)	(تفضّل ستريح)

5. Complete and read the following aloud:

a. il-mat9am laa ghaali wala rikhiis.   إلمطعم لا غالي ولا رِخيص

  li-ktaab _____   _____ لِـكْتاب

  is-sayyaara _____   _____ إلسَّيارة

  is-suug _____   _____ إلسّوگ

  il-akil _____   _____ إلأكل

  is-safar _____   _____ إلسَّفَر

  Baghdaad _____   _____ بـغداد

  il-9iraaq _____   _____ إلعراق

b. shmadrii aani na9saan?   شْمَـدْري آني نَعْسان؟

  shmadriiha _____?   ؟_____ شْمَـدْريها

  shmadriihum _____?   ؟_____ شْمَـدْريهم

  shmadriik _____?   ؟_____ شْمَـدْريك

  shmadriich _____?   ؟_____ شْمَـدْريـچ

  shmadriikum _____?   ؟_____ شْمَـدْريكم

c. <u>ish</u>-<u>sh</u>u<u>gh</u>ul laa <u>shiish</u> wala kabaab.   إلشُّـغـل لا شـيش ولا كـباب

    il-mat9am _____   _____ إلمطعـم

    il-akil _____   _____ إلأكـل

    is-suug _____   _____ إلسّـوگ

    ich-<u>ch</u>aay _____   _____ إلچّـاي

    il-gahwa _____   _____ إلـگَـهْوَة

6. Translate the following into Arabic:

She is an American. _____

The restaurant is okay. _____

We are not well today. _____

Please sit down (P). _____

He is an Iraqi. _____

They are in the airport. _____

neither expensive nor cheap _____

the reason for the visit _____

the post office near the embassy _____

What is your (F) name? _____

The car is not next to the hotel. _____

No, we are not hungry. _____

You (F) are in the Rashid Hotel. _____

There is no post office here. _____

neither from Basra nor Baghdad. _____

What is happening? _____

Creative Dialogues:

a.   ṭaalib 1:   ween Sa9ad?   وين سعد؟   :1 طالب

    ṭaaliba 2: Sa9ad msaafir   سعد مُسافر   :2 طالبة

    ṭaalib 1:   ween msaafir?   وين مُسافِر؟   :1 طالب

    ṭaaliba 2: huwwa msaafir l-Lubnaan.   هو مُسافِر لُ لبنان   :2 طالبة

    ṭaalib 1:   shgadd baaqi b-Lubnaan?   شگد باقي بُ لبنان   :1 طالب

    ṭaaliba 2: huwwa baaqi usbuu9.   هو باقي أُسبوع   :2 طالبة

    ṭaalib 1:   shunu sabab iz-ziyaara?   شنو سبب إلزّيارة؟   :1 طالب

    ṭaaliba 2: li-ziyaarat ahla b-Beerut.   لِزيارة أهلَه بُ بيروت   :2 طالبة

b.   ṭaaliba 1: aani raayḥa azuur Samiira.   آني رايْحة أزور سميرة   :1 طالب

    ṭaalib 2:   ween hiyya?   وين هي؟   :2 طالبة

    ṭaaliba 1: hiyya b- beetha.   هي بُ بيتها   :1 طالب

    ṭaalib 2:   beetha qariib loo bi9iid?   بيتها قريب لو بِعيد؟   :2 طالبة

    ṭaalib 1:   beetha laa qariib wala bi9iid.   بيتها لا قريب ولا بِعيد   :1 طالب

    ṭaalib 2:   hiyya shloonha?   هي شلونها؟   :2 طالبة

    ṭaaliba 1: laa shiish wala kabaab.   لا شيش ولا كباب   :1 طالب

For new words, see Glossary.

Ishtar Gate in the ancient city of Babylon

DARIS <u>KH</u>AMSA   دَرِس خَمْسَة

Arrival at Baghdad Airport, Part II

b-ma<u>t</u>aar Ba<u>gh</u>daad   بُ مَطار بَغْداد

Basma moves on to the customs inspector "mufatti<u>sh</u>."

Basic Dialogue (Audio)

1. mufatti<u>sh</u>: min fa<u>d</u>lich, iftahi j-jun<u>t</u>a.
   Please, open the luggage.

   مُفَتِّش: من فَضْلِج إفْتَحي الجُنْطة.

2. Basma: bi-kull suruur.
   With pleasure.

   بِسمة: بِكُل سُرور

3. mufatti<u>sh</u>: ma9ich a<u>sh</u>yaaʾ mamnuu9a?
   Do you have with you any illegal items?

   مُفَتِّش: مَعِج أشْياء مَمْنوعة؟

4. Basma: laa wa<u>ll</u>a, kullha malaabis <u>sh</u>a<u>kh</u>siyya.
   No, all are personal clothes.

   بِسمة: لا وللّٰه. كُلْها مَلابِس شَخْصِيَّة.

5. mufatti<u>sh</u>: <u>sh</u>gadd ma9ich fluus?
   How much money is with you?

   مُفَتِّش: شَگَد مَعِج فْلوس؟

6. Basma: ma9i hawaali alif duulaar.
   With me are about one thousand dollars.

   بِسمة: مَعي حَوالي ألِف دولار.

7. mufatti<u>sh</u>: ma9ich kaamira aw jigaayir?
   Do you have with you a camera or cigarettes?

   مُفَتِّش: مَعِج كاميرة أو جِگايِر؟

8. Basma: 9indi kaamira bass.
   I have a camera only.

   بِسمة: عِندي كاميرة بَسّ.

9. mufatti<u>sh</u>: <u>t</u>ayyib.
   Fine.

   مُفَتِّش: طَيِّب

10. Basma: min fadlak, ween it-taksi?   بسمة: من فضلك، وين إلتَّكْسي؟
    Please, where is the taxi?

11. mufattish: it-taksi hnaak giddaam   مُفَتِّش: إلتَّكْسي هُناك گِدّام المطار.
    il-mataar.
    The taxi is over there in front of the
    airport.

12. Basma: shukran, ma9a s-salaama.   بسمة: شكرا. مع السّلامة.
    Thanks, goodbye.

13. mufattish: safra sa9iida, inshaalla.   مُفَتِّش: سفرة سعيدة. إنشالله.
    Have a good trip, God willing.

Additional Expressions (Audio)

aku talifoon bil-mataar?	*Is there a telephone in the airport?*	أكو تَلِـفون بالمطار؟
hadiyya / hadaaya (S/P)	*gift/s*	هَديّـة / هَدايا
filim / aflaam (S/P)	*film/s*	فِـلِم / أفلام
filim kaamira	*camera film*	فِـلِم كاميرة
ma9i aflaam kaamira	*I have camera films.*	معي افلام كاميرة
majalla / majallaat (S/P)	*magazine/s*	مَجَلّـة / مَجَلّات
maa 9indi majallaat	*I do not have magazines.*	ما عندي مجلات
mufattish gamaarig	*customs inspector*	مُفَتِّـش گمارگ
daabut jawaazaat	*passport officer*	ضابُط جَوازات

Vocabulary (Audio)

iftah / iftahi / iftahu (M/F/P)	*you open (imp. verb)*	إفْتح / إفْتحي / إفْتحو
junta / junat (S/P)	*luggage/s, suitcase/s, purse/s*	جُنْطة / جُنَط
bi-kull	*with all (see below)*	بِـكُل
suruur	*pleasure*	سُرور
bikull suruur	*with (all) pleasure*	بكل سرور
ma9a + attached pronoun	*have, with (see below)*	مَعَ
9ind + attached pronoun, 9indi	*have (see lesson 14), I have*	عِـند. عِـندي
shii / ashyaaʾ (S/P)	*thing/s, something/s*	شي / أشْياء
mamnuu9 / mamnuu9a (M/F)	*illegal, forbidden (adj.)*	مَمْنوع / مَّمْنوعة
kullha	*everything, all*	كُلّـها
malaabis	*clothes*	ملابِـس
shakhsi / shakhsiyya (M/F)	*personal, private (adj.)*	شَخْصي / شَخْصيّة
shgadd?	*How much? How long?*	شْـگـد؟
fluus	*money*	فْـلوس
hawaali	*about, approximately*	حَوالي
alif	*one thousand*	أَلِـف
duulaar / duulaaraat (S/P)	*dollar/s*	دولار / دولارات
kaamira / kaamiraat (S/P)	*camera/s*	كاميرة / كاميرات

aw	*or*	أَو
jigaara / jigaayir (S/P)	*cigarette/s*	جِـگـارة / جِـگـايـر
bass	*only, enough, but*	بَـسّ
taksi	*taxi*	تَـكْـسي
giddaam	*in front, before, ahead*	گِـدّام
wara	*behind, in the back*	ورا
inshaalla	*God willing* (see below)	إنْـشالله
raqam / arqaam (S/P)	*number/s, numeral/s*	رَقَـم / أَرْقام

Grammar and Remarks

The Preposition ma9a   مَعَ   have, with (see also lessons 10 and 14)

The proposition **ma9a** is conjugated with the attached pronouns as follows:

ma9i	*I have (with me)*	مَعي
ma9aana	*we have (with us)*	مَعانا
ma9ak	*you* (M) *have (with you)*	مَعك
ma9ich	*you* (F) *have (with you)*	مَعـچ
ma9aakum	*you* (P) *have (with you)*	مَعاكـم
ma9aa	*he has (with him)*	مَعا
ma9aaha	*she has (with her)*	مَعاها
ma9aahum	*they have (with them)*	مَعاهـم

The Preposition Prefix b- / bi-   بْ / بِـ   in, by, at, with

The preposition prefix "**b-**" mostly corresponds to the English meanings "in" or "by," though in some contexts it also means "at" or "with." It occurs as a prefix with definite or indefinite nouns. When the prefix "**b-**" precedes a definite noun with the article " **il-**" (the), it takes the form "**bi-**" and the "**i**" of "**il**" drops. (Audio)

hiyya b-mataar	*She is in an airport.*	هي بْ مَطار
hiyya bil-mataar	*She is in the airport.*	هي بِالْـمطار
huwwa b-findiq	*He is in a hotel.*	هو بْ فِـنْـدِق
huwwa bil-findiq	*He is in the hotel.*	هو بِالْـفِـنْـدِق
misha b-sayyaara	*He went by a car.*	مِشـا بْ سَـيّـارة
misha bis-sayyaara	*He went by the car.*	مِشـا بِالسَّـيّـارة
saa9idni bij-junta	*Help me with the luggage.*	ساعِـدْني بِالْـجُـنْـطة

The Noun: il-isim   الإسـم

Arabic nouns have two grammatical genders, masculine (M) and feminine (F). In other words, things to Arabs are either masculine or feminine. There is no "it" as in English. These terms usually denote a natural gender, although inanimate (nonhuman) ones (book, library, etc.) must also be either masculine or feminine. (Audio)

taalib (M)	*student*	طالب	taaliba (F)	*student*	طالبة
khaal (M)	*uncle*	خال	khaala (F)	*aunt*	خالة
ktaab (M)	*book*	كتاب	maktaba (F)	*library*	مكتبة

As you can see from the above examples, the two genders are usually differentiated by the occurrence or the absence of the suffix "**a, ة**" at the end of the noun or the adjective. Almost all masculine words end in a consonant, and most feminine ones end with the suffix "**a ة**." The student, therefore, can change the gender of most words that refer to people by simply adding or omitting the feminine ending "**a ة**."

Most nouns have three numbers, singular (S); dual (D) for two persons or objects; and plural (P). (Audio)

diinaar (S) (one dinar)	دينار	diinaareen (D) (two dinars)	دينارين	danaaniir (P) (dinars)	دَنانـير
taalib (S) (one student M)	طالب	taalbeen (D) (two students M)	طالـْبين	tullaab (P) (students M)	طُّلاب
taaliba (S) (one student F)	طالبة	taalibteen (D) (two students F)	طالِبْتين	taalibaat (P) (students F)	طالِـبات

All nouns are either definite or indefinite. A noun is definite if it is preceded by the definite article "**il-** الـ" (*the*), has an attached pronoun, or is a proper name. Otherwise, it is indefinite. (Audio)

beet	*a house*	بيت	il-beet	*the house*	إلْبـيت
sayyaara	*a car*	سَيّارة	is-sayyaara	*the car*	إلسَّيّارة
beetna	*our house*	بـيتْنا	sayyaaratna	*our car*	سَيّارَتْنا

The Cardinal Numerals 1–10: arqaam أرْقـام (Audio)

1	waahid / wihda (M/F)	واحِـد / وحُـدة
2	thneen / thinteen (M/F)	ثْنـيـن / ثِنْـتين
3	tlaatha	تْلاثة
4	arba9a	أرْبَـعة
5	khamsa	خَمْسة
6	sitta	سِتَّة
7	sab9a	سَبْـعة
8	thmaanya	ثْمانْئَـة
9	tis9a	تِـسْعة
10	9ashra	عَشْـرة
0	sifir	صِفِـر

Idioms and Common Phrases (Audio)

The Arab people invoke **alla** الله (*God*) in their daily communication very often. The word **alla** is used in different contexts that do not necessarily reflect a religious significance but rather a cultural expression. Idiomatic phrases containing the word **alla** are used by secular and religious people alike, including non-Muslims. These invocations reflect the idea that health, sickness, success, failure, and other occurrences are the will of God. Below are some of the most common of these expressions. Notice that the word **alla** is almost always pronounced with emphatic "ḷ."

1. inshaaḷḷa   إنْـشـالله   *God willing, by the will of God, I hope.*

This idiomatic expression is one of the most commonly used in the Arabic language. It is used by speakers to express the hope that something has turned out or will turn out favorably. Nonnative speakers of Arabic must be very careful not to use this expression sarcastically. People who travel to the Middle East may see inshaaḷḷa done in beautiful Arabic calligraphy in homes, stores, cars, etc. (Audio).

safra sa9iida, inshaaḷḷa	*Have a happy trip, God willing.*	سَفْـرة سَعيدة. إنْشـالله
ashuufak baachir, inshaaḷḷa	*I will see you tomorrow, God willing.*	أشـوفك باجِـر، إنْشـالله
aani raayiḥ l-Baghdaad ba9ad usbuu9, inshaaḷḷa	*I am going to Baghdad in one week, God willing.*	آني رايح لُ بغداد بَعَـد اُسْبـوع، إنْشـالله
shloon shughlich?	*How is your (F) work?*	شُـلون شُـغْـلك؟ إنْشـالله
inshaaḷḷa zeen?	*Good, God willing?*	زين؟
shloonkum il-yoom?	*How are you (M) today?*	شُـلونْـكـم إلْـيـوم؟ إنْشـالله
ishaaḷḷa zeniin?	*Well, God willing?*	زينين؟

2. ilḥamdu lillaah   إلْـحَـمْـدُ لله   *Thanks be to God.*

This is one of the standard replies to a question about how a person is doing or how things are going (Audio).

shloon wildak?	*How are your (M) children?*	شُـلون ولـْدَك؟
zeeniin, ilḥamdu lillaah.	*Well, praise be to God.*	زينـين. إلحَمد لله
shloonak ilyoom ?	*How are you (M) today?*	شُـلونك إليـوم؟
zeen, ilḥamdu lillaah; or just	*Well, praise be to God.*	زين. إلحَمد لله
ilḥamdu lillaah	*Praise be to God.*	إلحَمد لله

3. alla ykhallii + attached pronoun   الله يُخَـلّـي   *May God preserve.*

Sometimes this phrase is used to request something from another person like min faḍlak مِن فَـضْلك (*please*). It may also be used as a response to a compliment (Audio).

min fadlak, ween it-taksi?	*Please, where is the taxi?*	من فضلك. وين إلتّـكسي؟
or		
alla ykhalliik, ween it-taksi ?	*Please, where is the taxi?*	الله يخليك. وين إلتّـكسي؟
min fadlich, iftahi ij-junta	*Please, open the luggage.*	من فضلِج.إفتحي الجُنطة
or		
alla ykhalliich, iftahi j-junta	*Please, open the luggage.*	الله يخليج. إفتحي الجُنـطة
min fadlich, ween il-bariid?	*Please, where is the post office?*	من فضلِج. وين البريد؟
or		
alla ykhalliich, ween il-bariid?	*Please, where is the post office?*	الله يخليج. وين البريد؟
min fadlak, saa9idni bij-junta	*Please, help me with the luggage.*	من فضلك. ساعِدني بالجُنـطة
or		
alla ykhalliik, saa9idni bij-junta	*Please, help me with the luggage.*	الله يخليك. ساعِدني بـالجُنـطة

4. yaa alla   يا الله   *Oh God.*

An exclamation said by someone who is about to begin something such as work, a trip, eating, sitting down, etc. (Audio).

5. yalla   يَـلّـلـه   *Hurry up.*

Idioms four and five are basically the same words, but notice the difference in pronunciation between them (Audio).

yalla, khalliina nruuh lil-beet	*Hurry up, let us go to the house.*	يَـلّـلـه. خلّـينا نروح للبيت
yalla, jiibi l-kursi	*Hurry up, bring (F) the chair.*	يَـلّـلـه. جيبي الكرسي
yalla, rah-yimshi l-qitaar	*Hurry up, the train will be leaving.*	يَـلّـلـه. رَح يمشي القطار
yalla, khalliina naakul	*Hurry up, let's eat.*	يَـلّـلـه. خلّـينا ناكل

6. walla   والله   *Really, definitely (lit., I swear by God, emphatic oath) (Audio).*

mufattish: ma9ich ashyaa° mmanuu9a?	*Do you have with you illegal items?*	مفتش: مَعِج أشياء ممنوعة؟
Basma: laa, walla	*No, definitely not.*	بسمة: لا. والله
walla, ma-shifit Baabil	*Really, I did not see Babylon.*	والله. مَ شفت بابل

| walla, ma-aruuh ma9ak | *Definitely not, I will not go with you* (M). | والله. ما روح معك |

7. balla? بَلْـكَـه؟ *Is it so? Is it true? Please* (with request) (lit., *in the name of God*).

il-findiq daraja uulaa	*The hotel is first class.*	إلفندق درجة أُولى
balla?	*Is it true?*	بَلْـكَـه؟
ujrat it-taxi hwaaya	*Taxi fare is expensive.*	أُجرت إلتّـكسي هواية
balla?	*Is it so?*	بَلْـكَـه؟
balla, fad jigaara	*A cigarette please* (would you give me...).	بَلْـكَـه. فَـد چِـكارة

8. muu balla? مو بَلْـكَـه؟ *Isn't it so? Isn't it?*

il-9iraaq balad qadiim, muu balla?	*Iraq is an ancient country.* *Isn't it?*	إلعراق بلد قديم. مو بَلْـكَـه؟
Amriika balad chibiir, muu balla?	*America is a large country.* *Isn't it?*	أمريكا بلد چبير. مو بَلْـكَـه؟
Basma Amriikiyya, muu balla?	*Basma is an American. Isn't it so?*	بسمة أمريكية. مو بَلْـكَـه؟

9. fiimaanillaa فيمانِـيـكـلا *goodbye* (lit., *in God's safety*)

| Basma: fiimaanillaa | *Basma: Goodbye* | بسمة: فيمانيـكـلا |
| Mufattish: fiimaanillaa | *Inspector: Goodbye* | مفتش: فيمانيـكـلا |

10. maashaalla ماشـالله *Praise be to God* (lit., *whatever God wills*).

Idiom of admiration used along with or instead of a direct compliment to avert the evil eye.

maashaalla, wildak kbaar	*Praise be to God, your children are big.*	ماشالله. ولـكـدَك كـبار
maashaalla, 9eeltak chibiira	*Praise God, your family is large*	ماشالله. عيلـكتك چِـبيرة
maashaalla, shughulkum zeen	*Praise be to God, your work is good.*	ماشالله. شُغـُلـكـكم زين

11. allaa(h)! ألـكـلاه! *How nice!* (Expression of admiration and the origin of the Spanish word "olé.")

allaah! shgadd hilu shaari9 Abu Nuwaas bil-leel?	*How nice is Abu Nuwas Street at night!*	ألـكـلاه! شگـد جِلو شارع ابو نواس بالـكـليل؟
allaah! shgadd hilu nahar Dijla bil-leel?	*How nice is the view of Tigris River at night!*	ألـكـلاه! شگـد جِلو نَـهر دِجْلة بالـكـليل؟
allaah ismich hilu!	*How nice your* (F) *name is!*	ألـكـلاه إسْمِچ حِلو!

Drills   tamaariin   تَمارين

1. Give appropriate oral replies to the following expressions:

min fa<u>d</u>lich ifta<u>h</u>i j-jun<u>t</u>a   من فضلج. إفتحي الجنطة

ween it-taksi, a<u>ll</u>a y<u>kh</u>alliik?   وين إلتـّكسي، اللّه يخلّيك؟

<u>sh</u>gadd ma9ich fluus?   شگـد معِـج فلوس؟

safra sa9iida, in<u>sh</u>aa<u>ll</u>a   سفرة سعيدة. انشالله

<u>a</u>ku talifoon bil-ma<u>t</u>aar?   أكو تلفون بالمطار؟

<u>sh</u>gadd baaqi b-Lubnaan?   شگـد باقي بـّلُبنان؟

ma9akum a<u>sh</u>yaaʾ mamnuu9a?   معـكم أشياء منوعة؟

9indkum kaamira wa aflaam?   عندكم كاميرة وأفلام؟

il-mufatti<u>sh</u> 9iraaqi loo Amriiki?   إلمفـتـّش عراقي لو أمريكي؟

<u>sh</u>loonkum? zeeniin in<u>sh</u>aa<u>ll</u>a?   شلونكم؟ زينين انشالله؟

2. Change the following masculine forms to feminine (F) and plural (P) forms:

ifta<u>h</u> ij-jun<u>t</u>a, min fa<u>d</u>lak   إفـتـح الجُـنْـطة. من فَـضْـلك

F:

P:

ma9ak kaamira wa filim   مَعَـك كاميرة وفِـلِـم؟

F:

P:

huwwa mufatti<u>sh</u> bil-ma<u>t</u>aar   هو مُفَـتـّش بـالـْمَطار

F:

P:

<u>sh</u>gadd inta baaqi hnaa?   شُگَـد إنت باقي هنا؟

F:

P:

beetak yamm is-suug   بـيـتك يَـم إلشّـوگ

F:

P:

inta muu ta9baan   إنت مو تَعُبان

F:

P:

aani muu zeen il-yoom   آني مو زين اليوم

F:

P:

huwwa muu juu9aan   هو مو جوعان

F:

P:

3. Read the following aloud:

a.   it-taksi giddaam il-maṭaar   إلتَّكسي گِدّام المطار

ij-junṭa giddaami   إلجُنطة گِدّامي

it-taksi giddaam il-findiq   إلتَّكسي گِدّام إلفندق

ij-junṭa giddaamna   إلجُنطة گِدّامنا

it-taksi giddaam il-bariid   إلتَّكسي گِدّام إلبريد

ij-junṭa giddaamak   إلجُنطة گِدّامك

it-taksi giddaam is-safaara   إلتَّكسي گِدّام إلسّفارة

ij-junṭa giddaamich   إلجُنطة گِدّامِچ

it-taksi giddaam il-beet   إلتَّكسي گِدّام إلبيت

ij-junṭa giddaamkum   إلجُنطة گِدّامُكم

it-taksi giddaam il-bank   إلتَّكسي گِدّام إلبنك

ij-junṭa giddaama   إلجُنطة گِدّامَه

it-taksi giddaam beethum   إلتَّكسي گِدّام بيتهم

ij-janṭa giddaamha   إلجُنطة گِدّامُها

it-taksi giddaam beetna   إلتَّكسي گِدّام بيتنا

ij-junṭa giddaamhum   إلجُنطة گِدّامُهم

b.   is-sayyaara wara is-safaara   إلسّيارة ورا السّفارة

it-ṭayyaara waraaya   إلطّيّارة ورايَه

is-sayyaara wara il-bank   إلسّيارة ورا البنك

it-ṭayyaara waraana   إلطّيّارة ورانا

is-sayyaara wara il-beet   إلسّيارة ورا البيت

it-ṭayyaara waraak   إلطّيّارة وراك

is-sayyaara wara il-bariid   إلسّيارة ورا البريد

	it-tayyaara waraa<u>ch</u>	إلطّيارة وراچ
	is-sayyaara wara beetkum	إلسّيارة ورا بيتكم
	it-tayyaara waraakum	إلطّيارة وراكم
	is-sayyaara wara beeta	إلسّيارة ورا بيته
	it-tayyaara waraa	إلطّيارة وراه
	is-sayyaara wara beetha	إلسّيارة ورا بيتها
	it-tayyaara waraaha	إلطّيارة وراها
	is-sayyaara wara beethum	إلسّيارة ورا بيتهم
	it-tayyaara waraahum	إلطّيارة وراهم
c.	ma9i malaabis wi-fluus	معي ملابس وفلوس
	ma9aa jigaayir hwaaya	مَعا چكاير هواية
	ma9aana malabis wi-fluus	مَعانا ملابس وفلوس
	ma9aaha jigaayir hwayya	مَعاها چكاير هُواية
	ma9ich junta <u>ch</u>ibiira	معج جُنطة چِبيرة
	ma9aakum junta <u>ch</u>ibiira	معاكم جُنطة چِبيرة
	ma9ak junta <u>ch</u>ibiira	معك جُنطة چِبيرة
	ma9aahum jigaayir hwaaya	معاهم جُنطة چِبيرة

4. Say the following in Arabic: aruu<u>h</u>   أروح   *I go*

I go to your (M) home by car.

I go home by train.

I go to the market today.

I go to Lebanon by an airplane, God willing.

I go to Babylon from the hotel.

Definitely, she is in the airport.

Definitely, they are in the American embassy in Baghdad.

Definitely, you (P) are in the Iraqi embassy in Washington.

Definitely, we are in the Saudi embassy in Jeddah.

Definitely, they are not from Jeddah.

Definitely they are neither Iraqis nor Americans.

Hurry up, open (M) the book.

Hurry up, open (M) the luggage.

Hurry up, open (F) the camera.

Hurry up, open (F) the film.

Hurry up, open (P) the door.

Hurry up, open (P) the embassy.

5. Complete and read the following aloud:

a.   alla ykhalliik, ween it-taksi?   الله يُخَـلّـيك. وين التَّكسي؟

     alla ykhalliich, _____?   ؟_____ الله يُخَـلّـيچ.

     alla ykhalliikum, _____?   ؟_____ الله يُخَـلّـيكم

     alla ykhalliik, ween findiq ir-Rashiid?   الله يُخَـلّـيك. وين فندق إلرّشيد؟

     alla ykhalliich, _____?   ؟_____ الله يُخَـلّـيچ.

     alla ykhalliikum, _____?   ؟_____ الله يُخَـلّـيكم.

b.   yalla, khalliina nruuh lis-safaara   يَـلّـه. خَـلّـينا نروح لِـلسّـفارة

     _____ lis-suug   لِـلسّـوگ _____

     _____ lil-findiq   لِـلْفِـندق _____

     _____ lil-bariid   لِـلْبريد _____

     _____ il-Baghdaad   إلْ بغـداد _____

     _____ lil-9iraaq   لِـلْعراق _____

     _____ lil-mataar   لِـلْمطار _____

     _____ lil-beet   لِـلْبيت _____

c.   maashaalla shughlak zeen   ماشـالله شُغْـلَـك زين

     _____ shughlich _____   _____ شُغْـلِـچ _____

     _____ shughulkum _____   _____ شُغْـلَـكم _____

     _____ shughli _____   _____ شُغْـلي _____

     _____ shughulna _____   _____ شُغْـلْها _____

     _____ shughla _____   _____ شُغْـلَـه _____

     _____ shughulhum _____   _____ شُغْـلْهم _____

6. Translate the following into English:

humma bil-findiq _____ هُمّه بـِالـعـراق

intu Amriikaan min Los Angeles _____ إنتو أمريكان مِن لوس انجَلوس

aani aruuh il-Baabil bis-sayyaara _____ آني أروحْ إلْ بابل بالسّـيارة

aani maa ruuh il-Baabil bil-qitaar _____ آني ما روحْ إلْ بابل بالقطار

aani hnaa li-ziyaarat il-aathaar _____ آني هُنا لـِزيارتْ إلآثار

ma9ich ashyaaᵓ mamnuu9a? _____ مـعـج أشياء مـمـنـوعة؟

walla, maa ma9i aflaam bij-junta _____ والله. ما مـعـي أفلام بالجّنطة

yalla, iftahu ij-junat _____ يَـلّـله. إفتحو الجّـنـط

is-sayyaara giddaam is-safaara _____ إلسّـيارة گـِـدّام إلسّـفارة

il-qitaar muu giddaam il-beet _____ إلقطار مو گـِـدّام إلبيت

il-akil laa ghaali wala rkhiis _____ إلأكل لا غـالي ولا رخيص

il-mat9am laa shiish wala kabaab _____ إلمطعم لا شـيش ولا كباب

shloon shughlak? zeen inshaalla? _____ شـلون شـُـغـلك؟ زين إنشـالله؟

yalla, rah-yimshi l-qitaar _____ يَـلّـله، رَحْ يِمشي القطار

Creative Dialogues

a. taalib 1:   ween sayyaartich?   طالب 1:   وين سيّـارْتـِـج؟

    taaliba 2:   haadhi sayyaarti   طالبة 2:   هاذي سَيّـارْتي

    taalib 1:   allaah, sayyaartich hilwa   طالب 1:   ألّـاه، سَيّـارتـِـج حِلـوَة هُواية
                 hwaaya

    taaliba 2:   shukran   طالبة 2:   شُـكـرا

    taalib 1:   yalla, khalliina nruuh   طالب 1:   يَـلّـله. خَـلّـينا نْروح لِـلْـمَـطعـم
                 lil-mat9am.

    taaliba 2:   ween il-mat9am?   طالبة 2:   وين الْـمَـطعـم؟

    taalib 1:   yamm findiq ir-Rashiid   طالب 1:   يَـم فِـنْـدِق إلـرّشـيـد

b. ṭaalib 1:   <u>sh</u>loona ibni<u>ch</u>, yaa Samiira?   شـلونَه إبْنِـچ. يا سـميرة؟ :1 طـالب

    ṭaaliba 2:   zeen, il<u>h</u>amdu lillaah   زين. إلْحَمُد للّه :2 طالبة

    ṭaalib 1:   beeti<u>ch</u> bi9iid, muu balla?   بـيتـج بِـعيد. مو بَـلَـكْله؟ :1 طالب

    ṭaaliba 2:   laa, muu bi9iid hwaaya   لا. مو بِـعيد هُوايه :2 طالبة

    ṭaalib 1:   <u>sh</u>u<u>gh</u>li<u>ch</u> zeen, in<u>sh</u>aa<u>ll</u>a?   شُـغلِـچ زين. إنشالله؟ :1 طالب

    ṭaaliba 2:   laa <u>sh</u>ii<u>sh</u> wala kabaab   لا شيش ولا كباب :2 طالبة

    ṭaalib 1:   fiimaanillaa   فـيماني‌كلا :1 طالب

    ṭaaliba 2:   fiimaanillaa   فـيماني‌كلا :2 طالبة

For new words, see Glossary.

Two bull men guard the gate of the ancient Assyrian city of Nimrud in northern Iraq

DARIS SITTA   دَرِس سِتَّة

Taking a Taxi

ta'jiir taksi   تَأجيـر تَكـئسـي

Basma walks to the front of the airport to take a taxi to the Rashid Hotel; she approaches a driver (saayiq) and says to him:

Basic Dialogue (Audio)

1. Basma: marhaba.
   Hello.

   بسـمة: مَرحبة.

2. saayiq: marhaba.
   Hello.

   سـايق: مَرحبة.

3. Basma: ariid aruuh il-findiq ir-Rashiid.
   I want to go to the Rashid Hotel.

   بسـمة: أريد أروح إلْ فِنـئدق إلرَّشـيد.

4. saayiq: 9ala 9eeni, tfaddali is9adi bis-sayyaara.
   With pleasure, please get in the car.

   سـايق: على عيني. تـئفَـضَّلي إصْعَدي بالسّيارة.

5. Basma: aku 9addaad bis-sayyaara?
   Is there a meter in the car?

   بسـمة: أكو عَدّاد بالسّيارة؟

6. saayiq: laa, maaku 9addaad.
   No, there is no meter.

   سـايق: لا. ماكـو عَـدّاد.

7. Basma: shgadd il-ujra?
   How much is the fare?

   بسـمة: شـئگَـد إلأُجْرَة؟

8. saayiq: 9ashir danaaniir.
   Ten dinars.

   سـايق: عَشـِر دَنـانير.

9. Basma: haadhi hwaaya, antiik sitt
   danaaniir.
   This is too much, I give you six dinars.

بسمة: هاذي هُوايَه. أنْطيك سِت دَنـانير.

10. saayiq: maykhaalif, tfaddali.
    Fine, please (get in.)

سايق: مَيْخالِف تفضّلـي.

11. Basma: il-findiq giriib loo bi9iid
    mnil-mataar?
    Is the hotel near or far from the airport?

بسمة: إلـفندق گـريب لو بِـعيد مُن لِـئَمطار؟

12. saayiq: laa giriib wala bi9iid.
    Neither near nor far.

سايـق: لا گِـريب ولا بِـعيـد.

13. Basma: shloona l-findiq?
    How is the hotel?

بسمة: شلـونـَه الـفِـندق؟

14. saayiq: daraja uulaa. wisalna, haadha
    huwwa l-findiq.
    First class. We've arrived, this is the hotel.

سايـق: دَرَجَة أولى. وصَلـئـنا هاذا هو الـفندق.

15. Basma: shukran, haak il-ujra.
    Thanks, take the fare.

بسمة: شكـرا. هاك الإجرة.

Vocabulary (Audio)

saayiq / saayqa (M/F)	*driver*	سايـق / سايْـقة
ariid	*I want* (see verbs, lesson 11)	أريد
aruuh	*I go* (see verbs, lesson 11)	أروح
9ala / 9a-	*on, upon, about* (see lesson 15)	عَـلى / عَ
9eeni	*my eye*	عـيني
9ala 9eeni	*with pleasure* (see below)	على عـيني
aku	*there is/are* (semi verb word)	أكـُو
maaku	*there isn't/aren't* (see below)	ماكـُو
is9ad / is9adi / is9adu (M/F/P)	*get in, go up* (imp. verb)	إصْعَد / إصْعَدي / إصْعَدو
9addaad	*meter* (car), *gauge*	عَـدّاد
ujra	*fare, fee, rate*	أُجـرَة
dinaar / danaaniir (S/P)	*dinar/s* (Iraqi currency)	دِينار / دَنـانير
haadha / haadhi / hadhoola (M/F/P)	*this, that* (demonstratives, see lesson 14)	هاذا / هاذي / هَذولـة
hwaaya	*much, many, a lot* (invariable)	هُوايَـه
antiik / antiich / antiikum	*I give you* (M/F/P)	أنْطيك / أنْطيج / أنْطيكـُم

maykhaalif	*fine, okay, it doesn't matter* (see lesson 14)	مَيْخالِف
giriib, qariib	*near, close by* (adj.)	گِـريب، قَـريب
bi9iid, ba9iid	*far away* (adj.)	بِـعـيد، بَـعـيد
loo	*or*	لـو
mni- < min	*from* (preposition. **min** becomes **mni** for phonetic reasons when it precedes the article **il-**)	مُن - > مِـن
daraja / darajaat (S/P)	*level/s, degree/s*	دَرَجَة / دَرَجات
uulaa / awwal (F/M)	*first* (ordinal numeral)	أُولى / أَوّل
wiṣalna	*we arrived, we have arrived.*	وِصَلْـنا
haak / haach / haakum (M/F/P)	*take* (imp. verb)	هاك / هاچ / هاكُم

Grammar and Remarks

The Adjective: iṣ-ṣifa   الصِّـفَـة

Arabic has three adjective forms: masculine, feminine, and plural. The masculine adjective is the simplest form with no added ending. The feminine has the ending "**a, ة**" like the feminine noun, sometimes with some changes in the underlying word, specifically the dropping of the stem vowel, "**i**" or "**u**," that precedes the last consonant in the word. There are two main forms of plural adjectives, a masculine plural formed by adding the suffix "**-iin**" and feminine plural formed by adding the suffix "**-aat**." A less common adjective form of the pattern CVCVVC (**kabiir**, *large*) is usually made plural in the pattern CCVVC (**kbaar**). For both noun and adjective agreement, see the section below. To decide the adjective form, the student must recognize the direction of the speech and determine whether the adjective is describing/modifying a male, a female, or a plural, and then select the appropriate form. Below is the declension of the adjective **zeen** (*well*) with the independent pronouns (Audio).

I	aani zeen / aani zeena (M/F)	*I am well*	آني زين / آني زينة
you	inta zeen (M)	*you are well*	إنت زين
you	inti zeena (F)	*you are well*	إنتي زينة
he	huwwa zeen	*he is well*	هو زين
she	hiyya zeena	*she is well*	هـي زينة
we	iḥna zeeniin / iḥna zeenaat M/F	*we are well*	إحْنا زينين / إحنا زينات
you	intu zeeniin / intu zeenaat (M/F)	*you are well*	إنْتو زينين / إنْتو زينات
they	humma zeeniin / humma zeenaat (M/F)	*they are well*	هُمّه زينين / هُمّه زينات

The Relative Adjective

This is a special form of adjective that reflects the meaning "of," "pertaining to," or "related to" the noun from which it is usually derived. It is an important and common construction in Arabic. It has three forms: masculine, feminine, and plural, just like the regular adjectives.

1. Masculine Singular and Plural: The masculine relative adjective is formed by adding the suffix "-i, ـِي" (singular) and the suffix "-iyyiin, ـِيِّين" (plural) to the noun (Audio).

Lubnaan	*Lebanon*	لُبْنان	9iraaq	*Iraq*	عِـراق
Lubnaani	*Lebanese*	لُبْناني	9iraaqi	*Iraqi*	عِـراقي
Lubnaaniyyiin	*Lebanese*	لُبْنانِيِّين	9iraaqiyyiin	*Iraqis*	عِـراقِـيِّـين
Tuunis	*Tunis*	تونِـس	Baghdaad	*Baghdad*	بَـغْـداد
Tuunisi	*Tunisian*	تونِـسي	Baghdaadi	*Baghdadi*	بَـغْـدادي
Tuunisiyyiin	*Tunisians*	تونِسِيِّـين	Baghdaadiyyiin	*Baghdadis*	بَغْـدادِيِّـين
			also: Bghaada	*Baghdadis*	بْـغـادَة

2. Feminine Singular and Plural: The feminine relative adjective is formed by adding the suffix "-iyya, ـِيَّة" (singular) and the suffix "-iyyaat, ـِيّات" (plural) (Audio).

Lubnaan	*Lebanon*	لُبْنان	9iraaq	*Iraq*	عِـراق
Lubnaaniyya	*Lebanese*	لُبْنانِيَّـة	9iraaqiyya	*Iraqi*	عِـراقِـيَّـة
Lubnaaniyyaat	*Lebanese*	لُبْنانِيّات	9iraaqiyyaat	*Iraqis*	عراقِـيّـات
gharb	*west*	غَـرْب	sharq	*east*	شَـرْق
gharbiyya	*westerner*	غَـرْبِـيَّـة	sharqiyya	*eastern*	شَـرْقِـيَّـة
gharbiyyaat	*westerners*	غَـرْبِـيّـات	sharqiyyaat	*easterners*	شَـرْقِـيّـات

There are some exceptions to the general rules outlined above.

Noun–Adjective Agreement

The adjective agrees with the noun it modifies in gender, number, and definiteness. If the noun is indefinite or definite, the adjective must also be indefinite or definite, respectively. (Audio)

beet jidiid	بيت جِـديد	il-beet li-jdiid	إلْبيت لِـجْـديد
a new house		*the new house*	
		beetna li-jdiid	بيتْنا لِـجْـديد
		our new house	
findiq rikhiis	فِندِق رِخيص	il-findiq li-rkhiis	إلفندق لِـرْخيص
a cheap hotel		*the cheap hotel*	

After a masculine or a feminine noun the adjective must be masculine or feminine, respectively. (Audio)

maktab jidiid	مَكتب جِديد	maktaba jidiida	مَكتبة جـِديدة
a new office		*a new library*	
walad <u>ch</u>ibiir	وَلـَد چـِبـير	bint <u>ch</u>ibiira	بِـنت چـِبـيرة
a big boy		*a big girl*	

With a masculine or feminine plural animate noun the adjective is also plural. With a nonhuman (inanimate) plural noun the adjective is usually feminine singular. (Audio)

tullaab 9iraaqiyyiin (M)	*Iraqi students*	طِلاب عِراقِيّـِين
taalibaat 9iraaqiyyaat (F)	*Iraqi students*	طـالِبـات عِراقِيـّـأت
kulliyya <u>ch</u>ibiira	*a large college*	كُلّـِية چـِبـيرة
kulliyyaat <u>ch</u>ibiira	*large colleges*	كُلّـِيـات چـِبـيرة
mifta<u>h</u> jidiid	*a new key*	مِفتاح جـِديد
mafaatii<u>h</u> jidiida	*new keys*	مَفاتيح جـِديدة

The Word aku   أكـّو   *there is / are*

The word **aku** (*there is/are*) is not a verb in Iraqi Arabic in spite of its meaning. It is made negative with the prefix "**ma-**."

aku sayyaara	*There is a car*	أكـو سَـيّارة
maaku sayyaara	*There isn't a car*	ماكـو سَـيّارة
aku mayy <u>h</u>aar	*There is hot water*	أكـو مَـيّ حار
maaku mayy <u>h</u>aar?	*There isn't hot water*	ماكـو مَيّ حار
aku sayyaaraat	*There are cars*	أكـو سَـيّارات
maaku sayyaaraat	*There aren't cars*	ماكـو سَـيّارات

The Cardinal Numerals 11–20   da9a<u>sh</u>–9i<u>sh</u>riin   دَعَـش ـ عِشّـرين (Audio)

11	da9a<u>sh</u>	دَعَـش
12	thna9a<u>sh</u>	ثـناعَـش
13	tla<u>t</u>-<u>t</u>a9a<u>sh</u>	تـلاطّـعَـش
14	arbaa-<u>t</u>a9a<u>sh</u>	أربـاطـعَـش
15	<u>kh</u>mus-<u>t</u>a9a<u>sh</u>	خـُمُصطـعَـش
16	sit-<u>t</u>a9a<u>sh</u>	سِـطّـاعَـش
17	sbaa-<u>t</u>a9a<u>sh</u>	سُـباطـعَـش
18	<u>th</u>mun-<u>t</u>a9a<u>sh</u>	ثـُمُنْطـعَـش
19	tsaa-<u>t</u>a9a<u>sh</u>	تـساطـعَـش
20	9i<u>sh</u>riin	عِـشرين

Idioms and Common Phrases (Audio)

1. 9ala 9eeni, 9ala raasi عَـلـى عيـني، عَـلـى راسـي *with pleasure (lit., on my eye, on my head)* Idiomatic expressions used to indicate the speaker's readiness and acceptance of what being is said or requested.

min fadlak, iftah il-baab	*Please open the door.*	مِن فَـضْلك إفْـتَـح الـبـاب
Reply: 9ala 9eeni	*With pleasure.*	عَـلـى عيـني
alla ykhalliik, saa9idni bij-junta	*Please, help me with the suitcase.*	اللّه يُخَلّـيـك، ساعِـدني بالجُـنطة
Reply: 9ala raasi	*With pleasure.*	عَـلـى راسـي
ariid aruuh il-findiq ir-Rashiid	*I want to go to the Rashid Hotel.*	أريد أروح إلْ فِـنْدق الرَّشـيـد
Reply: 9ala 9eeni, is9ad bis-sayyaara	*With pleasure, get in the car.*	عَـلـى عيـني، إصْعَـد بالسّيارة
min fadlich iftahi ish-shubbaach	*Please open the window.*	مِـن فَـضْلِـچ إفْـتَـحي الشّـبّـاچ
Reply: 9ala raasi	*With pleasure.*	عَـلـى راسـي

2. 9ala fikra عَـلـى فِـكْـرَة *by the way*

9ala fikra, shloona il-mat9am?	*By the way, how is the restaurant?*	على فِـكرة. شلـونَه المطعـم؟
9ala fikra, ween raayih?	*By the way, where are you going?*	على فِـكرة. وين رايح؟
9ala fikra, ween sayyaartak?	*By the way, where is your car?*	على فِـكرة. وين سيّـارتك؟
9ala fikra, shunu ismich?	*By the way, what is your name?*	على فِـكرة. شُـنـو إسْمِـچ؟

3. 9ala kull haal عَـلـى كُل حـال *in any case, anyway*

9ala kull haal, huwwa raayih lil-9iraq	*Anyway, he is going to Iraq.*	على كل حال، هو رايـح لِـلْعراق
9ala kull haal, huwwa ma-raayih lil-9iraq	*Anyway, he is not going to Iraq.*	على كل حال. هو مَ رايـح لِـلْعراق
Basma raayha lil-Basra, 9ala kull haal	*Basma is going to Basra, anyway.*	بسمة رايْحَة لِـلْبَصْرة. على كل حال
9ala kull haal, il-bariid muu bi9iid	*Anyway, the post office is not far.*	على كل حال، إلْبـريـد مُو بِـعيد
9ala kull haal, Laylaa muu 9iraaqiyya	*In any case, Laylaa is not an Iraqi.*	على كل حال، ليلى مُو عِراقيَّة

Drills   tamaariin   تَمارين

1. Give appropriate oral replies to the following statements:

ariid aruuh il-findiq ir-Rashiid	أريـد أروح إلّ فِـنْـدق الرّشـيـد
ween il-findiq, min fadlich?	وين إلْـفِـنْـدق، مِن فَـضُلـج؟
shgadd il-ujra mnil-mataar lil-findiq?	شْـگَـد الأجرة مُـن لْـمَطار لِـلْـفِـنْـدق؟
aku 9addaad bis-sayyaara?	أكو عَـدّاد بالسّيارة؟
il-findiq giriib loo bi9iid?	إلْـفِـنْـدق گِـريب لو بِـعيد؟
haak il-ujra	هاك الأجْـرَة
shloona findiq Baghdaad?	شْـلـونَه فِـنْـدق بـغداد؟
fiimaanillaa	فيمانيـٹلا
saayiq it-taksi 9iraaqi loo Amriiki?	سـايق إلتّـكْـسي عِـراقي لو أمْريكي؟
il-findiq ghaali loo rikhiis?	إلْـفِـنْـدق غالي لو رخيص؟

2. Make the following indefinite masculine noun–adjective phrases definite:

mataar jidiid	مَطار جـديد	saayiq Baghdaadi	سايق بغدادي
baasbort Amriiki	باسْبورْت أُمْريكي	taaliba kabiira	طالِـبة كَـبيرة
findiq bi9iid	فِـنْـدق بـعـيد	mufattish 9iraaqi	مُفَـتّـش عِـراقي
muwazzafa Lubnaaniyya	مُوَظَّـفَـة لُـبْنانية	junta chibiira	جنطة چِـبـيرة
mat9am zeen	مَطْـعَم زين	findiq rikhiis	فِـنـدق رِخيص
taksi ghaali	تَـكْـسي غالي	qitaar sarii9	قِـطار سَـريع

3. Make feminine and plural the following masculine statements and read aloud:

aani Amriiki	آني أمريكي	inta Almaani	إنت أمريكي

F:

P:

huwwa 9iraaqi	هو عراقي	ma9ak kaamira	معك كاميرا

F:

P:

ma9ak filim	معك فِـلِم	haak il-ujra	هاك الأجرة

F:

P:

aani mit°assif	آني مِتأسْف	iftah ij-junta	إفْتَح إلجُـنْطة
F:		F:	
P:		P:	
huwwa muu zeen	هو مو زين	aani muu Lubnaani	آني مو لُبناني
F:		F:	
P:		P:	
inta Masri loo Suuri	إنت مصري لو سوري؟		
F:			
P:			
inta laa juu9aan wala 9at shaan	إنت لا جوعان ولا عطشان		
F:			
P:			

4. Negate the following:

aku mataar b-Baghdaad	أكو مطار بْ بغداد
hiyya min Los Angeles	هي مـن لـوس انجلوس
inta Tuunisi loo Su9uudi?	إنت تونسـي لـو سُـعودي؟
humma Kuweetiyyiin	هُمّه كويـتـيِّـين
ma9i junta wihda	معـي جُنْطة وحْـدة
ma9ich baasbort?	معِـج باسْبـورت؟
aku tayyaaraat bil-mataar	أكو طَـيّـارات بـالـمَطار
ihna Amriikaan min Washington	إحنا أمريكان مِن واشنطن
hiyya raayha lis-suug	هي رايْحَـة لِـلـسّـوگ
it-taksi giddaam il-findiq	إلـتّـكـسـي گِـدّام الْـفِـنْدق
shaku il-yoom?	شَـكـو الـيـوم؟
shaku maaku 9ar-radio?	شكـو ماكـوَ الـرّاديـو؟

5. Make the following statements relative adjectives and read aloud:

Example: hiyya min Beeruut	*She is from Beirut.*	هي مِن بـيـروت
hiyya beeruutiyya	*She is Beiruti.*	هي بـيـروتـيِّـة
huwwa mnil-9iraaq هو مْـنِ لْـعْراق	Basma min Amriika	بسـمة من أمـريكا

Samiir min Baghdaad	سمير من بغداد	inta mnil-Kuweet	انت مِــن لكويت
intu (M) min Suurya	إنتو من سورية	inti min Liibya	إنتي من لـيبـيا
intu (F) min Urubbaa	إنتو من اوُروبا	humma min Lubnaan	هُــمّة من لبنان
humma (F) min Iraan	هُــمّه من ايران	laylaa min Maṣir	ليلى من مصر

6. Say the following in Arabic:

I am (M) an American.	I am (F) an American.
I am (M) a Canadian.	I am (F) a Canadian.
I am (M) an Iranian.	I am (F) an Iranian.
I am (M) a Sudanese.	I am (F) a Sudanese.
I am (M) a Mexican.	I am (F) a Mexican.
I am (M) a Turk.	I am (F) Turk.
I am (M) a Swede.	I am (F) a Swede.
I am (M) an African.	I am (F) an African.
I am (M) an easterner.	I am (F) an easterner.
I am (M) a westerner.	I am (F) a westerner.

7. Repeat the above statements in the plural forms, masculine and feminine:

Example: ihna Amriikaan	*We are* (M) *Americans.*	إحْــنا أمُريكان
ihna Amriikiyyaat	*We are* (F) *Americans.*	إحْــنا أمُريكِــيّــات

8. Count the following in Arabic:

one boy	two boys	ten boys
one girl	two girls	nine girls
one passport	two passports	six passports
one suitcase	two suitcases	four suitcases
one dinar	two dinars	seven dinars
one dollar	two dollars	five dollars
one hotel	two hotels	three hotels
one door	two doors	eight doors

9. Translate the following into English:

ma9akum kaamira bij-junṭa? _____ معكم كاميرا بالجُنطة؟

Basma bil-findiq _____ بسمة بالفندق

<u>sh</u>gadd fluus ma9i<u>ch</u>? _____ شُگَد فلوس معج؟

it-ṭayyaara bil-maṭaar _____ إلطيّارة بـالـمطار

il-findiq daraja uulaa _____ إلـفندق دَرَجة اُولى

muu baasbort 9iraaqi _____ مو باسُبورت عراقي

9ala 9eeni w raasi _____ على عيني وراسي

9ala fikra, ween Basma? _____ على فِكـرة. وين بسمة؟

yalla, <u>kh</u>alliina nruu<u>h</u> lil-beet _____ يَلـله خلّـينا نروح لِـلـبيت

il-ahal zeeniin, in<u>sh</u>aa<u>ll</u>a? _____ إلأهل زينين. إنشاالله؟

a<u>ll</u>a y<u>kh</u>alliik, ifta<u>h</u> is-sayyaara _____ الله يُخـلّـيك. إفتح السيّارة

9ala fikra, ween A<u>h</u>mad? _____ على فِكـرة. وين احمـد؟

aku maṭaareen ib-Ba<u>gh</u>daad _____ أكو مطارين بْ بغداد

9ala kull <u>h</u>aal, aani juu9aan _____ على كـل حال. آني جوعان

10. Complete and read the following aloud:

a. haak il-ujra	هاك الأجرة	haak il-baasbort	هاك الباسبورت
haa<u>ch</u> _____	_____ هاج	haa<u>ch</u> _____	_____ هاج
haakum _____	_____ هاكم	haakum _____	_____ هاكم
haak il-qalam	هاك القلم	haak ij-junṭa	هاك الجُـنطة
haa<u>ch</u> _____	_____ هاج	haa<u>ch</u> _____	_____ هاج
haakum _____	_____ هاكم	haakum _____	_____ هاكم

b.   9ala fikra, huwwa Iṭaali   على فِكْرة. هو إيطالي

_____ , hiyya _____   _____ هي _____

_____ , humma (M) _____   _____ هُمّة _____

_____ , humma (F) _____   _____ هُمّة _____

_____ , aani (M) _____   _____ آني _____

_____ , aani (F) _____   _____ آني _____

_____ , iḥna (M) _____   _____ إحنا _____

_____ , iḥna (F) _____   _____ إحنا _____

_____ , inta _____   _____ إنت _____

_____ , inti _____   _____ إنتي _____

_____ , intu _____   _____ إنتو _____

c.   9ala kull ḥaal, it-taksi muu ghaali bil-9iraaq   على كل حال، إلتّكسي مو غالي بالعراق

_____ b-Baghdaad   _____ بُ بغداد

_____ b-Lubnaan   _____ بُ لبنان

_____ b-Beeruut   _____ بُ بيروت

_____ b-Maṣir   _____ بُ مَصِر

_____ bil-Urdun   _____ بِالأُرْدُن

_____ b-9ammaan   _____ بُ عَمّان

_____ bis-Su9uudiyya   _____ بِالشّعودية

_____ bir-Riyaad   _____ بِالرّياض

Creative Dialogues

a. ṭaalib 1: tu9urfiin findiq zeen ib-Baghdaad?

طالب 1: تُعُرُفين فِندق زين بُ بغداد؟

ṭaaliba 2: na9am, a9ruf fanaadiq hwaaya.

طالبة 2: نعم. أعرف فنادق هُوايه

ṭaalib 1: ariid findiq rikhiis.

طالب 1: أريد فِندق رخيص

ṭaaliba 2: findiq 9ishtaar muu ghaali hwaaya.

طالبة 2: فِندق عِشتار مو غالي هُوايه

ṭaalib 1: ween haadha l-findiq?

طالب 1: وين هاذا الفندق؟

ṭaaliba 2: il-findiq ib-shaari9 is-Sa9duun.

طالبة 2: إلفِندق بُ شارع السَّعُدون

ṭaalib 1: huwwa bi9iid loo giriib?

طالب 1: هو بِعيد لو گِريب؟

ṭaaliba 2: bi9iid ishwayya.

طالبة 2: بِعيد شُوَيَّه

b. ṭaalib 1: inti 9iraaqiyya loo Iṭaaliyya?

طالب 1: إنتي عِراقيّة لو إيطاليّة؟

ṭaaliba 2: aani laa 9iraaqiyya wala Iṭaaliyya. aani Isbaaniyya.

طالبة 2: آني لا عِراقيّة ولا إيطاليّة آني إسبانيّة

ṭaalib 1: min ayy madiina?

طالب 1: مِن أي مَدينة؟

ṭaaliba 2: aani min madiinat Madriid.

طالبة 2: آني مِن مَدينة مَدُريد

ṭaalib 1: alla(h), haadhi madiina hilwa.

طالب 1: ألئَلاه. هاذي مَدينة حِلُوَة

ṭaaliba 2: shukran jaziilan.

طالبة 2: شُكراً جَزيلاً

For new words, see Glossary.

As-Safafier, an old market well-known for its copper and brass craftsmanship, in Baghdad

DARIS SAB9A   دَرس سَـبْعَـة

At the Rashid Hotel

b-findiq ir-Rashiid   بُ فِنْدِق الـرّشـيد

Basma gets out of the taxi at the Rashid Hotel and walks toward the reception desk to inquire about her room reservation. The receptionist (mudayyif) welcomes her saying:

Basic Dialogue (Audio)

1. mudayyif: ahlan wa sahlan. ayy khidma?
   Welcome. How can I serve you?
   مُضَيِّف: أهْلا وسَهْلا. أيّ خِدْمة؟

2. Basma: shukran, 9indi hajiz bil-findiq.
   Thanks, I have a hotel reservation.
   بسـمة: شُـكـرا. عِنْدي حَجِـز بالـّفِـندق.

3. mudayyif: shunu isim hadirtich?
   What is your name, please?
   مُضَيِّف: شُنو إسِم حَضِرْتِج؟

4. Basma: ismi Basma Adams.
   My name is Basma Adams.
   بسـمة: إسمي بسمة آدمز.

5. mudayyif: lahza min fadlich. na9am ghuruftich haadra, raqam 9ishriin.
   One moment, please. Yes, your room is ready, number twenty.
   مُضَيِّف: لَحْظَـة مِن فَـضْلِج. نعم غَـرُفْـتِـج حاضْرَة رَقَـم عِـشْرين.

6. Basma: shukran jaziilan.
   Thank you very much.
   بسـمة: شُـكـرا جَـزيلا.

7. mudayyif: il-baasbort, min fadlich.
   The passport, please.
   مَضَيِّف: إلباسْبـورت. من فَـضْـلِـج.

8. Basma: tfaddal, il-baasbort.
   Here is the passport.

   بسمة: تْفَـضَّل الـبَاسْبورت.

9. mudayyif: shukran. kam yoom baaqya?
   Thanks. How many days are you staying?

   مُضَيِّف: شُكْرا. كَم يوم باقْيَـة؟

10. Basma: baaqya usbuu9.
    I am staying for one week.

    بسمة: باقْيَـة اُسْبوع.

11. mudayyif: amrich. tfaddali l-miftaah.
    Certainly. Here is the key.

    مُضَيِّف: أمْرِج. تْفَـضَّلـي الـمِفْتاح.

12. Basma: gulli alla ykhalliik, il-ghurfa
    biiha hammaam wa mayy haarr?
    *Tell me please, does the room have a
    bathroom and hot water?*

    بسمة: كُلّـي الله يْخَـلّـيـك. الـغُـرْفة بـيها
    حَـمّـام ومَيّ حارّ؟

13. mudayyif: na9am, kullshi biiha,
    w-inshaalla ti9ijbich.
    *Yes, it has everything, and you will like it,
    hopefully.*

    مُضَيِّف: نعم، كُـلْـشـي بـيها. وانشاالله
    تِـعِـجْـبـج.

14. Basma: min fadlak, saa9idni bij-junta.
    Please, help me with the luggage.

    بسمة: من فضلك. ساعِدْني بالـجُـنْـطة.

15. mudayyif: 9ala 9eeni. haadha il-booy
    ysaa9dich.
    With pleasure. That bellboy will assist you.

    مُضَيِّف: على عيني. هاذا الـبُـوْيُ
    يُـساعِـدْج.

16. Basma: shukran, ma9a s-salaama.
    Thanks, goodbye.

    بسمة: شكرا. مع السّـلامة.

Vocabulary (Audio)

mudayyif / mudayyifa (M/F)	*host, hostess, stewardess*	مُضَيِّف / مُضَيِّفة
ahlan wa sahlan	*welcome*	أهلا وسهلا
ayy	*which?*	أيّ
khidma / khidmaat (S/P)	*service/s*	خِـدْمة / خِـدْمات
9indi	*I have (see lesson 15)*	عِـنْـدي
hajiz	*reservation*	حَـجِـز
lahza	*a moment*	لَـحْـظَـة
ghurfa / ghuraf (S/P)	*room/s*	غُـرْفة / غُـرَف
haadir / haadriin (M/P)	*ready*	حاضِر / حاضْرين
haadra / haadraat (F/P)	*ready*	حاضْرَة / حاضْرات
raqam / arqaam (S/P)	*number/s, numeral/s*	رَقَـم / أرقـام
jaziilan	*very, much (invariable)*	جَـزيلاً
kam, cham?	*how many? (see lesson 15)*	كَـم، چَـم؟
yoom / ayyaam (S/P)	*day/s*	يـوم / أيْـتام

baaqi / baaqya (M/F)	*staying*	باقي / باقْيَة
usbuu9 / asaabii9 (S/P)	*week/s*	أُسْبوع / أسابيع
amrich	*certainly, whatever you say (lit. your order)*	أمـْرِج
miftaah / mafaatiih (S/P)	*key/s*	مِفْتاح / مَفاتيح
gulli / gulliili / gulluuli (M/F/P)	*tell me (imp. verb, see below)*	گـُلّـي / گـُلّـيلي / گـُلّـلولي
biiha	*in it, it has (consists of preposition **bi** and attached pronoun **-ha**)*	
hammaam	*bathroom, Turkish bath*	حَمـّام
mayy	*water*	مَيّ
haarr	*hot*	حار
baarid	*cold*	بارد
kullshi	*everything*	
ti9ijbich / ti9ijbak / ti9jibkum (F/M/P)	*you like, it pleases you*	تِعـْجِـبِـج / تِعـْجِبَك / تِعـْجِـبْكم
ysaa9idni	*he helps me, he assists me*	يـْساعِـدني
booy	*bellboy (borrowed from the English word "boy," one who does manual service in hotels, restaurants, etc.)*	بـَوْي
ysaa9dich / ysaa9dak (F/M)	*he helps you*	يـْساعـْدِج / يـُساعـْدَك
aku	*there is/are (see lesson 6)*	أكو
nafis / nufuus (S/P)	*self/s*	نَـفِس / نـُفوس

Grammar and Remarks
Nouns of Occupations with Suffixes -chi and -chiyya ‏ــ چـي / ــ چِـيّـة

Iraqi Arabic has many nouns that refer to occupations or professions. These occupational nouns are derived from other nouns by adding the suffix "-**chi**" (singular) and the suffix "-**chiyya**" (plural). Adding these suffixes cause changes sometimes (shifting or omitting vowels) in the words (see below). This type of noun seems to occur in masculine form only. (Audio)

Noun	Meaning	Occupational Noun (S/P)		Meaning
chaay	*tea*	chaaychi	chaaychiyya	*tea vendor*
چاي		چايْـچي	چايْـچِـيّـة	
boosta	*post office*	boostachi	boostachiyya	*postman*
بوسْطة		بوسْـطَـچي	بوسْـطَـچِـيّـة	

shakar شَكَـر	sugar	shakarchi شَكَـرْچِي	shakarchiyya شَـكَـرْچِـيّـة	sweet seller
dumbug دُمْـبُـگ	drum	dumbagchi دُمْـبَـگْـچِي	dumbagchiyya دُمْـبَـگْـچِـيّـة	drummer
tanak تَـنَـك	tin	tanakchi تَـنَـكْـچِي	tanakchiyya تَـنَـكْـچِـيّـة	tinsmith
hammaam حَـمّـام	bath	hammamchi حَـمّـمْـچِي	hammamchiyya حَـمّـمْـچِـيّـة	bath keeper
saabuun صابون	soap	saabunchi صابونْـچِي	saabunchiyya صابونْـچِـيّـة	soap vendor
bistaan بِـسْـتـان	orchard	bistanchi بِـسْـتَـنْـچِي	bistanchiyya بِـسْـتَـنْـچِـيّـة	orchard keeper
qundara قُـنْـدَرَة	shoe	qundarchi قُـنْـدَرْچِي	qundarchiyya قُـنْـدَرْچِـيّـة	shoe repairman
gahwa گَـهْـوَة	coffee, cafe	gahawchi گَـهَـوْچِي	gahawchiyya گَـهَـوْچِـيّـة	cafe keeper

The Word abu أبــو *father (of)*

The word **abu** (*father*) and to a lesser extent the word **umm** (*mother*) are widely used with definite nouns by Iraqis to create an occupational noun. One can add **abu** to almost any of the above-mentioned definite nouns to indicate the related occupation or profession. (Audio)

Noun	Meaning		abu + Noun		Meaning
il-bariid	the post office	إلْـبَـريد	abu l-bariid	أبو الْـبَـريد	mailman
it-taksi	the taxi	إلتّـكْـسِي	abu t-taksi	أبو التّـكْـسِي	taxi driver
il-gahwa	the coffee	إلْـگَـهْـوَة	abu l-gahwa	أبو الـگَـهْـوَة	café keeper
is-saabuun	the soap	إلصّابون	abu s-saabuun	أبو الصّابون	soap vendor
il-haliib	the milk	إلْـحَـليب	umm il-haliib	أم الْـحَـليب	milk vendor (F)

The Imperative Verb: fi9il il-amur فِـعِـل الأمُـر

The imperative verb in Arabic is used in the same manner and it conveys the same meaning as the English counterpart, giving a command to a person who is present. It has three forms: masculine, feminine, and plural, all in the second person (you). The Arabic masculine form usually has no vowel ending, for example **jiib** (*bring*). It can be considered as the base form. The feminine form is obtained by adding the suffix vowel "**-i** ي ـ" to the masculine form, **jiibi** (*bring*), and the plural is formed by adding "**-u** و ـ" **jiibu** (*bring*). The addition of these suffixes often causes vowel changes in the underlying form, especially the dropping of the stem vowel. (Audio)

jiib (M)	جيب	jiibi (F)	جيبي	jiibu (P)	جيبو	*bring*	
is'al (M)	إسأل	is'ali (F)	إسألي	is'alu (P)	إسألو	*ask*	
saafir (M)	سافر	saafri (F)	سافري	saafru	سافرو	*travel*	
ruuh (M)	رُوح	ruuhi (F)	رُوحي	ruuhu (P)	رُوحو	*go*	
oogaf (M)	أوگـف	oogfi (F)	أوگـفي	oogfu (P)	أوگـفي	*stand up*	
sidd (M)	سِـدّ	siddi (F)	سِـدّي	siddu (P)	سِـدّو	*close*	

The negative imperative is expressed by adding the negative prefix "**la-**" to the second person indicative verb form and not to the command form. (Audio)

Imperative		Indicative		Negative Imperative	
ruuh (M)	روح	truuh	تروح	la-truuh	لـترو
go		*you go*		*don't go*	
ruuhi (F)	روحي	truuhiin	تروحين	la-truuhiin	لـتروحين
go		*you go*		*don't go*	
ruuhu (P)	روحو	truuhuun	تروحون	la-truuhuun	لـتروحون
go		*you go*		*don't go*	
sidd (M)	سِـدّ	tsidd	تسِـدّ	la-tsidd	لـتسِـدّ
shut		*you shut*		*don't shut*	
siddi (F)	سِـدّي	tsiddiin	تسِـدّين	la-tsiddiin	لـتسِـدّين
shut		*you shut*		*don't shut*	
siddu (P)	سِـدّو	tsidduun	تسِـدّون	la-tsidduun	لـتسِـدّون
shut		*you shut*		*don't shut*	

The Cardinal Numerals 20–100   9ishriin–miyya   عِشُـرين — مِـيّـة

In Arabic the numbers three through nine can be increased incrementally in tens by adding the suffix "**-iin** ين" after dropping out the final suffix "**a** ة" from the number. (Audio)

2	thneen	ثـنـيـن	20	9ishriin	عِشـرين	(special number)
3	tlaatha	ثـلاثة	30	tlaathiin	ثـلاثين	
4	arba9a	أربعة	40	arba9iin	أربـعين	
5	khamsa	خَـمسة	50	khamsiin	خَـمـسين	
6	sitta	سِـتّة	60	sittiin	سِـتّـين	
7	sab9a	سَـبـعة	70	sab9iin	سَـبـعين	
8	thmaany	ثـمانية	80	thmaaniin	ثـمانين	
9	tis9a	تِـسعة	90	tis9iin	تِـسعين	
			100	miyya	مِـيّة	

Numbers between twenty-one and twenty-nine or thirty-one and thirty-nine, etc., are read from right to left. For example, twenty-one is read as one-and-twenty. (Audio)

21	waahid - wa - 9ishriin	واحِد وعِشْرين
22	thneen - wa - 9ishriin	ثُنين وعِشْرين
23	tlaatha - wa - 9ishriin	ثلاثة وعِشْرين
24	arba9a - wa - 9ishriin	اربعة وعشْرين
25	xamsa - wa - 9ishriin	خمسة وعشْرين
26	sitta - wa - 9ishriin	سِتّة وعشرين
27	sab9a - wa - 9ishriin	سَبعة وعشرين
28	thmanya - wa - 9ishriin	ثمانية وعشرين
29	tis9a - wa -9ishriin	تِسعة وعشرين
30	tlaathiin	تْلاثِين
31	waahid- wi - tlaathiin	واحِد وتْلاثين

And so on with other numbers.

Idioms and Common Phrases (Audio)

1. sh9abaal + attached pronoun?   شْـعَـبال +؟   *What did (one) think otherwise? (lit., what was on someone's mind)*

sh9abaalak, Baghdaad sghayyra?	*What did you (M) think, Baghdad was small?*	شْـعَـبالَـك، بغداد صْغَـيـرَة؟
sh9abaalich, Basma 9iraaqiyya?	*What did you (F) think, Basma was an Iraqi?*	شْـعَـبالِـچ، بسمة عِـراقية؟
sh9abaalkum, il-9iraaq muu qadiim?	*What did you (P) think, Iraq was not ancient?*	شْـعَـبالـكُـم، العراق مو قـديم؟
sh9abaala, il-kabaab muu tayyib?	*What did he think, the kabab was not good?*	شْـعَـبالـه، الـكَـباب مو طَـيـب؟
sh9abaalha, is-suug muu bi9iid?	*What did she think, the market was not far?*	شْـعَـبالـها، السّـوگ مو بـعيـد؟
sh9abaalhum, is-safaara giriiba?	*What did they think, the embassy was close?*	شْـعَـبالـهُم، السّـفارة گِـريبة؟

2. maashi l-haal   ماشـي الـحـال   (invariable)   *Okay, not bad (lit., the condition is walking)*

Khaalid:	shloonich il-yoom?	*How are you today?*	خالـد: شلونِـچ اليوم؟
Basma:	zeena ilhamdu lillaah	*Good, praise God.*	بسمة: زينة. الـحَمْدُ لله
Khaalid:	shloon ish-shughul?	*How is the work?*	خالـد: شْـلون الشّـغُـل؟
Basma:	mashi l-haal	*Okay*	بسمة: ماشـي الـحـال

See below for more examples.

3. ya9ni يَعْنِي (invariable) *well, um, uh* (lit., *"it means, in other words"*).

It is used to fill pauses in speech.

Kariim: shloon ish-shughul?	*How is work?*	كريم: شلون الشّغل؟
Laylaa: ya9ni, maashi l-haal	*Well, okay.*	ليلى: يَعْني. ماشي الحال
Kariim: shloon l-ahal?	*How is the family?*	كريم: شلون الاهل؟
Laylaa: ya9ni, zeeniin il-hamdu lillaah	*Well, fine, praise God.*	ليلى: يَعْني. زينين الحمد لله

Drills   tamaariin   تَمارين

1. Give appropriate oral replies to the following expressions:

ahlan wa sahlan	أهلا وسهلا
aku hammaam bil-ghurfa?	أكو حَمّام بِالغُرفة؟
9indich hajiz bil-findiq?	عِنْدِج حَجِز بِالفندق؟
ween miftaah is-sayyaara?	وين مِفْتاح السّيارة؟
kam yoom baaqya hnaa?	كَم يوم باقْيَة هُنا؟
shaku maaku?	شَكو ماكو؟
ween miftaah il-ghurfa?	وين مِفْتاح الغُرُفة؟
aku mayy haar bil-hammam?	اكو مَيّ حار بِالحَمّام؟
shunu isim il-findiq?	شنو إسِم الفندق؟
min fadlak, saa9idni bij-junta	من فَضْلَك. ساعِدْني بِالجُنْطة
il-ghurfa haadra loo muu haadra?	إلغرفة حاضْرَة لو مو حاضْرَة؟
9ala 9eeni	على عيني

2. Negate the following:

aku nakhal (palms) hwaaya bil-9iraaq	أكو نَخَل هُواية بِالعِراق
shaku?	شُكو؟
aku booy bil-findiq	أكو بويْ بِالفندق
sidd il-baab, min fadlak	سِدّ الباب. مِن فَضْلَك
aku hammaam bil-ghurfa	أكو حَمّام بِالغُرُفة
ruuhi lil-mataar il-yoom	روحي لِلمَطار اليوم
9indi 9ishriin diinaar	عِندي عِشْرين دينار
it-taksi giddaam il-mataar	إلتَّكْسي گِدّام الٔمَطار
is°ali Laylaa ween il-bariid	إسْألي ليلى وين البَريد
ma9i kaamira bij-junta	مَعي كاميرا بِالجُنْطة

3. Change the following masculine imperative verbs (and anything else that needs to be changed) to feminine and plural forms:

min fadlak ruuh lil-beet	من فضلك. روح لِلبيت

F:

P:

saafir il-Baghdaad   سافر إلْ بغداد

F:

P:
tfaddal istariih   تْفَـضّـل إسْـتـريح

F:

P:
la-tsaafir il-Suurya   لتسافر إلْ سورية

F:

P:
gulli, shunu raqam il-ghurfa   گُـلْـلي، شـنـو رَقم الغرفة؟

F:

P:
iftah li-ktaab il-9arabi   إفتح لِـكْـتاب العربي

F:

P:
la-tjiib fluus   لَـتْـجيب فْـلوس

F:

P:
sidd li-ktaab li-Fransi   سِـدّ لِـكْـتاب لِـفْـرَنْـسي

F:

P:
la-tisʾal il-mufattish   لَـتِسْأل المـفـتـش

F:

P:

sh9abaalak, huwwa Itaali?   شْـعَبالـك هو إيطالي؟

F:

P:
la-toogaf giddaam il-qitaar   لـَتوگَف گِـدّام القطار

F:

P:
sh9abaalak, huwwa kaslaan?   شْـعَبالـك، هو كسلان؟

F:

P:

4. Say the following numbers in Arabic:

10	31	70	88	99	11	16	12	72
86	97	13	20	14	15	83	96	17
25	65	78	19	97	33	27	66	79
44	77	100	40	90	50	60	70	80

5. Complete and read the following aloud:

a. Saami haadir   سامي حاضِر   inta muu haadir   إنت مو حاضِر

    Basma _____   بسمة   inti _____   إنتي

    humma _____   هُـمّـه   intu (M) _____ إنتو

    huwwa _____   هو   intu (F) _____ إنتو

    aani (M) _____ آني   aani (F) _____   آني

    ihna (M) _____ إحنا   ihna (F) _____   إحنا

b. 9indi hajiz bil-findiq   عِندي حجز بالفندق
    maa 9indi hajiz bil-findiq   ما عندي حجز بالفندق

    _____ bit-tayyaara   بالطّيارة _____

    _____ bis-sayyaara   بالسّيارة _____

_____ bil-qitaar

بالقطار _____

_____ bis-siinama

بالسّينما _____

_____ il-yoom

اليوم _____

c. sh9abaalak, Basma 9iraaqiyya?

sh9abaalak, il-findiq muu bi9iid?

شْعَبالَك. بسِمة عراقيّة؟

شْعَبالَك.الـفندق مو بِـعيد؟

sh9abaalich, _____?

شْعَبالِـج. _____؟

_____, is-sayyaara muu jidiida?

إلسّيارة مو جِـديدة؟ _____

sh9abaalkum, _____?

شْعَبالكم. _____؟

_____, is-safaara muu giriiba?

إلسّفارة مو كِـريبة؟ _____

sh9abaala, _____?

شْعَبالَـه. _____؟

_____, it-taksi muu ghaali?

إلتّكسي مو غالي؟ _____

sh9abaalha _____?

شْعَبالْـها _____؟

_____, il-9iraaq muu qadiim?

إلعراق مو قديم؟ _____

sh9abaalhum, _____?

شْعَبالْـهم _____؟

_____, ich-chaay muu zeen?

إلچّـاي مو زين؟ _____

6. Translate into Arabic:

a. Please help (M) me with the luggage.

_____

help (F) me

_____

help (P) me

_____

b. You are (M) staying one week.

_____

(F)

_____

(P)

_____

c. He is staying two weeks.

_____

She is staying two weeks.

_____

They are (M) staying two weeks.

_____

They are (F) staying two weeks.

_____

We are (M) staying two weeks.

_____

We are (F) staying two weeks.

_____

d. He is going to Babylon.

_____

She is going to Babylon.

_____

They are (M and F) going to Babylon.

_____

I am (M and F) going to Babylon.

_____

We are (M and F) going to Babylon.

_____

You are (M, F, and P) going to Babylon.

_____

I am (M and F) ready.

_____

We are (M and F) ready.

_____

You are (M, F, and P) ready.

_____

He is ready.

_____

She is ready.

_____

7. Read the following aloud:

aku tanakchi zeen b-suug is-Safaafiir	أكو تَنَكْچي زين بُ سوگ الصّفافير
aku gahawchi zeen b-suug is-Safaafiir	أكو گَهَوْچي زين بُ سوك الصّفافير
aku kababchi zeen b-suug is-Safaafiir	أكو كَبَبُچي زين بُ سوگ الصّفافير
aku chaaychi zeen b-suug is-Safaafiir	أكو چايْچي زين بُ سوگ الصّفافير
aku shakarchi zeen b-suug is-Safaafiir	أكو شْكَـرْچي زين بسوگ الصّفافير
maaku bistanchi zeen b-suug is-Safaafiir	ماكو بِسْتَنْچي زين بُ سوگ الصّفافير
maaku hammamchi zeen b-suug is-Safaafiir	ماكو حَمّـمُچي زين بُ سوگ الصّفافير
maaku boostachi zeen b-suug is-Safaafiir	ماكو بوسْطَچي زين بُ سوگ الصّفافير
maaku qundarchi zeen b-suug is-Safaafiir	ماكو قُنْدَرْچي زين بُ سوگ الصّفافير

8. Make plural the following singular occupational nouns in parentheses:

aku (kababchi) tayyib b-suug is-Safaafiir	أكو (كَبَبُچي) طيّب بُ سوگ الصّفافير
(it-tanakchi) ta9baan il-yoom	(التّـنَكْچي) تَعُبان اليوم
huwwa khoosh (qundarchi)	هو خوش (قُنْدَرْچي)
inta laa (gahawchi) wala (bistanchi)?	انت لا (گَهَوْچي) ولا (بِسْتَنْچي)
(ish-shakarchi) bi9iid min findiq ir-Rashiid	(الشّكَـرْچي) بِعيد من فندق الرّشيد
(is-saabunchi) maa 9inda saabuun	(الصّابونْچي) ما عِنْدَه صابون

(il-boos<u>t</u>achi) Urduni min 9ammaan   (البوسْطَـچي) اُردني من عمّان

(il-bistan<u>ch</u>i) Ma<u>s</u>ri mnil-Qaahira   (البِسْتَـنْچي) مَصري مِن لْقاهرة

(i<u>ch</u>-<u>ch</u>aay<u>ch</u>i) 9iraaqi mnil-Ba<u>s</u>ra   (الجِّـايْـچي) عراقي مُن لْبَصْرة

Creative Dialogues

a.   <u>t</u>aalib 1:   ween naazla?   وين نازلَـة؟   طالب 1:

       <u>t</u>aaliba 2:   aani naazla b-findiq   آني نازْلَـة بْ فِـنْدق بغداد   طالبة 2:

            Ba<u>gh</u>daad

       <u>t</u>aalib 1:   <u>sh</u>loona haa<u>dh</u>a il-findiq?   شْلـونَه هاذا الْـفِـندق؟   طالب 1:

       <u>t</u>aaliba 2:   kulli<u>sh</u> zeen   كُلِّـش زين   طالبة 2:

       <u>t</u>aalib 1:   <u>gh</u>aali loo ri<u>kh</u>iis?   غالي لو رِخيص؟   طالب 1:

       <u>t</u>aaliba 2:   laa <u>gh</u>aali wala ri<u>kh</u>iis   لا غالٍ ولا رخيص   طالبة 2:

       <u>t</u>aalib 1:   shukran   شكراً   طالب 1:

       <u>t</u>aaliba 2:   ahlan wa sahlan   أهلاً وسهلاً   طالبة 2:

b.   <u>t</u>aalib 1:   abu it-taksi, ariid aruu<u>h</u>   ابو التّـكْـسي. أريد أروح إلْ فِـنْدق بغداد   طالب 1:

            il-findiq Ba<u>gh</u>daad

       <u>t</u>aaliba 2:   9ala 9eeni, tfa<u>dd</u>al is9ad   على عيني. تفضّـل إصْعَد بالسّـيارة   طالبة 2:

            bis-sayyaara

       <u>t</u>aalib 1:   gulliili findiq Ba<u>gh</u>daad zeen?   كُـلّـيلي فِـندق بغداد زين؟   طالب 1:

       <u>t</u>aaliba 2:   maa<u>sh</u>i l-<u>h</u>aal. findiq Fili<u>st</u>iin   ماشـي الحـال. فندق فِلِسطين كُلِّـش زين   طالبة 2:

            kulli<u>sh</u> zeen

       <u>t</u>aalib 1:   bi9iid loo qariib?   بِـعيد لو قَـريب؟   طالب 1:

       <u>t</u>aaliba 2:   bi9iid <u>sh</u>wayya   بِـعيد شْـوَيّـة   طالبة 2:

       <u>t</u>aalib 1:   la9ad, ruu<u>h</u> il-findiq   لَـعَـد. روح الْ فِـندق بغداد رجاءً   طالب 1:

            Ba<u>gh</u>daad, rajaaᵓan

       <u>t</u>aaliba 2:   iddallal   إدّلـلَـل   طالبة 2:

For new words, see Glossary.

The Abbaside Spiral Minaret in the city of Samarra, ninth century A.D.

DARIS THMAANYA   دَرِس ثْمانْئِيَـة

Introductions

تَـعـارُف   *ta9aaruf*

While Basma is strolling in the hotel lobby, she meets two people, Baasil (M) and Laylaa (F), and she greets them.

Basic Dialogue (Audio)

1. Basma: masaaʾ il-kheer.
   Good afternoon.

   بسـمة: مَسـاء الخير.

2. Laylaa: masaaʾ in-nuur.
   Good afternoon.

   ليلى: مَسـاء النّـور.

3. Basma: aani ismi Basma. shunu isimkum?
   My name is Basma. What are your names?

   بسـمة: آنـي اسـمـي بسـمة. شـنـو إسـمُكـم؟

4. Laylaa: aani ismi Laylaa, wa huwwa isma Baasil.
   My name is Laylaa and his name is Baasil.

   ليلى: آنـي اسمـي ليلى، وهـو إسْـمـه باسِـل.

5. Basma: tsharrafna biikum.
   Pleased to meet you (using the formal plural form).

   بسـمة: تْشَـرّفنـا بيكـم.

6. Laylaa and Baasil: w-ilna sh-sharaf.
   Pleased to meet you too.

   ليلى وباسـل: وِلْنا الشّـرَف.

7. Basma: mneen intu?
   Where are you from?

   بسمة: مُنين انتو؟

8. Laylaa: aani min Lubnaan, wa haa<u>dh</u>a zawji Baasil 9iraqi
   I am from Lebanon, and this is my husband Baasil, an Iraqi.

   ليلى: آني من لبنان. وهاذا زَوْجي باسِل عراقي.

9. Laylaa: w-inti mneen?
   And where are you from?

   ليلى: وِنْتي مُنين؟

10. Basma: aani Amriikiyya min Los Angeles.
    I am an American from Los Angeles.

    بسمة: آني أمريكية من لوس اﻧﺠﻠﻮس.

11. Laylaa: <u>sh</u>gadd <u>s</u>aarli<u>ch</u> hnaa?
    How long have you been here?

    ليلى: شْـﮔَـدّ صارْلِـﺞ هْـنا؟

12. Basma: <u>s</u>aarli hnaa yoomen.
    I have been here for two days.

    بسمة: صارْلي هـنا يومين.

13. Laylaa: aani <u>s</u>aarli sana b-baghdaad.
    I have been one year in Baghdad.

    ليلى: آني صارْلي سَـنة بُ بغداد.

14. Baasil: aani wiladit hnaa. zirti Baabil?
    I was born here. Have you visited Babylon?

    باسِل: آني وِلَـدِت هنا. زِرْتي بابل؟

15. Basma: laa, ba9ad maa zirit Baabil.
    No, I have not visited Babylon yet.

    بسمة: لا. بَـعَد ما زِرت بابل.

16. Baasil: aani <u>sh</u>ifit Baabil gabul sana.
    I saw Babylon a year ago.

    باسل: آني شِـفِت بابل ﮔَـبُل سَـنة.

17. Basma: fur<u>s</u>a sa9iida.
    A happy occasion (meeting you).

    بسمة: فُـرْصَة سَـعيدة.

18. Baasil and Laylaa: t<u>sh</u>arrafna
    Pleased to meet you.

    باسل وليلى: تْـشَـرَّفْـنا.

Vocabulary (Audio)

ta9aaruf	*introduction*	تَـعارُف
<u>sh</u>unu?	*what?*	شُنو؟
ismak / ismi<u>ch</u> / isimkum (M/F/P)	*your name*	إسْمَك / إسْمِـﺞ / إسِـمْكم
<u>sh</u>araf	*honor*	شَـرَف
t<u>sh</u>arrafna	*pleased to meet you (lit., we are honored)*	تْـشَـرَّفْـنا
biikum	*in you* (P) (word consists of " **bi-**" prefix and suffix pronoun "**-kum**")	بيـكُـم

ilna	*our ("* **il-** *" have and suffix pronoun "* **-na,** *" see lesson 14)*	إلْنا
w-ilna <u>sh</u>-<u>sh</u>araf	*pleased to meet you too (lit., the honor is ours)*	ولْنا الشَّرَف
mneen? or immeen?	*from where/where from?*	مْنين؟ إمّين؟
haa<u>dh</u>a	*this, that (demonstrative word, see lesson 14)*	هاذا
zawji, zooji	*my husband*	زَوْجي، زُوجي
zawijti, zoojti	*my wife*	زَوجْتي، زوجْتي
Lubnaan	*Lebanon*	لُبنان
9iraaqi (M)	*an Iraqi (relative adj., see lesson 6)*	عِراقي
Amriikiyya (F)	*an American (relative adj.)*	أمريكيّة
<u>sh</u>gadd?	*how long? how much?*	شْگَـد؟
<u>s</u>aarl	*to become, to have been (consists of* **<u>s</u>aar** *and* **-l** *)*	صارل
<u>s</u>aarli<u>ch</u>	*you have been*	صارْلِـج
<u>s</u>aarli	*I have been*	صارْلي
hnaa	*here*	هُـنا
yoom / yoomeen / ayyaam (S/D/P)	*one day/two days/days*	يوم / يومين / أيّام
sana / santeen / sniin (S/D/P)	*One year/two years/years*	سـنة / سَنْتيـن / سْـنين
wiladit	*I was born (see verbs below)*	ولـِدت
zirti	*you (F) visited*	زِرْتي
<u>sh</u>ifit	*I saw*	شـِفِت
fur<u>s</u>a	*occasion, opportunity*	فـُرْصَة
sa9iid / sa9iida (M/F)	*happy (adj.)*	سَعيد / سَعيدة
fur<u>s</u>a sa9iida	*happy occasion (meeting you)*	فـُرْصة سَعيدة

Grammar and Remarks
The Verb: il-fi9il   إلـْفِـعـِل

The Arabic verb consists of two basic parts: a stem and prefix/suffix. The stem gives the lexical meaning of the verb and the prefix/suffix indicates grammatical meanings, that is the person, the gender, and the number of the subject. For example, the past tense verb kitb**at** (*she wrote*) consists of the stem **kitb** (*wrote*) and the suffix **-at** (*she*), and the present verb **t**iktib (*she writes*) consists of the stem **ktib** (*to write*) and the prefix **t** (*she*).

The verb can be divided into two tenses: perfect and imperfect. These two tenses generally correspond to the English past and present/future tenses, respectively. In addition to the two tenses, most verbs have an imperative form, which you have already learned in lesson 7. To distinguish between the perfect/past and the imperfect/present verbs, one must notice that the former always takes a suffix and never a prefix (kitb**at**, *she wrote*); therefore, it is sometimes called the "suffix tense verb." The imperfect/present tense verb must always take a prefix and in some cases a suffix as well: **t**iktib, *she writes*, and **t**ikitb**uun**, *you write* (P). Consequently, it is also called the "prefix tense verb."

Each of the verb tenses has eight inflectional forms corresponding to the persons: **aani, iḥna, inta, inti, intu, huwwa, hiyya,** and **humma.** The verbs have four main types of roots: **regular, double, hollow,** and **weak.** The regular verb usually consists of three consonants that appear in all the words that are derived from that root as in **daras** (*he studied*). The double verb has also three consonants like the regular, except the last two consonants are identical as in **ḥabb** (*he liked*). The hollow verb usually has two consonants, and its third person masculine singular past tense form has a long vowel, "**aa**," between the two consonants as in **saaq** (*he drove*). The weak verb has also two consonants, and its third person masculine singular past tense ends in a final vowel as in **nisa** (*he forgot*). We shall begin with the past tense verb.

Note: Each verb has a past stem and present stem. Once the student memorizes the two stems of each verb, it should be easy to conjugate verbs since the prefixes of present verbs and the suffixes of past verbs never change.

The Past Tense Verb: il-fi9il il-maaḍi إلْـفِـعِـل الماضي

The base form for conjugating the past tense verb is the third person masculine singular because it is the simplest verb form, and the remaining forms are based on it. It is also the citation form used in most Arabic–English dictionaries.

Here are conjugation tables of the regular and the hollow verbs. (Audio)

The Regular Verb kitab *he wrote* كِـتَـب

Pronoun	Suffix	Verb Form				
huwwa	———*	kitab	*he wrote*	كِـتَـب	———	هو
hiyya	-at	kitbat**	*she wrote*	كِـتْـبَـت	ــَ ت	هي
humma	-aw	kitbaw**	*they wrote*	كِـتْـبَـوْ	ــَ وْ	هُـمّـه
inta	-it***	kitabit	*you wrote* (M)	كِـتَـبِـت	ــرت	إنت
inti	-ti	kitabti	*you wrote* (F)	كِـتَـبْـتـي	ــ تي	إنتي
intu	-tu	kitabtu	*you wrote* (P)	كِـتَـبْـتـو	ــ تـو	إنتو
aani	-it***	kitabit	*I wrote*	كِـتَـبِـت	ــِ ت	آني
iḥna	-na	kitabna	*we wrote*	كِـتَـبْـنـا	ــ نـا	إحنا

Remarks on the Regular Verb:

*No suffix added.

**The stem vowel "a" drops out in the she and they forms.

***Identical form.

The Hollow Verb shaaf *he saw* شاف

huwwa	——	<u>sh</u>aaf	*he saw*	شاف	——	هو
hiyya	-at	<u>sh</u>aaf**at**	*she saw*	شافَت	ـَ ت	هي
humma	-aw	<u>sh</u>aaf**aw**	*they saw*	شافَوْ	ـَ وْ	هُمّه
inta	-it	<u>sh</u>if**it***	*you saw*	شِفِت	ـِ ت	إنت
inti	-ti	<u>sh</u>if**ti**	*you saw*	شِفْتي	ـ تي	إنتي
intu	-tu	<u>sh</u>if**tu**	*you saw*	شِفْتو	ـ تو	إنتو
aani	-it	<u>sh</u>if**it***	*I saw*	شِفِت	ـِ ت	آني
ihna	-na	<u>sh</u>if**na**	*we saw*	شِفْنا	ـ نا	إحنا

Remarks on the Hollow Verb:

*The long vowel "**aa**" of the third person changes to the short vowel "**i**" in the second and first persons.

Idioms and Common Phrases (Audio)

1. diir baal + attached pronoun   دِيـــر بال +   *take care, watch out, give attention to* (lit., *turn around (your) mind*)

diir baalak mnis-sayyaara!	*Watch out for the car!*	دير بالَك مُن لسَّيّارة!
diiri baali<u>ch</u> 9ala binti<u>ch</u>!	*Take care of your daughter!*	دير بالِچ على بِنْتِچ!
diiru baalkum 9al-madrasa!	*Give your* (P) *attention to school!*	ديرو بالْكُم عَ الْمُدرسة!
Samiir, diir baalak 9ala nafsak!	*Samiir, take care of yourself!*	سمير، دير بالك على نَفْسك!

2. 9aa<u>sh</u> min <u>sh</u>aaf + attached pronoun   عاش مِــن شـاف +   *It has been a long time since I saw you* (lit., *lived he who saw you*).

haay ween inta? 9aa<u>sh</u> min <u>sh</u>aafak	*Where have you been? It has been a long time since I saw you* (M).	هايْ وين إنته؟ عاش مِن شافَك
haay ween inti? 9aa<u>sh</u> min <u>sh</u>aafi<u>ch</u>	*Where have you been? It has been a long time since I saw you* (F).	هايْ وين إنتي؟ عاش مِن شافِچ
haay ween intu? 9aa<u>sh</u> min <u>sh</u>aafkum	*Where have you* (P) *been? It has been long time since I saw you* (P).	هايْ وين إنتو؟ عاش مِن شافْكم

3. il-<u>kh</u>aatir   إلْ خاطِـر   *for someone's sake*

il-<u>kh</u>aatrak, ri<u>h</u>it il-Baghdaad	*For your* (M) *sake, I went to Baghdad.*	إلْ خاطْرَك، رِحـت إلْ بغداد
il-<u>kh</u>aatirkum, <u>sh</u>ifit Basma	*For your* (P) *sake, I saw Basma.*	إلْ خاطِـرُكم، شِـفِت بسمة

il-khaatrich, il-ujra diinaareen	*For your (F) sake, the rate is two dinars.*	إلْ خاطْرِج . الأجرة دينارين
il-khaatir alla, jiib li-ktaab	*For God's sake, bring the book.*	إلْ خاطِرِ الله. جيب لِكْتاب
il-khaatirhum, shifit il-mathaf	*For their sake, I saw the museum.*	إلْ خاطِرْهم. شِفِت المَتْحَف
il-khaatir Laylaa, ziritkum	*For Layla's sake, I visited you (P).*	إلْ خاطِرِ ليلى، زِرِتْكم

Drills   tamaariin تَمارين

1. Give appropriate oral replies to the following:

shinu ismich?	شِنُو إسْمِج؟
Laylaa 9iraaqiyya loo Lubnaaniyya?	ليلى عراقيّة لو لُبنانيّة؟
tsharrafna	تْشَرَّفْنا
imneen intu?	إمْنين إنـتو؟
shgadd saarilkum ib-Baghdaad	شْگَد صارِلْكم بُ بَغداد؟
aani 9iraaqi. w-inti?	آني عراقي. وانْتِ؟
fursa sa9iida	فُرْصة سَعيدة
ween wiladit?	وِيـن وِلَـدِت؟
ahlan wa sahlan	أهلا وسَهْلا
shifit loo maa shifit Baabil?	شِـفِت لو ما شِـفِت بابل؟
haay ween? 9aash min shaafkum	هاي وِين؟ عاش مِـن شافْكم
ween il-mathaf?	وِيـن الـمَتْحَف؟

2. Conjugate orally the following past tense regular and hollow verbs:

fitah baab	*He opened a door.*	فِـتَـح باب
zaar Baabil	*He visited Babylon.*	زار بابل
shirab mayy	*He drank water.*	شِـرَب مَيّ
saaq sayyaara	*He drove a car.*	ساق سَيّارة
diras ktaab	*He studied a book.*	دِرَس كْتاب
jaab miftaah	*He brought a key.*	جاب مِفْتاح
kisar qalam	*He broke a pen.*	كِـسَر قَـلَم
shaaf Laylaa	*He saw Layla.*	شاف ليلى
kitab risaala	*He wrote a letter.*	كِـتَب رسالة
raah lil-maktab	*He went to the office.*	راح لِـلْـمَكْتب
akal simach	*He ate fish.*	أكَل سِـمَج
taar ib-tayyaara	*He flew in an airplane.*	طار بُ طَـيّارة
hijaz ghurfa	*He reserved a room.*	حِـجَـز غُـرُفة

3. In the following sentences change orally the second person (M) singular past tense to second person (F) singular and plural forms; change anything else that must be changed:

Example:	fitaḥit il-baab	You (M) *opened the door.*	فِتَحِت الباب
	fitaḥti il-baab	You (F) *opened the door.*	فِتَحتي الباب
	fitaḥtu il-baab	You (P) *opened the door.*	فِتَحتو الباب

inta saafarit il-Lubnaan	إنت سافَرت إلَ لُبنان
inta wiladit ib-Baghdaad	إنت وِلَدِت بُ بغداد
siqit syyaara lil-findiq	سِقِت سَيّارة لِـلـئِـفِـنئِـدِق
ween shifit Basma?	وين شِـفِت بسمة؟
shgadd saarlak hnaa?	شَـگَـد صارلَك هنا؟
ḥijazit ghurfa bil-findiq	حِـجَـزت غُـرُفة بِـالـئِفِـندِق
inta 9iraaqi min ween?	إنت عراقي مِـن وين؟
inta zirit Baabil?	إنت زِرت بابل؟

4. Complete and read the following aloud:

a. aani 9iraaqi mnil-Baṣra	inta Su9uudi min Makka
آني عراقي مُـن لَـبَصْرة	إنت سُـعودي مِـن مَكّـة

iḥna (M) _____	إحنا	inti _____	إنتي
iḥna (F) _____	إحنا.	intu (M) _____	إنتو
hiyya _____	هي	intu (F) _____	إنتو
humma (M) _____	هُـمّة	humma (F) _____	هُـمّة

b. saarli yoom ib-findiq ir-Rashiid	صارلي يـوم بُ فِـندِق الرّشيد
saarli yoomeen ib-findiq ir-Rashiid	صارلي يومين بُ فِـندِق الرّشيد

saarilna shahar _____	صارِلـنا شَـهَر _____
saarilna shahreen _____	صارِلـنا شَـهْـرين _____
saarla usbuu9 _____	صارلَـه اُسبوع _____
saarilha usbuu9een _____	صارِلـها اُسبوعين _____
saarilhum saa9a _____	صارِلـهُم ساعة _____
saarilhum saa9teen _____	صارِلـهُم ساعـتين _____

saarlak sana _____   صارْلَك سَنة _____

saarlich santeen _____   صارْلِـج سَنْـتين _____

saarilkum daqiiqa _____   صارِلْكـم دَقيقة _____

saarilkum daqiiqteen _____   صارِلْكـم دَقيقْـتـين _____

c. haay ween? 9aash min shaaf Baasil   هايْ وين؟ عاش مِن شاف باسِل

_____ Khaalid   خـالــد _____

_____ Laylaa   لـيـلى _____

_____ Laylaa wa Basma   لـيـلى وبسـمة _____

_____ Baasil wa Khaalid   باسِـل وخـالِـد _____

_____ Zaki   زكـي _____

_____ Kariima   كـريـمة _____

d. il-khaatrak ujrat it-taksi diinaareen   إلْ خاطْـرَك أُجْـرَت التَّـكْـسـي دينارين

il-khaatrich _____   إلْ خاطْـرِج _____

il-khaatirkum _____   إلخاطِـرْكُـم _____

il-khaatra _____   إلْ خاطْـرَه _____

il-khaatirha _____   إلْ خاطِـرُها _____

il-khaatri _____   إلْ خاطْـري _____

il-khaatirna _____   إلْ خاطِـرْنا _____

e. diir baalak 9as-sayyaara!   ديـر بالَـك عَ الشَّـيارة!

diiri baalich _____!   ديـري بالِـج _____!

diiru baalkum _____!   ديـرو بالْـكم _____!

diir baalak mnis-sayyaara!   ديـر بالَك مُن لسَّيارة!

diiri baali<u>ch</u> _____!   !_____ ديري بالـچ

diiru baalkum _____!   !_____ ديـرو بالـكم

5. Read aloud the following imperative verbs/command sentences:

tfad<u>d</u>al zuurna bil-beet.   تـْفَـضـَل زورُنا بـالـْبيت

tfad<u>d</u>ali zuuriina bil-beet.   تـْفَـضـَلي زورينا بـالـْبيت

tfad<u>d</u>alu zuuruuna bil-beet.   تـْفَـضـَلو زورونا بـالـْبيت

min fa<u>d</u>lak, jiib Laylaa mnil-findiq.   مِن فَـضْلك. جيب ليلى مُن لُـفنـدق

min fa<u>d</u>lic, jiibi Laylaa mnil-findiq.   مِن فَـضْلـچ. جيبي ليلى مُن لُـفنـدق

min fa<u>d</u>ilkum, jiibu Laylaa mnil-findiq.   مِن فِضْلـكم. جيبو ليلى مُن لُـفنـدق

a<u>ll</u>a y<u>kh</u>alliik, la-tjiib Samiir mnil-ma<u>t</u>aar.   اللّٰه يْخـَلـَّيك. لَتـْئـْجيب سمير مُن لـْمطار

a<u>ll</u>a y<u>kh</u>alliich, la-tjiibiin Samiir mnil-ma<u>t</u>aar.   اللّٰه يْخـَلـَّيـچ. لَتـْئـْجيبين سمير مُن لـْمطار

a<u>ll</u>a y<u>kh</u>alliikum, la-tjiibuun Samiir mnil-ma<u>t</u>aar.   اللّٰه يْخـَلـَّيـكم. لَتـْئـْجيبون سمير مُن لـْمطار

6. Translate into Arabic:

My name is Laylaa, what is your name?

_____

We are honored; we are honored (in reply).

_____

I am (F) a Lebanese from Beirut.

_____

We are (F) Lebanese from Beirut.

_____

My husband is an American from New York.

_____

My wife is a German from Berlin.

_____

Are there palm trees in Iraq?

Where have you (P) been?

Where have you (F) been? It has been a long time since I saw you.

For your (M) sake, the fee is ten dollars.

For your (P) sake, I am staying in Baghdad.

Please where is the room key?

There is hot and cold water in the bathroom.

I have a hotel reservation.

Please help me.

Take care of yourself.

Watch out for the car.

Take care of the car.

Yes, she is my wife.

Creative Dialogues

a. taalib 1:   aani zirit il-9iraaq. inti zirti
                l-9iraaq?

    taaliba 2: na9am, zirit il-9iraaq. inta
                shwakit zirit l-9iraaq?

    taalib 1:   gabul shahar. w-inti?

    taaliba 2: gabul shahreen. shunu shifit?

    taalib 1:   shifit Baabil wa Naynawaa

    taaliba 2: aani shifit il-mathaf il-9iraaqi

    taalib 1:   ween haadha l-mathaf?

    taaliba 2: b-Baghdaad

b. taalib 1:   aani 9iraaqi. imneen Laylaa?

    taaliba 2: hiyya Lubnaaniyya min
                Beeruut

    taalib 1:   w-imneen Khaalid?

    taaliba 2: huwwa Suu9uudi min Makka

    taalib 1:   w-inti mneen?

    taaliba 2: aani min Beeruut

    taalib 1:   ya9ni, inti w Laylaa
                Lubnaaniyyaat

    taaliba 2: na9am

For new words, see Glossary.

طالب 1: آني زِرت العـراق. إنتي زِرتي
العـراق؟

طالبة 2: نعـم. زِرت العـراق. إنت شـوَكِت
زرت العـراق؟

طالب 1: گَـبُـل شَـهَر. ونْتـي؟

طالبة 2: گَـبُـل شَـهُرين. شـنُو شِـفِـت؟

طالب 1: شِـفِـت بابل ونَـيْـنَـوى

طالبة 2: آني شِـفِـت المتحف العراقي

طالب 1: وين هاذا المتحف؟

طالبة 2: بُ بغداد

طالب 1: آني عراقـي. إمْـنين ليلى؟

طالبة 2: هـي لبنانيّـة من بيروت

طالب 1: ومُـنـين خالـد؟

طالبة 2: هـو سُعـودي من مَـكّـة

طالب 1: ونْتـي منين؟

طالبة 2: آنـي من بيروت

طالب 1: يَـعـني، انتي وليلى لبنانـيّـات

طالبة 2: نعم

Houses in the mountains of northern Iraq

دَرس تِسْعَة   DARIS TIS9A

Speaking Arabic

il-lugha l-9arabiyya   إلْـلُّـغَـة الْـعَـرَبِـيَّـة

At the Rashid Hotel, Basma is sharing a dinner table with Mr. Maalik with whom she converses in Arabic.

Basic Dialogue (Audio)

1. Maalik: marhaba, shloon is-sihha?
   Hello, how are you?

   مالِـك: مرحبة. شلون الصّحّة؟

2. Basma: zeena, ilhamdu lillaah. w-inta shloonak?
   Well, thank God. And how are you?

   بسـمة: زينة. الحمد لله. وِانْت شـلـونك؟

3. Maalik: maashaalla, titkalmiin lugha 9arabiyya zeena.
   Praise be to God, you speak Arabic well.

   مالك: ماشالله. تِـتْـكَـلّـمِـين لُـغة عربية زينة.

4. Basma: ya9ni, shwayya.
   Well, a little.

   بسـمة: يَـعْـني. شْـوَيَّـة.

5. Maalik: ween t9allamti 9arabi?
   Where did you learn Arabic?

   مالك: وين تْـعَلَّـمْـتي عربي؟

6. Basma: dirasit 9arabi b-jaami9a Amriikiyya.
   I studied Arabic in an American university.

   بسـمة: دِرَسِـت عَربي بْ جامِـعَة أُمْـريكية.

7. Maalik: dirasti qraaya wi-ktaaba?
Did you study reading and writing?

مالك: دِرَسْتي قْرايةٍ وِكْتابةٍ؟

8. Basma: dirasit qraaya wi-ktaaba, bass nseetha shwayya
I studied reading and writing, but I have forgotten it a little.

بسمة: دِرَسْت قْرايةٍ وِكْتابةٍ. بَسّ نْسيتْها شْوَيّة.

9. Maalik: minu 9allamich 9arabi?
Who taught you Arabic?

مالك: مِنو عَلَّمِـچ عَربي؟

10. Basma: ustaadh 9raaqi min Baghdaad.
An Iraqi professor from Baghdad.

بسمة: أُسْتاذ عِراقي مِن بَغْداد.

11. Maalik: kam sana dirasti 9arabi?
How many years did you study Arabic?

مالك: كَم سَنة دِرَسْتي عَربي؟

12. Basma: hawaali santeen.
About two years.

بسمة: حَوالي سَنْتين.

13. Maalik: dirasti fus ha loo 9aammiyya?
Did you study the classical or the colloquial Arabic?

مالك: دِرَسْتي فُصْحى لو عامِّيّة؟

14. Basma: fus ha wa 9aammiyya.
The classical and the colloquial.

بسمة: فُصْحى وعامِّيّة.

15. Maalik: inti tih chiin 9iraaqi mumtaaz.
You speak excellent Iraqi Arabic.

مالك: إنتي تِحْچين عِراقي مُمْتاز.

16. Basma: shukran sayyid Maalik.
Thank you, Mr. Maalik.

بسمة: شكرا سَيّد مالِك.

Additional Expressions (Audio)

lugha Ingiliiziyya	*English language*	لُغة إنْگِليزِيّة
lugha Fransiyya	*French language*	لُغة فْرَنْسِيّة
lugha Almaaniyya	*German language*	لُغة أُمْريكِيّة
lugha Itaaliyya	*Italian language*	لُغة إطالِيّة
lugha Isbaaniyya	*Spanish language*	لُغة إسْبانِيّة
lugha Faarisiyya	*Persian language*	لُغة فارِسِيّة
lugha Ruusiyya	*Russian language*	لُغة روسِيّة
lugha Yaabaaniyya	*Japanese language*	لُغة يابانِيّة
lugha Hindiyya	*Hindi language*	لُغة هِنْدِيّة
lugha Turkiyya	*Turkish language*	لُغة تُرْكِيّة
lugha Kurdiyya	*Kurdish language*	لُغة كُرْدِيّة

Vocabulary (Audio)

sihha	*health*	صِحّة
shloon is-sihha?	*How are you?* (lit., *How is the health?*)	شْلون الصِّحّة؟

maashaalla	*Praise be to God* (see lesson 5)	ماشـالله
titkallam / titkallamiin / titkallamuun	*you speak* (M/F/P)	تِتْكَلَّم / تِتْكَـلَّـمين / تِتْكَـلَّـمون
lugha	*a language*	لُغَـة
9arabi / 9arabiyya (M/F)	*Arabic* (adj.)	عَـرَبي / عَـرَبيّـة
ya9ni	*well* (see lesson 7)	يَـعْني
shwayya	*a little* (invariable)	شْوَيّـة
t9allamit / t9allamti / t9allamtu	*you learned* (M/F/P)	تْعَلَّـمِت / تْعَلَّـمْتي / تْعَلَّـمْتو
dirasit	*I studied* (M and F)	دِرَسِـت
darras	*he taught*	دَرَّس
jaami9a / jaami9aat (S/P)	*university/ies*	جامِعة / جامِـعـات
tu9ruf / tu9urfiin / tu9urfuun	*you know* (M/F/P)	تُعُرُف / تُعُـرْفين / تُعُـرْفون
qraaya	*reading*	قْـرايَة
kitaaba	*writing*	كِـتابَـة
bass	*but, only*	بَـسّ
niseet (M/F)	*I forgot*	نِـسيـت
ustaadh / asaatidha (M/P)	*professor/s*	أُسْـتاذ / أساتِـذة
ustaadha / ustaadhaat (F/P)	*professor/s*	أُسْـتاذة / أُسْتاذات
sana / santeen / sniin (S/D/P)	*one year/two years/years*	سَـنة / سَنْتـين / سْـنين
hawaali	*about, approximately*	حَـوالي
fus ha	*classical, literary* (Arabic)	فُـصْحى
9aammiyya	*colloquial* (Arabic), *local*	عامِّـيّـة
loo	*or*	لـو
tihchi / tihchiin / tihchuun	*you speak* (M/F/P)	تْحْـچي / تْحْـچـين / تْحْـچـون
mumtaaz / mumtaaza (M/F)	*excellent*	مُمْتـاز / مُمْـتازة
sayyid / sayyida (M/F)	*Mr./Mrs.*	سَـيِّـد / سَـيِّـدَة

Grammar and Remarks
The Past Tense Verb: The Double and the Weak Verbs

As mentioned in lesson 8, the double verb is similar to the regular verb. It has three consonants but the last two are identical. The weak verb has two consonants and it ends in a final vowel in the third person masculine singular form. These two types are conjugated in the same way but both are conjugated differently from the regular and the hollow verbs (see below).

The Double Verb ḥabb   he liked/loved   حَبّ (Audio)

Pronoun	Suffix	Verb Form				
huwwa	——*	ḥabb	*he liked*	حَبّ	——	هو
hiyya	-at	ḥabbat	*she liked*	حَبَّت	ـَـت	هي
humma	-aw	ḥabbaw	*they liked*	حَبَّوْ	ـَوُّ	هُمّه
inta (M)	-eet**	ḥabbeet	*you liked*	حَبّيت	ـ يت	إنت
inti (F)	-eeti	ḥabbeeti	*you liked*	حَبّيتي	ـ يتي	إنتي
intu (P)	-eetu	ḥabbeetu	*you liked*	حَبّيتو	ـ يتو	إنتو
aani	-eet**	ḥabbeet	*I liked*	حَبّيت	ـ يت	آني
iḥna	-eena	ḥabbeena	*we liked*	حَبّينا	ـ ينا	إحنا

Remarks on the Double Verb:

Notice that suffixes added to the second and third persons are different from those added to the same persons of the regular and hollow verbs.

*No suffix added.

**Identical conjugation.

The Weak Verb misha   he walked/traveled   مِشَا (Audio)

Pronoun	Suffix	Verb Form				
huwwa	——	misha	*he walked*	مِشَا	——	هو
hiyya	-at	mishat	*she walked*	مِشَت	ـَـت	هي
humma	-aw	mishaw	*they walked*	مِشَوْ	ـَوُّ	هُمّه
inta (M)	-eet*	misheet	*you walked*	مِشيت	ـ يت	إنت
inti (F)	-eeti	misheeti	*you walked*	مِشيتي	ـ يتي	إنتي
intu (P)	-eetu	misheetu	*you walked*	مِشيتُو	ـ يتو	إنتو
aani	-eet*	misheet	*I walked*	مِشيت	ـ يت	آني
iḥna	-eena	misheena	*we walked*	مِشينا	ـ نا	إحنا

Remarks on the Weak Verb:

*Indicates identical conjugation.

The Past Tense Verb with Attached Pronoun

As mentioned in lesson 3, when an attached pronoun is added to a verb, it is the object of the verb. A verb with such a pronoun may undergo some vowel changes, such as the assimilation of the pronoun -a (*him*), the lengthening of the final vowel of the verb, or the dropping out of the stem vowel. These changes are especially frequent with the weak verb. See the conjugation table of the weak verb **niṭa** (*he gave*), and **nisaw** (*they forgot*) with the attached pronouns below. (Audio)

niṭa	*he gave*	نِطَا
niṭaani	*he gave me*	نِطاني

nitaana	*he gave us*	نِطانا
nitaak	*he gave you* (M)	نِطاك
nitaach	*he gave you* (F)	نِطاچ
nitaakum	*he gave you* (P)	نِطاكم
nitaa	*he gave him*	نِطاه
nitaahum	*he gave them*	نِطاهم
nisaw*	*they forgot*	نِسَوْ
nisooni	*they forgot me*	نِسُوني
nisoona	*they forgot us*	نِسُونا
nisook	*they forgot you* (M)	نِسُوك
nisooch	*they forgot you* (F)	نِسُوچ
nisookum	*they forgot you* (P)	نِسُوكم
nisoo	*they forgot him*	نِسُوه
nisoohum	*they forgot them*	نِسُوهم

*The suffix **-aw** changes to **-oo** with attached pronoun.

Idioms and Common Phrases (Audio)

1. lihusn il-hazz لِـحُـسْـن الْـحَـظ **or min husn il-hazz** مِن حُسْـن الْـحَـظ
fortunately, luckily

lihusn il-hazz, il-qitaar bil-mahatta	*Fortunately, the train is in the station.*	لِـحُـسْـن الْـحَـظ. الْـقطار بالْـمَـحَـطـة
lihusn il-hazz, il-bariid yamm is-suuq	*Fortunately, the post office is near the market.*	لِـحُـسْـن الْـحَـظ. البريد يَـم السوگ
lihusn il-hazz, Samiir bil-beet	*Fortunately, Samiir is home.*	لِـحُـسْـن الْـحَـظ. سمير بالْـبيت
lihusn il-hazz, dirasit qraaya wi-ktaaba	*Fortunately, I studied reading and writing.*	لِـحُـسْـن الْـحَـظ. دَرَسِـت قْـرايَة وكْـتابَة
lihusn il-hazz, zirit Baabil	*Luckily, I visited Babylon.*	لِـحُـسْـن الْـحَـظ. زِرت بابل

2. lisuuᵓ il-hazz لِـسُوء الْـحَـظّ or min suuᵓ il-hazz مِـن سوء الْـحَـظ
unfortunately

lisuuᵓ il-hazz, maa zirit Baabil	*Unfortunately, I did not visit Babylon.*	لِـسُـوء الْـحَـظ. ما زِرت بابل
lisuuᵓ il-hazz, il-bariid bi9iid mnis-suug	*Unfortunately, the post office is far from the market.*	لِـسُـوء الْـحَـظ. البريد بِـعـيد مُـن لْـسوگ
lisuuᵓ il-hazz, maa shifit Basma bil-findiq	*Unfortunately, I did not see Basma in the hotel.*	لِـسُـوء الْـحَـظ. ما شِـفِـت بسمة بـالْـفندق
lisuuᵓ il-hazz, Laylaa ta9baana	*Unfortunately, Laylaa is tired.*	لِـسُـوء الْـحَـظ. ليلى تَـعْـبانة

Drills   tamaariin   تمارين

1. Give appropriate oral replies to the following expressions:

shloon is-sihha?	شـلون الصّـحة؟
maashaalla, titkalmiin 9arabi zeen	ماشالله. تِتْكَلّمين عربي زين
ween t9allamti 9arabi?	وين تْعَلّمْتي عربي؟
t9allamit fus ha loo 9aammiyya?	تْعَلّمِت فُصْحى لو عامّيّـة؟
minu darraskum 9arabi?	مِـنو دَرّسْكـم عربي؟
kam sana dirastu 9arabi?	كم سـنة دِرَسْـتو عربي؟
tu9ruf qraaya wi-ktaaba?	تْعـرُف قْرايـة وكْتـابة؟
kam lugha tu9ruf?	كم لُغة تْعْـرُفَ؟
minu darrasich 9arabi?	مِـنو دَرّسِـچ عربي؟
kam lugha tih chi?	كم لُغة تِـحْـچـيـن؟

2. Conjugate orally the following past tense double and weak verbs:

bina	بِنَا	he built	liga	لِـگَـا	he found	ija	إجَـا	he came
sadd	سَـدّ	he closed	nita	نِطَا	he gave	dazz	دَزّ	he sent
nisa	نِسَا	he forgot	qira	قِـرَا	he read	gass	گَـصّ	he cut
hicha	حِـچَـا	he talked	hatt	حَـطّ	he put	shagg	شـگّ	he tore
misha	مِـشَـا	he walked	sawwa	سَـوّا	he made	ishtira	إشْـتِـرَا	he bought

3. Change orally the singular pronoun and verb in parentheses to the equivalent plural forms:

(inti titkallmiin) lugha 9iraaqiyya zeena	(إنتي تِتْكَلّـمين) لُغة عربية زينة
(t9allamit) il-lugha il-9arabiyya bij-jaami9a	(تْعَـلّـمِت) الـلغة العربية بالجَـامعة
(dirasat) qraaya wi-ktaaba	(دِرَسْـت) قْرايـة وكْـتابة
(kitab) risaala bil-9arabi	(كِـتـب) رسالة بالعَـربي
lisuu° il-hazz (aani niseet) ismak	لِـسوء الحَظّ (آني نِـسيت) اسُـمـك
(habbeet) il-lugha il-9arabiyya hwaaya	(حَـبّيت) الـلغة العربية هُـوايه
(hiyya qirat) ktaab Ingiliizi il-yoom	(هي قِـرَت) كِتاب انگِـليزي اليوم
(ijeet) bis-sayyaara loo bil-qitaar?	(إجـيت) بـالسّـيارة لو بالـقطار؟
(huwwa hatt) il-miftaah bil-ghurfa	(هو حَـطّ) الـمِفْتاح بـالـغُـرفة
(aani w hiyya dirasit) Ingiliizi w a9arabi	آني وهي (دِرَسِـت) انگـليزي وعربي

4. Conjugate the following sentences:

hatt il-qalam bid-daftar	(she, they, I, we)
حَـطّ القلم بالـدّفْـتَـر	
saarlak usbuu9 bil-Hilla (city name)	(you F, you P, he, she)
صـارْلَـك اُسْبوع بالـحِـلـة	
lisuu° il-hazz, niseet isimha	(you M, you F, you P)
لِـسوء الـحظ. نِـسيت إسِمُـها	

ijeena bit-tayyaara min Paariis	(*I, he, she, they*)	إجينا بالطّيّارة من پاريس
habb is-syyaara hwaaya	(*she, they, you* M)	حَبّ السّيّارة هُوايه
darras il-lugha il-9arabiyya bij-jaami9a	(*I, we, he, she, they*)	دَرّس الـلّـغة العربية بالجّامعة
lihusn il-hazz, shifit Samiir ib-Baghdaad	(*we, he, they*)	لـحُسن الحظّ. شـفـت سمير بُ بغداد

5. Replace the nouns or the pronouns in parentheses by their equivalent Arabic attached pronouns and add them to the verbs in the following sentences:

darras . . . 9arabi bij-jaami9a	(*Basma, them*)	دَرّس . . . عربي بالجـامعة
dazzat . . . lil-beet	(*Samiir, me, us*)	دَزّت . . . لِـلّـبيت
shifit . . . bil-findiq il-baarha	(*you* M, *you* F, *you* P)	شِـفـت . . . بالـفندق الـبارحة
jaab . . . bis-sayyaara il-yoom	(*him, them, me*)	جاب . . . بالسّيارة اليوم
qireet . . . bil-madrasa	(*risaala, jariida, kitaab*)	قِـريت . . . بـالـمَدُرَسة
shirbaw . . . bil-mat9am	(*mayy, haliib, Pipsi*)	شِـربَوْ . . . بِـالـمَطـعَم
hatteet . . . bil- beet	(*sayyaara, baasbort, them*)	حَطّيت . . . بِـالـبيت
habb . . . hwaaya	(*Laylaa, muwazzaf, you* P)	حَبّ . . . هُـوايه
zirit . . . gabul shahar	(*Baghdad, Babylon, Museum, all three*)	زِرت . . . گـبُـل شَـهَر

jaabat . . . lil-madrasa (walad, wilid, bint, banaat) جابَت . . . لِـلْـمَـدْرَسة

_____

siqna . . . lil-mahatta (sayyaara, qitaar, tayyaara) سِـقْـنا . . . لِـلْـمَـحَـطّة

_____

6. Complete and read the following aloud:

a. sadd baab il-ghurfa bil-miftaah   t9allam 9arabi w Almaani
سَـدّ باب الْـغُـرْفة بالْـمِـفْـتاح   تْـعَـلَّـم عَـرَبي وألْـماني

saddat _____ سَـدّت   t9allmat _____ تْـعَـلّـمت

saddaw _____ سَـدّوْ   t9allmaw _____ تْـعَـلّـمَـوْ

saddeet _____ سَـدّيت   t9allamit _____ تْـعَـلّـمِت

saddeeti _____ سَـدّيتي   t9allamti _____ تْـعَـلّـمْـتي

saddeetu _____ سَـدّيتو   t9allamtu _____ تْـعَـلّـمْـتو

saddeet _____ سَـدّيت   t9allamit _____ تْـعَـلّـمِت

saddeena _____ سَـدّينا   t9allamna _____ تْـعَـلّـمُـنا

b. ija lil-beet mnis-safaara   raah lil-findiq ib-sayyaara jdiida
إجَا لِـلْـبيت مُـن لسّـفارة   راح لِـلْـفندق ب سِـيّـارة جُـديدة

ijat _____ إجَـت   raahat _____ راحَـت

ijaw _____ إجَـوْ   raahaw _____ راحَـوْ

ijeet _____ إجَـيت   rihit _____ رِحِـت

ijeeti _____ إجَـيتي   rihti _____ رِحْـتي

ijeetu _____ إجَـيتو   rihtu _____ رِحْـتو

ijeet _____ إجَـيت   rihit _____ رِحِـت

ijeena _____ إجَـينا   rihna _____ رِحْـنا

c.   lihusn il-<u>h</u>azz, dirasit qraaya wi-ktaaba   لِحُسُن الْحَـظ . دَرَسِـت قَـْرايَة وِكْـتابَة

_____, dirasti _____   _____ دَرَسْـتي _____

_____, dirastu _____   _____ دِرَسْـتو _____

_____, diras _____   _____ دِرَس _____

_____, dirsat _____   _____ دِرْسَـت _____

_____, dirsaw _____   _____ دِرْسَـوْ _____

_____, dirasit _____   _____ دِرَسِـت _____

_____, dirasna _____   _____ دَرَسْـنا _____

d.   lisuuʾ il-<u>h</u>azz, ma-zaarna bil-beet   لِـسوء الْحَـظ. مَ زارْنا بِـالْبيت

_____, ma-zaaratna _____   _____ مَ زارَتْـنا _____

_____, ma-zaaruuna _____   _____ مَ زارُونا _____

_____, ma-ziritna _____   _____ مَ زِرَتْـنا _____

_____, ma-zirtiina _____   _____ مَ زِرْتِـيـنا _____

_____, ma-zirtuuna _____   _____ مَ زِرْتُـونا _____

7. Translate the following into Arabic:

He is a Frenchman from Paris.

_____

She is an Arab teacher from Lebanon.

_____

They are Americans (M) from Boston.

_____

They are (F) Americans and Canadians.

_____

You are (F) Japanese from Tokyo.

_____

You are (M) an Italian from Rome.

_____

They speak excellent Arabic, German, and English.

_____

Basma is a student and Khaalid is a professor.

_____

Khaalid is an Arabic professor at the university.

_____

They speak three languages.

_____

Maalik doesn't speak English very well.

_____

Unfortunately, I forgot the Arabic language a little.

_____

Creative Dialogues

a.   **taalib 1**: il-baarha chinit bil-beet. dirasit 9arabi, w-iktabit risaala l-Samiira. Samiira msaafra l-Berliin. ba9deen zirit Laylaa b-beetha. hnaak shifit zawijha Baasil. aani w Laylaa hicheena hwaaya 9an id-diraasa bij-jaami9a. Laylaa dirsat ib-jaami9at Beeruut wa ijat lil-9iraaq gabul sana. lihusn il-hazz, beet Laylaa muu bi9iid min beeti.

أ-   طالب 1: إلبارحة چِنِت بِالْبيت. دِرَسِت عربي، وكْتَبِت رسالة لْ سَميرة. سَميرة مُسافْرة لْ بَرْلين. بَعْدين زِرِت ليلى بْ بيتْها . هُناك شِفِت زَوْجْها باسِل. آني وليلى حِچينا هُوايه عَن الـدِّراسة بِالْجَامِعة. ليلى دِرْسِت بْ جامِعَة بيروت و إجَت لِلْعِراق گَبُل سَنة. لِحُسِن الْحَظ. بيت ليلى مو بِعيد مِن بيتي.

b. **taaliba 2**: aani chinit bil-9iraaq. hnaak t9allamit 9arabi l-lahcha l-9iraaqiyya. aani dira-sit b-jaami9at Baghdaad arba9 sniin. ustaadhi kaan 9iraaqi isma Jamaal Kaamil. huwwa kaan ustaadh mumtaaz. chinit aruuh lis-suug kull usbuu9 w-ashtiri ashyaaʾ 9iraaqiyya. zirit il-mathaf il-9iraaqi w Baabil. Ba9deen rija9it l- baladi Masir.

ب- طالبة 2: آني چِنِت بِالْعراق. هُناك تْعَلَّمِت عَرَبي الْلَـهْجَة العراقيّة. آني دِرَسِـت بُ جامِعَـة بغداد أرْبَع سْـنـين. أُسْـتاذي كان إسْمَه جَمال كامل, هو كان أُسْـتاذ مُـمْتاز. چِـنِـت أروح لِـلسّـوڨ كُل أُسْـبوع واشْـتِـرِيت أشْـيـاء عِـراقية. زِرت الْمَتْئحف العراقي وبابل. بَـعدين رِجَـعِـت لُ بَـلَـدي مَـصِر.

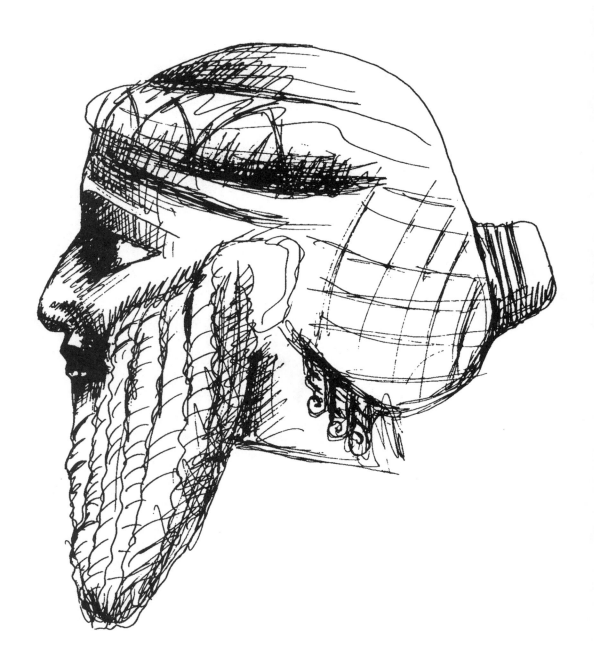

The bronze head of Sargon, king of ancient Akkad, third millenium B.C., Iraqi Museum

Telling Time

is-saa9a   الـسّـاعَة

Basma's watch is not working. She goes to the hotel information desk for help.

Basic Dialogue (Audio)

1. Basma: bee<u>sh</u> is-saa9a, min fa<u>d</u>lak?
   What is the time, please?

   بسمة: بـيش الـسّاعة. مِن فَـضْلَـك؟

2. mu<u>d</u>ayyif: is-saa9a tis9a.
   It is nine o'clock.

   مُضَـيِّـف: الـسّاعة تِـسْـعَة.

3. Basma: bass saa9ti <u>th</u>maanya illa rubu9.
   But my watch says a quarter to eight.

   بسمة: بَـسّ ساعْتِي ثْمانِئَة إلّـَ رُبُع

4. mu<u>d</u>ayyif: laazim saa9tich <u>kh</u>arbaana.
   Your watch must be broken.

   مُضَـيِّـف: لازِم ساعْتِـج خَـرْبانة.

5. Basma: <u>s</u>a<u>h</u>ii<u>h</u>. gulli tu9ruf mu<u>s</u>alli<u>h</u>
   saa9aat zeen?
   *True. Tell me, do you know a good watch
   repairman?*

   بسمة: صَحيح. گُـلْـلي تُـعْـرُف مُـصَلّـح ساعات زين؟

6. mu<u>d</u>ayyif: ʾii, aku mahal saa9aat
   bil-findiq.
   Yes, there is a watch store in the hotel.

   مُضَـيِّـف: ئِي، أكو مَحَل ساعات بِـالْـفندق.

Basma is in the watch store speaking to a salesman (bayyaa9).

7. Basma: saa9ti kharbaana wa tihtaaj tasliih.

   My watch is not working and needs repairing.

   بسمة: ساعُتي خربانة وتِحْتـاج تَصْليح.

8. bayyaa9: bikull suruur. haadhi saa9a hilwa bass qadiima.

   With pleasure. This is a nice watch but an old one.

   بيّاع: بِكُل سُرور. هاذي ساعة حِلْوَة بَـسّ قَديمة.

9. Basma: na9am, haadhi hadiyya min jiddi.

   Yes, this is a gift from my grandfather.

   بسمة: نعم، هاذي هَـدِيّـة من جِـدّي.

10. bayyaa9: 9idna saa9aat swiisriyya kullish zeena wa rikhiisa.

    We have very good and inexpensive Swiss watches.

    بيّاع: عِـدُنا ساعات سُـويـسْريّة كُـلِّـش زينة ورخيصة.

11. Basma: ba9deen ashuufha. shwakit tkhallis saa9ti?

    I will see them later. When will you finish my watch?

    بسمة: بَـعْدين أشوفْها. شْـوَكِت تْخَـلِّص ساعُتي؟

12. bayyaa9: baachir, is-saa9a tlaatha, inshaalla.

    Tomorrow at three o'clock, God willing.

    بيّاع: باچِـر الساعة تـلاثة. إنشاالله.

13. Basma: alla ykhalliik, diir baalak 9aleeha!

    Please, take care of it!

    بسمة: الله يُخَـلِّـيك، ديـر بالَـك عليها!

14. bayyaa9: mamnuun, 9ala 9eeni.

    Gladly, with pleasure. (emphasis)

    بيّاع: مَـمْـنـون، على عـيني.

Additional Expressions (Audio)

saa9a	*watch, clock, time, hour (depending on context)*	ساعَة
saa9at iid	*wrist watch*	ساعة إيـد
saa9at jeeb	*pocket watch*	ساعة جـيـب
saa9at haayit	*wall clock*	ساعة حايـط
saa9at tanbiih	*alarm clock*	ساعة تَـنْـبـيه
daqiiqa / daqaayiq (S/P)	*minute/s*	دَقـيقة / دَفايِـق
thaanya / thawaani (S/P)	*second/s*	ثانِـيَة / ثَـواني
rubu9	*one-quarter (fifteen minutes)*	رُبُـع

thilith	*one-third* (twenty minutes)	ثِلِث
nuss	*one-half*	نُصّ
illa	*of, before, except*	إلّكَ
gabul	*before, ago*	گَبُل
gabul saa9a	*one hour ago*	گَبُل ساعة
gabul iz-zuhur	*before noon (A.M.)*	گَبُل الظّهُر
ba9ad	*after*	بَعَد
ba9ad saa9a	*after one hour, in an hour*	بَعَد ساعة
ba9ad iz-zuhur	*afternoon (P.M.)*	بَعَد الظّهُر
zuhur	*noon (noun)*	ظُهُر
zuhran, iz-zuhur	*afternoon (adv.)*	ظُهُراً إلظّهُر
sabaah	*morning (noun)*	صَباح
sabaahan, is-subuh	*in the morning (adv.)*	صَباحاً. إلصُّبُح
9asir	*afternoon*	عَصِر
9asran, il-9asir	*in the afternoon (adv.)*	عَصُراً إلعَصِر
masaaᵓ	*evening (noun)*	مَساء
masaaᵓan, il-masaaᵓ	*in the evening (adv.)*	مَساءً. إلمَساء
leel	*night (noun)*	لِيل
laylan, bil-leel	*at night, nightly (adv.)*	لَيلاً بِاللِيل

Vocabulary (Audio)

beesh?	*How much?*	بِيش؟
saa9a / saa9aat (S/P)	*watch/es*	ساعة / ساعات
laazim (invairable)	*must, ought (semi verb)*	لازم
kharbaan / kharbaana (M/F)	*not working, broken (adj.)*	خَربان / خَربانة
sahiih	*true, correct (adj.)*	صَحِيح
musallih / musalliha (M/F)	*repairman/ repairwoman*	مُصَلِّح / مُصَلِّحَة
tasliih	*repairing, fixing*	تَصلِيح
ᵓii	*yes*	إِي
mahal / mahallaat (S/P)	*place/s, store/s, shop/s*	مَحَل / مَحَلات
tihtaaj / yihtaaj (F/M)	*she needs* (referring to the watch as a she) *he needs*	تِحتاج / يِحتاج
bayyaa9 / bayyaa9iin (S/P)	*salesman/en* (M)	بَيّاع / بَيّاعين
bayyaa9a / bayyaa9aat (S/P)	*saleswoman/en* (F)	بَيّاعة / بَيّاعات
qadiim / qadiima (M/F)	*old, ancient (adj.)*	قَدِيم / قَدِيمة
hadiyya / hadaaya (S/P)	*gift/s, present/s*	هَدِيّة / هَدايا
jidd / jidda (M/F)	*grandfather/grandmother*	جِدّ / جِدّة

swiisri / swiisriyya (M/F)	*Swiss*	سُويِسْري / سُويِسْرية
rikhiis / rikhiisa (M/F)	*inexpensive, cheap*	رخيص / رخيصة
ba9deen	*later on*	بَعُدِين
ashuufha	*I see it (referring to watches).*	أشوفْها
shwakit?	*when?*	شْوَكِت؟
tkhallis	*you (M) finish*	تْخَلَّص
baachir	*tomorrow*	باچِر
ayy?	*which?*	أيّ
yoom / yoomeen / ayyaam (S/D/P)	*day/two days/days*	يوم / يومين / أيّام
usbuu9 / usbuu9een / asaabii9 (S/D/P)	*week/two weeks/weeks*	أُسْبوع / أُسْبوعين / أسابيع
shahar / shahreen / ashhur (S/D/P)	*month/two months/months*	شَهَر / شَهْرين / أشْهُر
fasil / fusuul (S/P)	*season/s*	فَصِل / فُصُول
sana / santeen / sniin (S/D/P)	*year/two years/years*	سَنة / سَنْتين / سْنين
mamnuun	*gladly (idiom, see below)*	مَمْنون
diir baalak	*take care (idiom, see lesson 7)*	دير بالَك
alla ykhalliik	*please (idiom, see lesson 5)*	الله يْخَلِّيك

Grammar and Remarks
Time Expressions: il-waqit إلْوَقِـت

In Iraqi Arabic there are two ways of telling time:

is-saa9a wihda	or	is-saa9a bil-wihda	إلسّاعة بالْوُحُدة	إلسّاعة وُحُدة
is-saa9a arba9a	or	is-saa9a bil-arba9	إلسّاعة بِالأَرْبَعة	إلسّاعة أَرْبَعة

In the first column only the word **saa9a** takes the article "**il- > is-** (*the*)," whereas in the second column, the time number also takes the article "**il-**" as well as the prefix "**b-** (*at*)" as shown above. Both expressions are commonly used. Notice that the word **saa9a** is almost always mentioned when telling time. Below is a list of time expressions, using the first column form. (Audio)

is-saa9a wihda	*It is one o'clock.*	إلسّاعة وُحُدة
is-saa9a thinteen	*It is two o'clock.*	إلسّاعة ثِنْتين
is-saa9a tlaatha	*It is three o'clock.*	إلسّاعة تْلاثة
is-saa9a arba9a	*It is four o'clock.*	إلسّاعة أَرْبَعة

is-saa9a khamsa	*It is five o'clock.*	الساعة خَمُسة
is-saa9a sitta	*It is six o'clock.*	الساعة سِتّة
is-saa9a sab9a	*It is seven o'clock.*	الساعة سَبُعة
is-saa9a thmaanya	*It is eight o'clock.*	الساعة ثَمانْية
is-saa9a tis9a	*It is nine o'clock.*	الساعة تِسُعة
is-saa9a 9ashra	*It is ten o'clock.*	الساعة عَشْرة
is-saa9a da9ash	*It is eleven o'clock.*	الساعة دَعَش
is-saa9a thna9ash	*It is twelve o'clock.*	الساعة ثْناعَش
is-saa9a sitta w rubu9	*It is six-fifteen.*	الساعة سِتّة ورُبُع
is-saa9a sitta w thilith	*It is six-twenty.*	الساعة سِتّة وثْلِث
is-saa9a sitta w nuss	*It is six-thirty.*	الساعة سِتّة ونُص
is-saa9a sitta w nuss w khamsa	*It is six-thirty five.*	الساعة سِتّة ونص وخَمُسة
is-saa9a sitta w nuss illa khamsa	*It is six-twenty five.*	الساعة سِتة ونص إلّل خَمُسة
is-saa9a sitta illa rubu9	*It is quarter to six.*	الساعة سِتّة إلّل رُبُع
is-saa9a sitta illa thilith	*It is twenty to six.*	الساعة سِتّة إلّل ثْلِث
is-saa9a sitta illa 9ashra	*It is ten to six.*	الساعة سِتّة إلّل عَشْرة
is-saa9a sitta illa khamsa	*It is five to six.*	الساعة سِتّة إلّل خَمُسة

Days of the Week: ayyaam lis-buu9   أيّام لِسْبُوع (Audio)

Note: Except for Friday (**ij-jum9a**) and Saturday (**is-sabit**), the names of the weekdays are variant forms of the Arabic numerals.

---

shunu il-yoom?	*What day is today?*	شِنو الْيوم؟
il-yoom . . .	*Today is . . .*	إلْيوم . . .
yoom l-ahhad	*Sunday*	يوم الأحَّد
yoom li-thneen	*Monday*	يوم لِثْنين
yoom ith-thalaathaa	*Tuesday*	يوم الثَّلاثا
yoom il-arba9aa	*Wednesday*	يوم الأرُبَعا
yoom il-khamiis	*Thursday*	يوم الْخَميس
yoom ij-jum9a	*Friday**	يوم الجَّمُعَة
yoom is-sabit	*Saturday*	يوم السَّبِت

---

*The weekend day in the Arab and Islamic worlds.

Months of the Year: ashhur is-sana   أشْهُر السَّنَة (Audio)

Western/Gregorian Calendar			Eastern Calendar	
January	Yanaayir	يَنايِر	Kaanuun ith-Thaani	كانون الثاني
February	Fabraayir	فَبُرايِر	Shbaat	شْباط

Western/Gregorian Calendar			Eastern Calendar		
March	Maaris	مــارس	Aadhaar	آذار
April	Abriil	أبْـريل	Niisaan	نــيسان
May	Maayoo	مــايـو	Ayyaar/Maayis	أيّـار / مــايـس
June	Yoonyoo	يــونْيـو	Huzayraan	حُـزَيْـران
July	Yoolyoo	يــوليــو	Tammuuz	تَـمُّـوز
August	Ughustus	أغُسْـطِس	Aab	آب
September	Sibtambar	سِـبْـتَـمْـبَـر	Ayluul	أيْـلـول
October	Uktoobar	أكْـتـوبَـر	Tishriin il-Awwal	تِـشْرين الأول
November	Noovambar	نـوفَـمْـبَـر	Tishriin ith-Thaani	تِـشْرين الثّاني
December	Diisambar	ديسَـمْـبَـر	Kaanuun il-Awwal	كانون الأوّل

The Four Seasons: il-fusuul il-arba9a   إلـفُـصول الأرْبَـعَـة (Audio)

Spring	ir-rabii9	إلـرّبـيـع
Summer	is-seef	إلصّيـف
Autumn/Fall	il-khariif	إلـخَـريـف
Winter	ish-shita	إلشّـتـا

The Preposition wiyya   ويّـه   with

This preposition is used either with a proper name or a pronoun suffix (attached pronouns).
It is negated with **muu** مُـو. (Audio)

wiyya	with	ويّـه
wiyyaa	with him	ويّـا
wiyyaahum	with them	ويّـاهُـم
wiyyaak	with you (M)	ويّـاك
wiyyaach	with you (F)	ويّـاچ
wiyyaakum	with you (P)	ويّـاكُـم
wiyyaaya	with me	ويّـايَـه
wiyyaana	with us	ويّـانا
huwwa muu wiyyaana	He is not with us.	هو مو ويّـانا
Samiir muu wiyya Samiira	Samiir is not with Samiira.	سمير مُـو ويّـه سميرة
ruuhi wiyya Laylaa	Go (F) with Laylaa.	روحي ويّـه ليلى
la-truuhiin wiyya Khaalid	Don't go with Khalid.	لَـتْـروحين ويّـه خالد
ruuh wiyyaahum	Go (M) with them.	روح ويّـاهـم
la-truuh wiyyaahum	Don't go with them.	لَـتْـروح ويّـاهـم

Idioms and Common Phrases (Audio)

1. iddallal / iddallali / iddallalu (M/F/P) إِدَّلَـل / إِدَّلَـلي / إِدَّلَـلو   *as you wish, at your service* (an answer to a request, lit., *be spoiled*, imp. verb)

min faḏlak jiib is-sayyaara	*Please, bring the car.*	مِن فَضُلك جيب السّيارة
iddallal (in reply)	*As you* (M) *wish.*	إِدَّلَـل
diir baalak 9as-saa9a!	*Take care of the watch!*	دير بالك عَ الساعة
iddallali (in reply)	*As you* (F) *wish.*	إِدَّلَـلي
diir baalak 9al-wilid!	*Take care of the children!*	دير بالك عَ الوِلِد
iddallalu (in reply)	*As you* (P) *wish.*	إِدَّلَـلو
alla ykhaliik, saa9idni bij-junṭa	*Please, help me with the luggage.*	الله يُخَـلّيك. ساعِدُني بِالجُنْطة
iddallali (in reply)	*At your service.*	إِدَّلَـلي

2. mamnuun / mamnuuna / mamnuuniin (M/F/P) مَـمْنون / مَـمْنونة / مَـمْنونين   *to be indebted, grateful, thankful, pleased; gladly, with pleasure, you are welcome* (as a reply to a request or to the word thank you, shukran).

akuun mamnuun loo ijeet lil-beet	*I will be grateful if you come to the house.*	أكون مَـمْنون لو إجيت لِـلْبيت
shukran 9al-hadiyya	*Thanks for the gift.*	شكراً عَ الـهَـدِيـة
aani mamnuun (in reply)	*With pleasure.*	آني مَـمْنون
Maalik mamnuun minkum	*Maalik is indebted to you* (P).	مالِك مَـمْنون مِنْكم
Basma mamnuuna min Maalik	*Basma is grateful to Maalik.*	بسمة مَـمْنونة مِن مالِك
min faḏlak, saafir wiyya Laylaa	*Please, travel with Laylaa.*	مِن فضلك. سافِر ويَّـه ليلى
mamnuun (in reply)	*Gladly.*	مَـمْنون
ihna mamnuuniin min ustaaḏna	*We are grateful to our professor.*	إحنا مَـمْنونين من أُسْتاذنا

Drills   tamaariin   تَمارين

1. Give appropriate oral replies to the following questions:

min faḏlak, beesh is-saa9a?	مِن فَضُلك. بِـيش السّاعة؟
shwakit rihit il-maḥal is-saa9aat?	شــوَكِت رِحِـت إلْ مَحَل السّاعات؟
aku muṣalliḥ saa9aat bil-findiq?	اكو مُصَلّـح ساعات بالـفندق؟
saa9tich qadiima loo jidiida?	ساعْتِـچ قَديمة لو جِـديدة؟
kam saa9a bil-yoom?	كم ساعة باليوم؟
kam yoom bil-usbuu9?	كَـم يوم بالأسبوع؟
kam usbuu9 bish-shahar?	كم أسبوع بالشـّهر؟
kam yoom bish-shahar?	كَـم يوم بالشـّهر؟

kam shahar bis-sana   كَم شَهَر بالسَّنة؟

kam fasil bis-sana?   كَم فَصِل بالسَّنة؟

is-seef haar loo baarid bil-9iraaq?   الصّيف حار لو بارد بالعراق؟

Baghdaad haara loo baarda bish-shita?   بغداد حارّة لو بارْدَة بالشِّتا؟

2. Make the singular verb in parentheses plural in the following sentences:

(raahat) il-mahal saa9aat zeen bis-suug   (راحَت) إلْ مَحَل ساعات زين بالسّوگ

(shifit) Basma wiyya Kaamil wa Laylaa bil-findiq   (شِفِت) بسمة وِيّه كامل وليلى بالفندق

(huwwa sallah) is-saa9a ba9ad iz-zuhur   (هو صَلّح) السّاعة بَعَد الظّهُر

(inta wisalit) mataar Baghdaad yoom ij-jum9a   (إنت وِصَلِت) مَطار بغداد يوم الجُمْعَة

(hiyya taarat) bit-tayyaara yoom il-khamiis is-saa9a sab9a w nuss   (هي طارَت) بالطّيّارة يوم الخْميس السّاعة سَبْعَة ونُصّ

(aani zirit) il-mathaf is-saa9a tis9a is-subuh   (آني زِرِت) الْمتحف السّاعة تِسْعَة الصّبُح

(huwwa nisa) saa9ta bil-beet   (هو نِسَا) ساعْتَه بِالبيت

inta (hicheet) wiyyaahum is-saa9a 9ashra   (إنت حُچيت) وِيّاهم السّاعة عَشْرَة

(hiyya dirsat) 9arabi w-Ingiliizi bil-madrasa   (هي دِرْسَت) عَربي وانگليزي بالمدرسة

(inti t9allamti) qraaya wi-ktaaba bij-jaami9a   (إنتي تْعَـلّـَمْتي) قْـراية وِكْتابة بالجَامعة

3. Read the following aloud:

a.   ijeet lil-beet yoom l-ahhad is-saa9a khamsa w rubu9   إجيت لِلْبيت يوم الأحد السّاعة خَمْسة ورُبُع

ijeet lil-beet yoom li-thneen is-saa9a khamsa illa rubu9   إجيت لِلْبيت يوم لِثْنين السّاعة خَمْسة إلّـَ رُبُع

ijeet lil-beet yoom ith-thalaathaa is-saa9a khamsa w nuss   إجيت لِلْبيت يوم الثّـَلاثا السّاعة خَمْسة ونُصّ

ijeena lil-beet yoom il-arba9aa is-saa9a tis9a bil-leel   إجينا لِلْبيت يوم الأرْبَعا السّاعة تِسْعَة بالّليل

ijeena lil-beet yoom il-khamiis is-saa9a thinteen il-9asir   إجينا لِلْبيت يوم الخميس السّاعة ثِنْتين العَصِر

ijeena lil-beet yoom ij-jum9a is-saa9a tlaatha ba9ad iz-zuhur   إجينا لِلْبيت يوم الجُّمعة السّاعة تْلاثة بَعَد الظّهُر

ijeena lil-beet yoom is-sabit is-saa9a 9ashra is-subuh   إجينا لِلْبيت يوم السّبت السّاعة عَشْرَة الصّبُح

b.   shahar Yanaayir baarid bil-9iraaq   شهر يَناير بارد بالعراق

shahar Fabraayir baarid bil-9iraaq   شهر فَبْراير بارد بالعراق

shahar Maaris baarid shwayya bil-9iraaq   شهر مارس بارد شْوَيّه بالعراق

shahar Abriil laa haar wala baarid bil-9iraaq   شهر أبْريل لا حار ولا بارد بالعراق

shahar Maayoo laa ḥaar wala baarid bil-9iraaq	شهر مايو لا حار و لا بارد بالعراق
shahar Yoonyoo ḥaar shwayya bil-9iraaq	شهر يونيو حار شويّه بالعراق
shahar Yoolyoo ḥaar hwaaya bil-9iraaq	شهر يوليو حار هوايه بالعراق
shahar Ughusṭus ḥaar hwaaya bil-9iraaq	شهر اغسطس حار هوايه بالعراق
shahar Sibtambar laa ḥaar wala baarid bil-9iraaq	شهر سبتمبر لا حار ولا بارد بالعراق
shahar Uktoobar baarid shwayya bil-9iraaq	شهر اكتوبر بارد شويّه بالعراق
shahar Noovambar baarid bil-9iraaq	شهر نوفَمبَر بارد بالعراق
shahar Diisambar baarid hwaaya bil-9iraaq	شهر ديسَمبَر بارد هوايه بالعراق

4. Say the following times in Arabic:

3:20	12:05	5:15	9:30	3:30
12:40	4:45	8:25	2:35	10:55
4:50	9:35	4:45	11:45	5:55
2:20	2:15	11:15	10:10	7:10
8:35	2:00	10:11	6:50	9:12
8:00	10:49	6:25	7:20	9:45

5. Complete and read the following aloud:

a. aani mamnuun min Basma | آني مَمنون مِن بسمة

    aani mamnuuna _____ | _____ آني مَمنونة

    iḥna mamnuuniin _____ | _____ إحنا مَمنونين

    iḥna mamnuunaat _____ | _____ إحنا مَمنونات

    inta mamnuun _____ | _____ إنت مَمنون

    inti mamnuuna _____ | _____ إنتي مَمنونة

b. aani mamnuun mnil-mufattish | آني مَمنون مُن لمُفَتِّش

    intu mamnuunaat _____ | _____ إنتو مَمنونات

    huwwa mamnuun _____ | _____ هو مَمنون

    hiyya mamnuuna _____ | _____ هي مَمنونة

    humma mamnuuniin _____ | _____ هُمّه مَمنونين

    humma mamnuunaat _____ | _____ هُمّه مَمنونات

6. Replace the nouns or the pronouns in parentheses by their equivalent Arabic attached pronouns and add them to the preposition "wiyya" in the following sentences:

iqra 9arabi wiyya . . .   إقْرَه عربي ويّه . . .
(Basma and Laylaa)

lihusn ilhazz, raahaw wiyya . . .   لِحُـسن الحظ راحَوْ ويّه . . .
(you M, you P)

Basma tkallimat wiyya . . .bil-findiq   بسمة تْكَـلِـمَت ويّه . . . بالـفندق
(her, abu it-taksi)

ijeet wiyya . . . mnis-suug   إجيت ويّه . . . مْن السّوگ
(him, them)

dirasti il-lugha l-9arabiyya wiyya . . .   دِرَسْـتي الـلـغة العربية ويّه . . .
(me, us)

dazz ibna wiyya . . . lil-madrasa   دَزّ إبْـنه ويّه . . . لِـلـمَـدُرسة
(Samiira, you F)

kitab risaala wiyya . . . bil-beet   كِتَب رِسالة ويّه . . . بالـبيت
(us, them)

7. Translate the following into English:

is-seef haar wish-shita baarid ib-Baghdaad   إلصّيف حار ولِـشّـتَـه بارد بْ بغداد

_____

fasil ir-rabii9 tayyib ib-Baghdaad   فَـصِل الـرّبيع طَـيّبْ بْ بغداد

_____

is-sana arba9 fusuul   إلسّـنة أرْبَع فُـصول

_____

Basma 9idha saa9a hadiyya min jidha   بسمة عِـدْها ساعة هَـدِيّـة من جِـدْها

_____

saa9at Laylaa qadiima bass hilwa   ساعة ليلى قديمة بَـسّ حِـلْـوَة

_____

is-saa9a sittiin daqiiqa   إلسّاعة سِـتّـين دَقـيـقة

_____

id-daqiiqa sittiin thaaniya   إلـدّقيقة سِـتّـين ثانيـة

_____

il-yoom arba9a w 9ishriin saa9a

إليوم أرْبَـعـة وعِشرين ساعة

---

is-sana thna9ash shahar

إلسّـنـة ثْنَاعَش شَـهَر

---

ihna raayhiin, diiri baalich 9al-wilid!

إحْـنا رايْـحين. ديري بالِـج عَ الْـوِلِـد!

 °ii, iddallalu

ئِـي . إدّلّـلـو

Samiir chaan mamnuun minkum il-baarha

سمير چان مَـمْنون مِنْـكم الْبارْحة

Samiira chaanat mamnuuna minni qabul usbuu9

سميرة چانَـت مَـمْنونة مِنـي گَـبُـل اُسْـبـوع

Samiira muu mamnuuna min Jamaal

سميرة مُو مَـمْنونة مِن جمال

---

ihna muu mamnuuniin minhum

إحنا مو مَـمْنونين مِنْـهُم

---

lisuu° ilhazz, Ahmad ma-raah wiyyaahum

لِحُـسْن الْحَـظ. أحمد مَ راح وِيّـاهم

---

hiyya muu wiyya Khaalid

هي مو وِيّـه خالد

---

gulli tu9ruf mahal tasliih saa9aat zeen?

گُـلّـلي تُـعُـرُف مَحَـل سَـلِّيح ساعات زين؟

---

aku musallih sayyaaraat yamm il-findiq?

أكو مُـصَلِّح سَيّارات يَم الفندق؟

---

bayyaa9 is-saa9aat latiif

بَـيّاع الـسّاعات لَـطيف

---

shaafat Maalik ba9deen raahat lis-safaara

شافَت مالك بَعْدين راحَت لِسّْفارة

Creative Dialogues

a. taalib 1:   shwakit zirti l-9iraaq?

طالب 1: شْوَكِت زِرْتي العِراق؟

    taaliba 2:   zirit il-9iraaq bis-seef gabul shahar

طالبة 2: زِرت العِراق بالصّيف گـبـل شهـر

    taalib 1:   laazim chanat haara hwaaya

طالب 1: لازِم چانَت حارّة هُوايَه

    taaliba 2:   kullish haarra, bass muu ratba

طالبة 2: كُلِّـش حارّة. بَس مو رَطْـبة

    taalib 1:   shwakit ahsan waqit ib-Baghdaad?

طالب 1: شْـوَكِت أحْـسَـن وَقِت بُ بغـداد؟

    taaliba 2:   loo bir-rabii9 loo bil-khariif,

طالبة 2: لو بِالـرّبيع لو بِالـخَريف

    taalib 1:   leesh zirti il-9iraaq bis-seef?

طالب 1: لـيش زِرْتي العِراق بالصّيف؟

    taaliba 2:   lisuuʾ ilhazz, ma-kaan 9indi waqit thaani

طالبة 2: لِسوء الـحَـظ. ما كان عِـندي وَقِـت ثاني

b. taalib 1:   aani chinit bil-9iraaq

طالب 1: آني چِنِـت بالعِراق

    taaliba 2:   shunu sawweet hnaak?

طالبة 2: شـنُو سَـوّيت هُـناك؟

    taalib 1:   zirit ahli.

طالب 1: زِرت أهْلـي

    taaliba 2:   sh-aku bil-9iraaq?

طالبة 2: شَـكو بِـالـعِراق

    taalib 1:   il-9iraaq balad hilu wa ghani.

طالب 1: إلْعِراق بَـلَد حِـلُو وغَـني

    taaliba 2:   w huwwa balad qadiim jiddan

طالبة 2: وهو بَـلَـد قَـديم جِـداً

    taalib 1:   haadha sahiih. w bii aathaar hwaaya

طالب 1: هاذا صَـحيح، وبي آثار هُـوايَه

    taaliba 2:   ariid azuur il-9iraaq wiyyaak

طالبة 2: أريد أزور العِراق وِيّـاك

For new words, see Glossary.

The Iraqi Museum, Baghdad

Visiting the Iraqi Museum

ziyaara lil-mathaf il-9iraaqi زِـارَة لِـلْـمَـتْـحَـف الْـعِـراقي

Basma and Waliid (M) are on their way to the Iraqi Museum, which is located on the Karkh side of the Tigris River in Baghdad. The museum contains magnificent antiquities ranging from prehistoric to Islamic periods.

Basic Dialogue (Audio)

1. Basma: kam mathaf aku b-Baghdaad?
   How many museums are in Baghdad?

   بسـمة: كم مَتْـحَف اكو بُ بغداد؟

2. Waliid: aku mataahif hwaaya, bass ahsanha il-mathaf il-9iraaqi.
   There are many museums, but the Iraqi Museum is the best.

   وليد: اكو مَتاحف هُـوايه. بَس أُحْـسَـنْها الْـمتحف العراقي.

3. Basma: ween il-mathaf il-9iraaqi?
   Where is the Iraqi Museum?

   بسـمة: وين الْـمتحف العراقي؟

4. Waliid: qariib mnil-mahatta l-9aalamiyya.
   Near the International Train Station.

   وليد: قريب مُن لْـمَـحَـطّـة العالَـمية.

5. Basma: shunu haadhi l-binaaya l-kabiira?
   What is this large building?

   بسـمة: شُـنو هاذي الْـبِـناية الْـكَـبيرة؟

6. Waliid: haadha huwwa l-mathaf. khalliina nishtiri tadhaakir.
   This is the museum. Let us buy tickets.

   وليد: هاذا هو المتحف العراقي. خَلّـينا نِـشْـتِـري تَـذاكر.

7. Basma: wa daliil il-ma_t_haf, min fa_d_lak. وبَسمة: ودَليل الـمَتحَف، مِن فَـضُلك.
And the museum guide, please.

The two toured the museum and discussed the following on their way out.

8. Waliid: 9ijabi_ch_ il-ma_t_haf? وليد: عِـجَـبِـج الـمَتحَف؟
Did you like the museum?

9. Basma: na9am, 9ijabni hwaaya, wa بَسمة: نعم. عِجَـبْـني هْـوايَه. وخُـصُـوصاً
_kh_u_s_uu_s_an il-qaa9a s-Soomariyya. الـثـقاعة الـسّـومَريتة.
*Yes, I liked it very much, and especially the
Sumerian hall.*

10. Waliid: aani 9ijbatni l-qaa9a وليد: آني عِـجَـبَـتْـني الـثـقاعة الآشوريتة.
l-Aa_sh_uuriyya.
I liked the Assyrian hall.

11. Basma: il-9iraaq qadiim jiddan. بَسمة: العراق قَـديم جِـدّاً.
Iraq is a very ancient (country).

12. Waliid: na9am, huwwa aqdam min وليد: نعم. هو أقْـدَم مِن مَـصِـر.
Ma_s_ir.
Yes, it is older than Egypt.

13. Basma: ariid azuur madiinat Baabil بَسمة: أريد أزور مَـدينة بابل الـثـقَـديمة.
il-qadiima.
I want to visit the city of ancient Babylon.

14. Waliid: _kh_oo_sh_ fikra, _kh_alliina nruu_h_ وليد: خوش فِـكْـرَة. خَـلّـينا نُروح
siwiyya. سِـويّة.
A good idea, let us go together.

Additional Expressions (Audio)

qaa9at maa qabla t-taarii_kh_	*the prehistory hall*	قاعَـة ما قَـبُـلَ التاريخ
il-qaa9a l-Baabiliyya	*the Babylonian hall*	القاعَـة الـبـابِـلـيّـة
qaa9at il-_H_adar	*the Hatrian hall*	قاعَـة الـحَـضَـر
il-qaa9a l-Islaamiyya	*the Islamic hall*	الـثـقاعة الأسْـلامِـيّة
il-Ma_t_haf il-Qadiim	*the Ancient Museum* (capitalized because they are proper names)	إلـمَتحَف الـثـقَـديم
il-Ma_t_haf il-_H_adiith	*the Modern Museum*	إلـمَتحَف الـثـحَـديث
Ma_t_haf il-Fann il-_H_adiith	*the Museum of Modern Art*	مَتحَف الـثـفَـن الـثـحَـديث
il-Ma_t_haf il-_H_arbi	*the Military Museum*	الـمَتحَف الـثـحَـرْبي
il-Ma_t_haf il-9abbaasi	*the Abbasid Museum* (Islamic antiquities)	الـمتحف الـثـعَـبّاسي
Ma_t_haf _Kh_aan Mirjaan	*Khan Mirjan Museum* (Islamic remains)	مَتحف خان مِرْجان

Mathaf it-Taariikh it-Tabii9i	*the Natural History Museum*	مَتحف التّاريخ الطّبيعي
Mathaf al-Azyaaᵓ il-Wataniyya	*the Museum of National Costumes*	مَتحف الأزياء الوَطَنية

Vocabulary (Audio)

kam, cham?	*How many?* (see lesson 15)	كَـم چَـم؟
mathaf / mataahif (S/P)	*museum/s*	مَتـحَـف / مَتاحِف
aku	*there is/are* (see lesson 6)	أكـو
hwaaya	*many, much* (invariable, adj.)	هُـوابه
ahsan, ahsanha	*better, the best*	أحُسَـن. أحُسـنها
qariib, giriib	*near, close by*	قَـريب. گِـريب
mni < min	*from* (see lesson 3)	مُـن < مِـنْ
mahatta / mahattaat (S/P)	*station/s*	مَحَـطّـة / مَحَـطّـات
9aalam	*world, universe*	عالـَم
9aalami / 9aalamiyya (M/F)	*international* (relative adj.)	عالـَمي / عالـَميّة
binaaya / binaayaat (S/P)	*building/s*	بِـناية / بِـنايات
haadha / haadhi (M/F)	*this, that* (see lesson 14)	هاذا / هاذي
khalliina	*let us* (imp. verb)	خَلّـينا
nishtiri	*we buy*	نِشْتِـري
tadhkara / tadhaakir (S/P)	*ticket/s*	تَـذكَـرة / تَـذاكِـر
daliil	*guide*	دَلـيل
9ijabich	*You liked it.*	عِـجَبِـچ
9ijabni	*I liked it.*	عِجَـبْـني
khusuusan	*especially* (adv.)	خُـصُوصاً
qaa9a / qaa9aat (S/P)	*hall/s*	قاعَـة / قاعات
Soomar	*Sumer* (name of the ancient land of southern Iraq)	سُـومَر
Soomari / Soomariyyiin (M/P)	*Sumerian/s* (name of probably the first ancient people who inhabited southern Iraq)	سومَري / سومَريِّـين
Aashuur	*Assur* (name of the ancient land and main god of northern Iraq)	آشُور
Aashuuri / Aashuuriyya / Aashuuriyyiin (M/F/P)	*Assyrian/s* (name of the ancient people who inhabited northern Iraq)	آشُوري / آشُوريّـة / آشُوريِّـين

ariid	*I want*	أريـد
azuur	*I visit*	أزور
madiina / mudun (S/P)	*city, town/s*	مَديـنة / مُـدُن
Baabil	*Babylon (ancient)*	بابـل
qadiim / qadiima (M/F)	*old, ancient (adj.)*	قَـديم / قَـديـمة
aqdam	*older, more ancient*	أقـدَم
khoosh (M/F/P)	*good (invariable adj. precedes nouns)*	خـوش
fikra / afkaar (S/P)	*idea/s*	فِـكـرَة / أفـكار
nruuh	*we go*	نُـروح
siwiyya	*together*	سِـوِيّـة

Grammar and Remarks
The Present / Imperfect Tense Verb: il-fi9il il-mudaari9 إلْـفِـعِـل المُضارِع

The Arabic present tense verb differs from the past tense verb in one important feature. It must always have a prefix, as in **yiktib** يكـتب (*he writes*) although it also takes a suffix with certain persons to indicate gender or number, as in **yikitbuun** يكـتبون (*they write*). Therefore, the present verb consists of two and sometimes three elements: a prefix which indicates the subject marker, a stem which gives the lexical meaning, and sometimes a suffix (see lesson 8). The base form stem of the present tense verb is the same as that of the imperative verb stem preceded by the subject prefix, e.g. **ruuh** روح (*go*, M), **truuh** تـروح (*you go*, M).

Adding the prefixes to the present tense verb may create some variants depending on the type of the verb (regular or weak) or whether the stem has one initial consonant or more. Below are conjugation tables for the various types of the Iraqi present tense verbs and their prefix variants.

Notice that the third person feminine and the second person masculine of the present verbs have similar forms.

Important Note: At this stage of learning Arabic, the student is advised to learn the stem of the past and the present of each verb together (memorize verbs like: **raah, yruuh, kitab, yiktib**). By doing so, the student should be able to conjugate each type more easily. In the glossary of this book, and in almost in all the books that teach Arabic, the reader will find the verbs listed in the same manner, namely, third person masculine singular past tense first and its equivalent present tense second. For the future tense verb, see lesson 12.

The Present Tense Verb Paradigm (Audio)

Arabic Pronouns	Arabic Prefix/Suffix	Hollow Verb guul (*to say*)	Double Verb sadd (*to close*)
huwwa	y/yi/yu-	yguul	ysidd
hiyya	t/ti/tu- *	tguul	tsidd
humma	y/yi/yu ... uun	yguul**uun**	ysidd**uun**
inta	t/ti/tu- *	tguul	tsidd

Arabic Pronouns	Arabic Prefix/Suffix	Hollow Verb guul (*to say*)	Double Verb sadd (*to close*)
inti	t/ti/tu . . . iin	tguuliin	tsiddiin
intu	t/ti/tu . . . uun	tguuluun	tsidduun
aani	a-	aguul	asidd
ihna	n/ni/nu-	nguul	nsidd

يـُسِـدّ	يـُگـُول	يـْ / يـِ / يـُ ــ	هو
تـُسِـدّ	تـُگـُول	تـْ / تـِ / تـُ ــ*	هي
يـُسِـدّون	يـُگـُولون	يـْ / يـِ / يـُ . . . ون	هـُمّه
تـُسِـدّ	تـُگـُول	تـْ / تـِ / تـُ ــ*	إنت
تـُسِـدّين	تـُگـُولين	تـْ / تـِ / تـُ . . . يـُن	إنتي
تـُسِـدّون	تـُگـُولون	تـْ / تـِ / تـُ . . . ون	إنتو
أسِـدّ	أگـُول	أ ــ	آني
نـُسِـدّ	نـُگـُول	نـْ / نـِ / نـُ ــ	إحنا

*Identical conjugations.

Arabic Pronouns	Arabic Prefix/Suffix	Regular Verb ktib (*to write*), g9ud (*to sit*)		Weak Verb qra (*to read*)
huwwa	y/yi/yu-	yiktib	yug9ud	yiqra
hiyya	t/ti/tu-*	tiktib	tug9ud	tiqra
humma	y/yi/yu-. . .uun	yikitbuun	yugu9duun	yiqruun
inta	t/ti/tu-*	tiktib	tug9ud	tiqra
inti	t/ti/tu-. . .iin	tikitbiin	tugu9diin	tiqriin
intu	t/ti/tu-. . .uun	tikitbuun	tugu9duun	tiqruun
aani	a-	aktib	ag9ud	aqra
ihna	n/ni/nu-	niktib	nug9ud	niqra

يـِقـْره	يـُگـْعـُد	يـِكـْتـِب	يـْ / يـِ / يـُ ــ	هو
تـِقـْرا	تـُگـْعـُد	تـِكـْتـِب	تـْ / تـِ / تـُ ــ*	ي
يـِقـْرون	يـُگـْعـُدون	يـِكـْتـْبـُون	يـْ / يـِ / يـُ . . . ون	هـُمّه
تـِقـْرا	تـُگـْعـُد	تـِكـْتـِب	تـْ / تـِ / تـُ ــ*	إنت
تـِقـْرين	تـُگـْعـُدين	تـِكـْتـْبـِين	تـْ / تـِ / تـُ . . . يـُن	إنتي
تـِقـْرون	تـُگـْعـُدون	تـِكـْتـْبـُون	تـْ / تـِ / تـُ . . . ون	إنتو
أقـْرا	أگـْعـُد	أكـْتـِب	أ ــ	آني
نـِقـْرا	نـُگـْعـُد	نـِكـْتـِب	نـْ / نـِ / نـُ ــ	إحنا

*Identical conjugations.

Notes on the Verb Paradigm:

1. There are only four prefixes (**y-**, **t-**, **a-**, **n-**) to which the helping vowel "**i**" or "**u**" is added (**yi/yu, ti/tu, ni/nu**) when the prefixed stem has more than one initial consonant, as in the verbs **ktib**, **g9ud**, and **qra**. The helping vowel "**i**" is much more common than "**u**."

There is no established rule for adding "**i**" or "**u**" and the correct vowel is to be learned with each verb. However, there is a tendency toward vowel harmony; a verb with stem vowel "**i**" or "**u**" tends to take a similar helping vowel. The stem vowel is the vowel before the last consonant.

2. The hollow and the double verbs have one initial consonant. Therefore, its prefixes do not take a helping vowel.

3. The regular verbs **ktib** and **g9ud** have two initial consonants with "**i**" and "**u**" stem vowel, respectively. Therefore, their prefix takes similar helping vowels, namely "**i**" and "**u**." There are two variants to be noted in this type of verb (regular) which occur in the third person plural and the second person feminine and plural. First, when the suffix "**-uun**" or "**-iin**" is added there is an option of dropping out the prefix helping vowel, and second, the helping vowel is shifted from third to second position, as shown above.

4. The weak verb, such as **qra**, has two initial consonants and its prefix almost always takes the helping vowel "**i**." The final vowel in such a verb is always dropped out when a suffix beginning with a vowel is added, as in **tiqriin**.

Idioms and Common Phrases (Audio)

1. min waqit li-waqit مِن وَقِــت لِــوَقِــت *from time to time*

azuur il-9iraaq min waqit li-waqit	*I visit Iraq from time to time.*	أزور العراق مِن وَقِــت لِــوَقِــت
ihna nzuur 9ammaan min waqit li-waqit	*We visit Amman from time to time.*	إحنا نْزور عَمّــان مِن وَقِــت لِــوَقِت
huwwa yzuur Basma min waqit li-waqit	*He visits Basma from time to time.*	هو يْـزور بسمة مِن وَقِــت لِــوَقِت
inti tzuuriin Turkiya min waqit li-wqait	*You visit Turkey from time to time.*	إنتي تْـزورين تُرْكيا مِن وَقِــت لِــوَقِت
intu tzuuruun il-mathaf il-9iraaqi min waqit li-waqit	*You visit the Iraqi Museum from time to time.*	إنتو تْـزورون المتحف العراق مِن وَقِــت لِــوَقِت

2. min hissa w jay مِن هِـسّــه وجايْ *from now on*

min hissa w jaay, aruuh lil-mathaf kull shahar	*From now on, I will go to the museum every month.*	مِن هِـسّــه وجاي. أروح لِـلْـمَتحف كُل شهر
min hissa w jaay, ashrab gahwa	*From now on, I will drink coffee.*	مِن هِـسّــه وجاي. أشْـرَب گَـهْــوَة
min hissa w jaay, maa ashrab chaay	*From now on, I will not drink tea.*	مِن هِـسّــه وجاي. ما أشْـرَب چاي
min hissa w jaay, nzuurkum bil-beet kull usbuu9	*From now on, we will visit you at (your) house every week.*	مِن هِـسّــه وجاي. نْـزوركم بالبيت كُل اُسْبوع

min hissa w jaay, naakul kabaab ib-mat9am is-Salaam	*From now on, we will eat kebab in the Salaam restaurant.*	مِن هِسَّه وجاي، ناكُل كباب بُ مَطْعَم السَّلام
min hissa w jaay, adrus 9arabi kull yoom	*From now on, I will study Arabic every day.*	مِن هِسَّه وجاي، أدْرُس عربي كُل يوم
min hissa w jaay, laazim aqra taariikh il-9iraaq	*From now on, I must read the history of Iraq.*	مِن هِسَّه وجاي، لازِم أقْرَه تاريخ العراق

Drills   tamaariin   تَمارين

1. Give appropriate oral answers to the following questions:

il-mathaf il-9iraaqi chibiir loo saghiir?	المتحف العراقي چِبيــر لو صَغير؟
ween aku mataahif hwaaya?	وين أكو مَتاحف هُـوايه؟
ween il-mathaf il-9iraaqi?	وين الْمَتْحَف الْعراقي؟
minu zaar il-mathaf?	مِنو زار الْمتحف؟
ayy qaa9a 9ijbatich?	أيّ قاعة عِجْبَتِج؟
triidiin tzuuriin madinat Baabil?	تْريدين تْزورين مَدينة بابل؟
Baabil bi9iida loo qariiba min Baghdaad?	بابل بِعيدة لو قَريبة مِن بغداد؟
Baabil qadiima loo hadiitha?	بابل قَديمة لو حَديثة؟
shaku bil-mathaf il-9iraaqi?	شَكو بِالْمَتْحَف الْعراقي؟
aathaar il-9iraaq qadiima, muu balla?	آثـار الْعراق قَديمة. مُو بَـلْـلَـه؟
minu aqdam il-9iraaq loo Lubnaan?	مِنو أقْدم الْعراق لو لُبْنان؟
minu ahdath Masir loo Fransa?	مِنو أحْدَث مَصِر لو فْرَنْسا؟

2. Change the second person masculine to the second person feminine and plural:

ween thibb truuh?	khalliini ashtri tadhaakir
وين تْحِب تْروح؟	خَـلّيني أشتري تَذاكر

F:

P:

tshuuf il-aathaar	تْشوف الآثـار

F:

P:

tzuur Baabil baachir	تْزور بابل باچِـر

F:

P:

F:

P:

yi9ijbak il-mathaf?	يـِعِجْبَـك المتحف

F:

P:

tishrab chaay	تِشْـرَب چاي

F:

P:

tit9allam bij-jaami9a   تِـتْـعَـلّـم بالْجَـامِـعة   yzuurna bil-beet baachir   تْـزورنا بالْبيت باچِـر

F: F:

P: P:

tiqra w tiktib 9arabi   تِـقْـرا وتِـكْـئِـتِب عربي   titkallam 9iraaqi zeen   تِـتْـكَـلّـم عراقي زين

F: F:

P: P:

truuh lis-sinama hissa   تْـروح لِسِّـيـنَـما   thibb taariikh il-9iraaq?   تْـحِـب تاريخ العراق؟

F: F:

P: P:

3. Conjugate orally the following present tense verbs:

yruuh	he goes	يْـروح	yiji	he comes	يِـجي
yaakul	he eats	ياكُـل	yzuur	he visits	يْـزور
yishrab	he drinks	يِـشْـرب	yhutt	he puts	يْـحُـط
yriid	he wants	يْـريد	yudrus	he studies	يُـدْرُس
yiftah	he opens	يِـفْـتح	yuskut	he doesn't speak	يُـسْـكُـت
yshuuf	he sees	يْـشوف	yubqa	he stays	يُـبْـقـا
ynaam	he sleeps	يْـنام	yiktishif	he discovers	يِـكْـتِـشِـف
yguul	he says	يْـگـول	yoogaf	he stands up	يوگَـف
yudkhul	he enters	يُـدْخُـل	yiksir	he breaks	يِـكْـسِـر
yug9ud	he sits down	يُـگْـعُـد	ysidd	he closes	يْـسِـد

4. Complete and read the following sentences aloud:

a. huwwa yug9ud min in-noom is-saa9a sab9a   هو يُـوكْـعُـد من النّـوم السّاعة سَـبْـعَـة

hiyya _____ min in-noom is-saa9a sab9a   هي _____ من النّـوم السّاعة سَـبعة

humma _____ min in-noom is-saa9a sab9a   هُـمّـه _____ من النّـوم السّـاعة سَـبعة

inta _____ min in-noom is-saa9a 9ashra   إنت _____ من النّـوم السّـاعة عَـشْـرَة

inti _____ min in-noom is-saa9a 9ashra   إنتي _____ من النّـوم السّـاعة عَـشْـرَة

intu _____ min in-noom is-saa9a 9ashra   إنتو _____ من النّـوم السّـاعة عَـشْـرَة

aani _____ min in-noom is-saa9a sab9a w nu<u>ss</u>

آني _____ من النّـوم السّـاعة سَبعة ونُص

i<u>h</u>na _____ min in-noom is-saa9a sab9a w rubu9

إحنا _____ من النّـوم السّـاعة سَبعة ورُبُع

b. huwwa yi<u>sh</u>rab <u>ch</u>aay kull yoom i<u>s</u>-<u>s</u>ubu<u>h</u>   هو يِشْـرب چاي كُلُّ يوم الصُّـبُح

hiyya _____   _____ هـي

humma _____   _____ هُـمّـه

inta _____   _____ إنت

inti _____   _____ إنتـي

intu _____   _____ إنتو

aani _____   _____ آني

i<u>h</u>na _____   _____ إحنا

c. min hissa w jaay, Kaamil yiqra 9arabi kull yoom

مِن هِسّـه وجايْ. كامل يِـقرَه عربي كُلُّ يوم

_____ , Samiira _____   _____ سميرة _____

_____ , Maalik _____   _____ مالك _____

_____ , inta _____   _____ إنت _____

_____ , inti _____   _____ إنتـي _____

_____ , intu _____   _____ إنتو _____

_____ , aani _____   _____ آني _____

_____ , i<u>h</u>na _____   _____ إحنا _____

d. huwwa yudrus Ingiliizi kull usbuu9 is-subuh   هو يُدرُس إنگليزي كُلّ يوم الصُّبُح

_____ iz-zuhur   الظُّهُر _____

_____ il-9asir   الـعَصِر _____

_____ bil-masaaʾ   بالمَساء _____

_____ bil-leel   بالـليل _____

_____ gabul iz-zuhur   گَبُل الظّهُر _____

_____ ba9d iz-zuhur   بَعُد الظُّهُر _____

e. il-mathaf il-9iraaqi qariib loo bi9iid mnil-mahatta?

المتحف العراقي قريب لو بِعيد مُن لـمَحَطّة؟

_____ min Baabil?   مِن بابل؟ _____

_____ min nahar Dijla?   مِن نَهَر دِجلة؟ _____

_____ mnis-safaara?   مُن لـسّفارة _____

_____ mnil-findiq?   مُن لـفِنـدِق _____

_____ mnis-suug?   مُن لـسّوگ _____

_____ mnil-bariid?   مُن لـبَـريد _____

_____ mnij-jisir?   مُن لـجّسِـر _____

5. Read aloud the following sentences and translate them:

aku mataahif hwaaya b-Baghdaad   أكـو مَتاحف هُوايه بْ بغداد

aku sayyaaraat hwaaya bish-shaari9   أكـو سَيّارات هُوايه بالشّارع

aku tayyaaraat hwaaya bil-mataar   أكـو طيّارات هُوايه بالـمَطار

aku kutub hwaaya bil-maktaba   أكـو كُتُب هُوايه بالـمَكـتَبة

aku banaat hwaaya bil-madrasa   أكـو بَنات هُوايه بالـمَـدُرَسة

aku wilid hwaaya bij-jaami9a   أكـو ولِـد هُوايه بالجّامِعة

aku aathaar hwaaya bil-9iraaq   أكـو آثـار هُوايه بالعِراق

Basma w Maalik yruuhuun siwiyya l-Baabil   بسمة ومالك يُـروحون سِـويّـة لْ بابل

aani w-inta nruuh siwiyya lil-mathaf آني وانت نُروح سِـويّـه لِلْمَتحف

intu truuhuun siwiyya lis-siinama انتو تُروحون سِـويّـه لِلسّـينَـما

Laylaa w Samiir yshuufuun filim 9arabi siwiyya ليلى وسمير يُشـوفون فِلِـم عربي سِـويّـه

il-wilid yudursuun siwiyya bil-madrasa إلْـولِد يُـدُرسون سِـويّـه بالْـمَدْرَسـة

Basma tshuuf il-mathaf wiyya Waliid بسمة تُـشـوف الْـمَتْـحَف ويّـه وليد

Kariima tiqra 9arabi wiyya Samiira كريمـة تِـقـرَى عربي ويّـه سميرة

6. Translate the following into Arabic:

The Iraqi Museum is near the International Station.

_____

I like the Babylonian and the Assyrian halls.

_____

Please buy (F) the museum guide.

_____

There are many Islamic museums in Iraq.

_____

The Sumerian language is old.

_____

They visit the city of Babylon from time to time.

_____

From now on, I will speak Arabic every day.

_____

From now on, we will not drink coffee in the morning.

_____

Laylaa is thankful to you for the gift.

_____

I am indebted to my Arabic professor.

_____

You (M) say everything in English.

_____

They like to visit London in the summer.

_____

The summer is hot and the winter is cold in Baghdad.

_____

I go to sleep at night at eleven o'clock from time to time.

_____

Please take care (P) of my children.

_____

For your sake, I will study Arabic every day.

_____

Iraqi antiquities are very old.

_____

Creative Dialogues

a. taaliba 1: ariidak tiji wiyyaaya
               lil-mathaf
    taalib 2:   ayy mathaf triidiin tzuuriin?
    taaliba 1: 9ala keefak, mumkin
                il-Mathaf il-Islami
    taalib 2:   shaku bil-Mathaf il-Islaami?
    taaliba 1: aku aathaar Islaamiyya
    taalib 2:   shwakit triidiin truuhiin?
    taaliba 1: il-yoom is-saa9a tis9a
    taalib 2:   khoosh fikra

b. taalib 1:   shgadd saarlich bil-9iraaq?
    taaliba 2: saarli shahar
    taalib 1:   shwakit wisalti Baghdaad?
    taaliba 2: wisalit gabul shahar
    taalib 1:   b-ayy findiq naazla?

طالبة 1: أريدَك تْجي وِيّـايَه لِـلْـمتحف

طالب 2: أي مَتْحَف تْريدين تْزورين؟

طالبة 1: على كيفك، مُمْكِن المتحف الإسْلامـي

طالب 2: شَـكو بالْـمتحف الإسْلامـي؟

طالبة 1: أكـو آثـار إسْلامية

طالب 2: شْـوَكِـت تْريدين تْروحيـن؟

طالبة 1: الْـيوم السّاعَـة تِـسْعَـة

طالب 2: خُـوش فِـكْـرَة

طالب 1: شَـگَـد صـارْلِـچ بالـعراق؟

طالب 2: صـارْلـي شَـهَـر

طالب 1: شْـوَكِـت وِصَـلْـتي بـغداد؟

طالب 2: وصَـلِـت گَـبُـل شَـهَـر

طالبة 1: بْ أي فِـنْـدِق نازْلَـة؟

ṭaaliba 2:	naazla b-findiq 9i<u>sh</u>taar
ṭaalib 1:	<u>sh</u>loona haa<u>dh</u>a il-findiq?
ṭaaliba 2:	ya9ni, maa<u>sh</u>i il-<u>h</u>aal
ṭaalib 1:	<u>sh</u>unu zirti bil-9iraaq?
ṭaaliba 2:	zirit Baabil wa Naynawa

طالب 2: نازْلَـة بُ فَـنُـئدق عِشُـتار

طالبة 1: شـلـونَـة هاذا الْـفِنُـئدق؟

طالب 2: يَـعُـنـي، ماشـي الْـحال

طالبة 1: شُـنُـو زِرُتِي بالْعِراق؟

طالب 2: زِرت بابل ونَـيُـنَـوى

For new words, see Glossary.

An artist's reconstruction of ancient Babylon

Trip to Babylon

safra l-Baabil   سَـفْـرَة لُ بـابِـل

Basma goes to see Waliid, who is getting ready to go on a trip to the ancient city of Babylon.

Basic Dialogue (Audio)

1. Basma: <u>sh</u>-da-ssawwi?   بسـمة: شُـدَ سَّـوِّي؟
   What are you doing?

2. Waliid: da-ajma9 malaabsi. ra<u>h</u>-azuur   وليد: دَ أَجْمَع مَلابْسي. رَحُ أزور بابل باچِـر.
   Baabil baa<u>ch</u>ir.
   *I am collecting my clothes. I will visit
   Babylon tomorrow.*

3. Basma: ra<u>h</u>-truu<u>h</u> bis-sayyaara loo   بسـمة: رَحُ تْروح بالسَّـيارة لو بالْـقِطار؟
   bil-qitaar?
   Are you going by car or train?

4. Waliid: ra<u>h</u>-aruu<u>h</u> bis-sayyaara.   وليد: رَحُ أروح بالسَّـيارة.
   I will go by car.

5. Basma: mumkin aji wiyyaak?   بسـمة: مُمْكِـن أجي وِيَـاك؟
   Can I come with you?

6. Waliid: ahlan wa sahlan.   وليد: أهْلاً وسَـهْلاً.
   Welcome.

7. Basma: Baabil bi9iida min Ba<u>gh</u>daad?   بسـمة: بابل بِـعيدة مِـن بغداد؟
   Is Babylon far from Baghdad?

8. Waliid: laa, w hiyya kullish giriiba min
madinat il-Hilla

No, and it is very close to the city of Hila.

وليد: لا. وهي كُلّش گِريبة مِن مَدينة الحِلّة.

They reach the city outer wall of Babylon whose size impresses Basma.

9. Basma: walla, Baabil madiina dakhma!
shunu haadhi?

Indeed, Babylon is a huge city! What is that?

بسمة: والله. بابل مَدينة ضَخُمة! شُنو هاذي؟

10. Waliid: haadhi Bawwaabat 9ishtaar.

That is Ishtar Gate.

وليد: هاذي بَوّابة عِشتار.

11. Basma: hal hiyya l-Bawwaaba l-asliyya?

Is it the original gate?

بسمة: هَل هي الْبَوّابة الأَصليّة؟

12. Waliid: laa, il-Bawwaaba l-asliyya
b-mathaf Barliin.

No, the original gate is in the Berlin Museum.

وليد: لا. البَوّابة لأَصليّة بُ مَتحف برلين.

13. Basma: allaah, haadha Shaari9
il-Mawkib.

How nice, this is the Procession Street.

بسمة: ألّلاه. هاذا شارع الْمَوكِب.

14. Waliid: na9am, w haadha Asad Baabil
il-mashhuur.

Yes, and that is the famous Lion of Babylon.

وليد: نعم. وهاذا أسَد بابل الْمَشْهور.

15. Basma: la9ad, ween ij-Janaa'in
il-Mu9allaqa?

So, where are the Hanging Gardens?

بسمة: لَعَد. وين الجَّنائِن الْمُعَلَّقة؟

16. Waliid: b-qasir il-malik
Nabukhadnesser.

In King Nabuchadnezzer's palace.

وليد: بُ قَصِر الْمَلِك نَبوخَذنَصّر.

17. Basma: khalliina nruuh nshuuf Burij
Baabil.

Let us go to see the Tower of Babel.

بسمة: خَلّينا نُروح نُشوف بُرِج بابل.

18. Waliid: na9am, huwwa hnaak.

Yes, it is over there.

وليد: نعم. هو هُناك.

19. Basma: tara, Baabil chaanat madiina
9aziima!

You know, Babylon was a great city!

بسمة: تَرَا. بابل چانت مَدينة عَظيمة!

Additional Expressions (Audio)

tall / tuluul (S/P)	*tell/s, mound/s*	تَل / تُلول
athar / aathaar (S/P)	*antiquity/s, remains*	أثَر / آثار
athari / athariyya (M/F)	*archaeological, ancient* (relative adj.)	أثَري / أثَرِيَّة
tall athari / tuluul athariyya (S/P)	*archaeological mound/s*	تل أثري / تلول أثرية
aathaari / aathaariyya / aathaariyyiin (M/F/P)	*archaeologist/s*	آثاري / آثارية / آثارِّين
zaqquura / zaqquuraat (S/P)	*ziggurat/s*	زَقّورة / زَقّورات
Mudiiriyyat il-Aathaar il-9aamma	*Directorate General of Antiquities* (Iraq)	مُديرِيَّة الآثار العامة

Vocabulary (Audio)

sh-?	*what?* (see lesson 15)	شـ ــ
da-	*-ing* (see below)	دَ ــ
ssawwi < tsawwi	*You (M) do* (**t-** is assimilated for phonetic reasons)	سّوّي > تْسَوّي
ajma9	*I collect, I put together*	أجـمَع
rah-	*will, shall, going to* (see below)	رَح
malaabsi	*my clothes*	مَلابْسِي
walla	*indeed, really* (see also lesson 5)	والله
kullish	*very* (invariable)	كُلِّش
bi9iid / bi9iida / b9aad (M/F/P)	*far* (adj.)	بِعيد / بِعيدة / بُعاد
madiina / mudun (S/P)	*city/ies, town/s*	مَدينة / مُدُن
il-Hilla	*the city of Hilla* (near Babylon)	إلْحِلّة
haadha / haadhi (M/F)	*this, that* (see lesson 14)	هاذا / هاذي
dakhum / dakhma (M/F)	*huge* (adj.)	ضَخُم / ضَخْمَة
bawwaaba / bawwaabaat (S/P)	*gate/s*	بَوّابة / بَوّابات
Bawwaabat 9ishtaar	*Ishtar Gate*	بَوّابة عِشْتار
hal?	*What? Is it?* (see lesson 15)	هَـل؟
asli / asliyya (M/F)	*original, genuine*	أصْلي / أصْلِيَّة
allaah	*How nice!* (see lesson 5)	ألّاه
shaari9 / shawaari9 (S/P)	*street/s, road/s*	شارِع / شَوارِع
mawkib	*procession*	مَوْكِب
Shaari9 il-Mawkib	*Procession Street* (in Babylon)	شارع المَوْكِب
asad / usuud (S/P)	*lion/s*	أسَد / أسُّود
Asad Baabil	*the Lion of Babylon*	أسَد بابل

mashhuur / mashhuura (M/F)	*famous, well known* (adj.)	مَشْـهور / مَشْـهورة
la9ad	*in that case, so* (invariable, see below)	لَعَـد
ij-Janaaᵓin il-Mu9allaqa	*the Hanging Gardens* (one of the Seven Wonders of the world)	الجَنائـِن المُعَـلَّـقـة
qasir / qusuur (S/P)	*palace/s*	قَـصِر / قُـصُور
malik / miluuk (S/P)	*king/s*	مَـلِك / مِـلـوك
Nabukhadnesser	*Nabuchadnezzer* (king of Babylon who built most of what we see in Babylon today)	نَبوخَـذنَـصّـر
burij / abraaj (S/P)	*tower/s*	بُـرج / أبْـراج
Burij Baabil	*the biblical Tower of Babel*	
tara	*you know, otherwise,* or *else* (see below)	تَـرَا
chaanat (F)	*was* (see lesson 13)	چانـت
9aziim / 9aziima (M/F)	*great*	عَـظيم / عَـظيمة
gabul	*before, ago, previously*	گَـبُـل
idhaa	*if*	إذا

Grammar and Remarks
The Present Progressive Prefix da- دَ -*ing*

In Iraqi Arabic, the prefix "**da-**" is used with the present tense verb to indicate a progressive condition happening at the time of the speech, or an action going on currently. The composition of "**da-**" + **present tense** corresponds to the English verb + "-ing," as in **da-yishrab** (*he is drinking*). It is important to remember that the Iraqi present tense verb does not designate a progressive action but indicates a timeless habitual condition. (Audio)

nishrab chaay	*We drink tea.*	نِشْـرَب چاي
da-nishrab chaay	*We are drinking tea.*	دَ نِشْـرَب چاي
aakul khubuz	*I eat bread.*	آكُـل خُـبُز
da-aakul khubuz	*I am eating bread.*	دَ آكُـل خُـبُز
yijma9 fluus	*He collects money.*	يـِجْمَع فُـلوس
da-yijma9 fluss	*He is collecting money.*	دَ يـِجْمَع فُـلوس
ween truuh kull yoom?	*Where do you go everyday?*	وين تْـروح كـل يوم؟
ween da-truuh il-yoom?	*Where are you going today?*	وين دَ تْـروح اليوم؟
yili9buun tooba	*They play soccer (football).*	يـِلـِعْبون طوبَة
da-yli9buun tooba	*They are playing soccer.*	دَ يُلـِعْبون طوبَة

The Future Verb Prefixes rah-, ha- رَحْ، حَ ـ ـ *will, shall, going to*

The two prefixes "**rah-**" or "**ha-**" are added to the present tense verb to make a future tense verb equivalent to the English "will," "shall," or "going to." The future prefix "**rah-** رَحْ" has a variant form "**raah-** راح," however, we advise using the short form "**rah-**." (Audio)

adrus 9arabi	*I study Arabic.*	أُدْرُس عَـربي
rah-adrus 9arabi	*I shall study Arabic.*	رَحْ ادْرُس عَـربي
yiqra ktaab	*He reads a book.*	يـِقـْرَا كـْتاب
rah-yiqra ktaab	*He will read a book.*	رَحْ يـِقـْرَا كـْتاب

If the verb begins with two consonants, the helping vowel "**i**" is added to the beginning of the verb when it is preceded by "**rah-**."

nsaafir	*we travel*	نـْسـافِـر
rah-**i**nsaafir	*we shall travel*	رَحْ إنْسـافِر
tshuufiin	*you* (F) *see*	تـْشوفِـين
rah-**i**tshuufiin	*you will see*	رَحْ إتـْشوفِـين

The prefix "**ha-** ـ حَ" has the same meaning as "**rah-**" but sometimes connotes the immediate future, comparable to the difference between "I am going to go" and "I shall go" in English. When "**ha-**" precedes a first person singular verb, the prefix subject marker "**a**" of the verb is dropped out.

adrus	*I study.*	أُدْرُس	**ha-**drus	*I am going to study.*	حَ دُرُس
asaafir	*I travel.*	أسـافِـر	**ha-**saafir	*I am going to travel.*	حَ سـافِـر

Both prefixes "**rah-**" and "**ha-**" are negated with the word **ma-** (see lesson 4).

rah-adrus	*I shall study.*	رَحْ أُدْرُس	ma **rah-**adrus	*I shall not study.*	مَ رَحْ أُدْرُس
ha-drus	*I am going to study.*	حَ دُرُس	ma **ha-**drus	*I am not going to study.*	مَ حَ دُرُس

Idioms and Common Phrases (Audio)

1. la9ad لـَعَـد *then, so, in that case* (an invariable transitional word)

la9ad, leesh rihtu l-Baabil?	*Then why did you go to Babylon?*	لَعَـد. ليش رُحْـتو لْ بابل؟
la9ad, minu bina madinat Baabil?	*So, who built the city of Babylon?*	لَعَـد. مِنو بِـنَا مَدينـة بابل؟
la9ad, ta9aal zuurna baachir	*In that case, come to visit us tomorrow.*	لَعَـد. تـَعـال زورْنا باچِـر

| la9ad, shgadd il-ujra? | *So, how much is the rate?* | لَـعَـد. شْـگَـد الأَجْـرَة؟ |
| la9ad, ween il-bawwaaba l-asliyya? | *So, where is the original gate?* | لَـعَـد. وين الْـبَـوّابَـة الأَصْـلِـيّة؟ |

2. tara تَـرَا certainly, you know, otherwise (invariable transitional word used for confirmation)

tara, Baabil muu bi9iida min Baghdaad	*Certainly, Babylon is not far from Baghdad.*	تَـرَا. بابل مُـو بِـعـيدة مِـن بغداد
tara, aku aathaar hwaaya bil-9iraaq	*You know, there are many antiquities in Iraq.*	تَـرَا. أكـو آثـار هْـوايه بالعراق
la-tzuur Pariis, tara hiyya ghaalya hwaaya	*Don't visit Paris because it is very expensive.*	لَـتْـزور پاريس. تَـرَا هـي غالْـيَـة هُـوايه
has-sayyaara tara muu zeena	*You know, this car is not good!*	هَـالسَّـيـارة تَـرَا مو زيـنة
tara, Basma tu9ruf qraaya wi-ktaaba	*You know, Basma knows reading and writing.*	تَـرَا. بـسـمة تُـعْـرُف قْـرايَـة وكْـتابة
tara, az9al idhaa maa ijeet	*Otherwise, I will be upset if you don't come.*	تَـرَا. أزْعَـل إذا مـا إجـيـت

3. hal-ayyaam هَـلأيّـام these days, nowadays

id-dinya ghaalya, hal-ayyaam	*Life is expensive nowadays.*	إلـدّنْـيـا غالْـيَـة.هَـلأيّـام
hal-ayyaam, id-dinya haarra	*These days, it is hot.*	هَـلأيّـام. الـدّنْـيـا حارّة
hal-ayyaam, maaku safar lil-9iraaq	*These days, there is no traveling to Iraq.*	هَـلأيّـام. ماكـو سَـفَـر لِـلْـعـراق
hal-ayyaam, si9ir il-akil ghaali	*Nowadays, food prices are high.*	هَـلأيّـام. سِـعِـر الأكِـل غالي
hal-ayyaam, anaam is-saa9a 9ashra	*These days, I sleep at ten o'clock.*	هَـلأيّـام. أنـام السّـاعة عَـشْـرة
hal-ayyaam, hiyya masghuula hwaaya	*Nowadays, she is very busy.*	هَـلأيّـام. هـي مَـشْـغـولة هُـوايه

Drills tamaariin تَـمارين

1. Give appropriate oral replies to the following:

| Baabil bi9iida loo qariiba min Baghdaad? | بابل بِـعـيدة لو قَـريبة مِـن بغداد؟ |
| Baabil madiina sagiira loo chibiira? | بابل مَـدينة صَـغيرة لو چِـبـيـرة؟ |

Baabil madiina hadii<u>th</u>a loo qadiima?	بابل مَدينة حَديثة لو قَديمة؟
ween Baabil?	وين بابل؟
minu bina madinat Baabil?	مِنو بِنَا مَدينة بابل؟
ween Bawwaabat 9ish<u>t</u>aar il-a<u>s</u>liyya?	وين بَوّابة عِشتار الأَصليّة؟
Asad Baabil ma<u>sh</u>huur?	أَسَد بابل مَشهور؟
<u>sh</u>aku b-qa<u>s</u>ir Nabukhadne<u>ss</u>er?	شَكو بُ قَصِر نبوخدنصَر؟
<u>sh</u>wakit ra<u>h</u>-truu<u>h</u> l-Beeruut?	شُؤكِت رَح تُروح لُ بيروت؟

2. Make a progressive tense of the following sentences with "da-" (oral):

Example: yruu<u>h</u> lil-madrasa	*He goes to the school.*	يُروح لِلمَدرَسة
Answer: da-yruu<u>h</u> lil-madrasa	*He is going to the school.*	دَ يُروح لِلمَدرَسة
tudrus lu<u>gh</u>a 9arabiyya		تُدُرُس لُغة عَربية
azuur il-ma<u>th</u>af		أزور المَتحَف
n<u>sh</u>uuf aa<u>th</u>aar madinat Baabil		نُشوف آثار مَدينة بابل
<u>sh</u>unu yuqruun bij-jaami9a		شُنو يُقرُون بالجّامِعة؟
yibni Baabil hal-ayyaam		يِبني بغداد هَلأيّام
aani aqra w aktib 9arabi		آني أقرَا وكتِب عَربي
hal-ayyaam, y<u>sh</u>uufuun siinama hwaaya		هَلأيّام. يُشوفون سينما هُوايَه
tiktib risaala bil-9arabi		تِكتِب رسالة بالعَربي
y<u>sh</u>irbuun <u>ch</u>aay w gahwa, hal-ayyaam		يُشِربون چاي وگَهُوة. هَلأيّام
taakliin kabaab bil-ma<u>t</u>9am		تاكلين كَباب بالمَطعَم

3. Make a future tense of the following sentences with "rah- رَح" or "ha- حَ" (oral):

Example: tiktib risaala	*She writes a letter.*	تِكتِب رسالة
Answer: ra<u>h</u>-tiktib risaala	*She will write a letter.*	رَح تِكتِب رسالة
<u>h</u>a-tiktib risaala	*She is going to write a letter.*	حَ تِكتِب رسالة
yzuur Baabil yoom ij-jum9a		يُزور بابل يوم الجُمُعة
truu<u>h</u> lil-ma<u>th</u>af is-saa9a arba9a		تُروح لِلمُتحف السّاعة أَربَعة
at9allam qraaya wi-ktaaba kull yoom		أتعَلّم قُرايـة وكتابة كُل يوم
ysaafruun lil-9iraq ba9ad <u>sh</u>ahar		يُسافُرون لِلعِراق بَعَد شهر
<u>sh</u>wakit tijuun tzuuruuna bil-beet?		شُؤكِت جّون تُزورونا بِالبِيت؟
<u>sh</u>gadd tubqa b-Tuunis?		شُـگَد تُبُقا بُ تونِس؟
Waliid wa Layla ysaafruun bi<u>t</u>-<u>t</u>ayyaara		وليد وليلى يُسافُرون بالطّيارة
anaam is-saa9a da9a<u>sh</u> bil-leel		أنام السّاعة دَعَش باللِيل
yjiibuun Basma mnil-ma<u>t</u>aar baa<u>ch</u>ir		يُجيبون بسمة مُن المَطار باچِر
hiyya tsuuq is-sayyaara bi<u>sh</u>-<u>sh</u>aari9		هي تُسوق السّيارة بالشّارع

4. Negate the sentences of the drill 3 with the negation word "ma- مَ":

5. Change the following sentences to the opposite tense:

yriid yzuur il-mathaf yoom is-sabit

يُريد يُزور الْمتحف يوم السَّبت

---

tit9allam 9arabi bil-madrasa

تِتْعَلّم عَربي بالْمَدْرَسة

---

shaafaw il-Muusil gabul sana

شافَوْ الْمُوصِل گَبُل سَنة

---

dirsaw it-taariikh il-Islaami bij-jaami9a

دِرْسَوْ الـتَّاريخ الإسْلامي بالجّـامعة

---

yzuuruun il-mataahif ib-Baghdaad

يُزورون الْمَتاحِف بْ بغداد

---

sadd baab hammaam bil-findiq

سَـدّ باب الحَـمّام بالْفِـنْدِق

---

il-ustaadh ydarris Ingiliizi bij-jaami9a

إلأُسْتاذ يُـدَرِّس إنْگِـليـزي بالجّامعة

Basma saafrat min Los Angeles

بسمة سافْرَت مِن لوس انجلوس

Laylaa tuskun ib-Baghdaad yamm in-nahar

ليلى تُسْكُن بْ بغداد يَـمّ النَّهَـر

---

humma yaakluun siwiyya bil-beet

هُـمه ياكْلون سِـوِيَّه بالبيت

---

qreet ktaab 9arabi bil-maktaba

قْريت كتاب عَـربي بالْمَكْـتَـبَة

---

akalna kabaab bil-mat9am

أكَـلْنا كَـباب بالْمَطْـعَم

---

6. Complete and read aloud:

a. la9ad, lee<u>sh</u> ri<u>h</u>tu l-Ba<u>gh</u>daad?　لـَعـَد. لـيـش رِحـتـو لٌ بـغـداد؟

＿＿＿＿＿＿＿＿＿ lil-Ba<u>s</u>ra?　لِـلـبَـصْـرة؟ ＿＿＿＿＿＿＿＿＿

＿＿＿＿＿＿＿＿＿ lil-Muu<u>s</u>il?　لِـلـمُـوصِل؟ ＿＿＿＿＿＿＿＿＿

＿＿＿＿＿＿＿＿＿ lil-mat<u>h</u>af?　لِـلـمَـتْـحَـف؟ ＿＿＿＿＿＿＿＿＿

＿＿＿＿＿＿＿＿＿ lil-<u>H</u>illa?　لِـلـحِـلـّة؟ ＿＿＿＿＿＿＿＿＿

＿＿＿＿＿＿＿＿＿ il-Baabil?　لٌ بابـل؟ ＿＿＿＿＿＿＿＿＿

＿＿＿＿＿＿＿＿＿ lil-mataar?　لِـلـمَـطار؟ ＿＿＿＿＿＿＿＿＿

＿＿＿＿＿＿＿＿＿ lil-findiq?　لِـلـفِـنْـدِق؟ ＿＿＿＿＿＿＿＿＿

＿＿＿＿＿＿＿＿＿ lil-beet?　لِـلـبـيـت؟ ＿＿＿＿＿＿＿＿＿

b. id-dinya <u>h</u>aarra hal-ayyaam　الـدّنـيا حارّة هَـلأيّـام

＿＿＿＿＿＿＿＿＿ baarda hal-ayyaam　بـارْدَة هَـلأيّـام ＿＿＿＿＿＿＿＿＿

＿＿＿＿＿＿＿＿＿ ratba bil-Ba<u>s</u>ra　رَطْـبة بالبصرة ＿＿＿＿＿＿＿＿＿

＿＿＿＿＿＿＿＿＿ laa <u>h</u>aara wala baarda　لا حارّة ولا باردة ＿＿＿＿＿＿＿＿＿

＿＿＿＿＿＿＿＿＿ laa <u>sh</u>iish wala kabaab　لا شـيـش ولا كـباب ＿＿＿＿＿＿＿＿＿

＿＿＿＿＿＿＿＿＿ <u>s</u>a9ba hal-ayyaam　صَـعْـبة هَـلأيّـام ＿＿＿＿＿＿＿＿＿

＿＿＿＿＿＿＿＿＿ muu <u>s</u>a9ba hal-ayyaam　مو صَـعْـبة هَـلأيّـام ＿＿＿＿＿＿＿＿＿

c. hal-ayyaam, anaam is-saa9a 9a<u>sh</u>ra　هَـلأيّـام. أنام السّاعة عَـشْـرة

＿＿＿＿＿＿＿＿＿ tis9a　تِـسـعة ＿＿＿＿＿＿＿＿＿

＿＿＿＿＿＿＿＿＿ tis9a w nu<u>ss</u>　تِسْـعَة ونـُص ＿＿＿＿＿＿＿＿＿

＿＿＿＿＿＿＿＿＿ da9a<u>sh</u> illa rubu9　دَعَـش إلـّلَ رُبُـع ＿＿＿＿＿＿＿＿＿

＿＿＿＿＿＿＿＿＿ <u>th</u>na9a<u>sh</u> illa <u>kh</u>amsa　ثـنـاعَـش إلـّلَ خَـمْـسَـة ＿＿＿＿＿＿＿＿＿

_____ da9ash   دَعَش _____

_____ sitta   سِتَّة _____

d.   tara, aku aathaar hwaaya bil-9iraaq   تَرَا. أَكو آثار هُـوايَه بِـالْـعِراق

_____ b-Masir   بْ مَصِر _____

_____ bil-Ardun   بِـالأُرْدُن _____

_____ b-Turkiya   بْ تُرْكِـيا _____

_____ b-Suurya   بْ سُورْيا _____

_____ b-Lubnaan   ب لُبْـنان _____

_____ b-Tuunis   بْ تـونِس _____

_____ b-Liibya   بْ لـيـبْـيا _____

_____ b-Iraan   بْ إيـران _____

_____ bis-Suudaan   بِالسّـودان _____

7. Translate the following into English:

humma zaaru Baabil bis-sayyaara gabul usbuu9   هُـمّه زارُوْ بابل بِالسّـيارة گَبُل أُسْـبوع

_____

humma rah-yzuuruun madiinat Baabil ba9ad shahar   هُـمّه رَح يُزورون بابل بَـعَد شَـهَر

_____

humma da-yzuuruun madinat Naynawa il-yoom   هُـمّه دَ يُـزورون مدينة نَـيْـنوى الْـيوم

_____

Bawwaabat 9ishtaar b-Baabil muu asliyya   بَـوّابة عِشْـتار بْ بابل مو أَصْلِيّـة

_____

Baabil binaaha l-malik Nabukhadnesser   بابل بِـناها المَـلِك نبوخدنصّر

_____

Baabil biiha aathaar Baabiliyya kullish qadiima   بابل بيها آثار بابـليّـة كُلّـش قَديمة

---

hiyya ha-truuh il-madiinat il-Muusil bil-qitaar   هي حَ تُروح لُ مَدينة المَوصِل بالـْقِطار

---

inta tiktib risaala bil-9arabi loo bil-Ingiliizi?   إنت تِـكـْتـِب رِسالة بالعربي لو بالانگـْلـيزي؟

---

il-mathaf il-9iraaqi yamm il-mahatta l-9aalamiyya   إلمتحف العراقي يَـم الـْمَحَطة العالمية

---

huwwa ustaadh aathaar bij-jaami9a   هو أُسـْتـاذ آثـار بالجَـامِـعة

Asad Baabil mashhuur loo muu mashhuur?   أَسَد بابل مَشـْهور لو مو مَشـْهور؟

Maalik wa Basma rah-yruuhuun siwiyya lil-Hilla   مالك وبسمة رَح يُـروحون سِـوِيّه لِـلـْحِـلة

---

kam qaa9a bil-mathaf il-9iraaqi?   كم قاعة بالمتحف العراقي؟

---

aku aathaar Suumariyya wa Baabiliyya bil-9iraaq   أكو آثار سومَرِيّة وبابـِليّـة بالعراق

---

da-ydirsuun it-taariikh il-Islaami bij-jaami9a   دَ يـِدِرْسون التّـاريخ الاسلامي بالجَـامعة

Creative Dialogues

a.   taalib 1:   sh-da-ssawwiin il-yoom?   شْـدَدسّـوّين اليوم؟   :طالب 1

     taaliba 2:   da-aqra qussa bil-9arabi   دَ أقرَا قَصّة بالعربي   :طالبة 2

     taalib 1:   sh-rah-issawwiin baachir?   شُ رَح اسّـوّين باچِـر؟   :طالب 1

     taaliba 2:   rah-aruuh lil-madrasa   رَح أروح لِـلـْمَـدْرَسة   :طالبة 2

     taalib 1:   sh-rah-tudursiin hnaak?   شُ رَح تُـدُرْسين هُـناك؟   :طالب 1

     taaliba 2:   rah-adrus 9arabi   رَح أدْرُس عربي   :طالبة 2

     taalib 1:   w ba9deen sh-ha-ssawwiin?   وبِـعْدين شُ حَ سّـوّين؟   :طالب 1

taaliba 2:	ba9deen ha-rja9 lil-beet is-saa9a arba9a	بعدين حَ رْجَع لِـلْـبِـيت السّاعَـة اَرْبَعَـة	طالبة 2:
taalib 1:	9indich shughul bil-leel?	عِـنْـدِچ شُـغُـل بالْـبِـيت؟	طالب 1:
taaliba 2:	laa, ha-ruuh lis-siinama	لا، حَ رُوح لِـلسِّـيـنَـما	طالبة 2:

b.

taalib 1:	ween chinti il-baarha?	وين چِـنْـتي الْبارْحَة؟	طالب 1:
taaliba 2:	il-baarha chinit b-Baabil	إلْبارْحَة چِـنِـت بُ بابل	طالبة 2:
taalib 1:	sh-sawwati hnaak?	شُ سَـوَّتي هُـناك؟	طالب 1:
taaliba 2:	shifit aathaarha l-qadiima	شِـفِـت آثارُها الْقَـديمة	طالبة 2:
taalib 1:	shifti Asad Baabil?	شِـفْـتي أسَـد بابل؟	طالب 1:
taaliba 2:	tab9an, wa shifit Bawwaabat 9ishtaar	طَبُعاً، وشِـفِـت بَـوّابَة عِـشتار	طالبة 2:
taalib 1:	shgadd buqeeti b-Baabil?	شْـگَـد بُـقـيتي بُ بابل؟	طالب 1:
taaliba 2:	buqeet sitt saa9aat	بُـقيت سِـت ساعات	طالبة 2:
taalib 1:	inshaalla, 9ijbatich Baabil?	إنشالله. عِـجْـبَـتِـچ بابل؟	طالب 1:
taaliba 2:	9ijbatni hwaaya	عِـجْـبَـتْـني هُـوايَـه	طالبة 2:

For new words, see Glossary.

The lion of the ancient city of Babylon

13

At the Bank

bil-bank   بِالْـبَـنْـك

Basma goes to the Raafideen Bank to change some dollars to Iraqi dinars. After exchanging greetings with the teller/cashier (sarraaf), she asks him,

Basic Dialogue (Audio)

1. Basma: raja'an, ariid ta<u>s</u>riif miit duulaar ila danaaniir 9iraaqiyya.
   Please, I want to change 100 dollars to Iraqi dinars.

   بسـمة: رجاءً. أريد تضُـريف مية دُولار إلى دَنانير عراقية.

2. sarraaf: bikull suruur.
   With pleasure.

   صَـرّاف: بِـكل سُـرور.

3. Basma: agdar asarruf <u>sh</u>eekaat siyaahiyya?
   Can I change travelers' checks?

   بسـمة: أگـدَر أصَـرّف شيكات سِـياحِـية؟

4. sarraaf: na9am. i<u>sh</u>-<u>sh</u>eekaat bid-duulaar loo bil-istarliini?
   Yes. Are the checks in dollar or in sterling?

   صَراف: نعـم. الشَّـيكات بالـدّولار لو بالإسْـتَـرْليني؟

5. Basma: bid-duulaar. <u>sh</u>gadd si9ir it-ta<u>s</u>riif?
   In dollars. How much is the exchange rate?

   بسـمة: بالـدّولار. شَـگـدّ سِـعِـر التّـصريف؟

6. sarraaf: id-diinaar ysawwi tla<u>th</u> duulaaraat w rubu9.
   The dinar makes 3.25 dollars (old rate).

   صَراف: إلـدّينار يُـسَـوّي تلاث دولارات ورُبُـع.

7. Basma: haadha s-si9ir ir-rasmi loo si9ir
is-suug is-suuda?

*Is this the official rate or the black market
rate?*

بسمة: هاذا السِّعِـر الـرّسْمي لو سِعِر
السّوگ السّودَة؟

8. sarraaf: tab9an, haadha s-si9ir ir-rasmi!
maaku suug sooda bil-bank.

*Of course, this is the official rate! There is
no black market in the bank.*

صَرّاف: طبعاً، هاذا السِّعِـر الـرّسْمي! ماكو
سوگ سودة بالـبنك.

9. Basma: laazim amli ha-lis-stimaara?

Do I have to fill in this form?

بسمة: لازِم أمْـلي هَلْ الإسْتِـمارة؟

10. sarraaf: na9am. min fadlich ma9ich
baasbort?

*Yes. Please, do you have a passport with
you?*

صَرّاف: نعم. مِن فَضْلِـج مَعِـج
باسْـبورت؟

11. Basma: na9am, tfaddal.

Yes, here it is.

بسمة: نعم. تْـفَـضّـل.

12. sarraaf: shukran. raja°an, waqqi9i hnaa.

Thanks. Please sign here

صَرّاف: شكـراً. رَجاءً، وَقّـعي هُـنا.

13. Basma: tu9ruf ween aku maktab tasriif?

Do you know where is an exchange office?

بسمة: تُعْـرُف وين اكو مَكْـئتب
تَـصْريف؟

14. sarraaf: fii shaari9 is-Sa9duun.

In Saadun Street.

صَرّاف: في شارع السّـعْـدون.

Additional Expressions of Money Matters (Audio)

filis / fluus (S/P)	*penny/nies, money*	فِلِـس / فْـلوس
fluus 9iraaqiyya	*Iraqi money/currency*	فْـلوس عراقية
fluus Amriikiyya	*American money/currency*	فْـلوس أمُريكية
miit filis	*hundred pennies (fils)*	مية فِلِـس
diinaar / danaaniir (S/P)	*dinar/s (the currency of Iraq and some other Arab countries such as Jordan, Kuwait, etc.)*	ديـنار/ دَنـانير
rubu9 diinaar	*one-quarter of a dinar*	رُبُـع ديـنار
nuss diinaar	*one-half a dinar*	نُـص ديـنار
khurda	*small change*	خُـرْدة
sheekaat siyaahiyya	*traveler's checks*	شيكات سِـياحِيّـة
sakk / sukuuk, chakk / chukuuk (S/P)	*check/s*	صَكّ /صُكـوك، جَـكّ /جُـكـوك
chak khaas / chukuuk khaasa (S/P)	*personal check/s*	جَـك خاصّ / جُـكـوك خاصّة

9umla sa9ba	hard currency	عُمْلة صَعْبة
9indi credit card	I have a credit card.	عِندي كرِدت كارد
ariid wasil, min fadlak	I want a receipt, please.	أُريد وَصِل من فَضْلك
maktab viiza	visa office	مَكْتب فيزا
maktab American Express	American Express office	مكْتب أمَريكان إكْسبرَس
deen / diyuun (S/P)	debt/s	دِين / دْيون
qarid / quruud (S/P)	loan/s	قَرض / قُروض
hisaab / hisaabaat (S/P)	account/s	حِساب / حِسابات
hisaab jaari	checking account	حِساب جاري
hisaab tawfiir	savings account	حِساب تَوْفير

Vocabulary (Audio)

bank / bunuuk (S/P)	bank/s	بَنْك / بُنوك
masraf / masaarif (S/P)	bank/s	مَصْرَف / مَصارف
sarraaf / sarraafa (M/F)	teller, cashier	صَرّاف / صَرّافة
tasriif	change, exchange (money)	تَصْريف
asarruf, (sarraf, ysarruf)	I change	أصَرُّف (صَرّف، يْصَرّف)
raja°an	please (invariable)	رجاءً
ariid, (raad, yriid)	I want	أريد (راد، يْريد)
miit < miyya	one hundred	مِية > مِيّة
biduun (invariable)	without	بِدون
agdar (gidar, yigdar)	I can, I am able	أگْدَر (گِدَر، يِگْدَر)
siyaahi / siyaahiyya (M/F)	tourism, traveler (relative adj.)	سِياحي / سِياحِيّة
istarliini / istarliiniyya (M/F)	sterling (British pound)	إسْتَرْليني / إسْتَرْلينِيّة
si9ir / as9aar (S/P)	rate/s, price/s	سِعِر / أسْعار
ysawwi	it (he) makes	يْسَوّي
rasmi / rasmiyya (M/F)	official, formal (relative adj.)	رَسْمي / رَسْمِيّة
suug, suuq / aswaag (S/P)	market/s	سوگ، سوق / أسْواگ
aswad / sooda (M/F)	black (adj.)	أسْوَد / سُودّة
tab9an, bit-tabu9	of course, naturally	طَبْعاً، بالطَّبُع
laazim	must, ought to (invariable)	لازم
amli, (mila, yimli)	I fill	أمْلي، (مِلَا، يِمْلي)
istimaara / istimaaraat (S/P)	form/s, card/s	إسْتِمارة / إسْتِمارات
waqqi9 / waqqi9i / waqqi9u (M/F/P)	sign (imp. verb)	وَقّع / وَقّعي / وَقّعو
tu9ruf / tu9urfiin / tu9urfuun (M/F/P)	you know	تُعُرُف / تُعُرفين / تُعُرُفون

maktab / makaatib (S/P)	*office/s*	مَكْتَب / مَكاتِب
shaari9 is-Sa9duun	The name of one of the main streets in Baghdad.	شارِع السَّعـدون

Grammar and Remarks
The Participle raayih   رايـحْ   *going, having gone*

A participle is a word that has the characteristics of both a verb and an adjective. It behaves like an adjective because it has only three forms for gender and number: masculine, feminine, and plural (see adjectives, lesson 6). It functions like a verb in that it is usually negated by **ma-**, **ma-jaalis** مَ جالِـس (*not sitting*). (For negation, see lesson 14.) A participle can have an object, either a noun or an attached pronoun. The basic meaning of an active participle is "doing," or "having done," the English equivalent of an adjective or verb ending in "-ing." Participle words have several variant patterns depending on the verb stem from which they are derived from (regular, double, hollow, or weak, see lessons 8 and 9). Examples:

Regular:	jilas	to sit	جِلَـس	jaalis	sitting, having sat	جالِـس
Double:	dazz	to send	دَزّ	daazz	sending, having sent	دازّ
Hollow:	shaaf	to see	شاف	shaayif	seeing, having seen	شايِـف
Weak:	buqa	to stay	بُقـا	baaqi	staying, having stayed	بـاقـي

For the purpose of this book we shall discuss here only the participle word **raayih** رايـحْ (*going*), which is derived from the verb stem **raah** راح (*to go*), probably the most and commonly used participle in colloquial Arabic. Below is a conjugation table of **raayih** showing its three forms: masculine, feminine, and plural. (Audio)

aani raayih	*I am going* (M).	آني رايـح
aani raayha	*I am going* (F).	آني رايـحَة
ihna raayhiin	*We are going* (M).	إحنا رايـحين
ihna raayhaat	*We are going* (F).	إحنا رايـحات
inta raayih	*You are going* (M).	إنت رايـح
inti raayha	*You are going* (F).	إنتي رايـحَة
intu raayhiin	*You are going* (MP).	إنتو رايـحـين
intu raayhaat	*You are going* (FP).	إنتو رايـحات
huwwa raayih	*He is going.*	هو رايـح
hiyya raayha	*She is going.*	هي رايـحَة
humma raayhiin	*They are going* (M).	هُـمّه رايـحـين
humma raayhaat	*They are going* (F).	هُـمّه رايـحات

Notice that the stem vowel "**i**" in the masculine singular **raayih** drops out when a suffix beginning in a vowel is added in the feminine and plural forms. Occasionally, the forms of **raayih** are used in place of the future prefixes "**rah-**" and "**ha-**" to give a future meaning (*going to*). (Audio)

<u>sh</u>wakit raayi<u>h</u> tsaafir il-9ammaan?	*When are you going to travel to Amman?*	شْوَكِت رايِح تْسافِرِ لْ عَمّان؟
humma raay<u>h</u>iin lil-bank	*They are going to the bank.*	هُمَّه رايْحين لِلْبَّنك
raay<u>h</u>a truu<u>h</u> lil-beet	*She is going to go home.*	رايْحة تْروح لِلْبِيت
ween raay<u>h</u>aat baa<u>ch</u>ir?	*Where are you going tomorrow?*	وين رايْحات باچِر؟

The Demonstrative Words: asmaaᵓ il-i<u>sh</u>aara   أسْـماء الإشـارة

Iraqi Arabic has two groups of demonstrative words equivalent to the English demonstratives "this/these" and "that/those." Each group has three forms: masculine, feminine, and plural. Some of the words may have variants, but only the more common ones will be considered here. The demonstrative words agree with the noun in gender and number. There is only one plural form for both genders of each group.

This / That Group (Audio)

haa<u>dh</u>a	*this* (M)	هــاذا	haa<u>dh</u>a taalib	*This is a student.*	هاذا طالِب
haa<u>dh</u>i	*this* (F)	هاذي	haa<u>dh</u>i taaliba	*This is a student.*	هاذي طالبة
ha<u>dh</u>oola	*these* (M/F/P)	هَـذولـه	ha<u>dh</u>oola tullaab	*These are students.*	هَـذولة طُـلّاب
			ha<u>dh</u>oola taalibaat	*These are students.*	هَـذوله طالبات

That / Those Group (Audio)

ha<u>dh</u>aak	*that* (M)	هَــذاك	ha<u>dh</u>aak walad	*That is a boy.*	هَــذاك وَلَـد
ha<u>dh</u>ii<u>ch</u>	*that* (F)	هَـذيـچ	ha<u>dh</u>ii<u>ch</u> binit	*That is a girl.*	هذيـچ بِـنِـت
ha<u>dh</u>oolaak	*those* (M/F/P)	هَـذولاك	ha<u>dh</u>oolaak wilid	*Those are boys.*	هَـذولاك وِلِـد
			ha<u>dh</u>oolaak banaat	*Those are girls.*	هَـذولاك بَنات

The demonstrative words of both groups may be reduced to the short prefix "**ha-** هـ" if they precede a noun definite with the article "**il-** إلـ" (*the*) and that is the more common usage. (Audio)

hal-walad	*this/that boy*	هَالـوَلـد
hal-beet	*this/that house*	هَالـبـيـت
has-sayyaara	*this/that car*	هَالسَّـيـارة
ha<u>t</u>-taaliba	*this/that student*	هَالطّـالـبة

The demonstrative words are negated by placing the word "**muu** مُـو," (*not*) before the demonstrative if the noun is definite and after the demonstrative if the noun is indefinite. Notice the structural difference between the two: The first is a demonstrative noun phrase, whereas the latter is an equational statement. (Audio)

muu hal-beet	*not this house*	مُـو هَالـبيت
muu ha<u>dh</u>aak il-beet	*not that house*	مُـو هَـذاك الـبـيـت
ha<u>dh</u>aak muu beet	*That is not a house.*	هَـذاك مُـو بـيـت
ha<u>dh</u>oola muu tullaab	*These are not students.*	هَـذولة مُـو طلاب

Idioms and Common Phrases (Audio)

1. may<u>s</u>iir مَيْـصيـر *impossible, it can't be* (invariable idiomatic word consists of "ma-مَ," [*not*] and "y<u>s</u>iir يُـصيـر," [*to become*])

may<u>s</u>iir ti<u>sh</u>rab biira bi<u>sh</u>-<u>sh</u>aari9	*You can't drink beer in the street.*	مَيْـصيـر تشـرُب بـيرة بالشـتـارع
may<u>s</u>iir laazim n<u>sh</u>uuf Baabil siwiyya	*Impossible, we must see Babylon together.*	مَيْـصيـر لازم نـشـوف بابل سِـويّـه
may<u>s</u>iir tsaafir biduun viiza	*You can't travel without a visa.*	مَيْـصيـر تـسـافِـر بـيدون فـيـزة
may<u>s</u>iir tim<u>sh</u>uun ib-nu<u>ss</u> i<u>sh</u>-<u>sh</u>aari9	*You can't walk in the middle of the street.*	مَيْـصيـر تـمُـشون بـنُـص الشـتـارع
may<u>s</u>iir tzuurhum bil-leel	*You can't visit them at night.*	مَيْـصيـر تـزورُهم بالـلـيل

2. may<u>kh</u>aalif مَيْـخـالِـف *It is okay, it is permitted, it doesn't matter* (invariable idiomatic word consists of "ma-," [*not*] and "y<u>kh</u>aalif," [*to differ*]; it is the opposite of may<u>s</u>iir)

may<u>kh</u>aalif truu<u>h</u>iin wiyya Basma	*It is okay for you* (F) *to go with Basma.*	مَيْـخـالِـف تـروحين وِيّـه بسمة
may<u>kh</u>aalif tzuurhum bil-leel	*It is okay for you* (M) *to visit them at night.*	مَيْـخـالِـف تـزورُهم بالـلـيل
may<u>kh</u>aalif a<u>s</u>arruf fluus ib-maktab ta<u>s</u>riif	*It is permitted to change money in an exchange office.*	مَيْـخـالِـف أصَـرّف فلوس بـمَكـتب تـصُـريف
may<u>kh</u>aalif taa<u>kh</u>udh kaamira wiyyaak lil-mat<u>h</u>af	*It is permitted that you take a camera with you to the museum.*	مَيْـخـالِـف تاخُـذ كامِرا وِيّـاك لِـلـمتحف
may<u>kh</u>aalif aji wiyyaak?	*Is it okay I come with you* (M)?	مَيْـخـالِـف أجي وِيّـاك؟

3. hissa   هِسَّه   *now, right this moment, at the present time* (invariable)

hissa, laazim aruuh lil-beet	*Now, I must go home.*	هِسَّه، لازِم أروح لِلْبيت
hissa, wislat it-tayyaara	*Right this moment, the airplane arrived.*	هِسَّه، وِصْلَت الطَّيارة
hissa, toosal it-tayyaara	*Momentarily, the airplane will arrive.*	هِسَّه، توصَل الطَّيارة
hissa, il-mathaf masduud	*At the present time, the museum is closed.*	هِسَّه، الْمتحف مَسْدود
hissa, ariid fluusi	*Right this moment, I want my money.*	هِسَّه، أريد فْلوسي
min hissa lis-saa9a khamsa	*From now until five o'clock.*	مِن هِسَّه لِلسّاعَة خَمْسة

Drills   tamaariin   تَمارين
1. Give appropriate oral replies to the following:

haadhi fluus 9iraaqiyya loo Amriikiyya?	هاذي فلوس عراقية لو امريكية؟
9indak sukuuk khaasa loo sheekaat siyaahiyya?	عِنْدَك صُكوك خاصّة لو شيكات سِياحية؟
shgadd si9ir it-tasriif ir-rasmi bid-duulaar?	شْكَد سِعِر التَّصْريف بِالدّينار؟
kam filis bid-diinaar?	كَم فِلِس بِالدّينار؟
laazim ykuun ma9i baasbort?	لازِم يُكون مَعي باسْبورت؟
ween aku maktab tasriif?	وين اكو مَكْتَب تَصْريف؟
ween aku maktab siyaahi?	وين اكو مَكْتَب سِياحي؟
ir-Raafideen bank loo maktab?	الرّافِدين بَنْك لو مَكْتَب؟
kam duulaar bid-diinaar hissa?	كَم دولار بِالدّينار هِسَّه؟
triid wasil tasriif?	تْريد وَصِل تَصْريف؟
humma ween raayhiin?	هُمَّه وين رايْحين؟

2. Change the past tense sentences to the equivalent future tense and read aloud:

sarraf fluus 9iraaqiyya _____	صَرَّف فلوس عراقية
saafarit l-Baghdaad gabul shahar _____	سافَرِت لْ بغداد گَبُل شَهَر
raah lil-bank il-baarha _____	راح لِلْبنك البارْحة
shifit suug is-Safaafiir _____	شِفِت سوگ الصَّفافير
zirit il-mathaf wiyya Ahmad _____	زِرِت المتحف وِيَّه أحمد

raahaw lil-bariid siwiyya _____ راحـو لِلـْبَريد سِـويّه

jaabat Basma wiyyaaha _____ جابـت بسمة وِيّاها

akalna b-mat9am zeen _____ أكَلـْنا بُ مَطعم زين

3. Make the following sentences plural and read aloud:

raayha aruuh lil-madrasa baachir _____ رايـحة أروح لِـلـْمَدْرَسة باچر

raayih ydarris 9arabi bij-jaami9a _____ رايـح يُـدَرّس عربي بِالْجّامعة

shwakit rah-tsaafir il-Beeruut? _____ شْـوَكِت رَحْ تـْسافـرلُ بيروت؟

ariid asarruf fluus Almaaniyya _____ أريد أَصَرّف فلوس ألمانية

laazim yimli istimaara _____ لازم يـِمُلي إسْـتِمارة

maysiir, laazin tjiib il-baasbort wiyyaak _____ مَـيْصير. لازم تـْجيب الباسْبورت وِيّاك

maykhaalif la-tjiibiin il-baasbort _____ مَيْخالف لَتـْجيبين الباسْبورت

raja°an ariid wasil _____ رجاءً أريد وَصِل

haadha wasil tasriif? _____ هاذا وَصِل تصريف؟

ween raayha baachir? _____ وين رايـْحَة باچـر؟

haadha maktab tasriif loo bank? _____ هاذا مكتب تصريف لو بنك؟

maysiir tishrab biira bish-shaari9 _____ مَيْصير تِشـْرب بيرة بِالشّارع

haadhi taaliba loo ustaadha? _____ هاذي طالبة لو اُسْـتاذة؟

4. Complete and read aloud:

a. tab9an, yruuh wiyyaaya lil-bank   طَـبُعاً. يـَروح وِيّايَه لِـلـْبَـنـْك

_____ wiyyaana _____   _____ وِيّانا _____

_____ wiyyaak _____   _____ وِيّاك _____

_____ wiyyaach _____   _____ وِيّـاج _____

_____ wiyyaakum _____   _____ وِيّـاكـم _____

_____ wiyyaa _____   _____ وِيّـا _____

_____ wiyyaaha _____   _____ وِيّـاها _____

_____ wiyyaahum _____   _____ وِيّـاهـم _____

b. maysiir asaafir lil-9iraq biduun viiza   مَيْصير أسافِر لِلْعِراق بِدون فـيزة

_____ nsaafir _____   _____ نْسافر _____

_____ tsaafir _____   _____ تْسافر _____

_____ tsaafriin _____   _____ تْسافْرين _____

_____ tsaafruun _____   _____ تْسافْرون _____

_____ ysaafir _____   _____ يْسافِر _____

_____ tsaafir _____   _____ تْسافِر _____

_____ ysaafruun _____   _____ يْسافْرون _____

c. maykhaalif asarruf fluus 9iraaqiyya bil-bank مَيْخالف أصَرّف فْلوس عراقية بالْبَنْك

_____ nsarruf _____   _____ نْصَرُّف _____

_____ tsarruf _____   _____ تْصَرُّف _____

_____ tsarrufiin _____   _____ تْصَرّفين _____

_____ tsarrufuun _____   _____ تْصَرّفون _____

_____ ysarruf _____   _____ يْصَرَّف _____

_____ tsarruf _____   _____ تْصَرُّف _____

_____ ysarrufuun _____   _____ يْصَرّفون _____

d.   hissa, ariid fluus minnak   هِسَّه، أريد فْلوس مِنَّك

_____, nriid _____   _____ نْريد _____

_____, triid _____   _____ تْريد _____

_____, triidiin _____   _____ تْريدين _____

_____, triiduun _____   _____ تْريدون _____

_____, yriid _____   _____ يْريد _____

_____, triid _____   _____ تْريد _____

_____, yriiduun _____   _____ يْـريدون _____

5. Conjugate the following sentences with each of the demonstrative words, changing anything else that needs to be changed:

Example: haadha taalib yudrus 9arabi   هاذا طالِب يُـدْرُس عربي

haadhi taaliba tudrus 9arabi   هاذي طالْبة تُـدْرُس عربي

hadhoola tullaab yudursuun 9arabi   هَذوله طُلّاب يُـدُرْسون عربي

hadhoola taalibaat yudursuun 9rabi   هَذوله طالْبات يُـدُرْسون عربي

hadhaak taalib yudrus 9arabi   هَذاك طالِب يُـدْرُس عربي

hadhiich taaliba tudrus 9arabi   هَذيـج طالِبة تُـدْرُس عربي

hadhoolaak tullaab yudursuun 9arabi   هَذولاك طُلّاب يُـدُرْسون عربي

hadhoolaak taalibaat yudursuun 9arabi   هَذولاك طالِـبات يُـدُرْسون عربي

haadha sarraaf bil-bank   هاذا صَرّاف بالبنك

haadha raayih lil-beet   هاذا رايـح لِـلْـبـيت

haadha muwazzaf bil-findiq   هاذا مُـوَظّف بالفندق

haadha mudarris y9allim Ingiliizi   هاذا مُـدَرّس يُـعَلّم إنْـگـليزي

haadha bayyaa9 saa9aat bis-suug   هاذا بَـيّاع ساعات بالسّوگ

haadha aathaari yishtughul bil-mathaf   هاذا آثاري يِـشْـتُـغُـل بالمتحف

6. Replace the noun object in parentheses with the appropriate attached pronoun and read aloud:

agdar asarruf (sheekaat)? _____   أگْـدَر أصَـرّف (شيـكات)؟

laazim amli (istimaara) _____   لازم أمْـلي (إسْـتِـمارة)

ariid (waṣil), min faḍlak _____ أريد (وَصِل). مِن فَضْلك _____

nigdar niktib (risaala) bil-9arabi _____ نِگـدَر نِـكـئِتِب (رِسالة) بالعربي _____

huwwa da-yṣalliḥ (is-sayyaara) _____ هو دَ يُصَلّح (إلسّيارة) _____

saafraw (biṭ-ṭayyaara) min Baghdaad il-9ammaan _____ سافئَرُو (بالطّيارة) من بغداد إلْ عَمّان _____

maykhaalif truuḥiin wiyya (Basma) l-Beeruut _____ مَيْخالِف تـُروحين وِيّه (بسمة) لُ بيروت _____

maysiir taakh dhuun (kaamira) wiyyaakum! _____ مَيْـصير تاخُـذون (كاميرا) وِيّاكم! _____

maykhaalif la-tjiibiin (il-baasbort) wiyyaach _____ مَيْخالِف لَتـجِيـبين (الباسْبورت) وِتاچ _____

maysiir tishrab (biira) bish-shaari9 _____ مَيْـصير تِشـرَب (بيرة) بالشّارع _____

humma zaaraw (il-mathaf) yoom ij-jum9a _____ هُمّه زارَوْ (المتحف) يوم الجُمُعَة _____

il-malik Nabukhadnesser bina (Baabil) _____ الملك نبوخذنصر بِنـَا (بابل) _____

da-yaakul (kabaab) bil-maṭ9am _____ دَ ياكل (كباب) بالمطعم _____

rah-yjiibuun (Maalik w Basma) ba9ad saa9a _____ رَح يُجيـبون (مالك وبسمة) بَعَد ساعة _____

7. Make the words between parentheses in the following sentences plural:

Rajaaᵓan, ariid taṣriif (duulaar) ila (diinaar) _____ رجاءً. أريد تصريف (دولار) إلى (دينار) _____

9indi (ṣakk) khaaṣ _____ عِـندي (صَك خاص) _____

ṭab9an, (haadha si9ir rasmi) _____ طَـبْعاً. (هاذه سِعرِ رَسْمي) _____

ma laazim amli (istimaara) _____ مَ لازم أملي (إسْتِمارة) _____

tu9ruf ween aku (maktab) taṣriif? _____ تُعُرُف وين اكو (مَكْتب) تصريف؟ _____

aku (shaari9) ḥilu b-Baghdaad _____ اكو (شارع حِلو) بُ بغداد _____

rah-nzuur (il-mathaf) bil-9iraaq _____ رَح نْزور (المتحف) بالعراق _____

chaanat 9indha (sayyaara) sooda _____ چانت عِنْدها (سَيّارة) سـودة.

maysiir tsaafruun biduun (baasbort)! _____ مَيْصير تْسـافـْرون بدون (باسْبورت)

huwwa musallih (saa9a) zeen bil-findiq _____ هو مُصَلـّح (ساعة) زين بالفندق

aku (bank) ib-shaari9 ir-Rashiid _____ اكو (بنك) بُ شـارع الرّشيد

(haadha mat9am ghaali) _____ (هاذا مَطـْعـم غالي)

il-mathaf il-9iraaqi bii (qaa9a) hwaaya _____ المتحف العراقي بي (قاعة) هُوايه

8. Translate into Arabic:

I have opened an account in this bank yesterday. (two days ago, a week ago, five weeks ago, a month ago, two months ago, a year ago)

_____

_____

_____

_____

_____

_____

Did you have to fill in a form for this account? (money, amount, checks)

_____

_____

_____

_____

They want a loan from ir-Raafideen Bank. (a small loan, a big loan)

_____

_____

_____

He has an account with this bank. (he had, he will have, he is having)

_____

_____

_____

She wrote a letter in Arabic to the bank's director. (they, you [M], you [F], you [P], I)

_____

_____

_____

_____

It is okay, don't go with him. (her, them, me, us)

_____

_____

_____

_____

These days, life is expensive in Baghdad. (food, restaurants, travel, museums)

_____

_____

_____

_____

Is Babylon a modern or an old city? (a large or small, an Iraqi or Jordanian, a Babylonian or Assyrian)

_____

_____

_____

They will go from the city of Basra to Musil by car. (train, airplane)

_____

_____

We are drinking tea in a coffee shop. (coffee, water, Coca Cola)

_____

_____

_____

From now on, I will study the Arabic language every hour. (every day, every week, every month)

_____

_____

_____

From now until nine o'clock, we are going to read Arabic. (English, German, Italian, Spanish, history, archaeology)

_____

_____

_____

_____

_____

_____

_____

Creative Dialogues

a.   taalib 1:   ween raayha?   طالب 1: وين رائـحَة

      taaliba 2:   aani raayha lil-bank   طالبة 2: آني رائْحَة لِـلْبنك

      taalib 1:   ayy bank?   طالب 1: أي بَـنك؟

      taaliba 2:   bank ir-Raafideen   طالبة 2: بَـنك الـرّافدين

      taalib 1:   shaku 9indich bil-bank?   طالب 1: شَـكو عِـنْدِچ بِـالْبنك؟

      taaliba 2:   ariid aṣarruf haadhi   طالبة 2: أريد أصَرّف هاذي الشّـيكات

                     ish-sheekaat

      taalib1:   rah-aji wiyyaach   طالب 1: رَحْ أجي وِيّـاج

      taaliba 2:   yalla, khalli nruuh siwiyya   طالبة 2: يَـلّـه، خَلّـي نْروح سِـوَيّـه

b. taalib 1: min ween hadhoolaak il-banaat?   مِن وين هَذولاك البنات؟ :طالب 1

taaliba 2: humma min Baghdaad   هُــمّه مِن بغداد :طالبة 2

taalib 1: wa hadhoolaak il-wilid?   وهَذولاك الـوِلـد؟ :طالب 1

taaliba 2: humma min il-Muusil   هُــمّه من الموصِل :طالبة 2

taalib 1: sh-da-ysawwuun hnaak?   شْـدَيُـسـوّون هُـناك؟ :طالب 1

taaliba 2: yzuuruun aathaar Baabil il-qadiima   يُــزورون آثار بابل القديمة :طالبة 2

taalib 1: shgadd baaqiin b-Baabil?   شْـكـد باقين بْ بابل؟ :طالب 1

taaliba 2: humma baaqiin yoom waahid   هُــمّه باقـين يوم واحِد :طالبة 2

taalib 1: wenn humma saakniin?   وين هُــمّه ساكْنين؟ :طالب 1

taaliba 2: humma saakniin b-madiinat il-Hilla   هُــمّه ساكنين بْ مَدينة الحِلـة :طالبة 2

For new words, see Glossary.

Abu Nuwas Street along the Tigris River, Baghdad

دَرِس أَرْباطَعَـش DARIS ARBAA-TA9ASH

At the Post Office

bil-bariid بـالـكَـريــد

Basma goes to the post office to buy stamps. She walks toward one window and asks the man behind it,

Basic Dialogue (Audio)

1. Basma: haa<u>dh</u>a <u>sh</u>ubbaa<u>ch</u> it-tawaabi9?
   Is this the stamp window?

   بسـمة: هاذا شُـبّـاج الطّـوابع؟

2. muwa<u>zz</u>af: na9am, w haa<u>dh</u>a <u>sh</u>ubbaa<u>ch</u> il-hawaalaat il-maaliyya.
   Yes, and that is the window of money orders.

   مُوَظّـف: نعِم. وهاذا شُـبّـاج الـكَـحَـوالات الْـمالية.

3. Basma: min fadlak, ariid tawaabi9 l-Amriika.
   Please, I want stamps to America.

   بسـمة: مِن فضلك. أريد طَـوابع لُ أمُريكا.

4. muwa<u>zz</u>af: triidiin twaabi9 risaala loo bostkart?
   Do you want stamps for a letter or a postcard?

   مُوَظّـف: تريدين طوابع رِسالة لو بوسْكارت؟

5. Basma: ariid twaabi9 risaala.
   I want stamps for a letter.

   بسـمة: أريد طوابع رِسالة.

6. muwa<u>zz</u>af: risaala bil-bariid ij-jawwi loo il-9aadi?
   Air or regular mail letter?

   مُوَظّـف: رِسالة بالـكَـبريد الجَـوّي لو العادي؟

7. Basma: kam yoom bil-bariid ij-jawwi?
   How many days by airmail?

   بسمة: كَم يوم بالبَريد الجَّوّي؟

8. muwazzaf: usbuu9 bil-bariid ij-jawwwi,
   w-usbuu9een bil-9aadi.
   One week by air and two weeks by regular.

   مُوَظّف: أُسْبوع بالبريد الجَّوّي وأُسْبوعين بالعادي.

9. Basma: bil-bariid ij-jawwi, alla
   ykhalliik. shgadd si9ir it-tawaabi9?
   Airmail, please. How much are the stamps?

   بسمة: بالبريد الجَّوّي. الله يُخَلّيك. شَكَد سِعِر الطّوابع؟

10. muwazzaf: nuss diinaar.
    One-half of a dinar.

    مُوَظّف: نُص دينار.

11. Basma: ween aku sanduuq bariid?
    Where is a mail box?

    بسمة: وين أكو صَنئدوق بَريد؟

12. muwazzaf: hnaak.
    Over there.

    مُوَظّف: هُناك.

13. Basma: shukran jaziilan.
    Many thanks.

    بسمة: شكراً جزيلا.

14. muwazzaf: 9fwan.
    Don't mention it.

    مُوَظّف: عَفئواً.

Additional Expressions (Audio)

risaala musajjala	*registered letter*	رسالة مُسَجّلة
bariid sarii9	*express mail*	بَريد سَريع
zaruf / zuruuf (S/P)	*envelope/s*	ظَرُف / ظُروف
zuruuf tayyaara	*airmail envelopes*	ظُروف طَيّارة
zuruuf 9aadiyya	*regular envelopes*	ظُروف عادية
9unwaan / 9anaawiin (S/P)	*address/es*	عُنئوان / عَناوين
9unwaan il-mursil / il-mursila (M/F)	*address of the sender*	عُنئوان المُرسِل / المُرسِلة
9unwaan il-mustalim / il-mustalima (M/F)	*address of the addressee*	عُنوان المُسْتَلِم / المُسْتَلِمة
abu l-bariid	*mailman* (lit., *father of the post office,* see lesson 7)	أبو الَبَريد
poostachi	*mailman*	پوصْطَچـي
hawaala bariidiyya	*money/postal orders*	حَـوالة بَـريدِية
hawaala maaliyya	*money orders*	حَـوالة مالِية
ariid irsaal ruzma	*I want to send a package.*	أريد إرسال رُزمَة
talifoon / talifoonaat (S/P)	*telephone/s*	تَلِـفون / تَلِـفونات
mukhaabara / mukhaabaraat (S/P)	*telephone call/s*	مُخابَرة / مُخابَرات
mukhaabara daakhiliyya	*local telephone call*	مُخابَرة داخِلية
mukhaabara khaarijiyya	*long-distance telephone call*	مُخابَرة خارِجية

aku faaks bil-bariid?	*Is there a fax in the post office?*	اكو فاكـس بـالـبـريد؟
shgadd tkallif id-daqiiqa?	*How much is the cost of one minute?*	شَـگَـد تْـكَـلّـف الـدَّقـيـقـة؟

Vocabulary (Audio)

bariid	*post office, mail*	بَـريد
maktab bariid / makaatib bariid (S/P)	*post office/s*	مكتب بريد / مَكـاتِب بَـريد
shubbaach / shabaabiich (S/P)	*window/s*	شُـبّـاج / شَـبـابـيج
taabi9 / tawaabi9 (S/P)	*stamp/s*	طابـع / طوابـع
hawaala / hawaalaat (S/P)	*money order/s, note/s*	حَـوالة / حَـوالات
maal	*money, wealth, have (see below)*	مال
maali / maaliyya (S/F)	*money, financial*	مالـي / مالية
risaala / rasaaʾil (S/P)	*letter/s*	رسـالة / رَسـائـل
bostkart / bostkartaat (S/P)	*postcard/s*	بوسْـكـارت / بوسْـكَـرْتات
irsaal	*sending, mailing*	إرْسـال
jaww	*air, atmosphere*	جَـوّ
jawwi / jawwiyya (M/F)	*airmail, atmospheric*	جَـوّي / جَـوّيّة
9aadi / 9aadiyya (M/F)	*regular, usual*	عادي / عادِيّة
usbuu9 / asaabii9 (S/P)	*week/s*	أُسْـبـوع / أسـابـيـع
nuss	*one-half*	نُـصّ
sanduuq / sanaadiiq (S/P)	*box/es*	صَـنْـدوق / صَـنـاديـق
hnaak	*over there*	هُـنـاك

Grammar and Remarks

The Verb chaan / ykuun   چان / يُـكـون   *was, were/will*

The Iraqi **chaan** is a hollow verb and its use corresponds to the verb "to be" in English in the past tense, "was/were," but not in the present tense "is/are/am." The present form **ykuun** is used to convey future tense and usually comes with the future tense prefix "**rah-**." Notice that the Iraqis do not use the consonant "**ch**" of the past tense **chaan** with the present form **kuun**. Below is a conjugation table of the two forms. (Audio)

Past Tense: chaan   چـان

chaan naayim	*He was sleeping.*	چـان نـايـم
chaanat naayma	*She was sleeping.*	چـانَـت نـائـمَـة
chaanaw naaymiin	*They were sleeping* (M).	چـانَـوْ نـايـمـين
chaanaw naaymaat	*They were sleeping* (F).	چـانَـوْ نـائُـمـات
chinit naayim	*You were sleeping* (M).	چِـنِـت نـايـم
chinti naayma	*You were sleeping* (F).	چِـنْـتي نـائـمَـة

<u>ch</u>intu naaymiin	*You were sleeping* (MP).	چِـنْـتُو نايْـمِـين
<u>ch</u>intu naaymaat	*You were sleeping* (FP).	چِـنْـتُو نايْـمات
<u>ch</u>init naayim	*I was sleeping* (M).	چِـنِـت نايِـم
<u>ch</u>init naayma	*I was sleeping* (F).	چِـنِـت نايْـمَـة
<u>ch</u>inna naaymiin	*We were sleeping* (M).	چِـنْـتا نايْـمِـين
<u>ch</u>inna naaymaat	*We were sleeping* (F).	چِـنْـتا نايْـمات

Present / Future Tense: ykuun يُـكون

ykuun naayim	*He will be sleeping.*	يُـكون نايِـم
tkuun naayma	*She will be sleeping.*	تُـكون نايْـمة
ykuunuun naaymiin	*They will be sleeping* (M).	يُـكونون نايْـمِـين
ykuunuun naaymaat	*They will be sleeping* (F).	يُـكونون نايْـمات
tkuun naayim	*You will be sleeping* (M).	تُـكون نايِـم
tkuuniin naayma	*You will be sleeping* (F).	تُـكونين نايْـمة
tkuunuun naaymiin	*You will be sleeping* (MP).	تُـكونون نايْـمِـين
tkuunuun naaymaat	*You will be sleeping* (FP).	تُـكونون نايْـمات
akuun naayim	*I will be sleeping* (M).	أكون نايِـم
akuun naayma	*I will be sleeping* (F).	أكون نايْـمة
nkuun naaymiin	*We will be sleeping* (M).	نْـكون نايْـمِـين
nkuun naaymaat	*We will be sleeping* (F).	نْـكون نايْـمات

The form **<u>ch</u>aan** is also used as an auxiliary followed by a present verb or by a participle and in this case it modifies the time of the verb. (Audio)

<u>ch</u>aanaw saakniin bi9iid	*They were living far away.*	چـانَـوْ ساكْـنِـين بِـعيد
<u>ch</u>aanat tudrus 9arabi	*She was studying Arabic.*	چـانَـت تُـدْرُس عربي
aani <u>ch</u>init juu9aan	*I was hungry.*	آني چِـنِـت جوعان
<u>ch</u>intu laazim tudursuun bil-maktaba	*You* (P) *had to study in the library.*	چِـنْـتُو لازم تُـدْرُسون بالمـكْـتبة
<u>ch</u>aanat 9idha sayyaara	*She used to have a car.*	چـانَـت عِـدْها سَيّـارة
baa<u>ch</u>ir tkuun a<u>h</u>san, insh<u>aa</u>lla	*Tomorrow you will be better, God willing.*	باچِـر تُـكون أحْـسَـن. إنشالله
huwwa ra<u>h</u>-ykuun bil-beet	*He will be home.*	هو رَح يُـكون بالبِـيت
humma ykuunuun msaafriin baa<u>ch</u>ir	*They will be traveling tomorrow.*	هُـمّـه يُـكونون مُـسافْـرين باچِـر

The verb **<u>ch</u>aan / ykuun** is negated with the word "**ma-** مَ." (Audio)

ma <u>ch</u>aanaw saakniin bi9iid	*They were not living far.*	مَ چـانَـوْ ساكْـنِـين بِـعيد
aani ma <u>ch</u>init juu9aan	*I was not hungry.*	آني مَ چِـنِـت جوعان

humma ma-ykuunuun msaafriin baachir	*They will not be traveling tomorrow.*	هُـمّـه مَ يُكـونون مُسـافـئرين بـاچِـر
huwwa ma rah-ykuun bil-beet	*He will not be home.*	هو مَ رَحُ يُكون بالـبـيت

The Words il, 9ind, maal *"have"* and *"to"*

Arabic has no verb equivalent to the verb "to have" in English. In Iraqi Arabic, the meaning of possession (*to have*) is expressed by one of the words below combined with a proper attached pronoun (pronoun suffix).

1. The Preposition Prefix l- لُ *"to"*

The preposition takes form " **l-**" or " **li-** لِ ." It precedes definite nouns and proper names, therefore it should not be confused with the definite article "**il-**" (*the*), which is discussed in lesson 3. (Audio)

beetak	*your* (M) *house*	بـيتك	misha l-beetak	*He went to your house.*	مِشـا لُ بـيتك
maktabich	*your* (F) *office*	مَكـتبـبـج	misha l-maktabich	*He went to your office.*	مِشـا لُ مَكـتبـج
il-mataar	*the airport*	إلـمَطار	misha lil-mataar	*He went to the airport.*	مِشـا لـلـمَطار
il-findiq	*the hotel*	إلـفِـنـئدق	misha lil-findiq	*He went to the hotel.*	مِشـا لـلـفِـنـئدق
is-sayyaara	*the car*	إلسَّـيـارة	misha lis-sayyaara	*He went to the car.*	مِشـا لـلسَّـيـارة

Basma	بسمة	nita qalam l-Basma	*He gave a pencil to Basma.*	نطـا قلم لُ بسمة
Samiir	سمير	nita ktaab l-Samiir	*He gave a book to Samiir.*	نطـا كتاب لُ سـمير

2. The Preposition il- إلُ *"for, belonging to/have"*

It takes the form "**il-**" and is used with an attached pronoun or a proper name to express the meaning of possession (*to have*). This proposition prefix is negated with **muu** مو (*not*). Students should not confuse the "**il-**" (*have*) with the article "**il-**" (*the*) because the former must always take an attached pronoun, whereas the latter precedes nouns or adjectives and never takes attached pronouns. (Audio)

haadha ilich	*This is yours/belongs to you* (F).	هاذا إلـچ
haadha ili w ilak	*This is mine and yours/ belongs to me and you* (M).	هاذا إلـي وإلـك
ilkum haqq	*You* (P) *are right* (lit., *you have right*).	إلـكُم حَـق

haadha li-ktaab il-Samiira	*This book belongs to Samiira.*	هاذا لِكْتاب إلْ سميرة
haadha muu ilich	*This isn't yours* (F).	هاذا مو إلِجْ
haadha muu ili wala ilak	*This is neither mine nor yours* (M).	هاذا مو إلِي ولا إلَك
haadha li-ktaab muu il-Samiira	*This book doesn't belong to Samiira.*	هاذا لِكْتاب مو إلْ سميرة

3. The Preposition 9ind عِنْد "have, at the place of"

It has two meanings or usages. One usage expresses the meaning "in the possession of," in other words "to have" in English, when it is combined with an attached pronoun. Notice that with the pronouns for "she," "we," "you" (P), and "they" the consonant "**n**" of **9ind** drops out for phonetic reasons. (Audio)

9indi	*I have* (MF)	عِنْدي	9idna	*we have* (MF)	عِدْنا
9indak	*you* (M) *have*	عِنْدَك	9idkum	*you* (PM) *have*	عِدْكُم
9indich	*you* (F) *have*	عِنْدِج	9idkum	*you* (PF) *have*	عِدْكُم
9inda	*he has*	عِنْدَه	9idhum	*they* (M) *have*	عِدْهُم
9idha	*she has*	عِدْها	9idhum	*they* (F) *have*	عِدْهُم

The second usage conveys the meaning "at the place of," or "at the house of." (Audio)

il-walad 9ind Saami	*The boy is at Saami's house.*	إلْولد عِنْد سامي
ijeet min 9ind Saami gabul saa9a	*I came from Saami's house an hour ago.*	جيت مِن عِنْد سامي گَبُلْ ساعة
9ali 9ind il-ḥallaaq	*Ali is at the barber's (place).*	علي عِنْد الحَلّاق
Basma 9ind muṣalliḥ is-saa9aat	*Basma is at the watch repairman's (place).*	بسمة عِنْد مُصَلّح السّاعات

The preposition **9ind** that conveys the meaning "have" is made negative with **maa** ما and the one that has the meaning "at the house/place of" is negated with **muu** مو. (Audio)

maa 9indi sayyaara	*I don't have a car.*	ما عِندي سَيّارة
il-walad muu 9ind Saami	*The boy is not at Saami's house.*	إلْولد مو عِنْد سامي

4. The particle maal مالْ "of, belonging to/have"

It is widely used in the Iraqi dialect. The particle is used in two basic phrases. One uses the invariable form **maal** in a construction consisting of two nouns or noun phrases, usually definite, and separated by **maal**. The meaning of such a phrase is expressed in the English language with the "of" construction or the possessive "s." (Audio)

il-maktaba maal ij-jaami9a	*the library of the university*	المَكتبة مال الجامعة
il-baab maal il-beet	*the door of the house*	الباب مال البيت
is-sayyaara maal 9ali	*Ali's car*	السّيارة مال علي
dihin maal akil	*cooking oil*	دِهِن مال أكل
kulliyya maal banaat	*a girls' college*	كُلّية مال بنات

The second phrase of the particle consists of using **maal** with an attached pronoun (pronoun suffix). With this construction the particle has three forms, masculine **maal** مال, feminine **maalat** مالَت, and plural **maalaat** مالات. The gender and the number of the preceding word determines the form of **maal** and its attached pronoun. In other words, the form **maal** is used after a masculine singular word; the form **maalat** is used after a feminine singular, dual, or plural word/noun not referring to human beings (inanimate); and the form **maalaat** is used after plural word/noun referring to human beings (animate).

Note: Although **maal** suffixed with an attached pronoun conveys the same general meaning as that of a noun with an attached pronoun (see lesson 3), the construction of the two is different—an equational sentence in the former and phrase in the latter. (Audio)

Noun with Suffixed maal		Suffixed Noun	
il-qalam maali	إلقَلَم مالي	qalami	قَلَمي
The pencil is mine.		*my pen*	
is-sayyaara maaltak	إلسّيارة مالتَك	sayyaartak	سَيّارتَك
The car is yours (M).		*your* (M) *car*	
is-saayyaaraat maalatna	إلسّيارة مالَتنا	sayyaaraatna	سَيّارَتنا
The cars are ours.		*our cars*	
it-taaliba maalatkum	إلطّالبة مالَتكم	taalibatkum	طالِبَتكم
The student (F) *is yours* (P).		*your* (P) *student* (F)	
it-taalibaat maalaatkum	إلطّالبات مالاتكم	taalibaatkum	طالِباتكم
The students are yours.		*your* (P) *students* (F)	
li-ktaab maalhum	لِكتاب مالهُم	ktaabhum	كتابهُم
The book is theirs.		*their book*	
is-saa9a maaltich	إلسّاعة مالتِج	saa9tich	ساعتِج
The watch is yours (F).		*your* (F) *watch*	

Forms of **maal** are negated with **muu** مو, which is placed directly before the particle. (Audio)

kulliyya muu maal banaat	*A college is not for girls.*	كُلّية مو مال بنات
li-ktaab muu maala	*The book is not his.*	لِكتاب مو ماله
il-qalam muu maali	*The pen is not mine.*	إلقَلَم مو مالي
is-saa9aat muu maaltich	*The watches are not yours* (F).	إلسّاعات مو مالتِج

Idioms and Common Phrases (Audio)

1. b-ṣuura 9aamma   بُصُورَة عامّة   *in general, generally*

Basma thibb il-9iraaq b-ṣuura 9aamma	*Basma likes Iraq in general.*	بسمة تـُحِب العراق بـُصورة عامّـة
9ali ma-yhibb il-laham b-ṣuura 9aamma	*Ali doesn't like meat in general.*	علي مَ يـُحِب الْـلَـحَم بـُصورة عامّـة
il-ustaadh ydarris taariikh b-ṣuura 9aamma	*The Professor teaches history in general.*	الأُستاذ يـُدَرِّس تاريخ بـُصورة عامّـة
b-ṣuura 9aamma, aani ahibb is-safar	*In general, I like traveling*	بـُصورة عامّـة آني أحِب السَّـفَـر
b-ṣuura 9aamma, Laylaa tiqra lughaat ajnabiyya	*In general, Laylaa reads foreign languages.*	بـُصورة عامّـة . ليلى تـِقـْرَا لـُغات أجْنَبِـية

2. b-ṣuura khaaṣṣa   بُصُورَة خاصّة   *in particular, specially*

huwwa yhibb il-aathaar, b-ṣuura 9aamma, wib-ṣuura khaaṣṣa, Baabil	*He likes antiquities in general, especially Babylon.*	هو يُحِب الآثار بصورة عامة. وبُصورة خاصّة. بابل
mudun il-9iraaq hilwa, wib-ṣuura khaaṣṣa il-Baṣra	*Iraqi cities are pretty, especially Basra.*	مُدُن العراق حِلـْوة وبُصورة خاصّة البَصرة
ti9jibni il-aathaar, b-ṣuura 9aamma, wis-Suumariyya, b-ṣuura khaaṣṣa	*I am interested in antiquities in general and the Sumerian in particular.*	تِعـْجبْني الآثار بصوره عامة. والسّـومرية. بُصورة خاصّة

3. loo aani b-makaan or m-makaan + pronoun + chaan or verb
لو آني بُ مَكان. لو آني مُ مَكان + چان   *if I were you, if I were in your place*

loo aani m-makaanak, chaan zirit Baabil il-yoom	*If I were you, I would have visited Babylon today.*	لو آني مُ مَكانك. چـان زِرت بابل اليوم
loo aani m-makaanich, chaan dirasit 9arabi kull yoom	*If I were you, I would have studied Arabic every day.*	لو آني مُ مَكانـِچ. چـان دِرَسِـت عربي كل يوم
loo aani m-makaankum, aruuh baachir	*If I were you, I would go tomorrow.*	لو آني مُ مَكانـْكـُم. أروح باچـِر
loo aani m-makaanha, akhaabur ahli	*If I were she, I would call my family.*	لو آني مُ مَكانـْها. اخابـُر اهـْلي
loo aani m-makaanhum, maa aakul laham	*If I were they, I would not eat meat.*	لو آني مُ مَكانـْهم. ما آكـُل لـَحَم
loo aani m-makaana, aktib risaala	*If I were he, I would write a letter.*	لو آني مُ مَكانـَه. أكـْتِـب رِسالة

Drills   tamaariin   تَـمارين

1. Give appropriate oral replies to the following:

ween <u>sh</u>ubbaa<u>ch</u> it-tawaabi9?	وين شُبّاج الطَّوابـع؟
haa<u>dh</u>i risaala jawwiyya loo 9aadiyya?	هاذي رِسالة جَوِّيَّة لو عادِيّـة؟
ween <u>s</u>anduuq il-bariid?	وين صَنْدوق البَريد؟
<u>sh</u>gadd si9ir it-tawaabi9 l-Paaris?	شَكَـد سِعِـر الطّـوابـع لْ باريس؟
aku faaks bil-bariid?	أكو فاكْس بالبَريد؟
aku bariid yoom ij-jum9a?	أكو بَـريد يوم الجُمْـعة؟
aku talafoon bi<u>sh</u>-<u>sh</u>aari9?	أكو تَـلِـفون بالشـارع؟
ween aktib 9unwaan is-risaala?	وين أكْتِـب عُنْـوان الرِّسالة؟
kam <u>h</u>awaala maaliyya triid?	كـم حَوالة مالِيّـة تْريد؟
kam yoom il-bariid ij-jawwi min Amriika lil-9iraaq?	كـم يوم البريد الجَـوّي من امْريكا لِـلْعِـراق؟
<u>th</u>ibb irsaal risaala loo ruzma	تْـحِـب إرسال رِسالة لو رُزْمة؟

2. Conjugate the following sentences with each of the demonstrative words; change anything else that needs to be changed:

Example: haa<u>dh</u>a <u>t</u>aalib da-yudrus 9arabi:	هاذا طالب دَ يُدْرُس عربي
haa<u>dh</u>i <u>t</u>aaliba da-tudrus 9arabi	هاذي طالبة دَ تُـدْرُس عربي
ha<u>dh</u>oola <u>t</u>ullaab da-ydursuun 9arabi	هَـذوله طلاب دَ يُـدُرْسون عربي
ha<u>dh</u>oola <u>t</u>aalibaat da-ydursuun 9arabi	هَـذوله طالبات دَ يُـدُرْسون عربي
ha<u>dh</u>aak <u>t</u>aalib da-yudrus 9arabi	هَـذاك طالب دَ يُـدْرُس عربي
ha<u>dh</u>iich <u>t</u>aaliba da-tudrus 9arabi	هَـذيچ طالبة دَ تُـدْرُس عربي
ha<u>dh</u>oolaak <u>t</u>ullaab da-ydursuun 9arabi	هَـذولاك طلاب دَ يُـدُرْسون عربي
haa<u>dh</u>a <u>s</u>arraaf da-yu<u>sh</u>tughul bil-bank	هاذا صَرّاف دَ يُشْـتُغُـل بالبنك
haa<u>dh</u>a mudarris da-y9allim Ingiliizi	هاذا مُدَرّس دَ يْعَـلّـم انْگـليـزي
haa<u>dh</u>a <u>ch</u>aan saakin ib-Ba<u>gh</u>daad	هاذا چان ساكِـن بْ بغداد
haa<u>dh</u>a muwazzaf <u>h</u>ukuumi	هاذا مُوَظّف حُكـومي
haa<u>dh</u>a mu<u>s</u>alli<u>h</u> saa9aat zeen	هاذا مُصَلِّـح ساعات زين
haa<u>dh</u>a aa<u>th</u>aari bil-ma<u>th</u>af il-9iraaqi	هاذا آثاري بالمُتحف العراقي

3. Use the demonstrative short prefix "ha- هَـ" with the nouns in the following, oral:

Example: bariid bi9iid	بَريد بِـعيد
hal-bariid bi9iid	هَـالبَـريد بِـعيد
safaara yamm in-nahar	سَـفارة يَم النَّـهَر
has-safaara yamm in-nahar	هَـالسّفارة يَم النّـهَر
risaala musajjala	رِسـالة مُسَـجّلة
<u>t</u>aabi9 jawwi	طابع جَـوّي
<u>s</u>anduuq giddam il-bank	صَنْـدوق گِـدّام البنك
mudarris y9allim 9arabi bil-madrasa	مُدَرّس يْعَـلّـم عربي بالمدرسة

tullaab wa taalibaat yruuhuun lij-jaami9a	طلاب وطالبات يُروحون لِلـجّامعة
sayyaara hamra waagfa bish-shaari9	سَيّارة حَمرة واگـفة بالشّـارع
ustaadh ma-ydarris it-taariikh il-Islaami	أُستاذ مَ يُدَرّس التّاريخ الاسلامي
barrid bi9iid mnil-mahatta	بريد بـعيد مُن المحطـة
banaat rah-ysaafruun baachir lil-Muusil	بنات رَح يُسافرون باچـر لِلـمّوصل
wilid ma raayhiin lil-madrasa	ولـد مَ رايحين لـلـمدرسة
tayyaara rah-ittiir ba9ad saa9a	طيّارة رَح إطّـير بَعَد ساعة
qitaar yimshi mnil-mahatta ba9ad shwayya	قِطار يـمّشي مُن المحطـة بَعَد شـّوَيّة
maktab ysarruf duulaaraat Amriikiyya	مَكـتب يُصَرّف دولارات امُريكية
talafoon kharbaan, bass hadhaak yushtughul	تلـِفون خرُبان. بَس هَذاك يُشـتـُغـُل

4. Make plural the following masculine or feminine words of "have":

haadha ili w ilak	هاذا إلي وإلك	9indich khoosh fikra	عِنـدج خوش فِكـرة
ilha haqq	إلـها حَق	9idha shughul hwaaya	عِدُها شُغـُل هُوايه
ila 9indi alif diinaar	إلـه عندي ألـف دينار	9indi sayyaara jidiida	عِنـدي سَيّارة جـِديدة
maa 9inda fluus bil-bank	ما عِنـدَه فـلُوس بالـبنك		
il-kursi maalak	إلكـُرسي مالَك		
is-saa9a maaltich kharbaana	إلسّاعة مالـتِج خرُبانة		
li-ktaab muu maali	لـِكـتاب مو مالي		
il-ustaadh maalak raah lij-jaami9a	الأُستاذ مالَك راح لِلـجّامعة		
il-hadaaya maalatha hilwa	إلـهَدايا مالـتـها حِلـوَة		

5. Replace the possessive noun-pronoun construction with the maal مـال construction:

ktaabha jidiid

كْتابْها جِـديد

---

sayyaarathum bish-shaari9

سَيّـارَتْـهم بالشّـارع

---

risaaltak muu ṭiwiila

رِسالْتَك مو طِـويلة

---

madrastich zeena, b-ṣuura 9aamma

مَدرَسْتِـج زيـنة، بُصورة عامّة

---

baasborta muu qadiim

باسْبورْتَه مو قَـديم

ṭawaabi9kum jawwiyya

طَـوابِـعْكم جَـوّية

---

beetak qariib mnis-safaara

بـيـتَك قَـريب مْن السّـفارة

ḥsaabhum ib-bank ir-Raafideen

حُسابْـهـم بْ بَـنك الرّافِـدين

---

ibnak ṭaalib zeen bil-madrasa

إبنَك طالب زيـن بالـمدرسة

---

banaatkum muwazzafaat bil-bank

بناتْكـم مُـوَظّـفات بالـبَـنك

---

6. Complete and read the following aloud:

a. loo aani m-makaanak, chaan zirit Baabil

لو آني مَ مَكانَك، چان زِرِت بابل

_____ m-makaanich, _____

_____ مَ مَكانِـج، _____

_____ m-makaankum, _____

_____ مَ مَكانْكـم، _____

_____ m-makaana, _____   _____ م مَكانـه، _____

_____ m-makaanha, _____   _____ م مَكانئها، _____

_____ makaanhum, _____   _____ م مَكانئهم، _____

b. loo inta m-maakaani, <u>sh</u>i-ssawwi?   لو إنت م مَكانـي. شِـشّـوّي؟

_____ inti _____?   _____ إنتي _____

_____ intu _____?   _____ إنتو _____

_____ huwwa _____?   _____ هـو _____

_____ hiyya _____?   _____ هـي _____

_____ humma _____?   _____ هُـمّه _____

c. aani a<u>h</u>ibb il-aa<u>th</u>aar b-<u>s</u>uura 9aamma, wil-Baabiliyya, b-<u>s</u>uura <u>kh</u>aassa

آني أحِب الإثار بُصورة عامّة. وِالبابِلـِيَة بُصورة خاصّة

ihna _____ إحنا _____

inta _____ إنت _____

inti _____ إنتي _____

intu _____ إنتو _____

huwwa _____ هـو _____

humma _____ هُـمّه _____

d. il-akil il-9arabi <u>t</u>ayyib, b-<u>s</u>uura 9aamma, wil-Lubnaani b-<u>s</u>uura <u>kh</u>aassa

الأكل العربي طَـيّب بصورة عامّة. والـلُبناني بصورة خاصّة

_____ ghaali _____   _____ غالي _____

_____ ri<u>kh</u>iis _____   _____ رِخيص _____

_____ zeen _____   _____ زين _____

_____ muu ghaali _____   _____ مو غالي _____

_____ mumtaaz _____   _____ مُمتاز _____

_____ taaza _____   _____ تازة _____

e. yalla, khalliina nruuh l-Baabil bil-qitaar   يَلّه. خَلّينا نْروح لْ بابل بالْقِطار

_____ lil-mathaf bis-sayyaara   _____ لِلْمتحف بالسّيارة

_____ lis-safaara bil-baas   _____ لِلسّفارة بالْباص

_____ lil-bank bit-taksi   _____ لِلْبنك بالتّكْسي

_____ lil-9iraaq bil-baakhira   _____ لِلْعراق بالْباخِرة

_____ l-beet Khaalid mishi   _____ لْ بيت خالد مِشي

7. Translate the following into English:

alla ykhalliik, ariid tawaabi9 jawwiyya   ألله يُخَلّيك. أريد طوابع جَوّيّة

_____

9indi risaala musta9jala li-Fransa   عِنْدي رِسالة مُسْتَعْجَلة لِفْرَنْسا

_____

yishtiri hawaala maaliyya mnil-bariid   يِشْتِري حَوالة مالِية مُن البريد

_____

il-mukhaabaraat il-khaarijiyya ghaalya   إلْمُخابَرات الخارجِية غالْية

_____

tsarruf sheekaat siyaahiyya bil-bank   تْصَرّف شيكات سِياحية بالْبَنْك

_____

hiyya sarilha saa9a 9ind il-hallaaqa   هي صارِلْها ساعة عِنْد الْحَلاقة

_____

maaku talafoonaat ib-shawaari9 Baghdaad   ماكو تَلِفونات بْ شَوارِع بغداد

_____

haadhi tadhaakir maal il-mathaf il-9iraaqi   هاذي تَذاكِر مال المتحف العراقي

_____

humma ma-yruuḥuun lis-safaara bis-sayyaara

هُمّة مَ يُروحون لِلسّفارة بالسّيارة

---

hiyya raayḥa l-beet Kamaal

هـي رايْـحَـة لُ بِـيـت كامِل

Creative Dialogues

a. taalib 1:   ween ir-risaala maalti?   وين الرّسالة مالْتي؟   :طالب 1

    taaliba 2:   ayy risaala?   أي رسالة؟   :طالبة 2

    taalib 1:   ir-risaala maal Aḥmad   الرّسالة مال أحمد   :طالب 1

    taaliba 2:   maa adri, yimkin 9almeez   ما أدري. يِـمُكِن عَ الْـمِيز   :طالبة 2

    taalib 1:   ayy meez, meez il-ghurfa loo   أي ميز. ميز الغرفة لو المَطْبخ؟   :طالب 1
                 il-matbakh?

    taaliba 2:   yimkin meez il-ghurfa   يِـمُكِن ميز الغرفة   :طالبة 2

    taalib 1:   hiyya maakuu bil-ghurfa   هي ماكو بالغرفة   :طالب 1

    taaliba 2:   hissa tdhakkarit, hiyya   هِسّـه تْـذَكّـرِت. هي بالجـنْـطة   :طالبة 2
                 bij-junṭa is-sooda   السّـودة

b. taaliba 1:   shifit il-qaamuus il-9arabi   شِـفِت القاموس العربي مالي؟   :طالب 1
                 maali ?

    taalib 2:   laa. inti ween khalleetii?   لا. انتي وين خَـلّـيتي؟   :طالبة 2

    taaliba 1:   maa atdhakkar, loo   ما أتْـذكّـر. لو بالجّامعة لو   :طالب 1
                 bij-jaami9a loo bil-beet   بالـبّيت

    taalib 2:   triidiin asaa9dich?   تْـريدين أساعْـدِچ؟   :طالبة 2

    taaliba 1:   ii, shukran   ئـي. شكراً   :طالب 1

    taalib 2:   khalliina ndawwir bil-ghuraf   خَـلّـينا نْـدَوّر بالغُـرفة   :طالبة 2

    taaliba 1:   inta dawwir il-ghurfa maaltak   انت دَوّر بِـالغرفة مالْـتَك وآني   :طالب 1
                 w aani adawwir b-ghurufti   أَدوّر بُ غُـرُفْـتي

    taalib 2:   ligeet il-qaamuus hnaa   لِـگيت القاموس عَ الْـكُـرسي   :طالبة 2
                 9al-kursi

For new words, see Glossary.

Barbecuing the popular Masguf fish, Baghdad

DARIS KHMUS-TA9ASH دَرِس خْـمُصْطَعَـش

In the Restaurant

bil-mat9am بـِالـْمَطـْعَـم

Waliid invites Basma to a special dinner of fish called Masguuf, one of the most popular Iraqi dishes, at a restaurant on Abu Nuwaas Street, long considered the center of Baghdad night life along the Tigris River.

Basic Dialogue (Audio)

1. Waliid: aḥibb a9izmich 9ala aklat simach Masguuf.
   I would like to invite you to a dish of Masguuf fish.

   وليد: أحِب أعزِمـج على أكْلَـة سِمَـج مَسْـگـوف.

2. Basma: shukran. shunu simach Masguuf?
   Thank you. What is a Masguuf fish?

   بـسـمة: شكـراً. شُـنُو سِـمَـج مَسْـگـوف؟

3. Waliid: hiyya aṭyab akla b-Baghdaad.
   It is the most delicious dish in Baghdad.

   وليد: هي أطْيَب أكْـلَـة بُ بغداد.

4. Basma: la9ad, khalli nruuh. ween il-mat9am?
   So let us go. Where is the restaurant?

   بـسـمة: لَـعَـد. خَـلّـي نْـروح. وين الـْمطعم؟

5. Waliid: aku maṭaa9um hwaaya 9ala shaari9 Abu Nuwaas.
   There are many restaurants on Abu Nuwaas Street.

   وليد: أكـو مَطاعُم هُـوايه على شارع أبو نُـواس.

The two are sitting in a restaurant along "Nahar Dijla نَهَر دِجْلة," the Tigris River, and a waiter (booy بويْ) is approaching them.

6. Basma: allaah! shgadd hilu manzar in-nahar bil-leel!

   Oh my God! How pretty the view of the river is at night!

   بسمة: ألْلاه! شْـگَـد جِلُو مَنْظَر النّـهَر بالْـلَيل.

7. booy: shi-thibuun taakluun?

   What do you like to eat?

   بويْ: شِـتْـحِبّـون تاكْـلون؟

8. Basma: simach Masguuf, tab9an!

   Masguuf fish, of course!

   بسمة: سِـمَج مَسْگوف. طَـبْعـاً.

9. booy: triiduun shii wiyya s-simach?

   Do you want something with the fish?

   بويْ: تْـريدون شِـي وِيّـه السِـمَج؟

10. Basma: zalaata, min fadlak.

    Salad, please.

    بسمة: زَلاطة. مِن فَـضْـلَك.

11. booy: thibbuun tishirbuun shii?

    Do you like to drink something?

    بويْ: تْـحِـبّـون تِـشِـرْبون شِـي؟

12. Basma: 9idkum mashruubaat mithil biira wa 9arag?

    Do you have alcoholic beverages, such as beer and Arak?

    بسمة: عِـدْكُم مَشْـروبات مِـثِـل بـيرة وعَـرَگ؟

13. booy: kullshi 9idna. bass il-9arag zeen wiyya s-simach.

    We have everything. But Arak is good with the fish.

    بويْ: كُـلْـشي عِـدْنا. بَـس الْعَـرَگ زين وِيّـه السّـمَج.

14. Basma: min fadhlak, jiibilna 9arag wiyya mazza.

    Please, bring us Arak with appetizers.

    بسمة: مِن فضلَك. جيبـلْـنا عَرَگ وِيّـه مَـزّة.

15. booy: iddallalu.

    Whatever you wish.

    بويْ: إدَّلّـلو.

Additional Expressions (Audio)

aani juu9aan / juu9aana (M/F)	*I am hungry.*	آني جوعان / جوعانة
aani 9at shaan / 9at shaana (M/F)	*I am thirsty.*	آني عَطْـشان / عَطْـشانة
9idkum fawaakih?	*Do you have fruits?*	عِـدْكم فَـواكِه؟
akil sharqi	*Eastern food*	أكِل شَـرْقي
akil gharbi	*Western food*	أكِل غَـرْبي
shunu aklat il-yoom?	*What is today's dish?*	شُـنو أكْـلَـة اليوم؟
rajaʾan intiina li-hsaab	*Please, give us the bill.*	رجاءً إنْـطينا لِـحْـساب

| il-akil ṭayyib, bass ghaali | *The food is good, but expensive.* | الإكل طَيّب بَس غالي |
| il-akil laa ghaali wala rikhiis | *The food is neither expensive nor cheap.* (see lesson 4) | الإكل لا غالي ولا رخيص |

Vocabulary (Audio)

aḥibb	*I like*	أحِب
ḥabb, yḥibb	*to like, to love*	حَبّ، يْحِبّ
a9izmich	*I invite you* (F)	أعِزْمِج
9izam, yi9zim	*to invite* (to a dinner)	عِزَم، يِعْزِم
9aziima / 9azaayim (S/P)	*dinner invitation/s, banquet/s*	عَزيمَة / عَزايِم
akla / aklaat (S/P)	*dish/es* (of food)	أكْلَة / أكْلات
akil	*food* (collective word)	أكِل
simcha / simach (S/P)	*fish* (collective word)	سِمْچَة / سِمَج
Masguuf	*a popular Iraqi fish dish*	مَسْگوف
mat9am / mataa9um (S/P)	*restaurant/s*	مَطْعَم / مَطاعُم
Abu Nuwaas	*A street in Baghdad named after the famous Arab poet (eighth century)*	أبو نْواس
aḷḷaah!	*Oh my God!* (expression of appreciation)	ألّاه
shgadd?	*How much? How long?*	شْگَـد؟
hilu / hilwa (M/F)	*pretty, nice, sweet* (adj.)	حِلْو / حِلْوة
manẓar / manaaẓir (S/P)	*view, sight, scene/s*	مَنْظَر / مَناظِر
nahar / anhaar (S/P)	*river/s*	نَهَر / أنْهار
nahar Dijla	*Tigris River*	نَهَر دِجْلة
nahar il-Furaat	*Euphrates River*	نَهَر الـفُرات
booy / booyaat (S/P)	*waiter, bellboy/s* (the English "boy")	بُويْ / بُويات
taakul / taakliin / taakluun (M/F/P)	*you eat*	تاكُل / تاكْلين / تاكْلون
ṭab9an, biṭ-ṭabu9	*of course*	طَبْعاً، بالطَّبُع
zalaaṭa / zalaaṭaat (S/P)	*salad/s*	زَلاطة / زَلاطات
y9ijbak / y9ijbich / yi9jibkum (M/F/P)	*you like, it interests you*	يْعْجُبَك / يْعْجُبِج / يِعْجِبْكُم
tishrab / tishirbiin / tishirbuun (M/F/P)	*you drink*	تِشْرَب / تِشِرْبين / تِشِرْبُون
mashruub / mashruubaat (S/P)	*drink/s*	مَشْروب / مَشْروبات

mithil	*like, such as, similar*	مِثـِل
biira	*beer*	بـيـرة
9arag	*Arak (popular Iraqi alcoholic drink)*	عَرَگ
kullshi	*everything*	كُلْشـي
mazza / mazzaat (S/P)	*hors d'oeuvres, appetizer/s*	مَزّة / مَزّات
iddallal	*whatever you wish (see lesson 10)*	إدّلَـل
intiina	*give us (imp. verb)*	إنْطـيـنـا
nita, yinti	*to give (WV)*	نـِطـا، يـِنْطـي
hsaab / hisaabaat (S/P)	*bill, account/s*	حُسـاب / حِسـابات
bass	*but, enough*	بَـس
tayyib / tayyba (M/F)	*delicious, good, well* (adj.)	طَـيِّب / طَـيْـبَـة
ghaali / ghaalya (M/F)	*expensive* (adj.)	غـالـي / غـالـيَـة
rikhiis / rikhiisa (M/F)	*cheap, inexpensive* (adj.)	رخـيـص / رخـيـصَة
hatta	*in order to, until, till, as far as*	حَـتّـى

Additional Vocabulary Related to Food (Audio)

rayyuug / ftuur	*breakfast*	رَيّـوگ / فْـطور
ghada	*lunch*	غَـدَه
9asha	*dinner*	عَـشـا
khubuz	*bread*	خُـبُـز
sammuun	*(French) bread*	صَـمّـون
shoorba	*soup*	شـورْبَـة
doolma	*stuffed vegetable*	دولْـمَـة
baamya	*okra*	بامْـيَـة
gass	*grilled meat*	گَـص
jibin	*cheese*	جِـبِـن
hummus bi-t hiina	*chickpeas dip*	حُمّـص بِـطْـحـيـنة
baaba ghannuuj	*eggplant dip*	بابَـه غَـنـتوج
tabbuula	*chopped salad*	تَـبّـولة
kabaab	*kebab (minced meat)*	كَـبـاب
tikka	*chunks of meat*	تِكـّة
kubba	*meat with cracked wheat*	كُـبّـة
khudrawaat	*vegetable*	خُـضْـرَوات
busal	*onion*	بُـصَـل
tamaata	*tomato*	طَـماطة
tamur	*palm date*	تَـمُـر
halawiyyaat	*sweets*	حَـلَـويّـات
liban	*yogurt*	لِـبَـن

zibid	*butter*	زِبِد
fawaakih	*fruit*	فَواكِه
bee<u>d</u>	*eggs*	بِيض
la<u>h</u>am	*meat*	لَحَم
jaaj / dijaaj	*chicken*	جاج/ دِجاج
timman / ruzz	*rice*	تِـمّـَن/ رُز
milii<u>h</u>	*salt*	مِلِـح
filfil	*pepper*	فِلْفِل
mayy	*water*	مَيّ
<u>t</u>urshi	*pickles*	طُرْشـي
9a<u>s</u>iir	*juice*	عَصير
masluug	*boiled*	مَسْلـوگ
magli	*fried*	مَگْلـي
ma<u>sh</u>wi	*broiled*	مَشْوي
<u>th</u>alij	*ice*	ثَلِـج
manyoo	*menu*	مَنْيـو
istikaan	*tea glass*	إسْتِـكان
maa9uun	*plate, dish*	ماعُون
<u>gl</u>ass	*glass*	گْلاص
<u>s</u>iiniyya	*tray*	صِينِـيّة
<u>sh</u>ooka	*fork*	شُوكَة
si<u>ch</u><u>ch</u>iin	*knife*	سِچّـين
khaa<u>sh</u>uuga	*spoon*	خاشوگَـة

Grammar and Remarks

The Preposition 9ala / 9a- عَـ / عَلـى   *on, upon, about*

9ala is a common preposition in Arabic in general. In the Iraqi dialect it basically means "on" but also has variant meanings of "upon" and "about," depending on the context. The preposition is used with nouns or attached pronouns. If the noun is indefinite the complete form of **9ala** is used, whereas the shortened form "**9a-**" is used with the definite noun in conjunction with the article "**il-**" (*the*). (Audio)

9ala kursi	*on a chair*	على كُرْسي	**9al**-kursi	*on the chair*	عَ الْكُرْسي
9ala meez	*on a table*	على ميز	**9al**-meez	*on the table*	عَ الْميز
9ala jariida	*on a newspaper*	على جَريدة	**9aj**-jariida	*on the newspaper*	عَ الْجَريدة
9ala <u>s</u>iiniyya	*on a tray*	على صينِـيّة	**9as**-siiniyya	*on the tray*	عَ الصِّينِـيّة

When **9ala** is suffixed with an attached pronoun, it has the variant form **9alee-** plus the pronoun, except with the first person, which takes the form **9alayya**. (Audio)

9alee	on him	عَليه
9aleeha	on her	عَليها
9aleehum	on them	عَليهُم
9aleek	on you (M)	عَليك
9aleech	on you (F)	عَليچ
9aleekum	on you (P)	عَليكم
9alayya	on me	عَلَيَّه
9aleena	on us	عَلينا
li-hsaab 9alayya	The bill is on me.	لِحْساب عَلَيَّه
Basma tsallim 9aleekum	Basma says hello to you.	بسمة تْسَلِّم عليكم
9aleena shughul hwaaya	We have much work.	علينا شْغُل هُوايَه

The Interrogative Words: adawaat lis-tifhaam   أَدوات لِسْــتِــفْهام

Below is a list of most of the Iraqi interrogative words grouped together with examples for references. (Audio)

1. ween?	*Where?*	وين؟
ween il-mat9am?	*Where is the restaurant?*	وين المطعم؟
2. shwakit?	*When?*	شْوَكِت؟
shwakit zirtu Baabil?	*When did you (P) visit Babylon?*	شْوَكِت زِرْتو بابل؟
3. shloon?	*How? What kind of?*	شْلون؟
shloonkum?	*How are you (P)?*	شْلونْكُم؟
shloon madrasa?	*What kind of school?*	شْلون مَدْرَسة؟
4. shgadd?	*How much? How long? How far? (depending on context)*	شْكَد؟
shgadd il-ujra bis-sayyaara?	*How much is the car rate?*	شْكَد الأجرة بالسّيارة؟
shgadd saarlich hnaa?	*How long have you been here?*	شْكَد صارْلِچ هُنا؟
shgadd tib9id Baabil?	*How far is Babylon?*	شْكَد تِبْعِد بابل؟
5. beesh, ibbeesh?	*How much? What time?*	بيش، إبّيش؟
ibbeesh is-simach?	*How much is the fish?*	إبّيش إلسَّمَچ؟
beesh is-saa9a?	*What time is it?*	بيش السّاعة؟
6. shunu, sh- ?	*What?*	شُنو، شْ؟
shunu ismak? shi-smak?	*What is your name?*	شُنو إسْمَك؟ شِسْمَك؟
sh-da-taakul	*What are you eating?*	شْدَ تاكُل؟
sh-aku maaku il-yoom?	*What is happening today?*	شَكو ماكو اليوم؟

7. ay, yaa, yaahu?   *Which? Which one?*   أي. يا. ياهُو؟

    yaa bariid qariib?   *Which post office is near?*   يا بريد قريب؟

    yaahu ktaabak?   *Which one is your book?*   ياهُو كْتابَك؟

8. kam, cham?   *How many?*   كَـم، چَـم؟

    kam walad 9indi<u>ch</u>?   *How many boys do you (F) have?*   كَـم وَلَـد عِـنْـئِـدِج؟

    <u>ch</u>am miil min Bag<u>h</u>daad il-Baabil?   *How many miles from Baghdad to Babylon?*   چَـم ميل من بغداد لُ بابل؟

9. lee<u>sh</u>, ilwee<u>sh</u>, luwee<u>sh</u>?   *Why?*   ليـش، إلْـويـش، لُـويـش؟

    lee<u>sh</u> zaaraw 1-9iraaq?   *Why did they visit Iraq?*   ليـش زارَوُ العـراق؟

    ilwee<u>sh</u> ma zaaraw il-Basra?   *Why didn't they visit Basra?*   إلْـويـش مَ زارَوُ البصرة؟

    luwee<u>sh</u> tudrus 9arabi?   *Why does she study Arabic?*   لُـويـش تُـدْرُس عربـي؟

10. mneen, immeen?   *Where . . . from?*   مُـنيـن؟ إمْـيـن؟

    immeen <u>h</u>adirtak?   *Where are you from?*   إمْـيـن حَـضِـرْتَك؟

11. minu? ilman? maalman?   *Who? Whom? Whose?*   مِـنو، إلْـمَـن، مالْـمَـن؟

    minu huwwa?   *Who is he?*   مِـنو هو؟

    ilman <u>sh</u>iftu bil-findiq?   *Whom did you (P) see in the hotel?*   إلْـمَـن شِـفْـتو بالفندق؟

    maalman haa<u>dh</u>a l-baasbort?   *Whose is this passport?*   مالْـمَـن هاذا الباسْبورت؟

12. hal? (not used very much)   *is /are?*   هَـل؟

    hal hiyya 9iraaqiyya?   *Is she an Iraqi?*   هَـل هـي عراقية؟

    hal humma Lubnaaniyyiin?   *Are they Lebanese?*   هَـل هُـمَه لبنانيّـيـن؟

Idioms and Common Phrases (Audio)

1. 9eeb 9alee + Pronoun   عـيـب عَـليه   *Shame on (him)*

9eeb 9aleek, ma-ri<u>h</u>it lil-madrasa   *Shame on you, you didn't go to school.*   عيب عَـليك. مَ رحِت لِـلْـمَدْرَسة

9eeb 9alee<u>ch</u>, ma-ddursiin 9arabi   *Shame on you, you don't study Arabic.*   عيب عَـليـچ. مَ دُّرسـين عربـي

9eeb 9aleekum, taakluun hwaaya   *Shame on you, you eat too much.*   عيب عَـليكم. تاكْـلون هُـوايَه

9eeb 9alee, ykuun kaslaan   *Shame on him, he is lazy.*   عيب عَـليه. يْـكون كَـسْـلان

9eeb 9aleeha, tu<u>d</u>rub ibinha   *Shame on her, she hits her son.*   عيب عَـليها. تُـضُرب إبِـنْها

9eeb 9alayya, ma-zirit Baabil   *Shame on me, I didn't visit Babylon.*   عيب عَـلَـيَّـه. مَ زِرت بابل

2. shloon-ma thibb / ma-triid   شْـلون مَ تْحِب / مَ تْريد   *as you like, whatever you want* (conjunction, see lesson 20)

idrus shloon-ma thibb	*Study as you (M) like.*	إدْرُس شْـلون مَ تْحِب
idursuu shloon-ma thibbuun	*Study as you (P) like.*	إدْرُسُو شْـلون مَ تْحِبّـون
hiyya taakul shloon-ma thibb	*She eats whatever she likes.*	هي تاكُل شْـلون مَ تْحِب
huwwa ysallih is-sayyaara shloon ma-yhibb	*He repairs the car as he likes.*	هو يُـصَلّـح السّيارة شْـلون مَ يْحِب
ysaafruun shloon ma-yhibbuun	*They travel as they like.*	يُـسافْرون شْـلون مَ يْحِبّـون
nsaafir shloon ma-nriid	*We travel as we wish/want.*	نْـسافِر شْـلون مَ نْريد

3. sh-madrii + attached pronoun?   شْـمَدْري + ؟   *How does (he) know?*

sh-madriik aani 9iraaqiyya?	*How do you know I am an Iraqi?*	شْـمَدْريك آني عراقيـة؟
sh-madriich Basma raahat?	*How do you know that Basma has gone?*	شْـمَدْريج بسمة راحَت؟
sh-madriikum huwwa bil-beet?	*How do you know they are home?*	شْـمَدْريكم هو بالبيت؟
sh-madriiha l-Masguuf tayyib?	*How does she know that Masguuf is delicious?*	شْـمَدْريها المَسْـگـوف طَـيِّب؟
sh-madrii li-bnayya 9ind Khaalid?	*How does he know that the girl is at Khalid's house?*	شْـمَدْري لِـبْـنَـيَّـة عِـند خالد؟

Drills   tamaariin   تَـمارين

1. Give appropriate oral replies to the following:

ween shaari9 Abu Nuwaas?	وين شارع ابو نواس؟
minu 9izam Basma?	مِـنـو عِـزَم بسمة؟
li-hsaab 9layya loo 9aleech?	لِـحْساب عَلـيّـه لو عَليچ؟
il-Masguuf akla sharqiyya loo gharbiyya?	المَسْـگـوف أكْلـة شَرقية لو غَـريبة؟
sh-tishirbuun wiyya is-simach?	شْ تِـشِـرْبـون ويّـه السّـمـج؟
ween raah Waliid wa Basma?	وين راح وليد وبسمة؟
il-Masguuf ghaali loo rikhiis?	إلمَسْـگـوف غالي لو رخيص؟
shunu shirbaw wiyya il-Masguuf?	شْـنو شِـرْبَـو ويّـه المَسْـگـوف؟
Baghdaad 9ala ayy nahar?	بغداد على أي نَـهَـر؟
il-Msguuf aklat 9asha loo rayyoog?	إلمَسْـگـوف أكْـلـة عَشـا لو رَيُّـوگ؟
Baabil 9ala ayy nahar?	بابل على أي نَـهَـر؟
kam nahar chibiir bil-9iraaq?	كَم نَـهَر چِـبـيـر بـالـعراق؟

il-mat9am bii mashruubaat?   المطعـم بـي مَشـروبات؟

humma aklaw simich loo kabaab?   هُـمَّه أكْـلَـوْ سِـمَـچ لو كباب؟

shwakit raahaw lil-mat9am?   شْـوَكِت راحَـوْ لِـلْـمطعم؟

shunu shirbaw wiyya il-akil?   شُـنو شِـرْبَـوْ وِيَّـه الأكِـل؟

2. Make questions of the following sentences:

findiq ir-Rashiid ib-Baghdaad.   فندق الرّشيد بْ بغداد

Baabil qariiba mnil-Hilla.   بابـل قـريبة مُن الْـحِلـَّة

zirna Suurya gabul sana.   زِرْنا سوّرْيا گـَبُـل سنة

rah-nzuur Lubnaan ba9ad shahar.   رَح نْـزور لبنـان بَعَـد شهـر

Basma wa Kariim zeeniin.   بسمة وكريم زينيـن

aku simach 9ala shaari9 Abu Nuwaas.   اكو سِمَـچ على شارع ابو نواس

ujrat il-findiq muu rikhiisa.   أُجـرَت الفندق مو رخيصة

sarilhum usbuu9een ib-Baghdaad.   صارلْـهم اُسْبوعيـن بْ بغداد

hissa, is-saa9a tis9a.   هِسَّه. الساعة تِسْعة

keelu baamya b-arba9 danaaniir.   كيلو بامـيَة ب ارْبَع دنانـيـر

da-naakul doolma bil-mat9am.   دَ ناكل دولـئمة بالمطعم

aku aathaar hwaaya bil-mathaf.   اكو آثار هُوايـة بالمتحف

is-safaara l-Amriikiyya qariiba.   إلـسّفارة الأمريكية قـريبة

li-ktaab il-9arabi maali.   لِـكْـتاب العربي مالي

sittiin miil min Baabil il-Baghdaad.   سِـتّيـن ميل من بابل إلْ بغداد؟

arba9iin ghurfa bil-findiq.   أرْبَعين غُـرْفة بالفندق

Basma dirsat 9arabi hatta tzuur il-9iraaq.   بسمة دِرْسَت عربي حَتّى تْزور العراق

raahaw lil-mat9am hatta yaakluun simach.   راحَـوْ لِـلْـمطعم حَتـى ياكْـلون سِمَـچ

Abu it-taksi l-hamra min Beeruut.   أبو التـّكْـسي الحَمُـرة من بيروت

huwwa Abu il-bariid.   هو أبو البريد

is-sayyaara maal il-madrasa.   السّيارة مال الْـمَدْرَسة

Jamiila Almaaniyya min Berliin.   جميلة ألمانيّة من برلين

humma Su9uudiyyiin min Jidda.   هُـمَّه سَعـودِيِّيـن مِن جِـدّة

il-masguuf simach.   إلـمَسْـگـوف سِمَـچ

Basma shaafat Maalik wa Laylaa bil-findiq.   بسمة شافَت مالك وليلى بالفندق

3. Change the following past tense sentences to the present tense:

habbeet il-baamya l-9iraaqiya _____ حَـبّيت البامـيَة العراقية

akalit simach Masguuf _____ أكَـلِت سِمَـچ مسكوف

chaanat tzuur Baabil _____ چانت تْـزور بابل

humma raaḥaw lil-mataar bis-sayyaara _____ هُمّه راحَوُ لِـلُـمطار بِالسّيارة

dirasna il-lugha il-9arabiyya _____ دِرَسُنا اللغة العربية

inta saafarit il-Lubnaan _____ انت سافَـرِت إلُ لبنان

shwakit zirit il-matḥaf _____ شُـوَكِت زِرِت المتحف؟

ween akaltu kabaab wa kubba _____ وين أَكَـلُئتو كباب وكبّة؟

leesh chintu ta9baaniin? _____ ليش چِـنُئتو تعبانين؟

chaan 9indi sayyaarteen _____ چان عِنُئدي سَيّارُتـين

is-sayyaara maalti chaanat ḥamra _____ إلسّيارة مالُئتي چانت حَمُرة

loo aani m-makaanak, chaan zirit Baabil _____ لو آني م مَكانك. چان زِرِت بابل

chaan aku talafoon bish-shaari9 _____ چان اكـو تلفـون بِالشـّارع

hadhoola il-wilid chaanaw tullaab _____ هَـذوله الـوِلـد چانَـوُ طلاب

chinit tishrab 9arag bil-baar _____ چِـنِت تِشـُـرب عَرَگ بِالبار

chinna naakul kubba kull usbuu9 _____ چِـنّا ناكل كباب كُل اُسُبوع

Basma chaanat 9ind Samiir _____ بسمة چانت عِنُئد سمير

akalna baamya 9ind Sa9ad _____ أكَـلُئنا بامُيَة عند سَعَد

4. Fill in the blanks of the following:

Basma wa Waliid _____ simach Masguuf بسمة ووليد _____ سِـمَـج مَسُـكوف

Waliid 9izam _____ 9ala 9asha وليد عِزَم _____ على عَـشَّـا

aku _____ hwaaya 9ala shaari9 _____ اكو _____ هُـوايه على شارع _____

aku bil-mat9am _____ wa _____ اكو بالمطعـم _____ و _____

il-Masguuf akla _____

إلـمَسْكوف أكـْلة _____

rajaaʾn inṭiina _____

رجاءً إنـْطينـا _____

Baghdaad _____ nahar Dijla wa Baabil _____ nahar _____

بـغداد _____ نـَهَـر دِجْلة وبابل _____ نـَهَـر _____

il-mazza l-Lubnaaniyya _____

إلـمَـزّة الـلـُبنانية _____

id-doolma akla _____ loo _____

إلـدّولـمة أكـْلة _____ لو _____

il-walad _____ Samiir

إلـولد _____ سـمير

li-ḥsaab 9alayya loo _____

لِـحْساب عَلَـيَّه لو _____

Baabil madiina _____ loo _____

بابل مدينة _____ لو _____

usbuu9 bil-bariid _____ w-usbuu9een bil-bariid _____

أُسْـبوع بالبريد _____ واسْـبوعين بـالبريد _____

yṣarruf duulaaraat ila _____ bil-bank

يُـصَـرّف دولارات الى _____ بالبنك

hissa, laazim asaafir _____

هِـسّـه. لازم أسـافـر _____

9idhum ḥsaab _____ ir-Raafideen

عِـدهم حُـساب _____ الـرّافِـدين

maykhaalif taakhudh _____ lil-mathaf

مَيْخالف تاخُـذ _____ لِـلـْمتحف

maysiir truuhuun lil-9iraaq biduun _____

مَيْصير تـْروحون لِـلـْعراق بِـدون _____

Basma thibb il-aathaar _____

بسمة تـْحِب الآثار _____

5. Complete and read the following aloud:

a.   ḥsaab il-akil 9alayya hal-marra

حُـساب الأكـِل عَلـَيَّه هَالـْمَـرّة

_____ 9aleena _____

_____ عَلينا _____

_____ 9aleek _____

_____ عَلـيك _____

_____ 9alee<u>ch</u> _____   _____ عَليچ _____

_____ 9aleekum _____   _____ عَليكم _____

_____ 9alee _____   _____ عَليه _____

_____ 9aleeha _____   _____ عَليها _____

_____ 9aleehum _____   _____ عَليهم _____

b.   9eeb 9aleek, tiz9al wiyya Jaasim   عيب عَليك، تِزْعَل وِيّه جاسِم

9eeb 9alee<u>ch</u>, _____   _____ ،عيب عَليـچ

9eeb 9aleekum, _____   _____ ،عيب عَليكم

9eeb 9alee, _____   _____ ،عيب عَليه

9eeb 9aleeha, _____   _____ ،عيب عَليها

9eeb 9aleehum, _____   _____ ،عيب عَليهم

9eeb 9alayya, _____   _____ ،عيب عَلَيّه

9eeb 9aleena, _____   _____ ،عيب عَلينا

c.   <u>sh</u>-madriik Basma Amriikiyya?   شْـمَدُريك بسمة أمْريكية؟

<u>sh</u>-madrii<u>ch</u> _____?   شْـمَدُريـچ _____؟

<u>sh</u>-madriikum _____?   شْـمَدُريـكـم _____؟

<u>sh</u>-madrii _____?   شْـمَدُري _____؟

<u>sh</u>-madriiha _____?   شْـمَدُريـها _____؟

<u>sh</u>-madriihum _____?   شْـمَدُريـهم _____؟

<u>sh</u>-madriini _____?   شْـمَدُريـني _____؟

<u>sh</u>-madriina _____?   شْـمَدُريـنا _____؟

d. asawwi ish-shughul shloon ma-triid
أسَوّي الشّـتّـغـُل شْـلون مَ تْـريد

_____ ma-triidiin
مَ تْـريدين _____

_____ ma-triiduun
مَ تْـريدون _____

_____ ma-yriid
مَ يْـريد _____

_____ ma-triid
مَ تْـريد _____

_____ ma-yriiduun
مَ يْـريدون _____

_____ ma-ariid
ما ريد _____

_____ ma-nriid
مَ نْـريد _____

e. shloon saafarit il-Baghdaad?
شْـلون سافَـرِت إلْ بغداد؟

_____ saafarti lil-Hilla?
سافَـرْتي لِـلْـحِلـّة؟ _____

_____ saafartu lil-Muusil?
سافَـرْتو لِـلْـموصِل؟ _____

_____ saafar lil-Basra?
سافَـرْ لِـلْـبَصرة؟ _____

_____ saafrat l-Beeruut?
سافَـرَت لْ بيروت؟ _____

_____ saafraw l-9mmaan?
سافَـرَوْ لْ عَـمّان؟ _____

_____ saafarit lil-Qaahira?
سافَـرِت لِـلْـقاهِرة؟ _____

_____ saafarna l-Tuunis?
سافَـرْنا لْ تونِس؟ _____

6. Translate the following into Arabic:

Where did you (P) go?

_____

How is the food?

_____

When did you leave for Iraq?

_____

How long have you been in Baghdad?

_____

What is the name of the restaurant?

_____

Why do you study Arabic?

_____

Where are you from?

_____

What do you (F) like to eat?

_____

Is this the girls' college?

_____

I want airmail stamps.

_____

Please give me regular envelopes.

_____

I like the Iraqi okra and kubba.

_____

Who will pay the bill?

_____

Is the Masguuf a Syrian or Lebanese dish?

_____

I put everything in its place.

_____

Are there western restaurants in Baghdad?

_____

These cars are mine.

_____

Waliid sends his regards to you (P).

_____

These are boys and those are girls.

_____

We are eating and drinking in the restaurant.

_____

Creative Dialogues

a. taalib 1: sh-ithibiin taakliin?

طالب 1: شِـتْحِـبِّـين تاكـلِين؟

taaliba 2: aani aḥibb aakul simach. w-inta sh-ithibb?

طالبة 2: آني أحِب آكُل سِمَـچ. وإنـتَ شِـتْحِـب؟

taalib 1: aḥibb aakul dijaaj wa kabaab

طالب 1: أحِب آكُـل دِجاج وكَـباب

taaliba 2: bass haadha akil muu siḥḥi

طالبة 2: بَس هاذا أكِـل مو صِحّـي

taalib 1: leesh haadha akil muu siḥḥi?

طالب 1: لِيـش هاذا أكِـل مو صِحّـي؟

taaliba 2: li'ann ysammin

طالبة 2: لأنّ يُسَـمِّـن

taalib 1: kull il-akil ysammin?

طالب 1: كُل الأكِـل يُسَـمِّـن؟

taaliba 2: laa. loo aani m-makaanak aakul khuḍrawaat bass

طالبة 2: لا. لو آني م مَكانك آكُل خُـضْـرَوات بَـس

taalib 1: triidiini amuut mnij-juu9!

طالب 1: تْريدِيني أموت مُن الجُـوع!

b. taalib 1: il-yoom laazim nruuḥ il-beet Abu Jwaad

طالب 1: إلـيَـوم لازِم نْـروح لْ بِـيت أبو جُـواد

taaliba 2: shaku b-beet Abu Jwaad?

طالبة 2: شَـكـو بْ بِـيت أبو جُـواد؟

taalib 1: Aku 9ziima b-zawaaj Jwaad

طالب 1: أكو عَزِمة بْ زَواج جُـواد

taaliba 2: leesh maa gilitli ḥatta ashtiri hadiyya

طالبة 2: لِيـش ما گِـلِـتْلـي حَـتّى أشْـتِـري هَـدِيّـة

taalib 1: aani gilitlich, bass inti niseeti

طالب 1: آني گِـلِـتْـلِـچ. بَس إنتي نِـسِـيتي

taaliba 2: 9eeb 9aleena, nruuḥ biduun hadiyya

طالبة 2: عيب عَلِينا. نْروح بِـدون هَـدِيّـة

taalib 1:	la9ad shi-nsawwi?	طالب 1:	لَعَد شِنْسَوّي؟
taaliba 2:	inta ruuh ishtiri hadiyya bil-9ajal	طالبة 2:	إنت روح إشْتِري هَدِيّة بالْعَجَل
taalib 1:	hadiyya ghaalya loo rikhiisa?	طالب 1:	هَدِيّـة غالْيَة لو رِخيصة؟
taaliba 2:	laa ghaalya wala rikhiisa, wasat	طالبة 2:	لا غالْيَة ولا رِخيصة. وَسَط

For new words, see Glossary.

An Iraqi peasant woman selling daily yogurt

DARIS SIT-TA9ASH   دَرِس سِطْطَعَش

Family and Relatives

ahal wa garaayib   أهَـل وگَـرايِـب

Basma inquires about Waliid's family and relatives.

Basic Dialogue (Audio)

1. Basma: ween tuskun?
   Where do you live?

   بسـمة: وين تُسُكُـنْ؟

2. Waliid: aani askun wiyya ahli
   b-Baghdaad.
   I live with my family in Baghdad.

   وليد: آني أسُكُـن وِيّـه أهْلي بْ بغداد.

3. Basma: gulli shii 9an ahlak.
   Tell me something about your family.

   بسـمة: گُـلْـلـي شِـي عَن أهْلَـك.

4. Waliid: aani mizzawwij wa 9indi walad
   wi-bnayya
   I am married and have a boy and girl.

   وليد: آني مِـزّوّج وعِنْـدي وَلَـد وِبْنَـيّـة.

5. Basma: alla ykhalliilak yyaahum.
   May God keep them for you.

   بسـمة: الله يُخَـلّـيـلَـك ياهُم.

6. Waliid: shukran. waaldi w waalitti
   saakniin wiyyaana.
   *Thank you. My father and mother are
   living with us.*

   وليد: شكراً. والـدي ووالِـدْتي ساكـنين وِيّـانا.

7. Basma: 9indak ikhwaan wa khawaat?
   Do you have brothers and sisters?

   بسـمة: عِنْـدَك إخْـوان وخَـوات؟

8. Waliid: ii, 9indi akheen wa ukhut.
   Yes, I have two brothers and one sister.

وليد: ئِـي، عِنْدي أخّين وأُخُت.

9. Basma: 9idhum atfaal?
   Do they have children?

بسمة: عِدُهم أطْفال؟

10. Waliid: ii, 9idhum hwaaya atfaal.
    Yes, they have many children.

وليد: ئِـي، عِدُهم هُـواية أطفال.

11. Basma: ya9ni, inta 9amm wa khaal.
    Well, you are an uncle (paternal and maternal).

بسمة: يَـعْني. إنت عَـمّ وخال.

12. Waliid: wa 9indi 9amma wa khaala.
    And I have aunts (paternal and maternal).

وليد: وعِنْدي عَـمّة وخالة.

13. Basma: 9ammtak wa khaaltak, kam tifil 9idhum?
    Your aunts, how many children do they have?

بسمة: عَمْتَك وخالتك. كم طِفِـل عِـدُهم؟

14. Waliid: 9idhum wilid wa banaat kbaar.
    They have grown boys and girls.

وليد: عِدُهم ولِـد وبَنات كْبار.

15. Basma: maashaalla, 9eeltak chibiira.
    Praise God, your family is large.

بسمة: ماشاالله. عيلْـتَك چِـبِـيرة.

16. Waliid: na9am, ilhamdu lillaa. inti laazim tzuuriin ahli.
    Yes, thank God. You must visit my family.

وليد: نعم. إلحَمـدُ لله. إنتي لازم تْـزورين أهْـلي.

17. Basma: shukran, yimkin yoom ij-jum9a ij-jaayya.
    Thanks, perhaps next Friday.

بسمة: شـكراً. يِـمْكن يوم الجُـمْـعَـة الـجّـايَّة.

18. Waliid: ahlan wa sahlan.
    You are welcome.

وليد: أهلا وسَـهْلا.

Additional Kin Names (Audio)

jidd / jidda (M/F)	*grandfather/grandmother*	جِـدّ / جِـدّة
ab / aabaaʾ (S/P)	*father/s*	أب / آباء
umm / ummahaat (S/P)	*mother/s*	أُمّ / أُمَّـهات
hafiid / ahfaad (S/P)	*grandchild/ren*	حَـفيد / أحْـفاد
nasiib / nasiiba (M/F)	*relative* (in-law)	نَـسيب / نَـسيبة
ibin khaal / khaala	*cousin* (maternal)	إبن خال / خالة
ibin 9amm / 9amma	*cousin* (paternal)	إبن عَـمّ / عَـمّة
binit ukhut	*niece* (sister's side)	بِـنِـت أُخُـت
binit akh	*niece* (brother's side)	بِـنِـت أخ
ibin ukhut	*nephew* (sister's side)	إبِـن أُخُـت

ibin akh	*nephew (brother's side)*	إبِـن أخ
zooj ukhut	*brother-in law*	زوج أُخُـت
zoojat akh	*sister-in-law*	زوجَـة أخ
a9zab / 9izba (M/F)	*single, unmarried*	أعْـزَب / عِـزْبة

Vocabulary (Audio)

ahal	*family, relatives*	أهَـل
gariib / garaayib (S/P)	*relative/s*	گَـريب / گَـرايب
tuskun / tusukniin / tusuknuun	*you live (M/F/P)*	تُسْكُن / تُسُكْنين / تُسُكْنون
askun	*I live*	أسْكُن
wiyya	*with*	ويَّه
wiyyaana	*with us*	ويَـانا
gulli	*tell me (imp. verb)*	گُـلْلي
shii	*thing, something*	شِـي
9an	*about*	عَـن
mizzawwij / mizzawwija (M/F)	*married*	مِـزَّوِّج / مِـزَّوْجَة
walad / wilid (S/P)	*boy/s*	وَلَـد / ولِـد
binit / banaat (S/P)	*girl/s*	بِـنِت / بَـنات
bnayya / bnayyaat, banaat (S/P)	*girl/s*	بُنَيّـة / بُنَـيّات. بَـنات
alla ykhalliilak	*may God keep for you (see below)*	الله يُخَـلّيـلَك
yyaahum	*them (particle* **yyaa,** *see below)*	يّـاهُـم
waalid, ab	*father*	والِـد. أب
waalda, umm	*mother*	والْـدَة. أمّ
waalitti < waalidti	*my mother ("d" assimilated with feminine "t," see below)*	والِـدْتي
sikan, yuskun (RV)	*to live, to dwell*	سِـكَـن. يـسْكُن
saakin / saakna / saakniin (M/F/P)	*living, staying (participle)*	ساكِـن / ساكْـنة / ساكْـنين
akh / ikhwaan (S/P)	*brother/s*	أخ / إخْـوان
ukhut / khawaat (S/P)	*sister/s*	أخُـت / خَـوات
tifil / atfaal (S/P)	*child/ren*	طِـفِـل / أطْـفال
hwaaya	*many, much*	هُـوايَه
ya9ni	*well, oh, so (lit., it means)*	يَعْـني
9amm / 9amma (M/F)	*uncle/aunt (paternal)*	عَـم / عَـمّة
khaal / khaala (M/F)	*uncle aunt (maternal)*	خال . خالَـة

kabiir / kabiira / kbaar (S/F/P)	*big, large*	كَبِير / كَبِيرة / كُبار
chibiir / chibiira (M/F)	*big, large* (used only in singular form)	چِبِير / چِبِيرة
maashaalla	*Praise God* (see lesson 5)	ماشالله
ii	*yes*	ئِـي
jaay / jaayya / jaayyiin (M/F/P)	*coming* (participle)	جايُ / جايَّة / جايّيـن

Grammar and Remarks
The Particle yyaa- يّا

The particle **yyaa** has no meaning by itself. It serves as a stem to support an attached pronoun. In Iraqi Arabic there are verbs that may take two objects, the so-called direct and indirect objects in English. The direct object is usually in the form of an attached pronoun and the indirect object is a noun. But often the indirect object may be a pronoun also. Because two pronoun endings cannot be added to one verb in Arabic, the particle **yyaa** يّا or **iyyaa** إيّا is used as a stem to take the attached pronoun of the direct object while the verb takes the attached pronoun of the indirect object. (Audio)

alla ykhalliilak il-ahal	*May God keep the family for you.*	الله يُخَـلِّـيلَك الأهَل
alla ykhalliilak yyaahum	*May God keep them for you.*	الله يُخَـلِّـيلَك ياهُم
alla ykhalliilak il-binit	*May God keep the girl for you.*	الله يُخَـلِّـيلَك الـبِـنِـت
alla ykhalliilak yyaaha	*May God keep her for you.*	الله يُخَـلِّـيلَك ياها
ajiiblich li-ktaab	*I bring you the book.*	أجيبلِچ لِـكـتاب
ajiiblich iyyaa	*I bring it (him) to you.*	أجيْبلِـچ إيّـاه
aktiblak risaala	*I write you a letter.*	أكْتِـبُـلَـك رسالة
aktiblak iyyaaha	*I write it (her) to you.*	أكْتِـبُـلَـك إيّـاها
yintiini fluus	*He gives me money.*	يِـنْـطينـي فْلوس
yintiini yyaaha	*He gives it (her) to me.*	يِـنْـطينـي يّاها
intiini s-sayyaara	*Give me the car!*	إنْـطينـي سَـيّارة
intiini yyaaha	*Give it (her) to me!*	إنْـطينـي يّـاها

The Feminine "t ـة" Ending

As we discussed in lesson 6, nouns/things in Arabic are either masculine or feminine. There is no "it" as in English. Feminine nouns are usually marked by "**a**" in colloquial Arabic, the equivalent of the so-called feminine "**t** ـة"(**taa' marbuuṭa** تاء مَرْبوطة) ending in classical Arabic. When a feminine word is followed by another noun in a possession construction, the ending -**a** is pronounced -**at**. When an attached pronoun or other suffix is added, the -**at** ending is written as "ت."

Note: The feminine "**t** ـة" is always preceded by the short vowel "**a** ـَ." (Audio)

Masculine Nouns

<u>ch</u>alib	*a dog*	چَلِـب
<u>ch</u>albi	*my dog*	چَلـبي
<u>ch</u>albeen	*two dogs*	چَلـبين
<u>kh</u>aal	*an uncle*	خـال
<u>kh</u>aalha	*her uncle*	خـالـها
<u>kh</u>aaleen	*two uncles*	خـالـين
ṭaalib	*a student*	طالـب
ṭaalibna	*our student*	طالـبُنـا
sayyaara	*a car*	سَـيّارَة
ṭaalibat	*school student*	طالـبَـة
madrasa		مَدْرَسـة

Feminine Nouns

<u>ch</u>alba	*a dog*	چَلـبَة
<u>ch</u>alibti	*my dog*	چَلـبْـتـي
<u>ch</u>alibteen	*two dogs*	چَلـبْـتـين
<u>kh</u>aala	*an aunt*	خـالـة
<u>kh</u>aalatha	*her aunt*	خـالـتـها
<u>kh</u>aalteen	*two aunts*	خـالـتـين
ṭaaliba	*a student*	طالـبَة
ṭaalbatna	*our student*	طالـبَـتْـنا
sayyaarat Kariim	*Kariim's car*	سَـيّارَة كـريم

The idaafa إضافـة Construction

The **idaafa** construction in Arabic is an arrangement when two or more nouns join together (without interruption) to form an equivalent in English to a phrase with "of, " the possessive "s" phrase, or two (or more) nouns used as attributives. (Audio)

ṭaalib madrasa	*a school student* (M)	طالـب مَدْرَسَـة
ṭaalibat madrasa	*a school student* (F)	طالـبَـة مَدْرَسَـة
maktab Kaamil	*Kamil's office*	مَكـتب كامِل
maktabat Kaamil	*Kamil's library*	مَكـتبة كامِل
sayyaarat mat<u>h</u>af	*a museum car*	سَـيّارَة مَتْـحف
mufatti<u>sh</u> maṭaar	*an airport inspector*	مُفَتِّـش مطار
muwa<u>zz</u>af maktab bank	*a bank office employee*	مُوَظّـف مَكـتب بَـنك
muwa<u>zz</u>afat maktab bank	*a bank office employee* (F)	مُوَظّـفة مَكـتب بَـنك
miftaa<u>h</u> baab beet	*a house door key*	مِفْـتاح باب بيت
kursi maktab <u>ch</u>ibiir	*a large office chair*	كُـرُسـي مَكـتب چِـبـير
sayyaarat mat<u>h</u>af <u>ch</u>ibiira	*a large museum car*	سَـيّارَة مَتْـحف چِـبـيـرة

In definite **idaafa** only the last noun in the chain takes the definite article " **il-** الـ," which makes the whole phrase definite. Alternatively, the last noun can be a proper name, which is definite without **il-**. (Audio)

muwa<u>zz</u>af **il-**bank	*the employee of the bank*	مُـوَظّـف البنك
miftaa<u>h</u> baab **il-**beet	*the house door key*	مِـفْـتاح باب البيت
ṭaalibat jaami9at Ba<u>gh</u>daad	*the Baghdad University student*	طالـبَـة جامِـعَة بغداد
kursi **l-**maktab **ij-**jibiir	*the large office chair*	كُرسـي المَكـتب الجِّـبـير
sayyaarat **il-**mat<u>h</u>af **ij-**jibiira	*the large museum car*	سَـيّارَة المتحف الجِّـبـيـرة

Note: Sometimes there are inner vowel variations depending on whether the added suffix is a vowel or begins in a vowel or consonant.

Idioms and Common Phrases (Audio)

1. maaku luzuum   ماكو لـُزوم   *no need for* (invariable)

maaku luzuum truuh lil-bariid	You (M) *don't need to go to the post office.*	ماكو لـُزوم تـُروح لِـلْبَـريد
maaku luzuum tshuufuun Laylaa	You (P) *don't need to see Laylaa.*	ماكو لـُزوم تـْشوفون ليلى
maaku luzuum yjuun li-hnaa	*They don't need to come here.*	ماكو لـُزوم يـُجون لِـهْـنا
maaku luzuum adrus kull yoom	I *don't need to study every day.*	ماكو لـُزوم أُدْرُس كـُل يوم
maaku luzuum tzuuriin it-tabiib	You (F) *don't need to visit the doctor.*	ماكو لـُزوم تـْزورين الطـّبيب
maaku luzuum tijiin wiyyaahum	You (F) *don't need to come with them.*	ماكو لـُزوم تِـجين وِيّـاهم

2. bala adab   بَـلا أدَب   *impolite, with bad manners* (invariable)

huwwa bala adab	*He is impolite.*	هو بلا أدَب
humma bala adab	*They are impolite.*	هُـمّه بلا أدَب
Kariima taakul bala adab	*Kariima eats with bad manners.*	كريمة تاكـُل بلا أدَب
il-wilid yili9buun bala adab	*The boys play rudely.*	إلـْوِلِـد يِـلِـعْبون بلا أدَب
huwwa yimshi b-nuss ish-shaari9 bala adab	*He walks rudely in the middle of the street.*	هو يِـمْشي بْ نـُصّ الشـّـارع بلا أدَب

3. kullshi b-makaana   كـُلـْشِـي بْ مَكانـَه   *all right, exactly, everything in its place* (invariable)

kullshi b-makaana, mithil-ma triid	*It is exactly as you* (M) *want.*	كـُلـْشِـي بْ مَكانـَه. مِـثِـل مَ تـْريد
rah-akhalli kullshi b-makaana	I *will put everything in its place.*	رَحْ أخَـلـّي كـُلـْشِـي بْ مَكانـَه
la-tiqlaq kullshi b-makaana	*Don't worry, everything is all right.*	لَـتِـقـْلَق كـُلـْشِـي بْ مَكانـَه
khalleet il-kutub kullshi b-makaana	I *put the books in their places.*	خَـلـَّيت الكـُتب كـُلـْشِـي بْ مَكانـَه

Drills tamaariin تَمارين
1. Give appropriate oral replies to the following:

ween saakna?	وين ساكْنة؟
ahlak saakniin wiyyaak?	أهْلـك ساكْنين ويّـاك؟
kam walad 9indich?	كم وَلـد عِنْدِج؟
alla ykhalliilich yyaahum	الله يُخَـلّيـلِـج ياهُم
inta mizzawwij loo a9zab?	إنت مِـزّوّج لو أعْزَب؟
9eeltak chibiira loo saghiira?	عِيلْـتك چِـبيرة لو صَغيرة؟
shgadd 9umur ibnak?	شْـگَـد عَـمُر إبـنك؟
9indich ikhwaan wa khawaat?	عِـنْدِج إخْـوان وخَـوات؟
ibnak saghiir loo chibiir?	إبنك صَغير لو چِـبيـر؟
shgadd sarlich mizzawja?	شْـگَـد صارْلِـج مِـزّوّجَة؟
maashaalla, 9eelatkum chibiira	ماشاالله. عيلَـتْكم چِـبيرة
kam ukhut 9indak?	كم أُخُـت عِـنْدك؟
ahibb a9izmich 9idna bil-beet	أحب أعِـزْمِـج عِـدْنا بالبيت
thibbiin tzuuriin ahli?	تْـحِـبّيـن تْـزورين أهْـلي؟

2. Make the following singular sentences plural:

aani saakin wiyya ahli _____ آني ساكِـن وِيّـه أهْـلي

alla ykhallilak yyaaha _____ الله يُخَـلّـيـلَـك ياها

9inda akh wa ukhut _____ عِـنْـدَه أخ وأُخُـت

9indich walad wa binit kbaar _____ عِنْدِج وَلَـد و بِـنِـت كْـبار

inta mizzawwij? _____ إنت مِـزّوّج؟

shi-thibbiin tishurbiin wiyya is-simach? ____ شِـتْـحِـبّيـن تِـشـرْبين وِيّـه السِّـمَـچ؟

taalib jaami9i _____ طالِـب جامِـعـي

triid taabi9 jawwi loo 9aadi? _____ تْـريد طابِـع جَـوّي لو عادي؟

taaliba jaami9iyya _____ طالِـبة جامِـعِـيّة

arrid a9izmak 9ala simach _____ أريد أعِـزْمَـك على سِـمَـچ

maaku luzuum tijiin _____   ماكو لُزوم تجِـين

huwwa yaakul bala adab _____   هو ياكُل بلا أَدَب

wiyyaak _____   وِيّـاك

aani aḥibb il-akil il-9arabi _____   آني أَحِب الأكِل العربي

3. Fill in the blanks of the following:

hiyya _____ wiyya ahalha   هي _____ وِيّـه أهَـلـْها

sayyaarat _____ jidiida   سَيّارة _____ جِـديـدَة

iḥna _____ wiyya _____   إحُنا _____ وِيّـه _____

is-saa9a _____ Basma   السّاعة _____ بسمة

il-maktaba maal _____   إلـْمَكـْتَبة مال _____

aani muu mizzawwij, aani _____   آني مو مِـزَّوِّج، آني _____

ṭaabi9 _____ loo ṭaabi9 _____?   طابِـع _____ لو طابِـع _____؟

Baabil _____ min Baghdaad   بابل _____ مِن بغداد

ween aku ṣanduug _____?   وين اكو صَنـْدوك _____؟

_____ ṭifil 9indich?   طِـفِل عِنـْدِج؟ _____

9indi _____ wa _____   عَنـْدي _____ و _____

ḥsaab il-akil _____   حُساب الأكِل _____

4. Complete and read aloud:
a. alla ykhalliilak yyaa   الله يِـخـَلّـيـلَك يّـاه

_____ yyaaha   يّـاها _____

_____ yyaahum   يّـاهم _____

alla ykhalliilich yyaa   اللهُ يُخَلِّيلِچ يّاه

_____ yyaaha   يّاها _____

_____ yyaahum   يّاهم _____

alla ykhalliilkum yyaa   اللهُ يُخَلِّيلكُم يّا

_____ yyaaha   يّاها _____

_____ yyaahum   يّاهم _____

alla ykhallilak il-wilid   اللهِ يـخَلّيـلَك الـوِلِـد

_____ il-banaat   الـبنات _____

_____ l-atfaal   الأطْفال _____

_____ l-ahal   الأهَل _____

_____ il-9eela   الـعِيلة _____

b.   huwwa yih chi bala adab   هو يِـحْجي بَلا أدَب

hiyya _____   _____ هـي

humma _____   _____ هُـمَّه

inta _____   _____ إنت

inti _____   _____ إنتي

intu _____   _____ إنتو

aani _____   _____ آني

ihna _____   _____ إحنا

c.   sawweet ish-shughul kullshi m-makaana   سَـوّيت الشْـغُـل كُـلْشي مُ مَكانَـة

sawweena _____   _____ سَـوّينا

sawwa _____   _____ سَـوَّا

sawwat _____   _____ سَوَّت

sawwaw _____   _____ سَوَّوْ

sawweet _____   _____ سَوِّيت

sawweeti _____   _____ سَوِّيتي

sawweetu _____   _____ سَوِّيتو

d. maaku luzuum tijiin wiyyaa   ماكو لُزوم تِجِيـن وِيّـاه

_____ wiyyaaha   وِيّـاها _____

_____ wiyyaahum   وِيّـاهم _____

_____ wiyyaaya   وِيّـايَه _____

_____ wiyyaana   وِيّـانا _____

maaku luzuum aji wiyyaak   ماكو لُزوم أجي وِيّـاك

_____ wiyyaa<u>ch</u>   وِيّـاچ _____

_____ wiyyaakum   وِيّـاكم _____

5. Orally make the words in parentheses dual in the following sentences and change anything else that needs to be changed:

9indi (walad) wa (binit)   عِـنْدي (وَلَـد) و (بِنِـت)

9inda (<u>kh</u>aal) wa (<u>kh</u>aala)   عِـنْـدَه (خـال) و (خـالـه)

9idha (9mm) wa (9amma) kbaar   عِـدُها (عَـمّ) و (عَـمّة) كْبـار

(<u>t</u>aalib il-madrasa) zeen   (طـالِـب المَدْرسة) زين

(sayyaara) il-maktab <u>h</u>amra   (سَيّارة) المَكتب حَمْـرَة

(ustaa<u>dh</u>) maal jaami9a   (اسْتـاذ) مـال جامِعَـة

9idhum (<u>ch</u>alba) sooda bil-beet   عِـدُهم (چَـلْـبة) سودة بالـبْيـت

Maalik 9inda (<u>t</u>ifil)   مالِـك عِـنْـدَه (طِـفِـل)

ariid a<u>s</u>arruf (<u>h</u>awaala) bariidiyya   أريد أصَرُّف (حَـوالة) بَريديّة

(qaamuus) 9arabi jidiid   (قاموس) عربي جِـديـد

aku (bank) ib-<u>sh</u>aari9 ir-Ra<u>sh</u>iid   اكو (بَـنك) بْ شارع الـرَشـيد

(dijaaja) <u>t</u>ayba   (دِجاجَـة) طَـيْـبَة

6. Replace the words in parentheses with the right form of yyaa يّا :

Example: jiibli (il-binit) mnil-madrasa جيبْـلي (البِـنِت) مُن الْـمَدْرَسَة

jiibli yyaaha mnil-madrasa جيبْـلي يّـاها مُن الْـمَدْرَسَة

siddli (ish-shubbaach), min fadlak سِـدْلي (الشُّـبّاچ). مِن فضلك _____

dalliini (il-bariid), alla ykhalliik دَلّـيني (البريد). الله يُـخَـلّـيك _____

alla ykhalliilkum (il-wilid wil-banaat) الله يِخَـلّـيْلـكُم (الولد والبنات) _____

sallihli (is-sayyaara), min fadlak صَلّـحْلي (السّيارة). مِن فضلك _____

sallihiili (is-saa9aat) baachir صَلّـحِيلي (السّاعات) باچِـر _____

iqraali (ir-risaala) bil-9arabi إقْـرالي (الـرِّسالة) بالعربي _____

iktibli (il-9unwaan) bil-Ingiliizi إكْـتِـبْـلي (العُـنْـوان) بالانگليزي _____

ishtiriili (tawaabi9) 9aadiyya إشْـتِـريـلي (طَـوابِع) عاديّـة _____

i9zimli (Samiir) 9ala aklat Masguuf إعْزِمْـلي (سمير) على أكْـلـة مَـسْگـوف _____

khalliili (ij-junta) bil-beet خَـلّـيلي (الجّـنْـطة) بالبيت _____

7. Translate the following into Arabic:

May God keep them for you.

_____

May God keep the children for you (F).

_____

Let me bring you the car.

_____

I am bringing your (M) car.

_____

My nephew and my sister live in Basra.

_____

My family is large.

_____

I am living with my family.

_____

a college student (F)

_____

the employee (F) of the museum

_____

a wrist watch

_____

the American University of Beirut

_____

Basma's trip to Iraq is in one month.

_____

My aunt lives with us in the house.

_____

today's dish in the restaurant

_____

Our dog (F) has a bad manner.

_____

a car of a university student

_____

the university student's car

_____

I don't have today's newspaper.

_____

Creative Dialogues

a. taalib 1: Basma ta9aali wiyyaaya
   lil-beet

   taaliba 2: leesh shaku 9idkum?

   taalib 1: 9idna aziima il-yoom, w
   ahibb tkuuniin wiyyaana

   taaliba 2: bikull suruur, aani ahibb
   at9arraf 9ala ahlak

   taalib 1: rah-aji 9aleech is-saa9a sab9a

   taaliba 2: laa, ta9aal 9alayya is-saa9a
   thmaanya, raja'an

   taalib 1: luweesh?

   taaliba 2: laazim aruuh ashtiri hadiyya

   taalib 1: maaku luzuum lil-hadiyya

   taaliba 2: 9eeb 9alayya maa jiib hadiyya
   wiyyaaya

b. taalib 1: Basma haadhi zoojti Laylaa

   taaliba 2: tsharrafna, Laylaa

   taalib 1: wilna ish-sharaf. tfaddali
   stariihi hnaa

   taaliba 2: shukran. shloon l-atfaal,
   inshaalla zeeniin?

   taalib 1: zeeniin ilhamdu lillaah. bass
   ibni wakiih

   taaliba 2: luweesh huwwa wakiih?

   taalib1: yhibb yil9ab hwaaya. ta9aali
   a9arrfich 9ala ummi

   taaliba 2: tsharrafna umm Laylaa

   taalib 1: ahlan wa sahlan Basma

   taaliba 2: shukran. maashaalla
   9eelatkum chibiira

طالب 1: بسمة تَعالي وِيّاهَ لِلْبيت

طالبة 2: ليش شَكو عِدْكم؟

طالب 1: عِدْنا عَزِمة اليوم. وأحِب تْكونين وِيّانا

طالبة 2: بِكُل سُرور. آني أحَب أتْعَرَّف على أهْلَك

طالب 1: رَح أجي عليچ السّاعة سَبْعة

طالبة 2: لا. تَعال عَلَيْه السّاعة ثُمانِئة. رجاءً

طالب 1: لُويش؟

طالبة 2: لازم أروح أشْتِري هَدِيَّة

طالب 1: ماكو لُزوم لِلْهَدِيَّة

طالبة 2: عيب عَلَيْه ما جيب هَدِيَّة وِيّايَه

طالب 1: بسمة هاذي زُوجْتي ليلى

طالبة 2: تْشَرَّفْنا. ليلى

طالب 1: ولْنا الشَّرَف. تْفَضَّلي إسْتِريحي هُنا

طالبة 2: شكراً. شْلون لَطْفال. إنْشاللّه زينـين؟

طالب 1: زينـين الحَمْدُ للّه. بَس إبْني وَكيح

طالبة 2: لُويش هو وَكيح؟

طالب 1: يُحَب يِلْعَب هُوايَه. تَعالي أعَرْفِچ على اُمّي

طالبة 2: تْشَرَّفْنا أم لـيلى

طالب 1: أهلا وسهلا بسمة

طالبة 2: شكراً. ماشاللّه عيلَتْكم چِبيرة

For new words, see Glossary.

The Al–Hadba (tiled) Minaret in the city of Musil, twelfth century A.D.

DARIS SBAA-ȚA9ASH   دَرِس سُـباطعَـش

Medical Care

9inaaya ṭibbiyya   عِـنـايَـة طِـبّـيَّـة

Basma is not feeling well. She is at the doctor's office describing her condition to him.

Basic Dialogue (Audio)

1. ṭabiib: <u>sh</u>-bii<u>ch</u>?
   What is wrong with you?

   طبيب: شُـبـيـچ؟

2. Basma: a<u>h</u>iss ta9baana w 9indi wija9 raas.
   I feel tired, I have a headache.

   بسمة: أَحِـسّ تَـعُّبانة وعِـنْـدي وِجـع راس.

3. ṭabiib: <u>sh</u>wakit bidat 9indi<u>ch</u> haad<u>h</u>i l-a9raa<u>d</u>?
   When did you begin to feel these symptoms?

   طبيب: شْـوَكِـت بِـدَت عِنْـدچ هاذي الأعْـراض؟

4. Basma: gabul yoomeen.
   Two days ago.

   بسمة: گَـبُل يومين

5. ṭabiib: ifta<u>h</u>i <u>h</u>algi<u>ch</u>, w ṭal9i lsaani<u>ch</u>.
   Open your mouth and put your tongue out.

   طبيب: إفْـتَحي حَـلْـگِـج وطَـلْـعي لْـسانِـج.

6. Basma: aani mariida, jismi kulla yooja9ni.
   I am sick, my whole body hurts.

   بسمة: آني مَريضة. جِـسْـمي كُـلّـه يوجَـعْني.

7. ţabiib: 9indich haraara 9aalya. ukhdhi
   nafas 9amiiq, min fadlich.
   *You have a high temperature. Take a deep
   breath, please.*

   طبيب: عِنْدِچ حَرارة عالْية. اُخْـذي نَـفَـس عَميق. مِن فَضْلِـچ.

8. Basma: ţayyib.
   Fine.

   بسمة: طَـيِّـب

9. ţabiib: naami 9as-siriir, raja°an. ween
   il-alam?
   *Lay down on the bed, please. Where is the
   pain?*

   طبيب: نامي عَ السّرير رجاءً. وين الألَـم؟

10. Basma: baţni tooja9ni hwaaya.
    My abdomen hurts a lot.

    بسمة: بَطْـني توجَـعْني هُـوايَه.

11. ţabiib: 9indich iltihaab mi9da.
    You have a stomach infection.

    طبيب: عِنْدِچ إلْتِهاب مِـعْـدَة.

12. Basma: raḥ-tintiini diwa?
    Are you going to give me medicine?

    بسمة: رَح تِنْطيني دِوَا؟

13. ţabiib: na9am. haadhi wasfat hubuub
    antibaayootiks
    *Yes. This is a prescription for antibiotic
    tablets.*

    طبيب: نعم. هاذي وَصْفَـة حُبُوب أنْتي بايوتيكِـس.

14. Basma: kam habbaaya aakhudh
    bil-yoom?
    How many tablets should I take every day?

    بسمة: كَم حَـبّاية آخُـذ بالْيوم؟

15. ţabiib: tlath hubuub bil-yoom,
    il-muddat usbuu9.
    *Three tablets a day, for a period of one
    week.*

    طبيب: تلاث حُبُوب بالْيوم. إلْـمُـدَّة اُسْبـوع.

16. Basma: shukran jaziilan diktoor.
    Thank you very much, doctor.

    بسمة: شكراً جزيلاً دِكْتُور.

Additional Medical Expressions (Audio)

9iyaada / 9iyaadaat	*clinic/s*	عِـيادة / عِـيادات
ahtaaj ţabiib.	*I need a doctor.*	أَحْـتاج طبيب
haala mista9jila / idtiraariyya	*It is an emergency.*	حالَـة مِسْـتَـعْجِـلة / إضْـطِراريّـة
is9aaf	*emergency*	إسْعاف
sayyaarat is9aaf	*ambulance*	سَـيّارة إسْعاف
haaditha	*accident*	حادِثَـة
iltihaab 9een	*eye infection*	إلْتِهاب عـين
iltihaab idhin	*ear infection*	إلْتِهاب إذِن

s khuuna	*fever*	صُخونَة
9indi s khuuna	*I have a fever.*	عِنْدي صُخونَة
9indi nashla	*I have a cold.*	عِنْدي نَشْلَة
9indi gahha	*I have a cough.*	عِندي گَحَّة
gatra	*drops*	گَطْرَة
gatrat idhin	*ear drops*	گَطْرَة إِذِن
gatrat 9een	*eye drops*	گَطْرَة عين
hubuub musakkina	*pain killers*	حُبوب مُسَكِّنة
hubuub munawwima	*sleeping pills*	حُبوب مُنَوِّمَة
sinn / asnaan	*tooth / teeth*	سِنّ / أَسْنان
sihha	*health*	صِحَّة
9amaliyya / 9amaliyyaat	*operation/s, surgery/s*	عَمَلِيَّة / عَمَلِيّات
fahis	*check up, examination*	فَحِص
fihas, yifhas (RV)	*to check up, to examine*	فِحَص، يِفْحَص
tabiib asnaan	*dentist*	طَبيب أَسْنان
wija9 asnaan	*toothache*	وِجَع أَسْنان
wija9 zahar	*back pain*	وِجَع ظَهَر
wija9 galub	*chest (heart) pain*	وِجَع گَلُب
saydaliyya	*pharmacy*	صَيْدَلِيّة
saydali	*pharmacist*	صَيْدَلي
mustashfa / mustashfayaat	*hospital/s*	مُسْتَشْفى / مُسْتَشْفَيات

Vocabulary (Audio)

9inaaya	*treatment*	عِنايَة
tibb	*medical science*	طِبّ
tibbi / tibbiyya (M/F adj.)	*medical*	طِبّي / طِبِّيَّة
tabiib / atibbaa° (S/P)	*doctor/s (refers to physician only)*	طَبيب / أَطِبّاء
diktoor / dakaatra (S/P)	*doctor/s (refers to any type of doctor)*	دِكْتور / دَكاتْرَة
sh-biich?	*What is wrong? (lit. What's in you?)*	شْبيچ؟
ahiss	*I feel*	أَحِسّ
wija9 / awjaa9 (S/P)	*pain/s*	وِجَع ، أَوْجاع
wija9 raas	*headache*	وِجَع راس
raas / ruus	*head/s*	راس / روس
a9raad	*symptoms*	أَعْراض
gabul	*before, ago*	گَبُل
halig	*mouth*	حَلِگ
halgich	*your mouth*	حَلْگِچ

tal9i (imp. v. F)	*bring out*	طَـلْـعـي
lisaan / alsina (S/P)	*tongue/s*	لِـسـان / أَلْـسِـنة
mariid / mariida / mardaa (M/F/P)	*sick/s, ill/s* (adj.)	مَريض / مَريضة / مَرْضى
jisim / ajsaam (S/P)	*body/s*	جِـسِـم / أَجْـسام
kull	*all, whole*	كُـلّ
kulla	*all of it* (referring to the body)	كُـلّـه
yooja9	*It causes pain, it hurts.*	يوجَـع
yooja9ni	*It hurts me.*	يوجَـعْـني
haraara	*heat, temperature*	حَـرارة
9aalya	*high*	عالْـيَة
haraara 9aalya	*high temperature*	حَـرارة عالْـية
s khuuna	*fever*	صُـخونَـة
ukhdhi (imp. v. F)	*take*	أُخْـذي
nafas	*breath*	نَـفَـس
9amiiq	*deep*	عَـمـيـق
naami (imp. v. F)	*lie down, sleep*	نامي
alam / aalaam	*pain/s*	أَلَـم / آلام
batin	*abdomen, stomach*	بَـطِـن
iltihaab / iltihaabaat (S/P)	*infection/s*	إلْـتِهاب / إلْـتِهابات
mi9da / mi9ad	*stomach/s*	مِـعْـدَة / مِـعَـد
tintiini	*you (M) give me*	تِـنْطـيـني
duwa / adwiya (S/P)	*medicine/s*	دُوا / أدْوِية
wasfa	*prescription*	وَصْـفَـة
wasfat tabiib	*doctor's prescription*	وَصْـفَـة طَـبـيـب
habbaaya / hubuub (F/P), habb (col.)	*tablet/s, pill/s*	حَـبّـاية / حُـبوب. حَـبّ
aakhudh.	*I take*	آخُـذ
mudda	*period of time, while*	مُـدَّة

Some Additional Body Parts: (Audio)

Note that any part of the body which consists of two (e.g. two eyes, two hands, etc.) is generally feminine in Arabic.

arm	dhiraa9	ذِراع	*hair*	sha9ar	شَـعَر
blood	damm	دَمّ	*hand*	iid	إيـد
bone	9azum	عَظِـم	*knee*	rukba	رُكْـبَة
chest	sadir	صَدِر	*leg*	rijil	رجِـل
face	wajih	وَجِـه	*lip*	shiffa	شِـفّة
finger	isbi9	إضْبِع	*neck*	rugba	رُكْـبَة
foot	qadam	قَـدَم	*nose*	khashim	خَـشِـم

Grammar and Remarks

1. Ordinal Numbers First to Tenth:

The ordinal numbers in Iraqi Arabic are of two genders, masculine and feminine. Except for "first" the ordinal numbers have consistent forms. There are no ordinal numbers higher than tenth; the cardinal numbers are used instead. (Audio)

Numeral	Masculine	Feminine		
first	awwal	uulaa	أُولى	أوَّل
second	thaani	thaanya	ثانْيَة	ثاني
third	thaalith	thaaltha	ثالْثَة	ثالِث
fourth	raabi9	raab9a	رابْعَة	رابِع
fifth	khaamis	khaamsa	خامْسَة	خامِس
sixth	saadis	saadsa	سادْسَة	سادِس
seventh	saabi9	saab9a	سابْعَة	سابِع
eighth	thaamin	thaamna	ثامْنَة	ثامِن
ninth	taasi9	taas9a	تاسْعَة	تاسِع
tenth	9aashir	9aashra	عاشْرَة	عاشِر

Ordinal numbers may come either after or before nouns. After the noun they are regular adjectives and must agree with the noun in gender and in definiteness. Before the noun they must always be masculine singular and the noun indefinite although such phrases are definite in meaning. (Audio)

Masculine

taalib thaalith	*a third student*	طالب ثالِث
it-taalib ith-thaalith	*the third student*	إلطّالِب الثّالِث
maktab awwal	*a first office*	مَكْتب أوَّل
9aashir taalib	*the tenth student*	عاشِر طالِب
awwal maktab	*the first office*	أوَّل مَكْتب

Feminine

taaliba thaaltha	*a third student*	طالِبة ثالْثة
it-taaliba ith-thaaltha	*the third student*	إلطّالِبة الثّالْثة
maktaba uulaa	*a first library*	مَكْتبة أولى
9aashir taaliba	*the tenth student*	عاشِر طالِبة
awwal maktaba	*the first library*	أوَّل مَكْتبة

2. Cardinal Numbers Higher than 100

The words for "hundred, thousand, and million" are nouns and have three number forms: singular, dual, and plural (see lessons 5–7). (Audio)

miyya / miteen / miyyaat	one hundred/two hundred/ hundreds	مِيَّة / مِتـين / مِيـّات
alif / alfeen / aalaaf	one thousand/two thousand/ thousands	ألِـف / ألْـفين / آلاف
malyoon / malyooneen / malaayiin	one million/two million/ millions	مَلْـيون / مَلْـيونين / مَلايـيـن

Below are some examples with different numbers.

100	miyya	مِيَّة
101	miyya w waahid	مِيَّة وُواحِد
200	miiteen	مِيـتين
202	miiteen wi-thneen	مِيـتين وثـنين
300	tlath miyya	تْلَـث مِيَّة
310	tlath miyya w 9ashra	تْلَـث مِيَّة وعَشـرة
400	arba9 miyya	أرْبَـع مِيَّة
420	arba9 miyya w 9ishriin	أرْبَـع مِيَّة وعِشـرين
500	khamis miyya	خَـمِس مِيَّة
597	khamis miyya w sab9a w tis9iin	خَـمِس مِيَّة وسَبْـعة وتِسْـعين
600	sitt miyya	سِتّ مِيَّة
645	sitt miyya w khamsa w arba9iin	سِتّ مِيَّة وخَمْـسة وارْبَـعـين
700	sabi9 miyya	سَبـع مِيَّة
777	sabi9 miyya w sab9a w sab9iin	سَبـع مِيَّة وسَبْـعة وسَبْـعين
800	thman miyya	ثْمَـن مِيَّة
869	thman miyya w tis9a w sittiin	ثْمَـن مِيَّة وتِسْـعة وسِتَـيـن
900	tisi9 miyya	تِـسِـع مِيَّة
909	tisi9 miyya w tis9a	تِـسِـع مِيَّة وتِسْـعة

Note that the plural noun "taalaaf تالاف, thousands" is used only when the word is pre-ceded by one of the numbers 3–10.

1000	alif	ألِـف	1979	alif w tisi9 miyya w tis9a w sab9iin	ألِـف وتِـسِـع مِيَّة وتِسْـعة وسَبْـعين
2000	alfeen	ألْـفـين	2105	alfeen w miyya w khamsa	ألْـفـين ومِيَّة وخَـمْسَة
3000	tlat taalaaf	تْلَـت تالاف	3012	tlat taalaaf w thna9ash	تْلَـت تالاف وثْنَـعَـش
4000	arba9 taalaaf	أرْبَـع تالاف	4520	arba9 taalaaf w khamis miyya w 9ishriin	أرْبَـع تالاف وخَـمِس مِيَّة وعشـرين

5000	hkamis taalaaf	خَـمِس تالاف	5066	khamis taalaaf w sitta w sittiin	خَمِس تالاف وسِـتّـة وسِـتّـين
6000	sitt taalaaf	سِتّ تالاف	6004	sitt taalaaf w arba9a	سِتّ تالاف وارْبَـعَـة
7000	sabi9 taalaaf	سَبِـع تالاف	7900	sabi9 taalaaf w tisi9 miyya	سَبِـع تالاف وتِسِع مِيَّـة
8000	thman taalaaf	ثَـمَن تالاف	8751	thman taalaaf w sabi9 miyya w waahid w khamsiin	ثَـمَن تالاف وسَبِـع مِيَّـة وواحِد وخَـمُسـين
9000	tisi9 taalaaf	تِـسِـع تالاف	9225	tisi9 taalaaf w miteen w khamsa w 9ishriin	تِسِع تالاف ومِـيـتـين وخَـمُسَـة وعِـشْـرين

10,000	9ashir taalaaf	عَـشِـر تالاف
11,000	da9ash alf	دَعَـش ألـف
1,000,000	malyoon	مَـلْـيون
2,000,000	malyooneen	مَـلْـيونين
3,000,000	tlath malaayiin	تْـلَـث مَـلايِــيـن
4,000,000	arba9 malaayiin	أرْبَـع مَـلايِــيـن
5,000,000	khamis malaayiin	خَـمِس مَـلايِــيـن
6,000,000	sitt malaayiin	سِتّ مَـلايِــيـن
7,000,000	sabi9 malaayiin	سَبِـع مَـلايِــيـن
8,000,000	thman malaayiin	ثَـمَن مَـلايِــيـن
9,000,000	tisi9 malaayiin	تِـسِـع مَـلايِــيـن
10,000,000	9ashir malaayiin	عَـشِـر مَـلايِــيـن
one billion/two billions/ billions	milyaar / milyaareen / milyaaraat	مِلْـيار / مِلْـيارين / مِلْـيارات

3. Counting: hsaab   حُـسـاب

The Arabic system of counting (objects/nouns) requires attention from the student because of its number forms (S/D/P). Below are counting tables for two nouns (M and F). (Audio)

walad/wilid (M)	*boy/s*	وَلَـد / ولِـد
saa9a/saa9at (F)	*watch/s*	ساعَة / ساعات

Number			**Counting Masculine Nouns**	
1 waahid	واحِـد		walad (waahid)	وَلَـد (واحِد)
2 thneen	ثْـنين		waladeen	وَلَـدين
3 tlaatha	تَـلاثة		tlath wilid	تْـلَـث ولِـد

4	arba9a	أَرْبَعة	arba9 wilid	أربع ولِد
5	khamsa	خَمْسة	khamis wilid	خَمِس ولِد
6	sitta	سِتّة	sitt wilid	سِتّ ولِد
7	sab9a	سَبْعة	sabi9 wilid	سَبِع ولِد
8	thmaanya	ثَمانية	thman wilid	ثَمَن ولِد
9	tis9a	تِسْعَة	tisi9 wilid	تِسِع ولِد
10	9ashra	عَشْرَة	9ashir wilid	عَشِر ولِد
11	da9ash	دَعَش	da9ash walad	دَعَش وَلَد
12	thna9ash	ثْناعَش	thna9ash walad	ثْناعَش وَلَد
13	tlat-ta9ash	تْلاطَّعَش	tlat-ta9ash walad	تْلاطَّعَش وَلَد
14	arbaa-ta9ash	أرباطَعَش	arbaa-ta9ash walad	أرباطَعَش وَلَد

Counting Feminine Nouns

saa9a (wihda)	ساعة (وحُدَة)
saa9teen	ساعْتين
tlath saa9aat	تْلَث ساعات
arba9 saa9aat	أربع ساعات
khamis saa9aat	خَمِس ساعات
sitt saa9aat	سِتّ ساعات
sabi9 saa9aat	سَبِع ساعات
thman saa9aat	ثَمَن ساعات
tisi9 saa9aat	تِسِع ساعات
9ashir saa9aat	عَشِر ساعات
da9ash saa9a	دَعَش ساعة
thna9ash saa9a	ثْناعَش ساعة
tlat-ta9ash saa9a	تْلاطَّعَش ساعة
arbaa-ta9ash saa9a	أرباطَعَش ساعة

100	miyya	مِيَّة	miit walad	مِيت وَلَد
			miit saa9a	مِيت ساعة
200	miiteen	مِيتين	miiteen walad	مِيتين وَلَد
			miiteen saa9a	مِيتين ساعة
300	tlath miyya	تْلَث مِيَّة	tlath miit walad	تْلَث مِيت وَلَد
			tlath miit saa9a	تْلَث مِيت ساعة
400	arba9 miyya	أربع مِيَّة	arba9 miit walad	أربع مِيت وَلَد
			arba9 miit saa9a (to 900)	أربع مِيت ساعة
101	miyya w waahid	مِيَّة وواحِد	miit walad w walad	مِيت ولَد وولَد
			miit saa9a w saa9a	مِيت ساعة وساعة
102	miyya wi-thneen	مِيَّة وثْنين	miit walad w waladeen	مِيت ولَد وولَدين
			miit saa9a w saa9teen	مِيت ساعة وساعْتين
103	miyya wi-tlaatha	مِيَّة وثلاثة	miyya w tlath wilid	مِيَّة وتْلَث ولِد
			miyya w tlath saa9aat (to 110)	مِيَّة وتْلَث ساعات

Notes on Counting:

1. One (واحِد) and two (ثنـين) have exceptional forms, which are different from the more consistent numbers three to ten.

2. To say "one boy," only the word for boy needs to be uttered, although the number one "**waahid** واحِد" or "**wiḥda** وِحُدة ," depending on the gender of the word, can be added after the noun.

3. Counting two of one kind, there is a special dual form in Arabic, which is made by adding the suffix "**-een** or **-teen** يِن. تين" to the singular noun, masculine and feminine, respectively (see Lesson 5).

4. The counted noun is plural only from three to ten. Then from eleven and higher the noun must be singular again.

5. When counting from three to ten, the vowel ending "**a**" of the independent number must be omitted (see above). There are also other dropping, shifting and assimilation.

6. The independent number one hundred "**miyya** مِـيَّة" becomes "**miit** مِيت" in counting.

Idioms and Common Phrases (Audio)

1. sh-bii + attached pronoun? شِـبـيـي ؟ +   *What's wrong with (him)? (lit. What's in him?)*

sh-bii Salmaan?	*What's wrong with Salman?*	شِـبـيه سَـلمـان؟
sh-biiha Samiira il-yoom?	*What's wrong with Samiira today?*	شِـبـيـها سَميرة اليـوم؟
sh-biihum it-tullaab?	*What's wrong with the students?*	شِـبـيـهم الطُّـلّاب؟
sh-biik? leesh inta bil-mustashfa?	*What's wrong with you* (M)? *Why are you in the hospital?*	شِـبـيـك؟ ليش إنت بالـمُـسـتـشـفى؟

2. 9afya 9alee + attached pronoun عَـفْـيـه عَـلـي +   *Good for (him), bravo*

9afya 9aleek, tiḥ chi 9arabi zeen	*Good for you* (M), *you speak good Arabic.*	عَـفْـيـه عَـلـيك. تِـحْـچي عربي زين
9afya 9aleech, tudursiin bij-jaami9a	*Good for you* (F), *you are studying at the university.*	عَـفْـيـه عَـلـيـچ. تُـدُرسين بالجـامعة
9afya 9alee, siḥḥta kullish zeena	*Good for him, his health is very good.*	عَـفْـيـه عَـلـيه. صِحْـتـه كُـلّـش زينة
9afya 9aleeha, faazat bis-sibaaq	*Bravo, she won in the competition.*	عَـفْـيـه عَـلـيـها. فازَت بالسِّـبـاق

3. balkat, balki بَـلْـكَـتْ، بَـلْـكـي   *Perhaps, may (invariable)*

balkat yiji ba9ad shwayya	*Perhaps he will come shortly.*	بَـلْـكَـتْ يـجي بَـعَـد شْـوَيّـة
balki yruuḥuun ydursuun b-Baghdaad	*They may go to study in Baghdad.*	بَـلْـكـي يُـروحون يُـدُرسـون بْ بغداد
laazim ashuufa hissa, balkat ysaafir il-yoom	*I must see him now, he may travel today.*	لازم أشوفه هِـسّـه. بَـلْـكَـتْ يُسـافِر اليوم
balkat tshuufhum bil-9iraaq	*You may see them in Iraq.*	بَـلْـكَـتْ تْـشـوفْـهُم بالعراق

Drill   tamaariin   تَمارين

1. Give appropriate oral replies to the following:

sh-biiha Basma?	شْبيها بسمة؟
shunu yooja9 Basma?	شُنُو يوجَع بسمة؟
it-tabiib mara loo rijjaal?	إلطّبيب مَرَة لو رِجّال؟
sh-gaal it-tabiib lil-Basma	شْگَال الطّبيب لْ بسمة؟
sh-nita it-tabiib il-Basma?	شْنِطَه الطّبيب لْ بسمة؟
kam habbaaya taakhudh Basma bil-yoom?	كم حَبّاية تاخُذ بسمة باليوم؟
shgadd muddat id-diwa?	شْگَد مُدَّة الدّوا؟
Basma chaan 9idha iltihaab mi9da loo idhin?	بسمة چان عِدُها إلْتِهاب مِعْدة لو إذِن؟
ween Basma zaarat it-tabiib?	وين بسمة زارت الطّبيب؟
it-tabiib huwwa tabiib asnaan loo tabiib 9iyuun?	إلطّبيب هو طبيب أسْنان لو طبيب عِيون؟
kam marra Basma raahat lit-tabiib?	كم مَرَّة بسمة راحَت لِـلـطّبيب؟

2. Answer the following with true or false "sahh aw khataᵓ":

it-tabiib gaal l-Basma, "naami 9as-siriir."	إلطّبيب گال لْ بسمة "نامي عَ السّرير."
Basma ihtaajat tabiib 9iyuun.	بسمة إحْتاجَت طبيب عِيون.
Basma zaarat it-tabiib bil-mustashfa.	بسمة زارَت الطّبيب بالمُسْتَشْفى.
it-tabiib nita Basma hubuub munawwima.	إلطّبيب نطَا بسمة حُبوب مُنَوّمة.
Basma chaan 9idha gahha w-iltihaab idhin.	بسمة چان عِدُها گَحَّة والْتِهاب إذِن.
Basma chaanat kullish mariida.	بسمة چانت كُلِّش مَريضة.
Basma chaan 9idha wija9 raas w ta9baana.	بسمة چان عِدُها وجَع راس وتَعْبانة.
Basma zaarat it-tabiib marteen.	بسمة زارَت الطّبيب مَرّتين.
Basma zaarat it-tabiib awwal marra.	بسمة زارَت الطّبيب أوَّل مَرَّة.
Basma naamat usbuu9 bil-mustashfa.	بسمة نامَت أُسْبوع بالمُسْتَشْفى.
Basma raahat b-sayyaarat is9aaf lit-tabiib.	بسمة راحَت بْ سَيّارة إسْعاف لِـلـطّبيب.

3. Fill in the blanks of the following:

Saami zaar it-tabiib b- _____	_____ سامي زار طبيب بْ
diktoor aani mariid, w jismi kulla _____	_____ دِكْتور آني مَريض، وجِسْمي كُلّـه
shwakit _____ 9indich haadhi l-a9raad?	شْوَكِت _____ عِنْدِچ هاذي الأعْراض؟
aani 9indi wija9 _____ w-iltihaab _____	_____ والْتِهاب _____ آني عِنْدي وجَع
iftah halgak w talli9 _____	_____ إفْتَح حَلْگَك وطَلّع
Maryam tabiiba _____ mustashfa	مَرْيَم طبيبة _____ مُسْتَشْفى

9afya 9aleek, sihhtak _____ zeena

عَفْـيَه عليك. صِحُتك _____ زينة

9afya 9leekum, _____ lahja 9iraaqiyya

عَفْـيَه عَليكم، _____ لَـهْجَة عراقِـيَّة

_____ is9aaf _____ mustashfa

_____ إسْعاف _____ مُسْتَـشْـفى

Basma ma-shaafat _____ asnaan

بسـمة مَ شـافت _____ أسْنان

4. Say the following numbers in Arabic:

1995	the first month	the first student (F)
1988	the second year	the tenth car
2765	the fifth hospital on the right	1,000,100
400	the fifth chair in the classroom	10,000
545	the first, second, and third lessons	2,000,000
900	the seventh house on the left	200
3000	the tenth visit	600
1001	the fourth season	1,000,001
1002	the third exam	1,000,010

5. Count the following in Arabic:

1 doctor	2 doctors	10 doctors
1 hospital	3 hospitals	100 hospitals
1 ambulance	2 ambulances	200 ambulances
5 pills	10 tablets	2000 tablets
100 books	300 books	3000 books
1001 nights	365 days in the year	4 seasons in the year
12 months in the year	2005 years	100,000 universities in America
6,000 students	10 students	2 students (F)
600 miles	4 + 6 = 10	17 − 10 = 7

6. Complete and read aloud:

a. sh-bii il-yoom?   شـْبـِي الـيـوم؟

sh-biik _____?   ؟_____ شـْبـِيك

sh-biich _____?   ؟_____ شـْبـِيـچ

sh-biikum _____?   ؟_____ شـْبـِـيـكم

sh-bii _____?   ؟_____ شـْبـِـيـه

sh-biiha _____ ?	؟_____ شْـبِـيها
sh-biihum _____ ?	؟ _____ شْـبِـيهم
sh-biiyya _____ ?	؟_____ شْـبِـيَّـا
sh-biina _____ ?	؟_____ شْـبِـينا

b. 9afya 9alee, yitkallam w yiqra 9arabi   عَفْـيَـه عليه. يِـتْـكَـلَّـم ويِـقْـرَا عربي

     9afya 9aleeha, _____   _____ عَفْـيَـه عليها

     9afya 9aleehum, _____   _____ عَفْـيَـه عليهم

     9afya 9aleek, _____   _____ عَفْـيَـه عليك

     9afya 9aleech, _____   _____ عَفْـيَـه عليچ

     9afya 9aleekum, _____   _____ عَفْـيَـه عليكم

c. aani baaqi hnaa, balki yjuun ba9ad shwayya   آني باقي هُنا. بَـلْـكي يْجون بَعَـد شْـوَيّة

     ihna _____   _____ إحنا

     inta _____   _____ إنت

     inti _____   _____ إنتي

     intu _____   _____ إنتو

     huwwa _____   _____ هو

     hiyya _____   _____ هي

     humma _____   _____ هُـمَّـه

7. Make questions of the following sentences, using the appropriate form of "sh-bii?

؟"شْـبِـي":

Example: huwwa chaan mariid il-baarha.   هو چان مَريض البارْحة

        sh-bii chaan huwwa il-baarha?   شْـبِـيه چان هو البارْحَة؟

hiyya chaanat mariida il-baarha.   هي چانت مَريضة البارْحَة

humma <u>ch</u>aanaw mar<u>d</u>aa il-baar<u>h</u>a.	هُـمَّه چانَـوْ مَرْضى البارْحَة
inta <u>ch</u>init mariid il-baar<u>h</u>a.	إنت چِـنِـت مَريض البارْحَة
inti <u>ch</u>inti mariida il-baar<u>h</u>a.	إنتي چِـنْتـي مَريضة البارْحَة
intu <u>ch</u>intu mar<u>d</u>aa il-baar<u>h</u>a.	إنتو چِـنْتـو مَرْضى البارْحَة
aani <u>ch</u>init mariid il-baar<u>h</u>a.	آني چِـنِـت مَريض البارْحَة
aani <u>ch</u>init mariida il-baar<u>h</u>a.	آني چِـنِـت مَريضة البارْحَة
i<u>h</u>na <u>ch</u>inna mar<u>d</u>aa il-baar<u>h</u>a.	إحنا چِـنّـا مَرْضى البارْحَة

8. Put the following present tense sentences into past tense and translate them into English:

Kamaal ta9baan w yruu<u>h</u> lit-<u>t</u>abiib   كمـال تَـعْبان ويـروح لِـلـطّـبيب

---

aani mariid w aruu<u>h</u> lil-musta<u>sh</u>fa   آني مَريض وأروح لِـلْـمُسْـتَـشْـفى

---

huwwa da-yzuur it-<u>t</u>abiib bil-9iyaada   هو دَ يْـزور الطّـبيب بالْـعِـيادة

---

maktab it-<u>t</u>abiib bi9iid min beeti   مَكْـتَـب الطّـبيب بِـعيد مِن بـيتي

9afya 9aleekumm, tudursuun 9arab kull yoom   عَفْـيَه عليكم تُـدُرْسون عربي كُـل يوم

<u>sh</u>-biiha, lee<u>sh</u> hiyya raay<u>h</u>a lil-musta<u>sh</u>fa?   شِـبيها. ليش هي رايْـحَـة لِـلْـمُسْتَـشـفى؟

9indi haraara 9aalya w-iltihaab mi9da   عِـنْدي حَـرارة عالْـيَة والْـتِـهاب مِعْـدَة

---

nruu<u>h</u> lil-musta<u>sh</u>fa, <u>h</u>aala mista9jila   نْـروح لِـلْـمُسْتَـشفى، حالة مِـسْتَـعْجِـلة

Waliid saakin wiyya ahla bil-Mansuur   وليد ساكِـن وِيّـه أهْلَـه بالْـمَنْصور

---

azuurkum yoom ij-jum9a, in<u>sh</u>aalla   أزورْكُـم يوم الجُـمْـعَـة. إنْـشالله

---

9. Translate the following into Arabic:

Please lie down on the bed there.

_____

Basma is buying medicine at the pharmacy.

_____

You have a fever and stomach infection.

_____

Take one tablet a day for one week.

_____

I have a severe pain in my back.

_____

The hospital is not very far; it's near is-Safaafiir Market.

_____

She was the third girl in the class.

_____

Open (M) your mouth and put your tongue out.

_____

1,100,350 students

_____

There are about 200 doctors in the hospital

_____

Samiira was sick and stayed in the hospital for 4 weeks.

_____

The doctor gave me drops for my eyes and ears yesterday.

_____

I take sleeping pills every night.

_____

Last year was 2005 and this year is 2006.

_____

The year has 4 seasons, 12 months, 52 weeks, and 365 days.

_____

The doctor checks up on the patients in the hospital.

_____

They have good health, praise God.

_____

I am going to the doctor's office at 10:30.

_____

Creative Dialogues

a. taalib 1: ahiss ta9baan hwaaya

طالب 1: أحِسَّ تعبان هُـوايَه

taaliba 2: sh-biik? kheer inshaalla

طالبة 2: شْـبيك؟ خير إنْشـالله

taalib 1: ahtaaj tabiib yih chi Ingiliizi

طالب 1: أحْتاج طبيب يـحْچي إنْگـليزي

taaliba 2: aani a9ruf tabiib kullish zeen, w 9iyaadta qariiba

طالبة 2: آني أعْرُف طبيب كُـلّـش زين، وعِيادْتَه قَـريبة

taalib 1: yalla, khalli nruuh bil-9ajal, alla ykhalliich

طالب 1: يَـلّـه، خَـلّـي نْروح بالـعَجَل، الله يْـخَـلّـيـچ

taaliba 2: 9ala 9eeni. inshaalla inta muu kullish mariid

طالبة 2: على عيني. إنْشالله انت مو كُـلّـش مَريض

taalib 1: maa a9ruf, balkat it-tabiib yu9ruf

طالب 1: ما اعْرُف. بَـلْكَـت الطّـبيب يُعْرُف

taaliba 2: khalli asaa9dak, sihtak muu zeena

طالبة 2: خَـلّـي اساعْدَك، صِحْـتَـك مو زينة

taalib 1: sahih, shukran jaziilan

طالب 1: صَحـيح، شـكراً جزيلاً

taaliba 2: 9afwan

طالبة 2: عَفْـواً

b. taalib 1: ariid waahid ysaa9idni

طالب 1: أريـد واحِـد يُـساعِدْني

taaliba 2: aani asaa9dak. sh-biik?

طالبة 2: آني أساعْـدَك. شْـبيك؟

taalib 1: aani kullish mariid, ariid sayyaarat is9aaf

طالب 1: آني كُـلّـش مريض. أريد سَـيّارة إسْعاف

taaliba 2: hissa, akhaaburlak sayyaarat is9aaf

طالبة 2: هِـسّـه أخابُـرْلَك سَيّارة إسْعاف

taalib 1:	sayyaara durbatni. rijli maksuura	طالب 1: سَيّارة ضُرُبَتـْني. رِجْـلـي مَكـْسـورة
taaliba 2:	la-titharrak! ug9ud hnaa!	طالبة 2: لَـتِـتـْحَـرّك! اُكـْعُـد هُـنا!
taalib 1:	shwakit toosal sayyaarat l-is9aaf?	طالب 1: شـْوَكِـت توصَل سّـيّارة الإسْـعاف؟
taaliba 2:	wislat is-sayyaara. laazim aakh dhak lil-mustashfa	طالبة 2: وصْلَت السّـيّارة. لازم آخْـذك لِـلـْمُسْـتَـشـْفى
taalib 1:	shukran hwaaya 9ala musaa9adtich	طالب 1: شـكراً هُـوايَه على مُساعَـدْتِـچ

For new words, see Glossary.

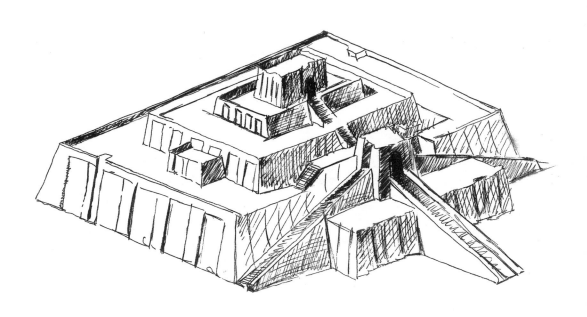

Ziggurat (staged monument) built by King Ur–Nammu (2112 B.C.), ancient Ur, the city of Abraham

DARIS THMUN-TA9ASH   دَرِس ثُـمُنْطَـعَـش

Media: Radio, Television, and Journalism

i9laam: raadyo, talfizyoon w sahaafa   إعْـلام: رادْيُـو وتَـلـئِـفِـزْيُـون وصَحافَة

Basma is visiting a radio and TV station in Baghdad. She is being given a tour of the station by its director.

Basic Dialogue (Audio)

1. mudiir: ahlan w sahlan bil-mahatta
   il-9iraaqiyya.
   Welcome to il-9iraaqiyya station.

   مُدير: أهْـلاً وسَـهْلاً بالـئَمَحَـطَّة العراقية.

2. Basma: shukran jaziilan.
   Thank you very much.

   بسـمة: شــكراً جــزيلاً.

3. mudiir: haadha qisim il-akhbaar
   bil-lugha il-9arabiyya wil-Ingiliiziyya.
   This is the news section in Arabic and English.

   مُدير: هاذا قِـسِم الأخْبـار بالـئَلُـغة العربية والإنـگِـليزية.

4. Basma: kam nashra akhbaariyya
   tdhii9uun bil-yoom?
   How many news bulletins do you broadcast a day?

   بسـمة: كم نَـشْـرة أخْبـارية تْـذيعون بِـالـئيـوم؟

5. mudiir: arba9 nashraat akhbaariyya
   bil-yoom.
   Four news bulletins a day.

   مُدير: أربع نَـشْـرات أخْـبـارية بِـالـئيـوم.

6. Basma: b-ayy waqit?
   At what time?

   بسـمة: بُأي وَقِـت؟

7. mudiir: <u>s</u>abaa<u>h</u>an w <u>z</u>uhran w 9a<u>s</u>ran w masaaʾan.

   In the morning, noon, afternoon, and evening.

مُدير: صَباحاً وظُهْراً وَعَصْراً ومَساءً.

8. Basma: 9idkum qisim tarjama?

   Do you have a translation section?

بَسمة: عِـدْكم قِسِم تَرْجَمَة؟

9. mudiir: tab9an, 9idna qisim kabiir lit-tarjama wit-ta<u>h</u>riir.

   Of course, we have a large section for translation and editing.

مُدير: طَبْعاً، عِـدْنا قِسِم كَبِير لِـلْتَرْجَمَة والـتَّحْرير.

10. Basma: 9idkum a<u>kh</u>baar b-lu<u>gh</u>aat ajnabiyya?

    Do you have news in foreign languages?

بَسمة: عِـدْكم أخبار بُـلُـغات أُجنَبِـيَّة؟

11. mudiir: na9am. 9idna a<u>kh</u>baar b-9iddat lu<u>gh</u>aat.

    Yes. We have news in a number of languages.

مُدير: نعم. عِـدْنا أخبار بِـعِـدَّة لُغات.

12. Basma: ayy noo9 baraamij t<u>dh</u>ii9uun?

    What types of programs do you broadcast?

بَسمة: أي نوع بَـرامِـج تُـذيعون؟

13. mudiir: baraamij mu<u>kh</u>talifa, siyaasiyya, w-iqti<u>s</u>aadiyya, w-ijtimaa9iyya, w <u>h</u>a<u>d</u>aariyya, w diniyya, w ta<u>th</u>qifiyya, w fanniyya.

    Different programs, political, economical, social, cultural, religious, educational, and artistic.

مُدير: بَـرامِـج مُـخْـتَـلِـفَـة سِـياسِـيّـة واقْتِصادِيّة وَحَضارِيّـة ودينِـيّـة وتَـثْـقـيـفِـيّة وفَـنَـيّـة.

14. Basma: maa<u>sh</u>aalla, 9idkum baraamij hwaaya.

    Praise be to God, you have many programs.

بَسمة: ماشالله. عِـدْكم بَـرامِـج هْوايَه.

15. mudiir: w 9idna muqaabalaat ka<u>th</u>iira ma9a masʾuuliin bil-<u>h</u>ukuuma.

    And we have many interviews with government authorities.

مُدير: وعِـدْنا مُقابَلات كَـثيرة مَعَ مَسْـؤولين بالْحُكـومَة.

16. Basma: shukran jaziilan 9ala hal-ma9luumaat.

    Thank you for this information.

بَسمة: شـكراً جَزيلاً على هَلْ مَعْـلومات.

17. mudiir: ahlan w sahlan aanisa Basma. <u>sh</u>arraftiina bi-zyaartich.

    Welcome Miss Basma. You honored us with your visit.

مُدير: أهلاً وسَـهْلاً آنِـسَة بَـسمة. شَـرَّفْـتـينا بِـزْيارْتِج.

Vocabulary (Audio)

i9laam	media	إعْـلام
raadyo	radio	راديو
idhaa9a / idhaa9aat (S/P)	radio station/s	إذاعَـة / إذاعات
talfizyoon / talfizyoonaat (S/P)	televisions/s	تَـلْـفِـزيون / تَـلْـفِـزيونات
sahaafa	press, journalism	صَحافَـة
sahafi / sahafiyya (M/F)	journalist	صَحَفـي / صَحَفِـيّة
mudiir / mudaraaʾ (S/P)	director/s, manager/s	مُدير / مُـدَراء
mahatta / mahattaat (S/P)	station/s (all kinds of stations)	مَـحَطّة / مَـحَطّـات
qisim / aqsaam (S/P)	section/s, division/s, department/s	قِسِـم / أقْسـام
qisim il-akhbaar	news section	قِسِم الأخْـبار
nashra / nashraat (S/P)	bulletin/s	نَـشْـرة / نَـشْـرات
nashra akhbaariyya	news bulletin	نَـشْـرة أخْبارية
tdhii9uun (HV)	You (P) broadcast.	تَـذيعـون
b-ayy?	at what?	بِـأيْ؟
waqit	time	وَقِـت
sabaahan (adv.)	in the morning	صَباحاً
zuhran (adv.)	at noon time	ظُهْـراً
9asran (adv.)	in the afternoon	عَـصْراً
masaaʾan (adv.)	at night	مَـساءً
tarjama / tarjamaat (S/P)	translation/s	تَـرْجَمَة / تَـرْجَمات
qisim tarjama	translation section	قِسِم تَـرْجَمة
tahriir	editing	تَـحْرير
muharrir	editor	مُـحَـرِّر
raʾiis qisim it-tahriir	editor-in-chief	رَئيس قِسِـم التَـحْرير
lugha / lughaat ajnabiyya	foreign language/s	لـُغَـة / لُـغات أجْـنَـبِـية
9idda	a number of, several	عِـدَّة
9iddat lughaat	a number of languages	عِـدَّة لُـغات
noo9 / anwaa9	type/s, kind/s	نوع / أنْـواع
barnaamij / baraamij	program/s	بَـرْنامِج / بَـرامِج
siyaasa	politics	سِـياسَـة
siyaasi / siyaasiyya (M/F adj.)	political	سِـياسي / سِـياسِـيّة
iqtisaad	economics	إقْـتِصاد
iqtisaadi / iqtisaadiyya (M/F adj.)	economical	إقْـتِصادي / إقْـتِصاديّة
ijtimaa9	meeting	إجْـتِماع
ijtimaa9i / ijtimaa9iyya (M/F adj.)	social	إجْـتِماعي / إجْـتِـماعِـيّة
hadaara	culture	حَـضارة
hadaari / hadaariyya (M/F adj.)	cultural	حَـضاري / حَـضاريّـة

thaqaafa	*education*	ثَقافة
tathqiifi / tathqiifiyya (M/F adj.)	*educational*	ثَقافِي / ثَقافِيَّة
diin / adyaan (S/P)	*religion/s*	دِين / أُدْيان
diini / diiniyya (M/F adj.)	*religious*	دِينِي / دِينِيَّة
fann / funuun (S/P)	*art/s*	فَنّ / فُنون
fanni / fanniyya (M/F adj.)	*artistic*	فَنّي / فَنِّيَّة
muqaabala / muqaabalaat (S/P)	*meeting/s, interview/s*	مُقابَلة / مُقابَلات
mas'uul / mas'uuliin (S/P)	*authority/s, person/s in charge*	مَسْؤول / مَسْؤولين
mas'uul hukuuma	*government official*	مَسْؤول حُكومة
hukuuma / hukuumaat (S/P)	*government/s*	حُكومة / حُكومات
ma9luumaat	*information*	مَعْلومات
aanisa / aanisaat (S/P)	*Miss/s*	آنِسَة / آنِسات
sayyida / sayyidaat (S/P)	*Mrs.*	سَيِّدَة / سَيِّدات
sharraftiina	*You (F) honored us.*	شَرَّفْتِينا
bi-zyaartich	*with your (F) visit*	بِزْيارتِج

Additional Vocabulary on Media (Audio)

akhbaar mahalliyya	*national news*	أخْبار مَحَلِّيَّة
akhbaar 9aalamiyya	*international news*	أخْبار عالَمِيَّة
mudhii9 / mudhii9a (M/F)	*broadcaster*	مُذيع / مُذيعَة
muraasil / muraasila (M/F)	*reporter, correspondent*	مُراسِل / مُراسِلة
muraasil ajnabi	*foreign reporter/correspondent*	مُراسِل أجْنَبي
majalla / majallaat (S/P)	*magazine/s*	مَجَلّة / مَجَلّات
jariida / jaraayid (S/P)	*newspaper/s*	جَريدة / جَرايد
sahiifa / suhuf (S/P)	*newspaper/s*	صَحيفة / صُحُف
barnaamij talfizyooni	*television program*	بَرْنامِج تَلْفِزْيوني
musalsala talfizyooniyya	*television series*	مُسَلْسَلة تَلْفِزْيونيّة
taqriir sahafi	*journalistic report*	تَقْرير صَحَفي
qanaat / qanawaat	*(TV) channel/s*	قَناة / قَنَوات
hurriyya / hurriyyaat	*freedom/s*	حُرِّيَة / حُرِّيّات

Grammar and Remarks
Comparative and Superlative:

The comparatives and the superlatives such as "taller, tallest," are predictable in Iraqi Arabic. They are usually derived from adjectives of associated meanings. They are invariable in form with no gender or number. The difference between the comparative and the superlative adjectives is in the structuring of the sentence. (Audio)

Adjectives			Comparatives/Superlatives		
kabiir	*big*	كَبِير	akbar	*bigger, biggest*	أكْبَر
saghiir	*small*	صَغير	asghar	*small, smallest*	أصْغَر
bi9iid	*far*	بِعـيـد	ab9ad	*farther, farthest*	أبْعَد
tiwiil	*tall, long*	طِويل	atwal	*taller, tallest, longer, longest*	أطْوَل
qasiir	*short*	قَـصير	aqsar	*shorter, shortest*	أقْـصَر
tayyib	*tasty*	طَـيّب	atyab	*tastier, tastiest*	أطْـيَب
jidiid	*new*	جِـديد	ajdad	*newer, newest*	أجْـدَد
qadiim	*old*	قَـديم	aqdam	*older, oldest*	أقْـدَم
sarii9	*fast*	سَريع	asra9	*faster, fastest*	أسْرَع
batii°	*slow*	بَطيء	abta°	*slower, slowest*	أبْطَـىء
kathiir	*much*	كَـثير	akthar	*more, most*	أكْثَر
qaliil	*little*	قَـليل	aqall	*less, least*	أقَـل
rikhiis	*cheap*	رخيص	arkhas	*cheaper, cheapest*	أرْخَص
ghaali	*expensive*	غالي	aghla	*more expensive, most expensive*	أغْـلى

1. Comparative: (Audio)

sayyaarti arkhas	*My car is cheaper.*	سَـيّارتي أرْخَـص
barnaamij atwal	*a longer program*	بَـرْنـامِـج أطْـوَل
Baabil aqdam	*Babylon is older.*	بابِل أقْـدَم

When two objects are compared, the preposition "**min مِــن**" is used, which is the equivalent of "than" in English in such constructions.

Laylaa akbar min Basma	*Laylaa is older than Basma*	ليلى أكْبَـر مِن بسمة
beetna asghar min beetkum	*Our house is smaller than your house.*	بيتْـنا أصْغَـر مِن بيتكم
Baabil aqdam min Baghdaad	*Babylon is older than Baghdad.*	بابِل أقْـدَم مِن بغداد

2. Superlative:

The superlative is usually constructed either with the comparative taking the definite article "**il- إلـ**, the," or with the following noun as a definite plural, or with a pronoun suffix attached to the comparative, depending on the context. (Audio)

Laylaa il-atwal	*Laylaa is the tallest.*	ليلى الأطْـوَل
Laylaa atwal il-banaat	*Laylaa is the tallest girl.*	ليلى أطْـوَل الـبَـنات
Laylaa atwalhum	*Laylaa is the tallest.*	ليلى أطْـوَلـهُم
Baabil il-aqdam	*Babylon is the oldest.*	بابل الأقْـدَم
Baabil aqdam il-mudun	*Babylon is the oldest city.*	بابل أقْـدَم الـمُـدُن
Baabil agdamhum	*Babylon is the oldest.*	بابل أقْـدَمُـهُم

There are certain adjectives such as "**mit'assif** مِتأسِّف (*to be sorry*), **farhaan** فَرحان (*happy*), and **juu9aan** جوعان (*hungry*)," that do not have associated comparative forms. In such cases the regular adjective is used with the comparative words "**akthar** أكثَر (*more*)," or "**aqal** أقَل (*less*)" as required. (Audio)

aani mit'assif akthar minnak	*I am more sorry than you.*	آني مِتأسِّف أكثَر مِنَّك
hiyya farhaana akthar minhum	*She is happier than they.*	هي فَرحانة أكثَر مِنهُم
intu ju9aaniin aqal min Basma	*You are less hungry than Basma.*	إنتو جوعانين أقَل مِن بسمة

The Colors: alwaan   ألوان

The color adjectives have three predictable forms: masculine, feminine, and plural. They must agree with the nouns in gender and number. (Audio)

Masculine		Feminine		Plural		Meaning
abyad	أبْيَض	beeda	بيضة	biid	بيض	*white*
aswad	أسوَد	sooda	سودة	sood	سود	*black*
ahmar	أحمَر	hamra	حَمرَة	humur	حُمُر	*red*
akhdar	أخضَر	khadra	خَضرَة	khudur	خُضُر	*green*
asfar	أصفَر	safra	صَفرَة	sufur	صُفُر	*yellow*
azrag	أزرَگ	zarga	زَرگَة	zurug	زُرُگ	*blue*
asmar	أسمَر	samra	سَمرَة	sumur	سُمُر	*brown*
ashgar	أشگَر	shagra	شگرَة	shugur	شُگُر	*blond*

Exceptional Colors: They have two genders, masculine and feminine only, with no plural. (Audio)

rumaadi	رُمادي	rumaadiyya	رُماديّة	——	——	*gray*
burtuqaali	بُرتُقالي	burtuqaaliyya	بُرتُقاليّة	——	——	*orange*
banafsaji	بَنَفسَجي	banafsajiyya	بَنَفسَجيّة	——	——	*purple*
bunni	بُنّي	bunniyya	بُنّيّة	——	——	*brown*

binit shagra	*a blond girl*	بِنِت شگرَة
il-binit ish-shagra	*the blond girl*	إلبِنِت الشگرَة
il-banat ish-shugur	*the blond girls*	إلبَنات الشگُر
sayyaara hamra	*a red car*	سَيّارة حَمرَة
is-sayyaara il-hamra	*the red car*	السَّيارة الحَمرَة
is-yayyaaraat il-hamra	*the red cars*	السَّيارات الحَمرَة
loon aswad	*black color*	لون أسوَد
alwaan sooda	*black colors*	ألوان سودَة

Idioms and Common Phrases (Audio)

1. 9ala jayya   على جَيَّـة   *On the way, coming, arriving soon* (invariable)

Q: ween Samiir?	*Where is Samir?*	وين سمير؟
A: huwwa bil-<u>idh</u>aa9a, bass 9ala jayya	*He is in the radio station, but arriving soon.*	هـو بالإذاعَـة. بَـس عـلـى جَـيَّـة
il-muraasil 9ala jayya mnil-maktab	*The reporter is coming from the office.*	إلـمُـراسِـل عـلـى جَـيَّـة مُـن الـمَـكْـتَـب
huwwa muu hnaa, bass 9ala jayya	*His is not here, but arriving soon.*	هـو مو هُـنا. بس عـلـى جَـيَّـة
ihna 9ala jayya mnil-mataar	*We are coming from the airport.*	إحْـنا عـلـى جَـيَّـه مُـن الـمَـطار

2. maaku <u>ch</u>aara   ماكـو چـارَة   *No cure, hopeless, no way out* (invariable)

maaku <u>ch</u>aara, laazim asaafir lil-9iraaq	*No way out, I must travel to Iraq.*	ماكـو چـارَة. لازِم أُسافِـر لِـلْـعِـراق
maaku <u>ch</u>aara, huwwa kulli<u>sh</u> mariid	*There is no hope, he is very sick.*	ماكـو چـارَة. هـو كُـلِّـش مَـريض
maaku <u>ch</u>aara il-marad is-sarataan	*There is no cure for the disease of cancer.*	ماكـو چـارَة. إلْ مَـرَض الـسَّـرَطان
huwwa muu <u>kh</u>oo<u>sh</u> rijjaal, maaku <u>ch</u>aara	*He is a bad man, hopelessly.*	هـو مو خوش رِجّـال. ماكـو چـارَة

Drill   tamaariin   تَـمارين

1. Give appropriate replies orally to the following:

<u>sh</u>unu zaarat Basma?	شُـنـو زارَت بسـمة؟
aku qisim tarjama bil-idhaa9a?	أكـو قِـسِـم تَـرْجَـمة بالإذاعة؟
b-kam lu<u>gh</u>a yd<u>h</u>ii9uun il-a<u>kh</u>baar?	بُـكـم لُـغَـة يُـذيعون الأخبار؟
Basma sahafiyya loo muraasila?	بسـمة صَحَفِـيّة لو مُـراسِـلة؟
kam marra bil-yoom yd<u>h</u>ii9uun il-a<u>kh</u>baar?	كـم مَـرّة بالـيـوم يُـذيعون الأخـبار؟
b-ayy waqit yd<u>h</u>ii9uun in-na<u>sh</u>raat il-a<u>kh</u>baariyya?	بُأي وَقِت يُـذيعون النَّـشرات الأخبارية؟
<u>sh</u>unu noo9 il-baraamij it-talfizyooniyya?	شُـنـو نوع البرامِـج التَّـلْـفِـزْيونية؟
Basma sayyida loo aanisa?	بسـمة سَـيِّـدة لو آنِـسَـة؟
minu <u>sh</u>awwaf Basma aqsaam il-idhaa9a?	مِـنـو شَـوَّف بسـمة أقسام الإذاعة؟
<u>sh</u>unu isim il-idhaa9a?	شُـنـو إسِـم الإذاعة؟

2. Fill in the blank with the appropriate form of comparative/superlative adjective:

Ba<u>gh</u>daad _____ min 9ammaan, w 9ammaan _____ min Beirut (rik<u>h</u>iis)

بغـداد _____ مِن عَـمّـان وعَـمّـان _____ مِن بيروت (رخيص)

London _____ il-mudun (ghaali)

لَنْدن ـــــــــــ المُـدُن (غالي)

aani _____ min ukhti, w ukhti _____ minni (kabiir, saghiir)

آني ـــــــــــ من اُخْـتي واُخْـتي ـــــــــــ مِـنّي (كبير، صغير)

hissa is-sayyaarat _____ min gabul (ghaali)

هِـسّـه السَّيارات ـــــــــــ مِن كَـبُل (غالي)

shahar fabraayir _____ shahar bis-sana (qasiir)

شَـهَر فَبْـرايِر ـــــــــــ شَـهَر بالسَّنة (قصير)

shahar Yoolyoo _____ shahar ib-Baghdaad (haar)

شَـهَر يوليو ـــــــــــ شَـهَر بْ بغداد (حار)

shahar Diisambar _____ shahar bil9iraq (baarid)

شَـهَر ديسَـمْبَـر ـــــــــــ شَـهَر بالعراق (بارد)

Lubnaan min _____ il-buldaan bish-Sharq il-Awsat. (hilu)

لُبنان مِن ـــــــــــ البُـلْـدان بالشَّـرْق الأوْسَط (حِـلو)

it-tayyaara _____ mnil-qitaar (sarii9)

إلطَّـيّـارة ـــــــــــ مُن القِطار (سَـريع)

in-nakhal (palms) _____ il-ashjaar bil-9iraaq (kathiir)

إلنَّخَـل ـــــــــــ الأشْـجار بالعراق (كثير)

minu _____ Baabil loo Naynawa? (qadiim)

مِـنو ـــــــــــ بابل لو نَـيْنَـوى؟ (قديم)

minu _____ Laylaa, Basma loo Samiira? (jamiil)

مِـنو _____ ليلى، بسمة لو سميرة؟ (جَميل)

inti mit°assfa hwaaya, bass hiyya mit°assfa _____ minnich (kathiir)

إنت مِتْئـاسّـف. بَس هي مِتْئـاسّـفة _____ مِنّـچ (كثير)

jaami9at UCLA min _____ ij-jaami9aat b-Amrica (shahiir)

جامِـعَة يو سي إلْ أي من _____ الجَـامِعات بُ امريكا (شَـهير)

3. Match the words in column one with their appropriate sentences in column two and translate them. Place the correct number from the list on the left on the correct space in the list on the right.

1. alwaan	_____ il-akhbaar arba9 marraat bil-yoom
2. il-9iraaq	_____ tlaathiin yoom
3. is-sahafi	_____ atwal nahar bil-9aalam
4. il-mudhii9	_____ asra9 il-qitaar, is-sayyara loo it-tayaara?
5. il-mahatta it-talfizyooniyya	_____ tihchi Fransi kullish zeen
6. it-tabiib	_____ yiji ba9ad shwayya
7. il-mariid	_____ il-mariid rah-ymuut
8. ydhii9uun	_____ 9ala jayya mnil-idhaa9a
9. 9afya 9aleek	_____ il-9alam il-Amriiki, ahmar, w abyad, w aswad, w azrag
10. ish-shahar	_____ min aqdam il-buldaan bil-9aalam
11. nahar il-Amazoon	_____ huwwa muraasil yiktib bil-suhuf wil-majallaat

12. yaahu   _____ huwwa rijjaal yu<u>sh</u>tughul bil-i<u>dh</u>aa9a

13. balki   _____ t<u>dh</u>ii9 baraamij siyaasiyya w <u>th</u>aqaafiyya

14. il-mudiir   _____ y9aalij il-mar<u>d</u>aa

15. maaku <u>ch</u>aara   _____ 9inda wija9 ib-jisma

1. ألْوان   _____ الأخبار أربع مَرّات باليوم

2. إلطّبيب   _____ تْلاثين يوم

3. إلصَّحَفي   _____ أطْوَل نَهَر بالعالم

4. إلْمذيع   _____ أسْرَع القطار، السَّيارة لو الطيّارة؟

5. إلْمَحَطّة التَّلْفِزْيونية   _____ تِحْچي فَرَنْسي كُلِّش زين

6. إلعراق   _____ يِجي بَعَد شْوَيّة

7. إلْمَريض   _____ الْعَلَم الأمريكي أحمر وابيض واسود وازرگ

8. يُذيعون   _____ على جَيّة

9. عَفْيَة عليك   _____ رَح يْموت

10. إلشَّهَر   _____ مِن أقدم الْبُلْدان بالْعالم

11. نَهَر الأمَزون   _____ هو مُراسِل يِكْتِب بالصُّحُف والْمَجَلات

12. ياهو   _____ هو رِجّال يُشْتُتْغُل بالإذاعة

13. بَلْكي   _____ تْذيع بَرامِج سِياسيّة وثْقافيّة

14. إلْمُدير   _____ يْعالِج المَرْضى

15. ماكو چارة   _____ عِنْدَه وجَع بُ جِسْمَه

4. Complete and read the following aloud:

a. Saami 9ala jayya min mahattat it-talfizyoon

سامي على جَيَّة مِن مَحَطَّة التَّلْئِفِزْيون

Samiira _____ min mahattat it-talfizyoon

سميرة _____ مِن مَحَطَّة التَّلْئِفِزْيون

humma _____ min mahattat it-talfizyoon

هُمَّه _____ مِن مَحَطَّة التَّلْئِفِزْيون

ihna _____ min mahattat it-talfizyoon　　إحْنا _____ مِن مَحَطَّة التَّلْئِفِزْيون

intu _____ min mahattat it-talfizyoon　　إنتو _____ مِن مَحَطَّة التَّلْئِفِزْيون

inta _____ min mahattat it-talfizyoon　　إنت .... مِن مَحَطَّة التَّلْئِفِزْيون

inti _____ min mahattat it-talfizyoon　　إنتي _____ مِن مَحَطَّة التَّلْئِفِزْيون

aani _____ min mahattat it-talfizyoon　　آني _____ مِن مَحَطَّة التَّلْئِفِزْيون

b. maaku chaara, huwwa kullish mariid bil-beet　　ماكو چارة . هو كُلِّش مَريض بالبيت

_____, hiyya kullish mariida bil-beet　　_____ ، هي كُلِّش مَريضة بالبيت

_____, humma kullish mardaa bil-beet　　_____ ، هُمَّه كُلِّش مَرْضى بالبيت

_____, inta kullish mariida bil-beet　　_____ ، إنت كُلِّش مَريض بالبيت

_____, inti kullish mariida bil-beet　　_____ ، إنتي كُلِّش مَريضة بالبيت

_____, intu kullish mardaa bil-beet　　_____ ، إنتو كُلِّش مَرْضى بالبيت

_____, aani kullish mariid bil-beet　　_____ ، آني كُلِّش مَريض بالبيت

_____, aani kullish mariida bil-beet　　_____ ، آني كُلِّش مَريضة بالبيت

_____, ihna kullish mardaa bil-beet　　_____ ، إحنا كُلِّش مَرْضى بالبيت

_____, ihna kullish mariidaat bil-beet　　_____ ، إحنا كُلِّش مَريضات بالبيت

c.   maaku <u>ch</u>aara, huwwa laazim ysawwi 9amaliyya   ماكو چارة. هو لازم يُـسَّـوّي عَمَـلِـيَّـة

     maaku <u>ch</u>aara, hiyya _____   _____ ماكو چارة. هي

     maaku <u>ch</u>aara, humma _____   _____ ماكو چارة. هُمَّه

     maaku <u>ch</u>aara, inta _____   _____ ماكو چارة. إنت

     maaku <u>ch</u>aara, inti _____   _____ ماكو چارة. إنتـي

     maaku <u>ch</u>aara, intu _____   _____ ماكو چارة. إنتو

     maaku <u>ch</u>aara, aani _____   _____ ماكو چارة. آني

     maaku <u>ch</u>aara, i<u>h</u>na _____   _____ ماكو چارة. إحنا

5. Translate the following into Arabic or English as required:

Mr. Najim is the editor-in-chief of the Lebanese *il-Nahar* newspaper.

_____

There are many newspapers and magazines in present-day Iraq.

_____

There are more newspapers in present-day Iraq than before.

_____

Radio stations broadcast interviews/discussions with government officials.

_____

Iraqis like international political and cultural news very much.

_____

The colors of the Iraqi flag are white, green, red, and black.

_____

Which country is the oldest: Greece, Egypt, or Iraq?

_____

At what times is the news broadcast in Baghdad?

Nowadays there are many foreign reporters in Iraq.

The year 1997 was a good year but the year 2001 was not a good year.

"Al-Ahram" is a well-known Egyptian newspaper.

---

il-Mustaqbal jariida 9raaqiyya mashhurra

"المُسْـتَـقْبَل" جَريدة عراقية مَشـْهورة

---

maaku chaara, il-mara kullish mariida w rah tmuut

ما كو چارة. إلمَرَة كُـلِّـش مريضة ورَح تْموت

---

la-truuh, il-muwazzaf il-hukuumi 9ala jayya

لَتْروح. المُوَظَّف الحُكومي على جَـيَّه

---

aani ahibb il-loon il-akhdar akthar minnak, w Laylaa thibb il-loon il-asfar more than me

آني أحِب الـلْون الأخضرأكْثر مِنَّك. وليلى تْحِـب الـلْون الأصْفر أكْـثر مِنِّي

---

leesh aku akthar min 170 jariida w majalla bil-9raq il-yoom?

ليش أكو أكْـثر من 170 جَـريدة ومَجَلَـة بالعراق الـيوم؟

---

ween atwal nahar bil-9aalam?

وين أطْـوَل نَـهَر بالـعالم؟

---

yaahu aqsar shahar bis-sana?

ياهو أقْـصَر شَـهَر بالسَّـنة؟

---

maaku chaara il-marad is-sarataan. huwwa akhtar il-amraad

ماكو چـارة إلْ مَرَض السَّـرَطان. هو أخْـطَـر الأمُراض

---

ydhii9uun il-akhbaar il-9aalamiyya is-saa9a thmaanya sabahan wis-saa9a sitta masaa°an

يُـذيعون الأخبار العـالمية السّاعة ثُمانْـيَة صَباحاً والسّاعة سِـتَّة مساءً

---

aku hurriyyat sahaafa bil-9iraaq il-yoom.

أكو حُـرِّـيَّة صَحافة بالعراق الـيْوم

---

mudiir il-idhaa9a da-yshawwif is-sayyid Muniir aqsaam il-mahatta

مُدير الإذاعة دَ يُـشـَوِّف السَّـيـد مُنيـر اقسام المَـحَطّة

---

ish-Sharq il-Awsat min ashhar il-jaraayid is-Su9uudiyya

"إلشـَّرْق الأوْسَط" مِـن أشْـهَر الجَّـرايـد السَّـعـوديَّـة

Sawt il-9arab ashhar idhaa9a Masriyya bil-9aalam il-9arabi

"صَوْت العرب" أشْـهَـر إذاعة مصرية بالعالم العربي

---

6. Answer the following in Arabic:

a. List names of some of the well-known Iraqi newspapers, radio, and TV channels.

b. List names of some of the well-known newspapers and magazines which are published in some of the Arab countries.

c. List names of some of the well-known international newspapers and magazines.

d. List names of some of the well-known American newspapers, magazines, and TV channels.

Creative Dialogues
muraasil ajnabi

Joon Dalas muraasil ajnabi min majallat il-Taaymz il-Amriikiyya. huwwa b-Baghdaad yhibb yiktib taqriir sahafi 9an il-hadaara il-9iraaqiyya il-qadiima. huwwa yriid ysawwi muqaabla wiyya muwazzaf ib-wizaarat il-I9laam ib-Baghdaad. hassal muqaabla ma9a sayyid Jamaal mas°uul qisim il-ajaanib bil-wizaara. il-muqaabala rah tkuun yoom il-arba9aa is-saa9a tis9a sabahan. il-muraasil Joon wil-muwazzaf Jamaal tqablaw ib-maktab Jamaal. awwal shii Jamaal si°al Joon idhaa kaan yhibb yishrab chaay loo gahwa. Joon tilab chaay saada w bida yis°al Jamaal as°ila hwaaya 9an aathaar w funuun il-9iraaq il-qadiim. il-muqazzaf kaan rijjaal min altaf in-naas w qaddam l-Joon akthar musaa9ada mumkina. Joon kaan masruur jiddan mnil-muqaabala w shikar Jamaal hwaaya 9ala ahsan il-ma9luumaat. Joon 9iraf ba9deen il-9iraaq huwwa min aqdam il-buldaan bil-9aalam.

مُـراسِـل أجْـنَـبـي

جون دالاس مُراسِل أجُنبي مِن مَجَلَّـة "التّايْـمز" الأمريكية. هو بُ بغداد يُـحِبّ يِكْـتِب تَـقْـرير صَحَفـي عَن الحضارة العِراقية القديمة. هو يُـريد يْـسَـوّي مُقابَـلة وِيَّـه مُوَظَّف بُ وزارة الأعْلام بُ بغداد. حَصَّل مُقابَـلة مَع سَـيِّد جَمال مَسْؤول قِسِم الأجانِب بالوِزارة. المُقابلة رَح تْكون يوم الاربعاء السّاعة تِسْـعـة صَبَاحاً. المُراسِل جون والمُوَظَّف جَمال تْـقابَـلوْ بُ مَكْـتِب جمال. أوَّل شِي جمال سِـأَل جون إذا كان يُـحِب يِـشْـرَب چاي لو گَـهْـوَة. جون طِـلَـب چاي سادة وبِـدَا يِـسْـأَل جمال أسْـئِـلـة هُوايـه عَن آثار وفُـنون العِراق الـقْديم. المُوَظَّف كان رِجّـال مِن ألْـطَف النّاس وقَـدَّم لُ جون أكْـثَر مُساعَـدة مُمْـكِـنة. جون كان مَسْرور جِـداً مَن الـمُقابَـلة وشِكَـر جمال هُـوايه على أحْسَن الـمَعلومات. جون عِـرَف بَـعْـدين العِراق هو مِن أقْـدَم البُلْـدان بِـالْـعالم.

7. Answer the following questions based on the previous passage:

minu Joon Dalas?	مِـنو جون دالاس؟
leesh Joon raah il-Baghdaad?	ليش جون راح لُ بغداد؟
b-ayy majalla yushtughul Joon?	بْـأي مَجَـلّة يُـشْـتُـغِل جون؟
minu qaabal il-muraasil Joon?	مِـنو قابَـل الـمَـراسِـل جون؟
ween yushtughul muwazzaf il-hukuuma?	وين يُـشْـتُـغِل مُوَظَّف الحكومة؟
shwakit chaanat il-muqaabala?	شْـوَكِـت چانت المقابلة؟
ween raah Joon l-muqaabalat Jamaal?	وين راح جون لُ مُقابَـلة جمال؟
shunu qaddam Jamaal l-Joon?	شُـنو قَـدَّم جمال لُ جون؟
9an shunu chaanat as°ilat Joon?	عَن شُـنو چانت أسْـئِـلَـة جون؟
Jamaal saa9ad loo ma-saa9ad Joon?	جمال ساعَد لو مَ ساعَد جون؟
shloon Jamaal saa9ad Joon?	شْـلون جمال ساعَد جون؟
sh-sawwa Joon ba9ad il-muqaabala?	شْـسَـوّه جون بَـعَـد المُقابَـلة؟
leesh il-muraasil chaan masruur kullish hwaaya?	ليش المُراسِل چان مَسْرور كُـلّـِـش هُـوايَه؟
min ayy balad Joon?	مِـن أي بَـلَـد جون؟
minu chaan min altaf in-naas?	مِـنو چان مِـن ألْـطَـف النّـاس؟

Mausoleum of Sitt Zumurrud Khatun (1202 A.D.), Abbasid Dynasty, Baghdad

Telephone Conversations

mukhaabaraat   مُخابَرات

Dialing telephone numbers in Iraq or in any other Arab country is similar to dialing in the western countries; numbers are read from left to right. Basma is making a telephone call to the home of a relative in Baghdad, and Kariim, her cousin, answers the phone.

Basic Dialogue (Audio)

1. Kariim: aloo, aloo. minu yitkallam?   كريم: ألو. ألو. مِـنو يِـتْكَـلَّـم؟
   Hello, hello. Who is speaking?

2. Basma: masaaʾ il-kheer . . . aloo . . .   بسـمة: مساء الخير . . . ألو . . .
   Good afternoon . . . hello . . .

3. Kariim: ma-da-asma9 zeen. il-khatt mshawwash.   كريم: مَ دَ أسْمَع زين. إلخَـط مُـشَـوَّش.
   I can't hear you well. There is static on the line.

4. Basma: hissa, tisma9ni ahsan?   بسـمة: هِـسَّه. تِسْـمَـعُني أحْـسَـن؟
   Now, do you hear me better?

5. Kariim: hwaaya ahsan. minu hadirtich?   كريم: هُـوايَـه أحْـسَـن. مِـنو حَـضِرْتِـچ؟
   Much better. Who are you?

6. Basma: aani Basma min Los Angeles.   بسـمة: آني بسمة مِن لوس انجْلوس.
   I am Basma from Los Angeles.

7. Kariim: Basma! ahlan w sahlan.
   il-hamdilla 9as-salaama.
   Basma! Welcome. Praise be to God for your
   safe arrival.

كريم: بسـمة! أهلاً وسـهلاً. الحَمْـدِلله عَ
السَّـلامة.

8. Basma: shukran jaziilan. shloonkum?
   inshaalla zeeniin?
   Thank you very much. How are you? Well,
   God willing?

بسمة: شكراً جزيلاً. شـلونـئكـم؟
إنْـشـاللـه زيـنيـن؟

9. Kariim: ihna zeeniin il-hamdu lillaah.
   9aash min sima9 sootich.
   We are well, thank God. Nice to hear your
   voice.

كريم: إحُـنا زيـنيـن الـحَـمدُ لله. عاش مِـن
سِـمَـع صُوتِـچ.

10. Basma: aani wsalit gabul yoomeen.
    haawalit akhaaburkum il-baarha, bass
    il-khatt chaan mashghuul.
    I arrived two days ago. I tried to call you
    yesterday but the line was busy.

بسمة: آنـي وُصَلِـت كَـبُـل يومين.
حاوَلِت أخابُـرْكـم البـارْحـة. بَس الخَـط چان
مَشْـغـول

11. Kariim: adri. binti Laylaa tih chi
    hwaaya 9at-talifoon.
    I know. My daughter Laylaa is always
    talking on the telephone.

كريم: أدْري. بِـنْـتي ليلـى تِـحْـچي هُـوايَه عَ
الـتَّـلِـفون

12. Basma: aani mushtaaqatilkum w ahibb
    azuurkum.
    I miss you and would like to visit you.

بسمة: آنـي مُشْـتـاقَـتِـلْكُـم وأحِـب
أزورْكـم

13. Kariim: ihna mushtaaqiin akthar. inti
    ween naazla?
    We miss you more. Where are you staying?

كريم: إحُـنا مُشْـتـاقـيـن أكْـثَـر. إنتـي وين
نازْلَـة؟

14. Basma: aani naazla b-findiq ir-Rashiid,
    ghurfa raqam 732.
    I am staying at the Rashid Hotel, room
    number 732.

بسمة: آنـي نـازْلَـة بُ فِـنْـدِق الـرَّشـيـد.
غُـرْفة رَقَـم 732

15. Kariim: shunu raqam talifoon il-findiq?
    What is the hotel telephone number?

كريم: شُـنُو رَقَـم تَـلِـفون الـفِـنْـدِق؟

16. Basma: raqam il-findiq: 772-5697
    The hotel number is 772-5697.

بسمة: رَقَـم الـفِـنْدِق: 772-5697

17. Kariim: aani hissa jaayy bis-sayyaara
    lil-findiq
    I am coming by car to the hotel right now.

كريم: آنـي هِـسَّـه جاي بالسَّـيارة
لِـلْـفِـنْـدِق

Vocabulary (Audio)

talifoon / talifoonaat (S/P)	telephone/s	تَلِفون / تَلِفونات
talifoon moobaayal	mobile/cell telephone	تَلِفون موبايَل
talifoon ardi	ground telephone	تَلِفون ارْضي
mukhaabara / mukhaabaraat (S/P)	telephone call/s	مُخابَرة / مُخابَرات
mshawwash / mshawwasha (M/F)	static, confused	مُشَوَّش / مُشَوَّشَة
ahsan (comparative adj. of zeen)	better	أَحْسَن
il-hamdilla (another form of il-hamdu lillaah)	Praise be to God.	الحَمْدِلله
9aash (HV)	He lived.	عاش
sima9 (RV)	He heard.	سِمَع
soot	voice, sound	صُوت
9aash min sima9 sootich (idiom, see below)	Nice to hear your voice.	عاش مِن سِمَع صُوتِج
khatt / khutuut (S/P)	line/s	خَط / خُطوط
mash ghuul / mash ghuula (M/F adj.)	busy	مَشْغول / مَشْغولة
khatt mash ghuul	busy line	خَط مَشْغول
il-baarha	yesterday	إلْبارْحَة
adri (WV)	I know.	أَدْري
mushtaaq / mushtaaqa/ mushtaaqiin (M/F/P)	to miss, to be lonesome	مُشْتاق / مُشْتاقة / مُشْتاقين
mushtaaqatilkum	I miss you (P).	مُشْتاقَتِلْكُم
akthar (comparative of kathiir and hwaaya)	more	أَكْثَر
ghurfa / ghuraf (S/P)	room/s	غُرْفَة / غُرَف
raqam / arqaam (S/P)	number/s	رَقَم / أرْقام
jaayy / jaayya (M/F part.)	coming	جايْ / جايَّة

Additional Vocabulary and Phrases on Telephone (Audio)

baddaala / baddaalaat (S/P)	telephone operator/s	بَدّالة / بَدّالات
umm il-baddaala, abu il-baddaala	female operator, male operator	أم البَدّالة. أبو البَدّالة
ghalat	wrong	غَلَط
raqam ghalat	wrong number	رَقَم غَلَط
kharbaan / kharbaana (M/F)	broken, out of order	خَرْبان / خَرْبانة
talifoon kharbaan	broken telephone	تَلِفون خَرْبان
mukhaabara daakhiliyya	domestic/national call	مُخابَرة داخِلِيَّة
mukhaabara khaarijiyya	international call	مُخابَرة خارِجِيَّة

Grammar and Remarks
Conditional Sentences (if):

Iraqi Arabic has two words used for the conditional sentences "if." The word " idhaa إذا, *if*" is used to express real and possible conditions (If you come we will go together.) and the word "loo لو, *if*" for unreal and impossible conditions (If you had come we would have gone together.).

1. Real Condition with idhaa   إذا   *if*

A sentence for a real and possible condition is expressed with the word "idhaa إذا , *if*," followed usually by a perfect (past) verb. However an imperfect (present) verb may also be used. Sentences with perfect or imperfect verbs have the same meaning in English. The verb in the second part of the sentence (the result clause) may be imperative or imperfect verb. (Audio)

idhaa riḥit l-Baghdaad, shuuf Baabil	*If you go (lit. went) to Baghdad, see Babylon.*	إذا رِحِت لُ بغداد شوف بابل
idhaa truuḥ l-Baghdaad, shuuf Baabil.	*If you go to Baghdad, see Babylon.*	إذا تُروح لُ بغداد شوف بابل
idhaa ykhaaburni asi°la	*If he calls me, I will ask him.*	إذا يُخابُرني أسِئلَـه
idhaa khaabarni asi°la	*If he calls (lit. called) me, I will ask him.*	إذا خابَـرني أسِئلَـه

2. Unreal Condition with loo   لو   *if*

The word "loo لو, *if*," is used for unreal and impossible conditions (contrary to the fact) followed usually by a participle or a perfect tense verb, although an imperfect verb may also be used. The verb in the second part of the sentence (the result clause) consists of "chaan چان" (invariable) followed by a perfect or imperfect verb conjugated to agree with the subject. (Audio)

loo raayḥiin lil-maktab, chaan shaafaw il-mudiir	*If they had gone to the office, they would have seen the director.*	لو رائِحين لِـلْمَكْتَب. چان شافَـوُ المُـدير
loo zaayir il-9iraaq, chaan shaaf nahar Dijla	*If he had visited Iraq, he would have seen the Tigris River.*	لو زايِـر العراق. چان شاف نَـهَر دِجْـلـة
loo jiit, chaan riḥna siwiyya	*If you had come we would have gone together.*	لو جيت. چان رُحْـنا سِـوِيَّـه
loo yu9ruf qraaya, chaan diras 9arabi	*If he knew reading, he would have studied Arabic.*	لو يُعُرُف قْـرايَـة. چان دِرَس عربي
loo 9indi waqit, chaan riḥit wiyyaak	*If I had the time, I would have gone with you.*	لو عِنْدي وَقِت. چان رِحِت وِيّـاك

The Relative Pronoun (i)lli إلِّـي Who(m), whose, that, which

The English relative pronouns "who, whom, whose, that, and which," whether they are referring back to people or things, masculine, feminine, singular, or plural, are expressed in Iraqi Arabic by the word "(i)lli إلِّـي." However, "(i)lli" is used only when the noun in the principal sentence is definite. There is no need for it if the noun is indefinite. "(i)lli" and the related word "min مِن, who" are also used in the beginning of phrases that correspond in English to "He who, whoever, anyone who, whatever, that which," sentences that usually have proverbial meanings. (Audio)

il-ustaadh illi ydarris 9arabi	the professor who teaches Arabic	الأسْتاذ إلِّـي يُـدَرِّس عربي
il-idhaa9a lli tdhii9 il-akhbaar	the radio station which broadcasts the news	الإذاعة الِّـي تُذيـع الأخْـبار
ween il-muraasiliin illi raayhiin lil-9iraaq?	Where are the reporters who are going to Iraq?	وين المُـراسِـلين إلِّـي رايْحين لِلْـعِراق؟
aku rijjal yriid ysallim 9aleek	There is a man who wants to greet you.	أكو رجّـال يُـريد يُـسَلِّـم عَـلـيك
9indi sayyaara tihtaaj tasliih	I have a car that needs repairing.	عِـنْدي سَـيّارة يِحْـتاج تَـصْلـيـح
illi y9iish yshuuf	He who lives will see (go through experience).	إلِّـي يُـعـيش يُـشوف
illi nkitab 9aj-jabiin laazim tshuufa il-9een	That which is written on the forehead must be seen by the eye (proverb).	إلِّـي نْكِـتَـب عَالجَّـبيـن لازِم تُـشوفـَه الـعـين

Idioms and Common Phrases (Audio)

1. 9aash min sima9 soot + attached pronoun + عاش مِـن سِـمَع صُـوت *Nice to hear your voice.* (lit. *He who hears [your] voice will live.* A compliment one says to another after an absence, see also lesson 8).

haay weenak? 9aash min sima9 sootak.	Where have you been? Nice to hear your voice.	هايْ وينـك؟ عاش مِـن سِـمَع صُـوتك
9aash min sima9 sootich. ween hal-gheeba?	Nice to hear your voice. Where have you been?	عاش مِـن سِـمَع صُـوتِـج. وين هَـلْ غِـيـبَة؟
aani mushtaaqlak. 9aash min sima9 sootak	I missed you. Nice to hear your voice.	آني مُشْـتاقْـلَـك. عاش مِـن سِـمَع صوتك
9aash min sima9 sootkum. safratkum tawlat	Nice to hear your voice. Your trip was long.	عاش مِـن سِـمَع صُـوتْكُـم. سَـفْـرَتْكـكُم طَـوُلَـت

2. minu abu baachir? مِنـو أبو باچِـر؟ *Who knows about tomorrow? Life is too short.*
(lit. *Who is the father of tomorrow?* Encourages one to enjoy life.)

ishtireet sayyaara jidiida.	*I bought a new car. Life is*	إشـتِـريت سَـيّـارة
minu abu baachir?	*too short.*	جِـديدة. مِـنـو أبو باچِـر؟
saafar il-Awrubba yitwannas.	*He went to Europe for fun.*	سافَـرَ لُ أُوَرِّبـا يِـتـوَنَّـس.
minu abu baachir?	*Life is too short.*	مِـنـو أبو باچِـر؟
minu abu baachir? khalli	*Who knows about*	مِـنـو أبو باچِـر؟ خَـلّي
nshuuf id-dinya	*tomorrow? Let us enjoy life.*	نْـشوف الـدِّنْـيا
leesh inta 9ussi? minu abu	*Why are you cheap? Who*	ليش إنت عُـصّي؟ مِـنـو
baachir?	*knows about tomorrow?*	أبو باچِـر؟

Drills   tamaariin تَـماريـن

1. Give appropriate replies orally to the following:

il-man khaabrat Basma?	إلْـمَـن خابَـرَت بسمة؟
minu jaawab it-talifoon?	مِـنـو جاوَب التَّـلِـفون؟
it-talifoon chaan kharbaan loo mshawwash?	إلتَّـلِـفون چان خَـرْبان لو مُشَـوَّش؟
min ween khaabrat Basma?	مِن وين خابَـرَت بسمة؟
leesh Kariim chaan farhaan hwaaya?	ليش كريم چان فَـرْحان هُـوايَه؟
minu yih chi hwaaya 9at-talifoon bil-beet?	مِـنـو يِـحْـچي هُـوايه عَ التَّـلِـفون بالبيت؟
leesh Basma khaabrat beet Kariim?	ليش بسمة خابَـرَت بيت كريم؟
il-mukhaabara chaanat daakhiliyya loo khaarijiyya?	إلْـمُخابَـرة چانت داخِـلِـيّـة لو خارجِـيّـة؟
ween Basma naazla b-Baghdaad?	وين بسمة نازْلَـة بُ بغداد؟
minu raah lil-findiq bis-sayyaara?	مِـنـو راحْ لِـلْـفِـنْـدِق بالسَّـيارة؟
leesh il-khatt chaan mash ghuul?	ليش الْـخَـطّ چان مَشْـغول؟
shgadd raqam ghurfat Basma bil-findiq?	شْـكَـد رَقَـم غُـرُفة بسمة بالـفِـنْـدِق؟

2. Fill in the blanks of the following sentences and translate them into English:

1. ma-da-asim9ak, il-khatt _____

2. khaabaritkum _____ bass talifoonkum chaan _____

3. raqam _____ bil-findiq 654

4. haadhi mukhaabara _____ loo _____?

5. mumking ah chi _____ Laylaa 9at-talifoon?

6. _____ rihtu l-jinuub il-9iraaq, zuru madiinat il-Basra

7. _____ 9indi fluus <u>ch</u>aan i<u>sh</u>tireet sayyaara

8. haa<u>dh</u>a huwwa l-mudiir _____ <u>sh</u>awwaf Samiira l-i<u>dh</u>aa9a

9. ha<u>dh</u>oola humma _____ illi yikitbuun b-jariidat il-A<u>kh</u>baar il-Ma<u>s</u>riyya

10. ween hal-<u>gh</u>eeba? _____

11. Kariim mi<u>sh</u>taaqlak _____ min Basma

12 nahar il-Amazoon _____ il-anhaar bil-9aalam

13. il-ma<u>t</u>9am _____ akalit bii kulli<u>sh</u> <u>gh</u>aali

14. ruu<u>h</u> <u>sh</u>uuf il-9aalam, _____?

15. aloo, aloo, raja°an sayyid _____ mawjuud?

١. مَ داسِمـْعَك. الـْخط _____

٢. خابَرِتْكـم _____ بَس تَـلِـفونْكـم چان _____

٣. رَقَـم _____ بالـْفندق 654

٤. هاذي مُخابَـرَة _____ لو _____؟

٥. مُمْكِـن أحچي _____ ليلى عَ التَّـلِـفون؟

٦. _____ رِحـْـتو لْ جِـنوب العراق. زورو مَدينة الـْبَصْرة

٧. _____ عِنـْدي فلوس چان اشـْتِريت سَـيّارة

٨. هاذا هو المدير _____ شَـوّف سميرة الإذاعة

٩. هَذولـه هُمّـه _____ إلّـي يُـكِـتْبون بْ جَريدة الأخْبار الـْمَصْريّة

١٠. وين هَـلْ غِـيبة؟ _____

١١. كـريم مُشـْتاقـْلَـك _____ مِن بسمة

12. نَهَر الأمَزون ــــــــــــــــــ الأنـهار بالعـالم

13. إلمَـطعَم ــــــــــــــــــ أكَـلِـت بي كُـلّـش غالي

14. رُوح شـوف العـالم، ــــــــــــــــــ

15. ألـو. ألـو. رجاءً سَـيّـد ــــــــــــــــــ مَـوجُود؟

3. Change the "idhaa إذا" real conditional sentence to the "loo لـو" unreal conditional sentence and vice versa, changing anything else that needs to be changed in the sentence:

idhaa truuh lil-9iraaq zuur jaami9at Baghdaad	إذا تـروح لِـلـعـراق زور جامعَة بغداد
idhaa shifit Ahmad sallimli 9alee	إذا شِـفِـت أحمد سَـلّـمُـلـي عليه
idhaa taakul hwaaya tsiir simiin	إذا تاكُل هُـوايَه تـصير سِـمـين
idhaa jiit il-yoom nruuh siwiyya	إذا جيت اليوم نُـروح سِـوِيَّه
idhaa dirasti 9arabi abuuch ykuun masruur	إذا دَرَسْـتي عربي أبوچ يُـكون مَسـرور
loo jiit chaan shifit Basma	لو جيت چان شِـفِـت بسمة
loo a9ruf 9arabi chaan zirit 9ammaan	لو أعُـرُف عربي چان زرت عَـمّـان
loo zaayir it-tabiib chaan sihtak saarat ahsan	لو زايِـر الطّـبـيب چان صِـحتـك صارَت أحُـسَـن
loo beeti muu bi9iid chaan ziritkum kull usbuu9	لو بيتي مو بِـعيد چان زِرتـكـم كُل اسبـوع

4. Make plural the following relative pronoun phrases and sentences:

il-ustaadh illi ydarris it-taariikh il-Islaami	الأستاذ إلّـي يُـدَرّس التّاريخ الإسْلامي
it-taaliba lli tit9alaam il-lugha il-9arabiyya	الطّـالِـبة إلّـي تِـتـعَـلّـم اللغة العربية
ween il-mudhii9 illi ydhii9 akhbaar il-yoom?	وين المُـذيع إلّـي يُـذيع أخبار اليوم؟
9aash min sima9 sootak	عاش مِن سِمَع صوتَك
haay weenich? 9aash min shaafich	هاي وينـِـچ؟ عاش مِن شافِـچ
minu is-sahafi lli kitab it-taqriir?	مِـنو الصّحَـفي إلّـي كِـتَب التّـقـريـر؟
ween it-talifoon illi chaan 9al-meez?	وين التّـلِـفون إلّـي چان عَ المِـيز؟
ween raah it-tabiib illi fuhas Jamiila?	وين راح الطّـبـيب إلّـي فُحَـص جَميلة؟
haadhi t-tayyaara illi truuh l-Paariis	هاذي الطّـيّـارة إلّـي تـروح لُ پاريس
qreet il-maqaala illi kitabha l-muraasil	قـريت المَـقالة إلّـي كِـتَـبُـها المُـراسِل

5. Complete and read aloud:

a. leesh inta 9ussi? minu abu baachir?   ليش إنت عُـصّي؟ مِـنو أبو باچِـر؟

    leesh inti 9ussiyya? _____?   ليش إنتي عُـصّـيّـة؟ _____؟

    leesh intu 9ussiyyiin? _____?   ليش إنتو عُـصّـيّـين؟ _____؟

leesh intu 9ussiyyaat? _____?   ليش إنتو عُصِّيّات؟ _____؟

leesh huwwa 9ussi? _____?   ليش هو عُصِّي؟ _____؟

leesh hiyya 9ussiyya? _____?   ليش هي عُصِّيَّة؟ _____؟

leesh humma 9ussiyyiin? _____?   ليش هُمّه عُصِّيّين؟ _____؟

leesh humma 9ussiyyaat? _____?   ليش هُمّه عُصِّيّات؟ _____؟

leesh aani 9ussi? _____?   ليش آني عُصِّي؟ _____؟

leesh aani 9ussiyya? _____?   ليش آني عُصِّيَّة؟ _____؟

leesh ihna 9ussiyyiin? _____?   ليش إحْنا عُصِّيّين ؟ _____؟

leesh ihna 9ussiyyaat? _____?   ليش إحْنا عُصِّيّات؟ _____؟

b. ween hal-gheeba? 9aash min sima9 sootak   وين هَلْ غيبة؟ عاش مِن سِمَع صُوتَك

_____? 9aash min sima9 sootich   _____؟ عاش مِن سِمَع صُوتِچ

_____? 9aash min sima9 sootkum   _____؟ عاش مِن سِمَع صُوتْكم

_____? 9aash min sima9 soota   _____؟ عاش مِن سِمَع صُوتَه

_____? 9aash min sima9 sootha   _____؟ عاش مِن سِمَع صُوتْها

_____? 9aash min sima9 soothum   _____؟ عاش مِن سِمَع صُوتْهُم

c. aani mushtaaqlak, ween hal-gheeba?   آني مُشْتاقْلَك، وين هَلْ غيبَة؟

aani mushtaaqlich, _____?   آني مُشْتاقْلِـچ، _____؟

aani mushtaaqilkum, _____?   آني مُشْتـاقِـلْـكم، _____؟

aani mushtaaqla, _____?   آني مُشْتـاقْلَـه، _____؟

aani mushtaaqilha, _____?   آني مُشْتـاقِـلْـها، _____؟

aani mushtaaqilhum, _____?   آني مُشْتـاقِـلْـهم، _____؟

6. Translate the following into Arabic:

The operator (F) who works in the office is not here.

International phone calls are more expensive than local calls.

The operator (M) gave me the wrong telephone number.

If you (F) had gone to the school you would have seen Professor Khaalid.

If you come to my home, we will study the French language together.

He misses his son who has been studying engineering in Germany since 2003.

There are some visitors who want to see the director of the radio/TV station.

There are many newspapers and magazines in Iraq nowadays.

What are your room number and the hotel telephone number?

He who brought the magazines went to his home.

A Thousand and One Nights is an Arabic book.

I must go to my doctor's clinic; I have a cold and high fever.

My home is the fifth yellow house on the right side of the street.

Hello, hello! Can you hear better now?

_____

Who is the teacher who taught them Arabic at the university?

_____

7. Make two meaningful sentences of each of the following idiomatic phrases:

9aa<u>sh</u> min <u>sh</u>aaf . . .   عاش مِـن شـاف . . .

_____

_____

9aa<u>sh</u> min sima9 <u>s</u>oot . . .   عاش مِـن سِـمِع صُـوت . . .

_____

_____

minu abu baa<u>ch</u>ir?   مِـنو أبو باچِـر؟

_____

_____

maaku <u>ch</u>aara   ماكو چارة

_____

_____

9ala jayya   على جَيَّة

_____

_____

balki   بَـلْكي

_____

_____

<u>sh</u>bii . . . ?

شِبِي . . . ؟

_____

_____

Creative Dialogues

a. <u>t</u>aalib 1:   aloo.   طالب 1:   ألو

      <u>t</u>aaliba 2:   <u>s</u>abaa<u>h</u> il-<u>kh</u>eer. raja²an mudiir il-i<u>dh</u>aa9a mawjuud?   طالبة 2:   صَباحِ الخَيْرِ. رجاءً مُدير الإذاعة مَوْجود؟

      <u>t</u>aalib 1:   minu <u>h</u>adirtich?   طالب 1:   مِنو حَضِرْتِج؟

      <u>t</u>aaliba 2:   anni ismi Juudi Kaartar, min <u>s</u>a<u>h</u>iifat "it-Taaymz" il-Landaniyya.   طالبة 2:   آني إسمي جودي كارْتَر، مِن صَحيفَة "التّايمْز" الـلَـنْـدَنِـيّة

      <u>t</u>aalib 1   ahlan w sahlan. <u>sh</u>i-triidiin min il-mudiir is-sayyid Kamaal?   طالب 1:   أهلاً وسهلاً. شِـتْريدين مِن المُدير السَّـيِّد كمال؟

      <u>t</u>aaliba 2:   a<u>h</u>ibb asawwi muqaabal <u>s</u>ahafiyya wiyyaa   طالبة 2:   أحِبّ أسَوّي مُقابِـلة صَحَفِـيَّة ويّاه

      <u>t</u>aalib 1:   muqaabla <u>s</u>ahafiyya, 9an <u>sh</u>unu?   طالب 1:   مُقابَـلَـة صَحَفِـيَّة. عَـن شُـنو؟

      <u>t</u>aaliba 2:   9an baraamijkum il-i<u>dh</u>aa9iyya wit-talfizyooniyya?   طالبة 2:   عَـن بَرامِـجْـكم الإذاعِـيَّة والتَّـلْـفِـزْيونية

      <u>t</u>aalib 1:   <u>t</u>ayyib. bass sayyid Kamaal ma-mawjuud bil-maktab hissa   طالب 1:   طَيِّب. بَس سَيِّد كمال مَ مَوْجود بِالمَكْتب هِـسَّه

      <u>t</u>aaliba 2:   <u>sh</u>wakit ykuun bil-maktab?   طالبة 2:   شْـوَكِـت يُـكون بِـالمَكْـتب؟

      <u>t</u>aalib 1:   huwwa ykuun hnaa ba9ad nu<u>ss</u> saa9a   طالب 1:   هو يُـكون هُـنا بَعَد نُصّ ساعة

      <u>t</u>aaliba 2:   mumkin aji aqaabla ba9ad saa9a?   طالبة 2:   مُـمْـكِـن أجي أقابْـله بَعَد ساعة؟

      <u>t</u>aalib 1:   aani agulla min yirja9   طالب 1:   آني أڱـولّـه مِـن يِـرْجَـع

      <u>t</u>aaliba 2:   <u>sh</u>ukran jaziilan, ma9a s-salaama   طالبة 2:   شُـكراً جزيلاً. مَعَ السَّـلامة

b. <u>t</u>aalib 1:   aloo.   طالب 1:   ألو

      <u>t</u>aaliba 2:   mar<u>h</u>aba. min fa<u>d</u>lak sayyid <u>H</u>amiid mawjuud?   طالبة 2:   مَـرْحَبَـة. مِن فَـضْلَـك سَـيِّد حَـميد مَوْجود؟

ṭaalib 1:	laa, ma-mawjuud. minu yitkallam rajaaᵓan?	طالب 1: لا. مَ مَـوْجود. مِـنو يِـتْـكَـلَّـم رجاءً؟
ṭaaliba 2:	aani Basma Adams. ween huwwa?	طالبة 2: آني بسمة آدَمْـز. وين هو؟
ṭaalib 1:	raaḥ yjiib binta mnil-madrasa	طالب 1: راح يُـجيب بِـنْـتَـه مُـن المَدرَسَة
ṭaaliba 2:	mumking atrukla khabar wiyyaak?	طالبة 2: مُـمْـكِـن أتْـرُكْـلَـه خَـبَر وِيّـاك؟
ṭaalib 1:	ii, tfaḍḍali	طالب 1: ئي، تْـفَـضَّـلي
ṭaaliba 2:	rajaᵓan, gulla Basma b-Baghdaad wi-thibb tshufak	طالبة 2: رجاءً. گـُـلَّـه بسمة بْ بغداد وتْـحِبّ تْـشوفَـك
ṭaalib 1:	shgadd raqam talifoonich?	طالب 1: شْـكَـد رَقَـم تَـلِـفونچ؟
ṭaaliba 2:	raqam talifooni, 422-0629	طالبة 2: رَقَـم تَـلِـفوني 422-0629
ṭaalib 1:	khalli a9iid ir-raqam, 422-0629	طالب 1: خَـلّـي أعـيـد الـرَّقم 422-0629
ṭaaliba 2:	ṣaḥiiḥ. la-tinsa rajaᵓan	طالبة 2: صَـحيح. لَـتِـنْـسى رجاءً
ṭaalib 1:	laa, maa ansa. 9ala 9eeni	طالب 1: لا ما أنْـسى. على عيني
ṭaaliba 2:	shukran	طالبة 2: شُـكـراً

For new words, see Glossary.

Marble statue of a princess (138 A.D.), ancient Hatra, Northern Iraq

Cultural and Folkloric Tales

qusas hadaariyya wa sha9biyya قُـصَـصْ حَـضاريَّـة وشَـعْـبِـيَّـة

Modern Iraq was ancient Mesopotamia, the land between the two rivers, the Tigris and the Euphrates. Most historians call ancient Iraq the cradle of civilization. Its archaeological remains date as far back as the Paleolithic Age, 100,000 years ago. Mesopotamia contributed many inventions and innovations to civilization: the first writing, school, law, map, math, irrigation, wheel, chariot, contract and court, the first kingdom and empire, metallurgy, astronomy, and literature. The "Epic of Gilgamesh," about five thousand years old, is a magnificent literary work that preceded Homer's *Iliad* and *Odyssey* by more than two thousand years. Ancient Mesopotamians were sophisticated builders who built great monuments and cities, among them Ur, Uruk, Nineveh, and Babylon. Babylon was the city where the "Hanging Gardens," one of the world's Seven Wonders, once stood. After a few centuries of foreign occupation, Iraq flourished again in the 8th century, when Baghdad became the capital of the Islamic empire. Baghdad's scientists, scholars, philosophers, mathematicians, educators, physicians, writers, translators, poets, singers, musicians, artists, traders, and artisans are all to be found in the tales of *A Thousand and One Nights*, which speaks of the glorious city that was Baghdad. One can imagine that with such a long history Iraq must have had very rich traditions of legends and tales of fabled cities, caliphs, kings, princes, wise men, jinns, and animals.

Basma is strolling in the book market "Suug is-Saraay," one of oldest markets in Baghdad. She stops by a bookstore inquiring about some old books about Baghdad, when the owner of the shop begins to intrigue her with folk tales on the literary history of the city.

1. The Story of the Caliph Harun ir-Rashid and Abu Nuwas

The Caliph Harun ir-Rashid, whose reign is considered to be the golden age of the Islamic empire, ruled from 786 to 809. Abu Nuwas was a famous poet whose life was full of intrigues.

Title: "il-9udhur aqbah mnidh-dhanib" (Audio)

yoom mnil-ayyaam il-Khaliifa Haruun ir-Rashiid chaan da-yitmashsha b-hadiiqat qasra.

w shaaf Abu Nuwaas da-yishrab nabiidh bil-hadiiqa.

il-Khaliifa ghidab hwaaya li°an il-Khalifa huwwa Amiir il-Mu°miniin.

lamman Abu Nuwaas shaaf il-Khaliifa khaaf w damm butil in-nabiidh waraa.

il-Khaliifa si°al abu Nuwaas "haay shunu daamm wara zahrak?"

Abu Nuwaas gaal " butil mayy, mawlaay."

il-Khaliifa galla "khalliini ashuufa."

Abu Nuwaas shawwaf il-butil lil-Khaliifa.

il-Khaliifa shaaf il-butil bii nabiidh ahmar, w galla "shloon il-mayy ykuun ahmar?"

Abu Nuwaas galla "mawlaay, il-mayy min shaafak khijal minnak w saar ahmar."

il-Khaliifa kullish ghidab 9ala Abu Nuwaas w haddada bil-qatil.

bass Abu Nuwas twassal bil-Khaliifa hatta yi9fi 9anna.

il-Khaliifa galla "a9fi 9annak bi-sharit waahid, huwwa tintiini 9udhur aqbah mnidh-dhanib."

Abu Nuwaas galla "mawlaay, shloon agdar antiik 9udhur aqbah mnidh-dhanb?"

il-Khaliifa galla "maa a9ruf. loo tintiini 9udhur aqbah mnidh-dhanib loo aqutlak." w raah.

ba9ad kam yoom, Abu Nuwaas shaaf il-Khaliffa da-yitmashsha bil-hadiiqa. raah wara il-Khaliifa w girasa min tiiza.

il-Khaliifa gumaz wi-t9ajjab. minu yigdar yigrus Amiir il-Mu°miniin b-qasra?

il-Khaliifa indaar da-yshuuf minu girasa, shaaf abu Nuwaas. galla "haay shloon tijjarra° tugrus Amiir il-Mu°miniin?!"

Abu Nuwaas galla "il-9afu mawlaay, aani fakkarit inta Zubayda."

il-Khaliifa ghidab akthar li°ann Zubayda hiyya zawijta. w galla "shloon tijjarra° tugrus zawijti Zubayda, Umm il-Mu°miniin?!"

Abu Nuwaas galla "mawlaay, aani maa ajjara° agrus Zubayda, bass haadha 9udhri. inta tidhdhakkar tilabit minni antiik 9udhur aqbah mnidh-dhanib?"

il-Khaliifa Harun ir-Rashiid dihak hwaaya, w 9ifa 9an Abu Nuwaas.

عُنْوان: "إلْعُـذر أقْبَح مُن الـذّنـِب"

يوم مُن الأيَام، إلْخَليفة هارون الـرَّشـيـد چان دَيـتْمَشـّا بْ حَديقَة قَصْرَه.

وشاف ابو نُواس دَ يـشْـرَب نـَبـيـذ بالحَـديقة.

إلْخَليفة غـِضَب هُـوايَه لأن الخَليفة هو أمير المُؤمنين.

لَـمَّـن ابو نواس شاف الخَليفة خاف وضَمّ بُـطِل الـنَّـبـيـذ وَراه.

الخليفة سِئـتـل ابو نواس "هاي شُـنُو ضام وَرا ظَـهَـرَك؟"

ابو نواس گال "بُطِل مَيْ، مَـوْلاي."

الخليفة گَـلْـلَـه "خَـلّـيـنـي أشُـوفه."

ابو نواس شَـوَّف البُطِل لِـلْخليفة.

الخليفة شاف البُطِل بي نَبيذ أحْمَر، و گَـلْـلَـه "شْـلون الْـمَـيْ يُـكون أحْمَر؟"

ابو نواس گَـلْـلَـه "مَـوْلاي، الْـمَـيْ مِـن شافَك خِـجـل مِـنَّك وصار أحْمَر."

الـخليفة گَـلّـش غِـضَب عَلى ابو نواس وهَـدَّدَه بِـالْـقَـتِـل.

بَـس ابو نواس تَـوَسَّـل بِـالْخليفة حتّى يِـعْـفـي عَـنّه.

الخليفة گَـلْـلَـه "أعْـفـي عَـنّـك بِـشَـرْط واحِد، هو تِـنْطيـني عُـذر أقْـبَح مُـن الـذَّنـِب."

ابو نواس گَـلْـلَـه "مَـوْلاي، شْـلون أ گْـدَر أنْطيك عُـذر أقْـبَح مُـن الـذَّنـْب؟"

الخليفة گَـلْـلَـه "ما أدري. لو تِـنْطيـني عُـذرُ أقْـبَح مُـن الـذَّنـِب لو أقْتُـلَـك". وراح.

بَـعَـد كَم يوم، ابو نواس شاف الخليفة دَيِـتْمَـشّـه بالحديقة. راح وَرا الخليفة و گِـرَصّه مِن طيـزَه. الخليفة گُـمَـز وتْـعَـجَّـب. مِنو يِـگْـدَر يُـگْـرُص أمير الْـمُـؤمِنين بْ قَـصْـرَه؟ الخليفة إنْدار دَ يْـشُـوف مِـنو گِـرَصَّه. شاف ابو نواس. گَـلْـلَـه "هاي شْـلون تِـجَّـرَّأ تُـگْـرُص أمير الْـمُؤمِنين؟!"

ابو نواس گَـلْـلَـه "إلْـعَـفو مَـوْلاي. آني فَـكَّـرت إنت زُبَـيْـدَة."

الخليفة غِـضَب أكْـثَـر أكْـثَـر لأن زُبَـيْـدَة هي زَوجْـتَـه. و گَـلْـلَـه "شْـلون تِـجَّـرَّأ تُـگْـرُص زَوجْـتـي زُبـيْـدَة، أُم الْـمُـؤمِنين؟!"

ابو نواس گَـلْـلَـه "مَـوْلاي، آني ما أجَّـرَّأ أكُـرْص زُبَـيْـدَة. بَـس هاذا عُـذري. إنت تِـذكَّـر طِلَبِـت مِـنّـي أنْطيك عُـذرُ أقْـبَح مُـن الـذَّنـِب؟"

الخليفة هارون الـرَّشـيـد ضِحَـك هُـوايَه. وعَـفـا عَـن ابو نواس.

Translation: *"The excuse is worse than the misdeed."*

Once upon a time, the Caliph Harun ir-Rashid was strolling in his palace garden.

He saw Abu Nuwas in the garden drinking wine.

The Caliph was very angry because he was the Prince of the Believers.

When Abu Nuwas saw the Caliph he was afraid and hid the wine bottle behind his back.

The Caliph asked Abu Nuwas, "What are you hiding behind your back?"

Abu Nuwas said to him, "A bottle of water my lord."

The Caliph said to him, "Let me see it."

Abu Nuwas showed the bottle to the Caliph.

The Caliph saw the bottle with red wine in it and said to him, "How come the water is red?"

Abu Nuwas said to him, "My lord, when the water saw you it became abashed and turned red."

The Caliph was very angry with Abu Nuwas and threatened him with death.

But Abu Nuwas begged the Caliph to forgive him.

The Caliph said to him, "I would forgive you on one condition: that you give me an excuse that is worse than the misdeed."

Abu Nuwas said to him, "My lord, how could I give you an excuse that is worse than the misdeed?"

The Caliph said "I don't know. Either you give me an excuse that is worse than the misdeed or I shall kill you."

A few days went by, Abu Nuwas saw the Caliph walking in the garden. He went behind him and pinched him on his buttocks.

The Caliph jumped in surprise and wondered who would to do that to him in his palace.

When the Caliph turned around to see who pinched him, he saw Abu Nuwas. He said to him, "How dare you pinch the Prince of the Believers?!"

Abu Nuwas said to him, "Sorry my lord, I thought you were Zubayda."

The Caliph became even angrier because Zubayda was his wife, and said to him, "How dare you pinch my wife Zubayda, the Mother of the Believers?!"

Abu Nuwas said, "My lord, I don't dare pinch Zubayda, but this is my excuse. Do you remember your demand from me that I give you an excuse that is worse than the misdeed?"

The Caliph Harun ir-Rashid laughed and forgave Abu Nuwas.

(The well-known saying of this story, "The excuse is worse than the misdeed," is cited when somebody makes a mistake, doesn't perform his/her duty etc., then gives a stupid excuse for the misdeed.)

Vocabulary (Audio)

adab / aadaab (S/P)	literature/s	أَدَب / آداب
qussa / qusas (S/P)	tale/s, story/s	قُصّة / قُصَص
hadaara / hadaaraat	culture/s, civilization/s	حَضارَة / حَضارات
hadaari / hadaariyya (M/F adj.)	cultural	حَضاري / حَضارِيَّة
sha9ab	people	شَعَب
sha9bi / sha9biyya (adj.)	folkloric, popular	شَعْبي / شَعْبِيَّة
khaliifa / khulafaaʾ (S/P)	caliph/s	خَليفة / خُلَفاء
9udhur / a9dhaar (S/P)	excuse/s	عُذر / أعْذار
aqbah < qabiih (adj.)	worse < bad (lit. ugly)	أقْبَح > قَبيح
dhanib / dhunuub (S/P)	misdeed/s, sin/s	ذَنِب / ذْنوب
yitmashsha	He strolls/walks.	يِتْمَشّى
hadiiqa / hadaayiq (S/P)	garden/s	حَديقة / حَدايِق
qasir / qusuur (S/P)	palace/s	قَصِر / قُصور
nabiidh	wine	نَبيذ
ghidab, yigh dab	to become angry	غِضَب، يِغْضَب
amiir / umaraaʾ (S/P)	prince/s	أمير / أمَراء
muʾmin / muʾminiin (S/P)	believer/s	مُؤْمِن / مُؤْمِنين
Amiir il-Muʾminiin	Prince of Believers (Caliph's title)	أمير المُؤْمِنين
lamman	when, at the time	لَمَّن
khaaf, ykhaaf	to be afraid	خاف، يُخاف

ḏamm, yḏumm (DV)	*to hide*	ضَـمّ، يُـضُـمّ
ḏaamm (part.)	*hiding*	ضَامّ
buṭil / bṭaala (S/P)	*bottle/s*	بُـطِل / بُـطَالَـة
haay (invariable)	*his/that* (see also lesson 14)	هَايْ
wara	*behind, in the back*	وَرَا
zahar	*back*	ظَـهَـر
gaal, yguul (HV)	*to say*	گَال، يُـگـول
galla	*He said to him.*	گَـلْـلَـه
ashuuf	*I see.*	أشـوف
shawwaf, yshawwif	*to show*	شَـوّف، يُـشَـوّف
mawlaay	*my lord*	مَـوْلَاي
khijal, yikhjal (RV)	*to become abashed/ashamed*	خِـجَـل، يِـخْـجَـل
haddad, yhaddid	*to threaten*	هَـدّد، يُـهَـدّد
qatil	*murder, killing*	قَـتِـل
aqutlak	*I kill you* (M).	أقُـتْـلَـك
twassal, yitwassal	*to beg*	تْـوَسّـل، يِـتْـوَسّـل
yi9fi	*He forgives.*	يِـعْـفِي
sharṭ / shuruuṭ (S/P)	*condition/s*	شَـرْط / شُـرُوط
tinṭiini	*You give me.*	تِـنْـطِيـني
anṭiik	*I give you.*	أنْـطِيـك
agdar	*I can. I am able.*	أگْـدَر
a9ruf	*I know.*	أعْـرُف
giras, yugrus (RV)	*to pinch*	گِـرَص، يُـگْـرُص
ṭiiz / ṭyaaza (S/P)	*buttocks*	طِـيـز / طْـيَازَة
gumaz, yugmuz (RV)	*to jump*	گُـمَـز، يُـگْـمُـز
t9ajjab	*He was surprised.*	تْـعَـجّب
ndaar, yindaar	*to turn around*	نْـدار، يِـنْـدار
ijjarraᵓ < itjarraᵓ	*He dared.*	إجَّـرَّأ > إتْـجَـرَّأ
tidhdhakkar (RV)	*You (M) remember.*	تِـذَّكَّـر
fakkar, yfakkir (RV)	*to think*	فَـكّـر، يُـفَـكّـر
fakkarit	*I thought.*	فَـكّـرت
Zubayda	*name of the Caliph's wife*	زُبَـيْـدَة
liᵓann	*because*	لأَنّ
umm	*mother*	أمّ
Umm il-Muᵓminiin	*Mother of the Believers* (title)	أمّ الـمُـؤمنيـن
ṭilabit	*You (M) demanded. You requested.*	طِـلَـبِـت
minni	*from me*	مِـنّي
anṭiik	*I give you* (M).	أنْـطِيـك
ḏiḥak, yiḏḥak (RV)	*to laugh*	ضِـحَـك، يِـضْـحَـك
9ifa, yi9fi (WV)	*to forgive*	عِـفَا، يِـعْـفِي

2. The Story of the Lion and the Wolf
Title: "sh-ṣaarat khoo muu farwat sabi9?"

fad yoom is-sabi9 (Abu Khmuyyis) malik il-ḥaywaanaat chaan kullish 9aṭ shaan w
    da-ydawwir 9ala mayy.

shaaf biir mayy. lamman baawa9 bil-biir shaaf dhiib waagi9 bil-biir.

is-sabi9 sallam 9adh-dhiib. widh-dhiib jaawaba "ahlan w sahlan yaa Abu Khmuyyis."

is-sabi9 galla "sh-da-ssawwi jawwa bil-biir?"

idh-dhiib jaawaba "aani da-asawwi farwa."

is-sabi9 galla "yaa dhiib, ij-jaw baarid bish-shita, aani ariid farwa hamm."

idh-dhiib galla "zeen, asawwilak farwa, bass rah aḥtaaj jilid ṭili".

is-sabi9 raah w rija9 ba9ad saa9a ṣaayid ṭiliyyeen smaan. w rima iṭ-ṭiliyyeen lidh-dhiib
    bil-biir.

idh-dhiib galla "bass haadha muu kaafi aḥtaaj ṭilyaan hwaaya. ṭili waaḥid loo thneen
    bil-yoom."

is-sabi9 gaam kull yoom yjiib ṭili loo ṭiliyyeen lidh-dhiib. w kull marra yisʔal "khilṣat
    il-farwa?"

idh-dhiib yjaawba "aḥtaaj ba9ad jilid".

ba9deen is-sabi9 khilaṣ ṣabra, liʔann kull marra yjiib ṭili, idh-dhiib yintii 9udhur jidiid
    "chinit mariiḍ, chaan aku 9iid."

bass Abu Khmuyyis zihag, w gaal lidh-dhiib "laazim tkhalliṣ il-farwa!"

idh-dhiib jaawaba "ba9ad yoomeen".

is-sabi9 rija9 ba9ad yoomeen, bass idh-dhiib galla "il-ubra inkisrat, ta9aal baachir w jiib
    ḥabil wiyyaak."

is-sabi9 riji9 thaani yoom w nazzal il-ḥabil bil-biir ḥatta yis ḥab il-farwa.

is-sabi9 bidda yis ḥab il-farwa, w fakkar il-farwa laazim zeena liʔannha chaanat thigiila.

bass huwwa ma-chaan yidri idh-dhiib mit9allig bil-ḥabil wi-mghatti raasa b-jilid ṭili.

awwal-ma wiṣal idh-dhiib l-ḥaaffat il-biir, rima ij-jilid 9ala wijih is-sabi9 wi-nhizam.

lamman Abu Khmuyyis shaal ij-jilid min 9ala wijha, idh-dhiib ṣaar bi9iid w nija b-nafsa.

عُنْوان: "شْصارَت خُو مُو فَرْوَت سَبِع؟"
فَد يوم السَّبِع (أبو خُمَيِّس) مَلِك الحَيْوانات چان كُلِّش عَطْشان و دّ يُدَوِّر على مَيّ.
شاف بير مَيّ. لِمَّن باوَع بالبير شاف ذِيب واگِع بالبير.
السَّبِع سَلَّم عَ الذِّيب. والذِّيب جاوَبَه "أهْلا وسَهْلا يا أبو خُمَيِّس."
السَّبِع گَلْلَه "شْدَسّوّي بالبير؟"
الذِّيب جاوَبَه "آني داسَوّي فَرْوَة."
السَّبِع گَلْلَه "يا ذِيب، الجَوّ بارِد بالشِّتا، آني أريد فَرْوَة هَمّ."
الذِّيب گَلْلَه "زين، بَس رَح أُحْتاج جِلِد طِلي."
السَّبِع راح و رجَع بَعَد ساعة صايِدْلَه طِلِيِّين سُمان. ورمى الطِّلِيِّين لِلذِّيب بالبير.
الذِّيب گَلْلَه "بَس هاذا مُو كافي، اُحْتاج طِلي واحِد لو طِلِيِّين بالْيوم."

إلسَّبع گـام كُل يوم يُجيب طِلي لو طِلِيّـــين لِــلذيب. وكُل مَـرَّة يِسْأَل "خِـلْـصَت الفَـرْوَة؟"

إلذيب يُجاوْبه "أحْتاج بَـعَد جِلـد."

بَعْـدين الشّبع خِلـص صَبْره. لأن كُل مَـرَّة يُجيب طِلي، الـذيب يِنْطي عُذُر جديد "چِنـت مَريض، چان أكو عِيد."

بَس ابو خُمُـيِّس زهَك، وگـال لـلـذيب "لازم تْخَلّـص الفَـرْوَة!"

إلذيب جاوَبَه "بَعَد يومين."

الشّبع رجَع بعد يومين، بَس الـذيب گـلّـه "الأبْرَة إنْكِـسـرَت، تـعال باچِر وجيب حَبـل ويّـاك."

إلشّبع رجَع ثاني يوم ونَـزّل الحَبـل بالبير حَتّى يِسْحَب الفَـرْوَة.

إلشّبع بِدَا يِسْحَب الفَـرْوَة. وفَكّـر الفَـرْوَة لازم زينة لأنّها چانت ثِـگِـيلة.

بَس هو مَ چان يِـدْري الـذيب مِتْعَلّگ بالحَبـل ومُـغَـطّـي راسَـه بِجِلـد طِلي.

أوّل مَ وصَل الذيب حافّة البِـير، رمى الجِلـد على وجِـه الشّبع ونْـهِـزَم.

لـمَّـن ابو خُمُـيِّس شال الجِـلـد مِن على وجْـهَـه، الـذيب صار بِـعيد ونْجى بْ نَفْسَه.

Translation: *"What happened? It's not the lion's fur coat!"*

One day, the lion (Abu <u>Kh</u>muyyis), the king of the beasts, was very thirsty looking for water.

He saw a well. When he looked down into the well he saw a wolf.

The lion greeted the wolf and the wolf said to him, "Welcome Abu <u>Kh</u>muyyis."

Said the lion, "What are you doing down there?"

The wolf replied, "I am making a fur coat."

The lion said, "O wolf, the winter is cold and I would like to have a fur coat, too."

Said the wolf, "Okay, but I will need sheepskins."

The lion went and came back after one hour having hunted two fat sheep and threw them down the well to the wolf.

The wolf said, "But this is not enough. I shall need one or two sheep every day."

The lion began to bring one or two lambs every day to the wolf, and asked him each time, "Is the fur coat done?"

The wolf would respond "I need more skin."

Then the lion ran out of patience because each time he brought a lamb, the wolf gave him new excuses for not finishing the coat, "I was ill, there was a feast," etc.

But the lion got fed up and said to the wolf, "You must finish the coat!"

Said the wolf, "In two days."

When the lion returned after two days, the wolf said to him, "The needle broke. Come tomorrow and bring a rope with you."

The lion came the next day and threw the rope down the well to pull up the fur coat.

As he began to pull up the coat he thought it must be a fine one since it was heavy.

But he did not realize that the wolf was hanging on the rope after covering his head with a sheepskin.

As soon as the wolf was drawn to top of the well, he threw the skins in the lion's face and fled.
By the time Abu Khmuyyis lifted the skins off his face the wolf was far away and saved himself.

(The saying of this story: "What happened? It's not the lion's fur coat!" is cited when delivering a job, especially if a garment is postponed a few times—E.S. Stevens, *Folk-Tales of Iraq*, Oxford University Press, London 1931.)

Vocabulary (Audio)

sh-saarat?	What happened? (lit. *What has become of it?*)	شُـصـارَت؟
khoo	interjection implying apprehension or hope	خـو
farwa / farwaat (S/P)	fur/s	فَـرْوَة / فَـرْوات
sabi9 / sbaa9 (S/P)	lion's	سَـبِـع / سُـباع
Abu Khmuyyis	lion's nick name (lit. *father of five referring to the lion's five claws*)	أبو خْـمَـيِّـس
haywaan / haywaanaat (S/P)	animal/s, beast/s	حَـيْوان / حَـيْوانات
ydawwir	He searches/looks for.	يْـدَوِّر
biir / byaara (S/P)	well/s	بـير / بْـيارَة
lamman	when, at the time	لَـمَّـن
baawa9, ybaawi9	to look/see	باوَع، يْـباوِع
dhiib / dhyaaba (S/P)	wolf/s	ذيـب / ذيـابَة
waagi9 (part.)	falling, fallen	واگِـع
jaawab, yjaawib	to answer	جاوَب، يْـجاوِب
jawwa	inside, underneath	جَـوَّه
jaw	weather, climate	جَـوْ
hamm	also, too	هَـمّ
asawwi	I make	أسَـوّي
asawwilak	I make for you.	أسَـوّلَـك
da-asawwi	I am making	داسَـوّي
ahtaaj	I need	أحْـتاج
jilid /jluud (S/P)	skin/s, leather/s	جِـلِـد / جُـلـود
saayid (part.)	hunting, hunted	صايـد
tili / tilyaan (S/P)	sheep, lamb/s	طِـلِـي / طِـلْـيان
tiliyyeen	two sheep	طِـلِـيِّـيـن
simiin / smaan (S/P M)	fat	سِـمـين / سْـمان
rima, yirmi	to throw	رِمَا، يِـرْمي
kaafi	enough	كافي

gaam	*He stood up. He began to . . . (in association with another verb).*	گـام
marra	*once, one time*	مَـرَّة
kull marra	*each time, every time*	كُل مَـرَّة
khilsat	*It is finished/done.*	خِلْـصَت
sabur	*patience*	صَبُـر
sabra	*his patience*	صَبْـرَه
khilas sabra	*He ran out of patience.*	خِلَـص صَبْـرَة
li'ann	*because*	لأن
9iid / a9yaad (S/P)	*feast/s, festival/s*	عِـيـد / أعْـيـاد
zihag	*He is fed up/disgusted.*	زهَـگ
ubra / ubar (S/P)	*needle/s*	أُبْـرَة / أُبَـر
inkisar, yinkisir (RV)	*to be broken*	إنْـكِـسَـر، يِنْـكِـسِـر
ta9aal	*come (imp. v.)*	تـعـال
habil / hbaal (S/P)	*rope/s*	حَـبِـل / حُبال
nazzal	*He lowered.*	نَـزَّل
yis hab	*He pulls.*	يِـسْـحَب
fakkar	*He thought.*	فَـكَّر
thigiil / thigiila (M/F)	*heavy*	ثـگِـيـل / ثـگِـيـلة
mit9allig	*hanging on*	مِتْـعَلّـگ
mghatti	*covering*	مُغَـطّـي
awwal-ma	*as soon as (injunction)*	أوّل مَ
wisal, yoosal	*to reach/arrive*	وصَـل، يوصَل
haaffa / haaffaat (S/P)	*edge/s*	حافـّة / حافـّات
wijih	*face*	وجِـه
nhizam, yinhizim (RV)	*to run away, to flee*	نْـهِـزَم، يِـنْـهِـزِم
shaal, yshiil (HV)	*to lift off, to carry*	شـال، يُـشـيـل
nija, yinja (WV)	*to be saved*	نْـجَـا، يِـنْـجَـا
nafis	*self, being, soul*	نَـفِـس
nafsa	*himself*	نَـفْـسَه
lizam, yilzam	*to catch, to hold*	لِزَم، يِـلْـزَم
kidhab, yikdhib	*to lie*	كِـذب، يِـكْـذِب

Grammar and Remarks
Conjunctions:

Conjunctions are used to connect words, phrases or clauses, e.g. and, or, if, etc. Several conjunctions have already appeared in the book. There are two types of conjunctions in Iraqi Arabic: simple conjunctions and those which are formed by adding the suffix "**-ma**" to certain prepositions, interrogatives, or nouns. Below is a list of the most common conjunctions of the two types with examples. (Audio)

1. Simple Conjunctions:

w/wa و *and*

Kaamil w Samiira w Laylaa 9iraaqiyyiin	*Kamil and Samira and Laylaa are Iraqis.*	كامل وسميرة وليلى عراقيِّين

bass بَس *but, only, enough*

aani khaabartak, bass il-khat chaan mashghuul	*I called you, but the line was busy.*	آني خابَرْتك. بَس الخَط چان مَشْغول
dirasna 9arabi bass	*We studied Arabic only.*	دِرَسْنا عربي بَس
haadha w bass	*This is enough.*	هاذا وبَس

laakin لاكِن *but*

laakin inti tidriin aani ta9baan!	*But you know I am tired!*	لاكِن إنتِ تِدْرين آني تَعْبان!

aw أوْ *or*

inta 9iraaqi aw Masri?	*Are you Iraqi or Egyptian?*	إنت عِراقي أوْ مَصْري؟

loo لو *or*

hiyya 9arabiyya loo Turkiyya?	*Is she an Arab or a Turk?*	هي عَرَبِيَّة لو تُرْكِيَّة؟

loo لو *if* (see also lesson 19)

loo jiit chaan rihna siwiyya	*If you had come we would have gone together.*	لو جيت چان رِحْنا سِوِيَّه

idhaa إذا *if* (see also lesson 19)

idhaa truuh lil-9iraq zuur Baabil	*If you go to Iraq, visit Babylon.*	إذا تْروح لِلْعِراق زور بابل

li'ann لأن *because*

huwwa yudrus hwaaya li'ann 9inda mtihaan	*He is studying very much because he has an exam.*	هو يُدْرُس هُوايَه لأن عِنْدَه امْتِحان

hatta حَتّى *in order to, so (that), until*

jiibli jilid hatta asawwilak farwa	*Bring me skins so that I will make you a fur coat.*	جيبْلي جِلِد حتّى أسَوِّلَك فَرْوَة

laa . . . wala لا . . . ولا *neither . . . nor, not . . . and not* (see also lesson 4)

il-mat9am laa ghaali wala rikhiis	*The restaurant is neither expensive nor cheap.*	إلمَطْعَم لا غالي ولا رخيص

min مِن *when*

min yiji nruuh siwiyya   *When he comes we will go together.*   مِن يِجي نْروح سِـوِيَّـه

walaw ولَـوْ *although, even though*

raahaw lil-9iraaq walaw   *They went to Iraq although*   راحَوْ لِـلْـعراق ولَـوْ مَ

ma-yihchuun 9arabi   *they don't speak Arabic.*   يِـحْـچـون عَربي

2. Conjunctions with Suffix -ma مَ:
a. With Interrogatives:

ween? *(where?)*	ween-ma *(wherever)*	وين مَ
	ween-ma truuh aruuh wiyyaak *(Wherever you go, I go with you.)*	وين مَ تْروح أروح وِيّاكَ
shwakit? *(when?)*	shwakit-ma *(whenever)*	شْـوَكِـت مَ
	shwakit-ma triidiin *(Whenever you [F] want.)*	شْـوَكِـت مَ تْريدين
shloon? *(how?)*	shloon-ma *(however, any way that)*	شْـلـون مَ
	shloon-ma triidiin *(Any way you [F] want.)*	شْـلـون مَ تْريدين
shunu? sh- ? *(what?)*	shunu-ma, sh-ma *(whatever)*	شْ مَ
	sh-ma triid antiik *(I give you [M] whatever you want.)*	شْ مَ تْريد أنْطيك
shgadd? *(how much?)*	shgadd-ma *(no matter how much)*	شْـگَـد مَ
	ariid is-sayyaara shgadd-ma ykuun si9irha *(I want the car, no matter how much its price.)*	أريد الـسَّـيّـارة شَـگَـد مَ يْـكون سِـعِـرُها
minu? *(who?)*	minu-ma *(whoever)*	مِنو مَ
	minu-ma yiji yaakhudh li-ktaab *(Whoever comes takes the book.)*	مِنو مَ يِـجي ياخُـذ لِـكْـتاب
mneen? *(from where?)*	mneen-ma *(from wherever)*	مْنـين مَ
	mneen-ma ijeet ahlan biik *(Wherever you came from, you are welcome.)*	مْنـين مَ إجيـت أهْـلاً بـيـك

b. With Prepositions:

gabul (*before*)	gabul-ma (*before*)	گَبُل مَ
	huwwa raah gabul-ma ijeetu (*He left before you arrived.*)	هو راح گَبُل مَ إجيتو
ba9ad (*after*)	ba9ad-ma (*after*)	بَعَد مَ
	ruuh ba9ad-ma tshuuf Laylaa (*Go, after you see Laylaa.*)	روح بَعَد مَ تْشوف ليلى
been (*between*)	been-ma (*while*)	بيـن مَ
	hiyya wislat been-ma aani naayim (*She arrived while I was asleep.*)	هي وِصْلَت بيـن مَ آني نايـم
mithil (*like, similar to*)	mithil-ma (*as, the way that*)	مِـثِـل مَ
	sawweet ish-shughul mithil-ma triid (*I did the work the way that you wanted.*)	سَـوّيت الشُّـغـل مِـثِـل مَ تْـريد

c. With Some Nouns:

yoom (*day*)	yoom-ma (*the day when*)	يـوم مَ
	akuun farhaan yoom-ma azuur Baghdad (*I will be happy when I visit Baghdad.*)	أكون فَـرْحان يوم مَ أزور بغداد
saa9a (*hour*)	saa9at-ma (*the hour when*)	ساعَة مَ
	frahit hwaaya saa9at-ma shiftich (*I was very happy when I saw you.*)	فْـرَحِت هُـوايه ساعَة مَ شِـفْتِـج
mahall (*place*)	mahall-ma (*the place where*)	مَحَـل مَ
	raahaw mahall-ma shiftak (*They went to the place where I saw you.*)	راحَـوُ مَحَـل مَ شِـفْتَك

Idioms and Common Phrases (Audio)

1. makaan (ak) khaali مَكانَك خالي *(You) were missed. (lit. Your place was vacant.)*

il-baarha zirna Baabil, makaanak khaali	*Yesterday we visited Babylon. We missed you.*	إلبارْحة زِرْنا بابل، مَكانَك خالي
leesh ma-jiitu lil-hafla, makaankum khaali	*Why didn't you come to the party? We missed you.*	ليش مَ جيتو لِلْحَفْلة؟ مَكانْكُم خالي
Laylaa makaanha khaali, hiyya muu hnaa	*Laylaa is missed, she is not here.*	ليلى مَكانْها خالي، هي مُو هْـنا
yoom ij-jum9a akalit ib-mat9am zeen, makaanich khaali	*On Friday I ate in a good restaurant. I missed you there.*	يوم الجُّـمْعَة أكَـلِت بْ مَطْعَم زين، مَكانِـج خالي

2. 9aashat iid + pronoun   + عاشَت إيــد   *well done* (lit. *long live (your) hand.*)

It is said to someone who has done a good job.

9aashat iidak haadha khoosh shughul	*Well done, this is good work.*	عاشَت إيدَك هاذا خوش شُغُل
9aashat iidkum akilkum tayyib	*Well done, your food is tasty.*	عاشَت إيدُكُم أُكِلْكُم طَيِّب
9aashat iidich sallahti is-saa9a b-sur9a	*Well done, you fixed the watch quickly.*	عاشَت إيدِج صَلَّحْتي السّاعة بْ سُرْعَة

Drill   tamaariin   تَمارين

1. Answer orally the following questions based on folktale number 1:

ween il-Khaliifa chaan da-yitmashsha?	وين الخَليفة چان دَيِتْمَشّا؟
ilman shaaf il-Khaliifa bil-hadiiqa?	إلْمَن شاف الخَليفة بالْحَديقة؟
sh-da-ysawwi Abu Nuwaas bil-hadiiqa?	شْـدَ يُسَـوّي ابو نواس بالْحَديقة؟
sh-sawwa Abu Nuwaas min shaaf il-Khaliifa?	شْ سَـوّى ابو نواس مِن شاف الْخَليفة؟
Abu Nuwaas chaan da-yishrab mayy loo nabiidh?	ابو نواس چان دّ يِشـرب مَي لو نبيـذ؟
leesh il-Khaliifa ma-yriid ahad yishrab ib-qasra?	ليش الخَليفة مَ يُريد أحَد يِشرب بْ قصرة؟
shunu shart il-Khaliifa hatta yi9fi 9an Abu Nuwaas?	شُنو شَـرْط الخَليفة حَتّى يِـعْفي عَن ابو نواس؟
ba9deen sh-sawwa Abu Nuwaas lil-Khaliifa?	بَعْدين شْ سَوّى ابو نواس لِلْخَـليفة؟
min shunu t9ajjab il-Khaliifa?	مِن شُنو تْعَـجّب الْخَليفة؟
sh-gaal Abu Nuwaas lil-Khaliifa ba9ad-ma girasa?	شْگـال ابو نواس لِلْخليفة بَعَد مَ گِـرَصَه؟
leesh il-Khaliifa ghidab akthar 9ala Abu Nuwaas?	ليش الخَليفة غِضَب أكْثَر على ابو نواس؟
shunu chaan jawaab Abu Nuwaas lil-Khaliifa?	شُنو چان جَواب ابو نواس لِلْخَـليفة؟
shunu isim zawjat il-Khaliifa?	شُنو أسِم زَوْجَة الْخَليفة؟
leesh 9ifa il-Khaliifa 9an Abu Nuwaas?	ليـش عِـفـا الْخَليفة عَـن ابو نواس؟

2. Answer orally the following questions based on folktale number 2:

minu malik il-haywaanaat?	مِـنو مَلِك الحَيْوانات؟
leesh is-sabi9 chaan da-ydawwir 9ala mayy?	ليش السَّـبِع چان دَ يُدَوِّر على مَيّ؟
sh-shaaf is-sabi9 bil-biir?	شْ شاف السَّـبِع بالْبير؟
sh-raad is-sabi9 mnidh-dhiib?	شْ راد السَّـبِع مُـن الـذّيب؟

sahiih idh-dhiib chaan da-ysawwi farwa?	صَحيح الـذّيب چان دّ يُسَوّي فَـرْوَة؟
sh-tilab idh-dhiib mnis-sabi9?	شُ طِلَب الـذّيب مُن السَّـبـع؟
kam tili raad idh-dhiib bil-yoom?	كـم طِلـي راد الـذّيب بالـيوم؟
leesh is-sabi9 khilas sabra?	ليـش السَّـبـع خِلَـص صَبْـرَه؟
leesh idh-dhiib raad tilyaan akthar?	ليـش الـذّيب راد طِلـيان أكـثَـر؟
shloon is-sabi9 sihab il-farwa mnil-biir?	شـلون السَّـبـع سِحَب الفروة مُن الـبير؟
leesh il-farwa chaanat thigiila?	ليـش الفروة چانـت ثِـكـيلة؟
sh-sawwa idh-dhiib min wisal haaffat il-biir?	شُ سَـوّى الـذّيب مِن وصَل حافة البير؟
leesh Abu Khmuyyis ma-gidar yilzam idh-dhiib?	ليـش ابو خمُـيّـس مَ كِـدَر يِلـئزَم الـذّيـب؟
leesh idh-dhiib kidhab 9as-sabi9?	ليـش الـذّيب كِـذب عَ السَّـبـع؟

3. Fill in the blanks using the conjunctions listed below:

bass	min	gabul-ma	yoom-ma
loo	ween-ma	ba9ad-ma	shgadd-ma
hatta	laakin	been-ma	minu-ma
idhaa	shwakit-ma		

_____ 9inda fluus chaan ishtira sayyaara

raahat lil-madrasa _____ ma-dirsat 9arabi

laazim ykuun 9indak fiiza _____ truuh lil-9iraaq

_____ khaabartak il-khatt chaan mashghuul

Samiir habb Samiira _____ shaafha

antiik fluus _____ triid

ijiit azuurak _____ inta ma-chinit bil-beet

_____ shifit Basma sallimli 9leeha

ta9aal lil-beet _____ truuh lij-jaami9a

aruuh wiyyaak _____ triid

zaaraw il-9iraaq _____ zaaraw Lubnaan

wiṣal Khaalid _____ aani <u>ch</u>init bil-madrasa

_____ taakliin aakul wiyyaa<u>ch</u>

_____ tzuur aruu<u>h</u> wiyyaak

بَس	مِن	گَبُل مَ	يوم مَ
لو	وين مَ	بَعَد مَ	شْگَـد مَ
حَتّى	لاكِن	بين مَ	مِنو مَ
إذا	شْوَكِت مَ		

_____ عِنئَدَه فلوس چان إشْتِرا سَيّارة

_____ مَ دِرْسَت عَربي راحَت لِلْمَدرسة

لازم يْكون عَندك فيزَة _____ تْروح لِلْعِراق

_____ خابَرْتك الْخَط چان مَشْغول

سمير حَب سميرة _____ شافْها

أنْطيك فلوس _____ تْريد

إجيت أزورَك _____ إنت مَ چِنِت بالْبيت

_____ شِفِت بسمة سَلّمْلي عَليها

تَعال لِلْبيت _____ تْروح لِلْجّامِعَة

أروح وِيّاك _____ تْريد

زارَوْ العراق _____ زارَوْ لُبنان

وِصَل خالد _____ آني چِنِت بِالْمَدْرَسَة

_____ تاكْلين آكُل وِيّاچ

_____ تْزور أروح وِيّاك

4. Put the following in complete sentences:

mahal-ma   مَحَل مَ

---

saa9at-ma   ساعَة مَ

---

mithil-ma   مِثـِل مَ

---

mithil   مِثـِل

---

l'iann   لأن

---

laa ... wala   لا ... ولا

---

minu?   مِنو؟

---

minu-ma   مِنو مَ

---

makaanak khaali   مَكانك خالي

9aashat iidak   عاشت إيدَك

---

aw   أوْ

---

mneen?   مُنين؟

---

mneen-ma   مُنين مَ

---

5. Complete and read the following aloud:

a. il-filim <u>ch</u>aan kulli<u>sh</u> zeen, makaanak <u>kh</u>aali   إلْفِـلِم چان كُـلّـش زين. مَكانَك خالي

_____ , makaani<u>ch</u> <u>kh</u>aali   مَكانِـج خالي ,_____

_____ , makaankum <u>kh</u>aali   مَكانْكُم خالي ,_____

_____ , makaana <u>kh</u>aali   مَكانَه خالي ,_____

_____ , makaanha <u>kh</u>aali   مَكانْها خالي ,_____

_____ , makaanhum <u>kh</u>aali   مَكانْـهُم خالي ,_____

b. 9aa<u>sh</u>at iidak (M), sawweet i<u>sh</u>-<u>sh</u>ughul ib-sur9a   عاشِت إيـدَك. سَـوّيت الشّـغُـل بْ سُـرْعَة

(inti) _____   _____ (إنتـي)

(intu) _____   _____ (إنتو)

(huwwa) _____   _____ (هـو)

(hiyya) _____   _____ (هـي)

(humma) _____   _____ (هُـمَّه)

6. Translate the following into Arabic:

Whenever I go to the school garden I see Samar there.

_____

Iraq is one of the most ancient countries in the world.

_____

Mesopotamia means the land between the two rivers, the Tigris and the Euphrates.

_____

Harun ir-Rashid was the most famous caliph of the Islamic Empire.

_____

The "Epic of Gilgamesh" is the oldest literary tale; it preceded Homer's *Iliad* by more than two thousand years.

_____

Harun ir-Rashid, Prince of the Believers, was married to Zubayda, Mother of the Believers.

_____

Was Abu Nuwas a well-known poet or a musician in the caliph's palace?

_____

The lion is stronger than the wolf, but the wolf is smarter than he is.

_____

The wolf had fallen in the well and he tricked the lion to take him out of the well.

_____

The wolf lied to the lion because he wanted to save himself.

_____

The lion ran out of patience after many excuses from the wolf.

_____

Better to have a good brain than strength without a brain.

_____

Whenever I go home I find my sister watching TV.

_____

After I study Arabic here, I shall go to the University of Cairo in Egypt for two years.

_____

I would have gone to Baghdad if I had spoken Iraqi Arabic better.

_____

What have you learned from these two old folktales?

_____

7. Write two short paragraphs: one telling about an experience you might have had similar to the folktale, "The excuse is worse than the misdeed," and the second similar to the folktale, "What happened? It's not the lion's fur coat."

GLOSSARY

Please read the notes below.

This glossary contains the words, expressions, phrases, and idioms that occur in this book. It is organized as follows:

Both the Arabic–English and the English–Arabic sections are arranged alphabetically. The Arabic–English section is listed according to the Iraqi Arabic letters and symbols, which are shown in lesson 1 (ء ʾ, ب b, پ p, ت t, ث th, ج j, چ ch, ح ḥ, خ kh, د d, ذ dh, ر r, ز z, س s, ش sh, ص ṣ, ض ḍ, ط ṭ, ظ ẓ, ع 9, غ gh, گ g, ف f, ق q, ك k, ل l, ڵ l, م m, ن n, ھ h, و w, ي y). The English–Arabic section is listed in the English alphabetical order.

1. A cross-reference system is used in the glossary. References are made to the relevant discussion, structure, or grammar either in the text or to another heading in the glossary. A word that occurs or constitutes part of a common phrase/idiom is listed under that word.

2. Since the glottal stop sound, the so-called **hamza** (ʾ), is not rendered graphically in this text when it occurs in the beginning of the word, the reader will find the words that begin with one of the vowels, "**a**," "**i**," or "**u**" listed in that vowel order under the heading (ʾ) in the glossary.

3. Verbs are listed, as usual, under the third person masculine singular form (he) in the past tense followed by the present tense.

4. Nouns and adjectives (including relative adjectives) are listed without the definite article "**il-**" in their singular forms followed by the plural, masculine, and feminine forms.

Arabic–English

ء   ع

hamza (glottal stop)

A   أ

Aashuur	*Ashur*, name of ancient land and god of northern Iraq	آشــور
Aashuuri / Aashuuriyyiin (M)	*Assyrian/s*, ancient people of northern Iraq	آشـوري / آشوريّــين
Aashuuriyya / Aashuuriyyaat (F)	*Assyrian/s, Assyriology*	آشوريّـة / آشوريّات
aani	*I* (independent pronoun, see lesson 2)	آني
aanisa / aanisaat (S/P)	*Miss/s*	آنِسَة / آنِسات
sayyida / sayyidaat (S/P)	*Mrs./s*	سَـيِّـدَة / سَـيِّـدات
ab / aabaaʾ (S/P)	*father/s*	أب / آبــاء
waalid	*father*	والِـد
abjadi / abjadiyya (M/F)	*alphabetical, alphabetically*	أُبْجَدي / أَبَجَديّـة
il-huruuf il-abjadiyya	*the alphabet*	إلـحُـروف الأبْجَـدِيّـة
Abu Nuwaas	A proper name of the night-life street in Baghdad named after the famous Arab poet who lived in the eighth century.	أبو نُـواس
athar / aathaar (S/P)	*antique/s, antiquity/s, ruin/s*	أثَـر / آثـار
athari / athariyya (M/F)	*archaeological, ancient*	أثَـري / أَثَـريّـة
aathaari / aathaariyya / aathaariyyiin (M/F/P)	*archaeologist/s*	آثاري / آثاريّـة / آثاريّـين
ajjar, yʾajjir (RV)	*to rent, to lease*	أجَّـر / يـأجِـر
ahhad	*one, someone*	أحَّـد
ahsan	*better* (for comparative see lesson 18)	أحْـسَن
ahmar / hamra (M/F/)	*red* (for colors see lesson 18)	أحْمَر / حَمْرَة
akh / ukhwaan (S/P)	*brother/s*	أخ / أخْـوان
akhadh, yaakhudh (RV)	*to take*	أخَـذ، يـاخُـذ
akhbaar mahalliyya	*national news*	أخْـبار مَـحَـلِّـيّـة
akhbaar 9aalamiyya	*international news*	أخْـبار عالَـمِيّـة
adab / aadaab (S/P)	*literature/s*	أدَبْ / آداب
bala adab	*impolite, with no manner*	بَلا أدَبْ

arba9a	*four*	أَرْبَعَة
arbaa-ta9ash	*fourteen*	أَرْباطَعَش
arba9iin	*forty* (see lesson 7)	أَرْبَعين
raabi9 / raab9a (M/F)	*fourth* (ordinal number see lesson 17)	رابِع / رابْعَة
asaas / usus (S/P)	*basis, foundation/s*	أَساس / أُسُس
asaasi / asaasyyiin (M)	*basic*	أَساسي / أَساسِيّين
asaasiyya / asaasiyyaat (F)	*basic*	أَساسِيَّة / أَساسِيّات
asad / usuud (S/P)	*lion/s*	أَسَد / أُسود
Asad Baabil	*the Lion of Babylon* (in Babylon)	أَسَد بابل
as-salaamu 9alaykum	*Peace be upon you.* (Always in plural form, it is the most common formal greeting that can be used any time of the day, see lesson 2.)	ألسَّلامُ عَلَيْكُم
wa 9alaykum is-salaam	*And peace be upon you* (in reply).	وَعَلَيْكُم إلسَّلام
aswad / suud (M)	*black/s* (colors, see lesson 18)	أسْوَد / سود
sooda / soodaat (F)	*black/s*	سودَة / سودات
asfar / sufur (M)	*yellow/s*	أصْفَر / صُفُر
safra / safraat (F)	*yellow/s*	صَفْرة / صَفْرات
asil	*origin*	أصِل
asli / asliyyiin (M)	*original*	أصْلي / أصْلِيّين
asliyya / asliyyaat (F)	*original*	أصْلِيَّة / أصْلِيّات
a9raad	*symptoms*	أعْراض
a9zab / 9uzzaab (M)	*single/s, unmarried*	أعْزَب / عُزّاب
9izba / 9izbaat (F)	*single/s, unmarried*	عِزْبَة / عِزْبات
Akad	*Akkad* (name of ancient land and city in Iraq)	أكَد
Akadi / Akadiyya / Akadiyyiin (M/F/P)	*Akkadian/s* (name of ancient people)	أكَدي / أكَدِيَّة / أكَدِيّين
akal, yaakul (RV)	*to eat*	أكَل، ياكُل
akil	*food* (collective word)	أكِل
akil sharqi	*eastern food*	أكِل شَرْقي
akil gharbi	*western food*	أكِل غَرْبي
akla / aklaat (S/P)	*dish/es of food*	أكْلَة / أكْلات

aklat il-yoom	*today's dish*	أكْلَـة إلْيـوم
aku	*there is/are* (see lesson 7)	أكـو
maaku	*there isn't / aren't*	ماكـو
aqba<u>h</u> < qabii<u>h</u> (adj.)	*worse < bad* (lit. *ugly*)	أقْبَـح > قَبيـح
alam / aalaam	*pain/s*	ألَـم / آلام
alif / aalaaf (S/P)	*thousand/s* (see lesson 17)	ألِـف / آلاف
a<u>ll</u>a	*God*	ألله
a<u>ll</u>a y<u>kh</u>alliik	*May God preserve you* (see lesson 5).	ألله يُخَـلّيـك
a<u>ll</u>aa(h)	*How nice* (expression of admiration, see lesson 5).	ألْـلاه
a<u>ll</u>aa bil-<u>kh</u>eer	*God bless* (see lesson 5)	ألله بِـالْخيـر
Amriika	*America*	أمْريكا
Amriiki / Amriikaan (M)	*American/s*	أمْريكـي / أمُريكـان
Amriikiyya / Amriikiyyaat (F)	*American/s*	أمُريكِـيَّـة / أمُريكِـيّـات
amiir / umaraaᵓ (S/P)	*prince/s*	أميـر / أُمَـراء
amur / awaamir (S/P)	*order/s, matter/s*	أمُـر / أوامِـر
ahal, 9eela	*family*	أهَـل، عـيـلَـة
ahlan wa sahlan	*welcome* (very common phrase)	أهْلاً وسَهْلاً
aw, loo	*or*	أوْ، لـو
Awrubba	*Europe*	أوْروبـا
awwal / uulaa (M/F)	*first* (see ordinal number lesson 17)	أوَّل / اُولى
awwal-ma	*as soon as* (see lesson 20)	أوَّل مَ
ayy, yaa, yaahu?	*which?* (see lesson 15)	أي، يـا، يـاهو

ا   إ

ii, na9am	*yes*	ـي، نَـعَـم
ibin / abnaaᵓ (S/P)	*son/s* (for more terms, see lesson 16)	إبِـن / أبْـناء
ibin a<u>kh</u>	*nephew* (brother's side)	إبِـن أخ
ibin u<u>kh</u>ut	*nephew* (sister's side)	إبِـن اُخُـت
ibin <u>kh</u>aal	*male cousin* (maternal)	إبِـن خـال
binit <u>kh</u>aal	*female cousin* (maternal)	بِـنِـت خـال
ibin 9amm	*male cousin* (paternal)	إبِـن عَـم
binit 9amm	*female cousin* (paternal)	بِـنِـت عَـم
ithneen / thinteen (M/F)	*two* (cardinal)	إثْـنيـن / ثِـنْـتيـن
thaani / thaanya (M/F)	*second* (ordinal)	ثاني / ثانِـيَـة

ija, yiji (irregular WV)	*to come*	إجَا. يِجي
ijtimaa9	*meeting*	إجْـتِـماع
ijtimaa9i / ijtimaa9iyya (M/F adj.)	*social*	إجْـتِـماعي / إجْـتِـماعِـيّة
ihna	*we (independent pronoun, see lesson 2)*	إحْنا
ijjarra° < itjarra°	*to dare*	إجَّـرَّأ > إتْجَـرَّأ
iddallal / iddallali / iddallalu (M/F/P)	*whatever you wish, at your service (see lesson 10)*	إدَّلَـلْ / إدَّلَـلـي / إدَّلَـلو
idhaa	*if (see lesson 19)*	إذا
idhaa9a / idhaa9aat (S/P)	*radio station/s*	إذاعَـة / إذاعات
idhin	*ear*	إذِن
ir-Rashiid	*proper name*	إلـرَّشـيد
shaari9 ir-Rashiid	Name of one of the oldest main streets in Baghdad, named after the Caliph Harun ir-Rashid (786–809).	شـارِع الـرَّشـيد
isim / asmaa° (S/P)	*name/s*	إسِـم / أسْـماء
asmaa° il-ishaara	*demonstrative words*	أسْـماء الإشارَة
is9aaf	*emergency*	إسْـعاف
sayyaarat is9aaf	*ambulance*	سَـيّـارَة إسْـعاف
Islaam	*Islam*	إسْـلام
Islaami / Islaamiyyiin (M adj.)	*Islamic*	إسْـلامي / إسْـلامِـيّـين
Islaamiyya / Islaamiyyaat (F adj.)	*Islamic*	إسْـلامِـيّة / إسْـلامِـيّـات
istarliini / istarliiniyya (M/F)	*sterling (British pound)*	إسْتَـرْليني / إسْتَـرْلِـينِـيّة
istikaan / istikaanaat (S/P)	*(tea) glass/es*	إسْتِـكان / إسْتِـكانات
istimaara / istimaaraat (S/P)	*form/s, card/s*	إسْتِـمارة / إسْتِـمارات
idaafi / idaafiyya (M/F)	*additional*	إضافي / إضافِـيّة
i9laam	*media*	إعْـلام
iqtisaad	*economy, economics*	إقْتِـصاد
iqtisaadi / iqtisaadiyya (M/F adj.)	*economical*	إقْتِـصادي / إقْتِـصادِيّة
il-	*the (see lesson 2)*	إلْـ
il	*have (see lesson 14)*	إلْ
il-baarha	*yesterday*	إلْـبـارْحَة
iltihaab / iltihaabaat	*infection/s*	إلْتِـهاب / إلْتِـهابات

il-<u>h</u>amdu lillaah	*Thanks be to God* (see lesson 5)	إلـحَـمْـدُ لله
il-<u>H</u>illa	*Hilla (a city near Babylon)*	إلـحِـلّـة
ij-Janaaʾin il-Mu9allaqa	*the Hanging Gardens*	إلجَّـنـائِـنِ الـمُـعَـلَّـقة
illa	*of, before, less than* (telling time)	إلّـلَ
illi	*who, whom, which, that* (depending on context, relative clause, see lesson 19)	إلْـلي
ilman?	*whom?* (see lesson 15)	إلْـمَـن؟
ilwee<u>sh</u>?	*why?* (see lesson 15)	إلْـويش؟
immeen, mneen?	*where from?* (see lesson 15)	إمْـين. مُـنـين؟
inta	*you* (M) (independent pronoun, see lesson 2)	إنت
indaar, yindaar (HV)	*to turn around*	إنْـدار، يِـنْـدار
in<u>sh</u>aalla	*God willing* (see lesson 5)	إنْـشـالله
inkisar, yinkisir (RV)	*to be broken*	إنْـكِـسَـر، يِـنْـكِـسِـر

U أَ

ubra / ubar (S/P)	*needle/s*	أُبْـرَة / أُبَـر
ujra / ujar (S/P)	*fee/s, rate/s*	أُجْـرة /أَجَـر
u<u>kh</u>ut / <u>kh</u>awaat (S/P)	*sister/s*	أُخُت / خَـوات
usbuu9 / asaabii9 (S/P)	*week/s*	أُسْـبوع / أسابـيـع
ustaa<u>dh</u> / asaati<u>dh</u>a (M)	*professor/s*	أُسْـتـاذ / أسـاتِـذة
ustaa<u>dh</u>a / ustaa<u>dh</u>aat (F)	*professor/s*	أُسْـتاذة / أُسْـتـاذات
umm, waalda	*mother*	أُم. والـكَـدة

B ب

b- / bi-	*in, by, at, with* (preposition, see lesson 5)	بْ / بِـ
baab / bwaab (S/P)	*door/s*	بـاب / بُـواب
baaba <u>gh</u>annuuj	*eggplant dip*	بـابَـة غَـنّـوج
Baabil	*Babylon (ancient city)*	بـابِـل
Baabili / Baabiliyyiin (M)	*Babylonian/s*	بـابِـلي / بابِـلِـيِّـين
Baabiliyya / Baabiliyyaat (F)	*Babylonian/s*	بـابِـلِـيَّـة / بابِـلِـيّـات
baa<u>ch</u>ir	*tomorrow*	بـاجِـر
il-yoom	*today*	إلْـيـوم
baarid / baarda (M/F)	*cold*	بـارِد / بـارْدة

baasbort / baasbortaat (S/P)	*passport/s* (borrowed from English)	باسْبورْت / باسْبورْتات
Jawaaz / jawaazaat	*passport/s*	جَـواز سَـفَـر
baas / baasaat (S/P)	*bus/es* (borrowed from English)	باص / باصات
baa9, ybii9 (HV)	*to sell* (see lesson 8)	بـاع، يُـبيع
baaqi / baaqiin (M)	*staying* (participle, see lesson 13)	باقي / باقئين
baaqya / baaqyaat (F)	*staying*	باقئَة / باقئيات
baamya	*okra*	بـامْـيَـة
baawa9, ybaawi9	*to look/see*	باوَع، يُـباوع
baayi9, bayyaa9/ bayyaa9iin (M)	*salesman/en*	بايـع، بَـيّاع / بَـيّاعِـين
bayyaa9a / bayyaa9aat (F)	*saleswoman/en*	بَـيّاعَـة / بَـيّاعات
baddaala / baddaalaat (S/P)	*telephone operator/s*	بَـدّالة / بَـدّالات
bariid	*post office, mail*	بَـريد
bariid jawwi	*airmail*	بَـريد جَـوّي
bariid 9aadi	*regular mail*	بَـريد عـادي
bariid sarii9	*express mail*	بَـريد سَـريع
maktab bariid / makaatib bariid	*post office/s*	مَكْـتب بريد / مكاتب بريد
abu l-bariid	*mailman* (see lesson 7)	أبو الْـبـريد
sanduuq bariid	*mail box*	صَنْـدوق بريد
barnaamij / baraamij	*program/s*	بَـرْنامِج / بَـرامِج
bass	*but, only, enough*	بَـسّ
batin / butuun	*abdomen/s, stomach/s*	بَطِـن / بُطون
ba9ad	*after*	بَـعَـد
ba9d iz-zuhur	*afternoon, P.M.*	بَـعَـد الظّـهُـر
ba9ad-ma	*after* (conjunction, see lesson 20)	بَـعَـد مَ
ba9deen	*later on* (invariable)	بَـعْـدين
bala adab	*impolite, with bad manners*	بلا أدَب
balam	*boat*	بَـلَـم
balkat, balki	*perhaps, may be* (invariable, see lesson 17)	بَـلْـكَـتْ، بَـلْـكي
balla?	*is it so? is it true?* (idiom, see lesson 5)	بَـلْـلَـه
muu balla?	*isn't it so? isn't it?* (idiom, see lesson 5)	مُـو بَـلْـلَـه

bank / bunuuk (S/P)	*bank/s*	بَنْك / بُـنوك
bawwaaba / bawwaabaat (S/P)	*gate/s*	بَوّابَة / بَـوّابات
beet / buyuut (S/P)	*house/s, home/s*	بيت / بُـيـوت
bee<u>sh</u>, ibbee<u>sh</u>?	*how much?* (see lesson 15)	بـيـش. إبّـيـش؟
bee<u>d</u>	*egg* (collective)	بـيـض
bee<u>d</u>a / bee<u>d</u>aat (S/P)	*egg/s*	بـيـضة / بيـضات
been-ma	*while* (conjunction, see lesson 20)	بـيــن مَ
biir / byaara (S/P)	*well/s*	بـيـر / بُـيـارَة
biira	*beer*	بـيـرَة
bit-taᵓkiid	*certainly*	بِـتّـأكِـيد
biduun	*without*	بِـدون
bistaan	*orchard*	بِـسْـتـان
bistan<u>ch</u>i / bistan<u>ch</u>iyya (S/P)	*orchard keeper/s* (see lesson 7)	بِـسْـتَـنـجي / بِـسْـتَـنْـجِـيّـة
b-<u>s</u>uura <u>kh</u>aa<u>s</u>a	*in particular, especially* (see lesson 14)	بُـصُـورة خاصّـة
b-<u>s</u>uura 9aamma	*in general, generally* (see lesson 14)	بُـصُـورة عـامّـة
bi<u>t</u>-<u>t</u>abu9, <u>t</u>ab9an	*of course*	بِـالطَّـبُـع، طَـبْـعـاً
bi9iid / bi9iida / b9aad (M/F/P)	*far*	بـعـيـد / بِـعـيـدة / بُـعـادِ
bikull . . .	*with all . . .*	بِـكُـل . . .
bikull suruur	*with pleasure*	بِـكُـل سُـرور
bina, yibni (WV)	*to build* (see lesson 9)	بِـنـا، يِـبْـني
binit, bnayya / banaat (S/P)	*girl/s, daughter/s* (see also **ibin**)	بِـنِـت، بْـنَـيّـة / بَـنـات
binit a<u>kh</u>	*niece* (brother's side)	بِـنِـت أخ
binit u<u>kh</u>ut	*niece* (sister's side)	بِـنِـت أخُـت
binit <u>kh</u>aal	*cousin* (maternal)	بِـنِـت خـال
binit 9amm	*cousin* (paternal)	بِـنِـت عَـم
booy / booyaat (S/P)	*bellboy/s, busboy/s* (English)	بـوي / بُـوياَت
boskaart / boskaartaat (S/P)	*postcard/s* (from English, also poskaart)	بُـسْـكـارْت / بُـسْـكـارْتـات
Burij Baabil	*the biblical Tower of Babel*	بُـرج بابل
bu<u>s</u>al	*onion* (collective)	بُـصَـل
raas bu<u>s</u>al	*one onion* (lit., *a head of onion*)	راس بُـصَـل
bu<u>t</u>il / b<u>t</u>aala (S/P)	*bottle/s*	بُـطِـل / بْـطـالـة

buqa, yubqa (WV)	*to stay* (see lesson 9)	بُـقـا، يُـبْـقـا
bsaat / busut (S/P)	*kilim/s*	بُساط / بُسُط

P پ

paasbort / paasbortaat (S/P)	*passport/s* (borrowed from English)	پـاسْبـوْرت / پـاسْبـوْرْتات
poskaart / poskaartaat (S/P)	*postcard/s*	پُـسْكـارْت / پُـسْكـارْتات

T ت

taariikh / tawaariikh (S/P)	*history/s, date/s*	تاريخ / تَـواريخ
taaza	*fresh*	تازة
tabbuula	*chopped salad*	تَـبُّـولة
tahiyya / tahiyyaat (S/P)	*greeting/s*	تَـحِـيَّـة / تَـحِـيّـات
tahriir	*editing*	تَـحْـرير
muharrir	*editor*	مُـحَـرِّر
raʾiis qisim it-tahriir	*editor-in-chief*	رَئـيـس قِـسـم الـتَـحْـرير
tadhkara / tadhaakir (S/P)	*ticket/s*	تَـذْكَـرَة / تَـذاكِـر
tara	*you know, otherwise, certainly* (invariable, see lesson 12)	تَـرَه
tarjama / tarjamaat (S/P)	*translation/s*	تَـرْجَـمَة / تَـرْجَـمات
qisim tarjama	*translation section*	قِـسِـم تَـرْجَـمة
tasriif	*change, exchange* (also see **sarraaf**)	تَـصْريف
tasliih / tasliihaat (S/P)	*repair/s, fixing/s*	تَـصْليح / تَـصليحات
ta9aal	*come*	تَـعال
ta9aaruf	*introduction*	تَـعارُف
ta9baan / ta9baaniin (M)	*tired*	تَـعْبان / تَـعْبانـين
ta9baana / ta9baanaat (F)	*tired*	تَـعْبانـة / تَـعْبانات
taksi / taksiyyaat (S/P)	*taxi/s*	تَـكْسي / تَـكْسِـيّـات
abu t-taksi	*taxi driver* (also see **abu**, lesson 7)	أبـو الـتَّـكْسي
talifoon / talifoonaat (S/P)	*telephone/s*	تَـلِـفـون / تَـلِـفـونات
talifoon moobaayal	*mobile/cell telephone*	تَـلِـفـون مُـوبايَـل
talifoon ardi	*ground telephone*	تَـلِـفـون أرْضي
talfizyoon / talfizyoonaat (S/P)	*televisions/s*	تَـلْـفِـزيون / تَـلْـفِـزيونات
tall / tuluul (S/P)	*tell/s, mound/s*	تَـل / تُـلول
tamur	*palm date* (collective)	تَـمُـر

tamra / tamraat (S/P)	*one date/s*	تَمْرَة / تَمْرات
tanak	*tin*	تَنَك
tanakchi / tanakchiyya (S/P)	*tinsmith/s* (see lesson 7)	تَنَكْچِي / تَنَكْچِيَّة
tamriin / tamaariin (S/P)	*drill/s, exercise/s*	تَمْرين / تَمارين
tis9a	*nine*	تِسْعَة
tsaa-ta9ash	*nineteen*	تْساطَعَش
tis9iin	*ninety* (see lesson 7)	تِسْعين
taasi9	*ninth* (see lesson 17)	تاسِع
ti9ab, yit9ab (RV)	*to get tired*	تِعَب، يِتْعَب
tsharraf, yitsharraf (RV)	*to be honored, to be pleased (meeting someone)*	تْشَرَّف، يِتْشَرَّف
timman, ruzz	*rice*	تِمَّن، رُزّ
t9ajjab, yit9ajjab	*to be surprised*	تْعَجَّب، يِتْعَجَّب
t9allam, yit9allam (RV)	*to learn*	تْعَلَّم، يِتْعَلَّم
tfaddal / tfaddali / tfaddalu (M/F/P)	*please (common expression used when someone is offering something)*	تْفَضَّل / تْفَضَّلي / تْفَضَّلو
tfaddal istariih	*please sit down*	تْفَضَّل إسْتَريح
min fadlak / min fadlich / min fadilkum (M/F/P)	*please (used when someone is requesting something)*	مِن فَضْلَك / مِن فَضْلِج / مِن فَضِلْكَم
tkallam, yitkallam (RV)	*to speak, to talk*	تْكَلَّم، يِتْكَلَّم
tlaatha	*three*	تْلاثَة
tlat-ta9ash	*thirteen*	تْلَطَّعَش
tlaathiin	*thirty*	تْلاثين
thaalith	*third* (see lesson 17)	ثالِث
twassal, yitwassal	*to beg*	تْوَسَّل، يِتْوَسَّل
twannas, yitwannas	*to have fun*	تْوَنَّس، يِتْوَنَّس

TH   ث

thaanya / thawaani (S/P)	*second/s*	ثانْيَة / ثَواني
thalij	*ice*	ثَلِج
thigiil / thigiila (M/F)	*heavy*	ثِگيل / ثِگيلة
thilith	*one-third*	ثِلِث
thoob / thyaab (S/P)	*dress/es, shirt/s, clothes*	ثوب / ثياب
thmaanya	*eight*	ثْمانْيَة
thman-ta9ash	*eighteen*	ثَمَنْطَعَش
thmaaniin	*eighty*	ثْمانين
thaamin	*eighth*	ثامِن

<u>th</u>neen / <u>th</u>inteen (M/F)	*two*	ثُنيـن / ثِنْتيـن
<u>th</u>na9a<u>sh</u>	*twelve*	ثُناعَـش
<u>th</u>aani	*second* (see lesson 17)	ثـاني

J ج

jaab, yjiib (HV)	*to bring*	جـاب، يُـجيب
jaaj	*chicken* (collective)	جـاج
jaaja / jaajaat (S/P)	*chicken/s*	جـاجَـة / جـاجـات
dijaaja / dijaaj (S/P)	*chicken/s*	دِجاجَـة / دِجاج
jaami9 / jawaami9 (S/P)	*mosque/s*	جامِـع / جَـوامِـع
jaami9a / jaami9aat (S/P)	*university/s*	جامِـعَـة / جامِـعات
jaawab, yjaawib	*to answer*	جاوَب، يُجاوِب
jaay / jaayya / jaayyiin (M/F/P)	*coming* (part.)	جايْ / جايَّـة / جايِّيـن
jayya / jayyaat	*arrival/s*	جَـيَّـة / جَيّـات
9ala jayya	*coming, arriving soon* (invariable idiom, see lesson 18)	علـى جَـيَّـة
jadwal / jadaawil (S/P)	*table/s, chart/s, small water canal/s*	جَـدْوَل / جَـداوِل
jaziilan	*much, very* (invariable)	جَـزيلاً
jaww	*weather, climate*	جَـوّ
jaww / ajwaaᵓ (S/P)	*atmosphere/s, air*	جَـوّ / أجْـواء
jawwi / jawwiyya (M/F)	*air, aerial*	جَـوّي / جَـوّيَّـة
bariid jawwi	*airmail*	بَـريد جَـوّي
jawwa	*inside, underneath*	جَـوّه
jawaaz / jawaazaat (S/P)	*passport/s, permit/s*	جَـواز / جَـوازات
baasbort / baasbortaat (S/P)	*passport/s*	باسْبورت / باسْبورْتات
jibin	*cheese*	جِـبيـن
jidd / jduud (M)	*grandfather/s*	جِـدّ / جُـدود
jidda / jiddaat (F)	*grandmother/s*	جِـدَّة / جِـدّات
jiddan	*very* (invariable)	جِـدّاً
jidiid / jidiida / jdaad (M/F/P)	*new*	جِـديـد / جِـديـدَة / جُـداد
jisir / jisuur (S/P)	*bridge/s*	جِـسِـر / جِـسور
jisim / ajsaasm (S/P)	*body/s*	جِـسِـم / أجْـسام
jigaara / jigaayir (S/P)	*cigarette/s*	جِـگارة / جِـگايِـر
jilid / jluud (S/P)	*skin/s, leather/s*	جِـلِـد / جُـلود
juu9	*hunger*	جُـوع

juu9aan / juu9aaniin (M)	*hungry*	جُـوعان / جُـوعانين
juu9aana / juu9aanaat (F)	*hungry*	جُـوعانـة / جُـوعانات
ju<u>n</u>ta / juna<u>t</u> (S/P)	*suitcase/s, purse/s, briefcase/s*	جُنْطَـة / جُنَـط

CH چ

<u>ch</u>aan (kaan), ykuun	*was/were, will be/shall be* (see lesson 13)	چان (كان). يُـكـون
<u>ch</u>aay / <u>ch</u>aayaat (S/P)	*tea/s*	چـائْ / چـايات
<u>ch</u>aay<u>ch</u>i / <u>ch</u>aay<u>ch</u>iyya (S/P)	*tea vendor/s (in coffee shop)*	چـائْـچـي / چـائْـچِـيَّـة
<u>ch</u>alib / <u>ch</u>laab (M)	*dog/s*	چَـلِـب / چُـلاب
<u>ch</u>alba / <u>ch</u>albaat (F)	*dog/s*	چَـلْـبَة / چَـلْـبات
<u>ch</u>am, kam?	*How many?* (see lesson 15)	چَـم، كَـم؟
<u>ch</u>ibiir / <u>ch</u>ibiira / kbaar (M/F/P)	*big, large, old* (person)	چِـبـيـر / چِـبِـيـرة / كُـبار
kabiir / kabiira / kbaar	*big, large, old* (person)	كَـبـيـر / كَـبِـيـرة / كُـبار

H ح

<u>h</u>a-	*will, shall, going to* (prefix see lesson 12)	حَـ
<u>h</u>aadi<u>th</u>a	*accident*	حادِثَـة
<u>h</u>aadir / <u>h</u>aadriin (M)	*ready, present*	حاضِر / حاضُرين
<u>h</u>aadra / <u>h</u>aadraat (F)	*ready, present*	حاضُرَة / حاضُرات
<u>h</u>aarr / <u>h</u>aarra (M/F, adj.)	*hot, warm*	حارّ / حارَّة
<u>h</u>aaffa / <u>h</u>aaffaat (S/P)	*edge/s*	حافَّة / حافّـات
<u>h</u>aal	*condition*	حـال
maa<u>sh</u>i il-<u>h</u>aal	*okay, not bad* (see lesson 7)	ماشي الْحـال
<u>h</u>abb, y<u>h</u>ibb (DV)	*to like, to love* (see lesson 9)	حَـبّ، يُـحِـبّ
<u>h</u>abbaaya / <u>h</u>ubuub		حَـبّـاية / حُـبوب
<u>h</u>ubuub musakkina	*pain killers*	حُـبـوب مُـسَـكِّـنة
<u>h</u>ubuub munawwima	*sleeping pills*	حُـبـوب مُـنَـوِّمَة
<u>h</u>abil / <u>h</u>baal (S/P)	*rope/s*	حَـبِـل / حُـبال
<u>h</u>atta	*in order to, until, till, as far as*	حَـتَّـى
<u>h</u>adra / <u>h</u>adraat (S/P)	*presence of a person (expression of addressing, see lesson 2)*	حَـضْـرة / حَـضْـرات
<u>h</u>ajiz	*reservation*	حَـجِـز
<u>h</u>adii<u>th</u> / <u>h</u>adii<u>th</u>a / <u>h</u>daa<u>th</u> (M/F/P)	*modern*	حَـديث / حَـديثة / حُـداث
a<u>h</u>da<u>th</u>	*more recent* (see lesson 18)	أحْـدَث

hadiiqa / hadaayiq (S/P)	*garden/s*	حَـديقة / حَـدايِـق
haraara (Noun)	*heat, temperature*	حَرارة
harb / huruub (S/P)	*war/s*	حَـرُب / حَـروب
harbi / harbiyya / harbiyyiin (M/F/P)	*military*	حَرْبي / حَرْبِيَّة / حَرْبِـيِّـين
haruf / huruuf (S/P)	*letter/s, consonant/s*	حَـرُف / حُـروف
huruuf abjadiyya	*alphabet*	حُـروف أبْجَـدِيَّة
huruuf 9illa	*vowels*	حُـروف عِـلَّة
hatt, yhutt (DV)	*to put (see lesson 9)*	حَطّ، يُـحُطّ
hadaara / hadaaraat	*culture/s, civilization/s*	حَـضارَة / حَـضارات
hadaari / hadaariyya (M/F adj.)	*cultural*	حَـضاري / حَـضارِيَّـة
hafiid / ahfaad (M)	*grandchild/children*	حَـفيـد / أَحْـفـاد
hafiida / hafiidaat (F)	*grandchild/children*	حَـفيـدَة / حَـفيـدات
halawiyyaat	*sweets*	حَـلَـويـّات
halig	*mouth*	حَـلِـگ
hammaam / hammaamaat (S/P)	*bath/s, bathroom/s*	حَـمّـام / حَـمّـامات
hammamchi / hammamchiyya (S/P)	*bathhouse keeper/s (see lesson 6)*	حَـمّـمْـچـي / حَـمّـمْـچِـيَّـة
mirhaad	*toilet*	مِـرْحـاض
hawaala / hawaalaat (S/P)	*money order/s*	حَـوالة / حَـوالات
hawaala bariidiyya	*money order*	حَـوالَـة بريـدِيَّـة
hawaala maaliyya	*money order*	حَـوالة مالِـيَّـة
hawaali	*about, approximately*	حَـوالي
hawwal, yhawwil (RV)	*to change, to exchange, to move*	حَـوَّل، يُـحَـوِّل
haywaan / haywaanaat (S/P)	*animal/s, beast/s*	حَـيْـوان / حَـيْـوانات
hicha, yih chi (WV)	*to speak (see lesson 9)*	حِـچـا، يِـحْـچـي
hilu / hilwiin (M)	*pretty, nice, sweet*	حِـلـو / حِـلْـوين
hilwa / hilwaat (F)	*pretty, nice, sweet*	حِـلْـوَة / حِـلْـوات
htaaj, yihtaaj (WV)	*to need, to require*	حْـتاج، يِـحْـتاج
hsaab / hisaabaat (S/P)	*account, bill, invoice, arithmetic (see lesson 17)*	حْـساب / حِـسابات
hsaab tawfiir	*savings account*	حْـساب تَـوْفـيـر
hsaab jaari	*checking account*	حْـساب جاري
hmaar / hamiir (S/P)	*donkey/s*	حْـمار / حَـمـيـر
hurriyya / hurriyyaat	*freedom/s*	حُـرِّيَـة / حُـرِّيّـات
hukuuma / hukuumaat (S/P)	*government/s*	حُـكـومة / حُـكـومات

hummus	*chickpeas*	حُـمَّـص
hummus bi-t hiina	*chickpea dip* (consists of chickpeas, sesame oil, garlic, lemon, and olive oil)	حُـمَّـص بِـطْـحِـيـنَـة

KH خ

khaabar, ykhaabur (RV)	*to telephone* (see lesson 8)	خَـابَـرٍ، يْخَابُـر
mukhaabara	telephone call	مُخَابَـرَة
khaashuuga / khwaashiig (S/P)	*spoon/s*	خاشوگَـة / خْـواشيـگ
mil9aqa / malaa9iq (S/P)	*spoon/s*	مِلْعَقَـة / مَلاعِـق
khaas	*special, private*	خاص
khusuusan (adv.)	*especially*	خُـصوصاً
khusuusi / khusuusiyya (M/F, adj.)	*private, privately*	خُـصوصي / خُـصوصيّـة
kharbaan / kharbaaniin (M)	*broken, not working*	خَـرْبان / خَـرْبانيـن
kharbaana / kharbaanaat (F)	*broken, not working*	خَـرْبانـة / خَـرْبانات
khashsh, ykhushsh (DV)	*to enter* (see lesson 9)	خَـشّ، يُخُـشّ
khatt / khutuut (S/P)	*line/s*	خَـط / خُـطوط
khaaf, ykhaaf (HV)	*to be afraid* (see lesson 8)	خاف، يُـخاف
khaal / khwaal (M)	*uncle/s* (maternal, also see **9amm**)	خال / خْـوال
khaala / khaalaat (F)	*aunt/s* (maternal)	خالـة / خالات
khalla, ykhalli (WV)	*to let, to leave behind* (see lesson 9)	خَـلّـا، يْخَـلّـي
khaliifa / khulafaaʾ (S/P)	*caliph/s*	خَـليفة / خُـلَـفاء
khalliina	*let us*	خَـلّـيـنا
khalliina nruuh	*let us go*	خَـلّـيـنا نْـروح
khamsa	*five*	خَمْسَـة
khmus-ta9ash	*fifteen*	خْمُـصْطَـعَـش
khamsiin	*fifty*	خَمْسيـن
khaamis	*fifth* (ordinal see lesson 17)	خامِـس
kheer / kheeraat (S/P)	*good, goodness, blessing/s*	خيـر / خيـرات
b-kheer	*well, good, fine*	بْ خيـر
alla bil-kheer	*God bless* (see lesson 5)	ألله بِالخيـر
khijal, yikhjal (RV)	*to become abashed/ashamed*	خِـجَـل، يِـخْـجَـل

khidma / khidmaat (S/P)	*service/s*	خِـدْمَة / خِـدُمات
khoo	interjection implying apprehension or hope.	خــو
khoosh	*good* (invariable word that precedes nouns)	خوش
khoosh fikra	*a good idea*	خوش فِـكْـرَة
khubuz	*bread* (collective)	خُـبْـز
sammuun	*bread* (French style)	صَـمُّـون
khurda	*small change*	خُـرْدَة
khudrawaat	*vegetables*	خُـضْـرَوات

D د

da-	A prefix that precedes the present tense verb to indicate present progressive tense (see lesson 12).	دَ
daraja / darajaat (S/P)	*level/s, degree/s, mark/s*	دَرَجَـة / دَرَجات
daris / duruus (S/P)	*lesson/s*	دَرس / دُروس
darras, ydarris (RV)	*to teach*	دَرَّس، يْـدَرِّس
dazz, ydizz (DV)	*to send* (see lesson 9)	دَزّ، يْـدِزّ
da9ash	*eleven*	دَعَـش
daqiiqa / daqaayiq (S/P)	*minute/s*	دَقـيـقـة / دَقايِـق
dawwar, ydawwir (HV)	*to search, to look for*	دَوَّر، يْـدَوِّر
deen / diyuun (S/P)	*debt/s*	دَيـن / دُيـون
dira, yidri (WV)	*I know.*	دِرَا، يِـدْري
diinaar / danaaniir (S/P)	*dinar/s* (the currency of Iraq and some other Arab countries)	دينار / دَنانـير
nuss diinaar	*one-half of a dinar*	نُـص دينار
rubu9 diinaar	*one-quarter of a dinar*	رُبُـع دينار
diin / adyaan (S/P)	*religion/s*	ديـن / أَدْيـان
diini / diiniyya (M/F adj.)	*religious*	ديـني / دينِـيّـة
dijaaja / dijaaj (S/P)	*chicken/s* (also see **jaaj**)	دِجاجَـة / دِجاج
Dijla	*Tigris*	دِجْـلَـة
nahar Dijla	*Tigris River*	نَـهَـرْ دِجْـلَـة
nahar il-Furaat	*Euphrates River*	نَـهَـرُ الـفُـرات
diras, yudrus (RV)	*to study* (see lesson 8)	دِرَس، يُـدْرُس
diktoor / dakaatira (S/P)	*doctor/s* (MD and Ph.D)	دِكْـتـور / دَكاتِـرَة
diwa / adwiya (S/P)	*medicine/s*	دِوَا / أَدْوِيَة

doolma	*stuffed vegetables* (dish)	دولْكَمَة
doomna	*domino*	دومْنَة
duulaar / duulaaraat (S/P)	*dollar/s*	دولار / دولارات
dukkaan / dakaakiin (S/P)	*shop/s, store/s*	دوكّان / دَكاكـين
dumbug	*drum*	دومْبُگ
dumbagchi /	*drummer/s* (see lesson 7)	دومْبَـگْچي /
dumbagchiyya (S/P)		دومْبَـگْچِـيَّة

DH ذ

dhaa9, ydhii9 (HV)	*to broadcast*	ذاع، يَـذيـع
dhahab	*gold*	ذَهَب
fudda	*silver*	فُضّة
dhanib / dhunuub (S/P)	*misdeed/s, sin/s*	ذَنِب / ذْنوب
dhiib / dhyaaba (S/P)	*wolf/s*	ذيـب / ذيابَة

R ر

raah, yruuh (HV)	*to go* (see lesson 8)	راح، يْـروح
raad, yriid (HV)	*to want, to wish* (see lesson 8)	راد، يُـريد
raadyo / raadyowaat (S/P)	*radio/s*	رادْيـو، رادْيُـوات
raas / ruus	*head/s*	راس / روس
raayih / raayhiin (M, part.)	*going, going to* (see lesson 13)	رايِـح / رايْحـين
raayha / raayhaat (F)	*going, going to*	رايْـحَة / رايْـحات
rajaaᵓan	*please* (invariable when requesting something)	رَجـاءً
rah-	*will, shall, going to* (future tense prefix, see lesson 12)	رَح
rasmi / rasmiyyiin (M)	*official, formal*	رَسْمي / رَسْمِـيّـين
rasmiyya / rasmiyyaat (F)	*official, formal*	رَسْمِـيَّة / رسْمِـيّات
ratub / ratba (M/F)	*moist, humid*	رَطْب / رَطْبَة
raqam / arqaam (S/P)	*number/s numeral/s*	رَقَـم / أرْقـام
rayyuug, futuur	*breakfast*	رَيّوگ، فُـطور
ghada	*lunch*	غَـدا
9asha	*dinner*	عَـشـا
rijjaal / ryaajiil (S/P)	*man/men*	رِجّـال / رْيـاجيل
mara / niswaan (S/P)	*woman/en*	مَـرَة / نِـسْوان
rikhiis / rikhiisa / rkhaas (M/F/P)	*cheap, inexpensive*	رِخـيص / رِخيصَة / رْخاص
ghaali / ghaalya / ghaaliin (M/F/P)	*expensive*	غـالي / غالْـيَة / غالِـين
risal, yirsil (RV)	*to send*	رِسَل، يـرْسِل

risaala / rasaaʾil (S/P)	*letter/s*	رِسالَة / رَسائِل
risaala musajjala	*registered letter*	رِسالَة مُسَجَّلَة
rima, yirmi	*to throw*	رِمَا، يِرْمي
ruzz, timman	*rice*	رُزّ، تِمَّن
ruzma / ruzam (S/P)	*package/s*	رُزْمَة / رُزَم

<h2 style="text-align:center">Z ز</h2>

zaar, yzuur (HV)	*to visit* (see lesson 8)	زار، يِـزور
zalaaṯa / zalaaṯaat (S/P)	*salad/s*	زَلاطَة / زَلاطات
zawj / azwaaj (M)	*husband/s* (also see **zooj** below)	زَوْج / أَزْواج
zawja / zawjaat (F)	*wife/s*	زَوْجَة / زَوْجات
zeen / zeeniin (M, adj.)	*well, fine, good, okay*	زين / زيـنـين
zeena / zeenaat (F)	*well, fine, good, okay*	زينَة / زينات
zibid	*butter*	زِبِـد
zihag, yizhag	*to be fed up/disgusted*	زَهَـگ، يِـزْهَـگ
zooj / azwaaj (M)	*husband/s* (see above)	زوج / أَزْواج
zooj ukhut	*brother-in-law*	زوج أُخَـت
zoojat akh	*sister-in-law*	زوج أخ

<h2 style="text-align:center">S س</h2>

saa9a / saa9aat (S/P)	*watch/es, clock/s, hour/s, time*	ساعَة / ساعات
saa9at iid	*wrist watch*	ساعَة إيـد
saa9at jeeb	*pocket watch*	ساعَة جـيـب
saa9at ḥaayiṯ	*wall clock*	ساعَة حايـط
saa9at tanbiih	*alarm clock*	ساعَة تَنْبـيـه
saa9at-ma	*the hour when* (conjunction see lesson 20)	ساعَة مَ
saa9ad, ysaa9id (RV)	*to help, to assist*	ساعَد، يُساعِد
saafar, ysaafir (RV)	*to travel* (see lesson 8)	سافَر، يُسافِر
saaq, ysuuq (HV)	*to drive*	ساق، يُسوق
saakin / saakniin (M, part.)	*living, residing*	ساكِـن / ساكْـنين
saakna / saaknaat (F)	*living, residing*	ساكْـنَة / ساكْـنات
saayiq / saayqa / suwwaaq (M/F/P)	*driver/s*	سايِـق / سايْـقَـة / سُـوّاق
saayiq taksi	*taxi driver*	سايِـق تَـكْـسي
abu t-taksi	*taxi driver* (also see **abu**, lesson 7)	أبو الـتَّـكْـسي
sabab / asbaab (S/P)	*reason/s*	سَـبَـب / أسْباب
sabi9 / sbaa9 (S/P)	*lion's*	سَـبـع / سُباع
asad / usuud	*lion/s*	أسَـد / أسود

sab9a	seven	سَـبْـعَة
sbaa-ta9ash	seventeen	سَـباطْـعَـش
sab9iin	seventy	سَـبْـعـين
saabi9	seventh (ordinal see lesson 17)	سابِـع
sadd, ysidd (DV)	to close, to shut	سَـدّ، يْـسِـدّ
sarii9 / sarii9a (M/F)	fast, express	سَـريع / سَـريـعَة
sa9iid / sa9iida (M/F)	happy	سَـعـيد / سَـعـيدة
Sa9duun	(proper name)	سَـعْـدون
shaari9 is-Sa9duun	Name of one of the main streets in Baghdad.	شارِع الـسَّـعْـدون
safaara / safaaraat (S/P)	embassy/ies	سَـفارَة / سَـفاراّت
qunsiliyya / qunsiliyyaat (S/P)	consulate/s	قُـنْـصِـلِـيَّـة / قُـنْـصِـلِـيّات
safra / safraat (S/P)	trip/s, travel/s	سَـفْـرَة / سَـفْـرات
safra sa9iida	good trip, farewell	سَـفْـرَة سَـعـيدة
salaama	safety	سَـلامَة
ma9a s-salaama	goodbye	مَـع الـسَّـلامَة
samman, ysammin (RV)	to make (someone) fat	سَـمَّـن، يُـسَـمِّـن
sana / sniin (S/P)	year/s	سَـنَة / سْـنـين
sawwa, ysawwi (WV)	to make, to do	سَـوّا، يُـسَـوّي
sayyid / saada (M)	Mr./Messrs.	سَـيِّـد / سادَة
sayyida / sayyidaat (F)	Mrs., lady/ies	سَـيِّـدَة / سَـيِّـدات
sayyaara / sayyaaraat (S/P)	car/s	سَـيّارة / سَـيّارات
sayyaarat is9aaf	ambulance	سَـيّارة إسْـعاف
siʾal, yisʾal (RV)	to ask	سِـئـل، يِـسْـأَل
sitta	six	سِـتّة
sit-ta9ash	sixteen	سِـطْـطَـعَـش
sittiin	sixty	سِـتّـين
saadis	sixth (ordinal see lesson 17)	سادِس
sihab, yis hab	to pull	سِـحَب، يِـسْـحَب
sichchiin / sichaachiin (S/P)	knife/knives	سِـچّـين / سِـچاچـين
si9ir / as9aar (S/P)	price/s, rate/s	سِـعِـر / أسْعار
sikan, yuskun (RV)	to live, to reside	سِـكَن، يُـسْكُن
simcha / simach (S/P)	fish/es	سِـمْـچَة / سِـمَـچ
simach Masguuf	Masguuf fish	سِـمَـچ مَـسْـكوف
simiin / smaan (S/P M)	fat	سِـمـين / سْـمان

sinn / asnaan (S/P)	*tooth/s*	سِـــن / أَسْـنان
siwiyya	*together* (invariable)	سِـويّـه
siyaaha / siyaahaat (S/P)	*tour/s, tourism*	سِـياحَة / سِـياحات
siyaahi / siyaahiyyiin (M)	*tourism, tourist/s*	سِـياحي / سِـياحِـيِّـين
siyaahiyya / siyaahiyyaat (F)	*tourism, tourist/s*	سِـياحِـيَّـة / سِـياحِـيّـات
siyaasa	*politics*	سِـياسَة
siyaasi / siyaasiyya (M/F adj.)	*political*	سِـياسِـي / سِـياسِـيَّـة
sooda / soodaat (F)	*black* (also see **aswad**)	سـودَة / سـودات
Soomar	*Sumer* (ancient land of southern Iraq)	سـومَر
Soomari / Soomariyyiin (M)	*Sumerian/s* (ancient people of Iraq)	سـومَري / سـومَـرِّيـِّـين
Soomariyya / Soomariyyaat (F)	*Sumerian/s*	سـومَرِيَّـة / سـومَـرِيّـات
suug, suuq / swaag (S/P)	*market/s*	سـوك. سـوق / سُـواك
suug sooda	*black market*	سـوك سـودَة
suug is-Safaafiir	Name of a famous, old market in Baghdad known for its brass, copper, and tin craftsmanship	سـوك الصَّـفافير
suruur	*pleasure, happiness*	سُـرور
bikull suruur	*with pleasure*	بِـكُـل سُـرور
(i)stariih	*rest, sit* (imp. verb)	إسْـتَـريـح
tfaddal stariih	*Please sit down* (also see lesson 2)	تْـفَـضَّـل إسْـتَـريح
Swiisra	*Switzerland*	سْـويسْـرا
Swiisri / Swiisriyyiin (M)	*Swiss*	سْـوِيسْـري / سْـوِيسْـرِّيـِّـين
Swiisriyya / Swiisriyyaat (F)	*Swiss*	سْـوِيسْـرِيَّـة / سْـوِيسْـرِيّـات
syaaqa	*driving*	سْـياقَـة

SH ش

sh- / shunu?	*what?* (see lesson 15)	شَـ / شُـنو؟
sh-madriik?	*how do you know?* (idiom, see lesson 15)	شْـمَـدْريك؟
shaaf, yshuuf (HV)	*to see, to look* (see lesson 8)	شاف، يُـشوف
shaal, yshiil (HV)	*to lift, to carry*	شـال، يُـشيل
shakhis / ash khaas (S/P)	*person/s*	شَـخِص / أشْـخاص
shakh si (M)	*personal, private*	شَـخْـصِي

shakh siyya / shakh siyyaat (F/P)	*personality/ies, identity/ies*	شَخْصِيَّة / شَخْصِيّات
sharaf	*honor*	شَرَف
sharraf, ysharruf (RV)	*to honor, to arrive* (see lesson 8)	شَرَّف. يُشَرُّف
shart / shuruut (S/P)	*condition/s*	شَرْط / شُرُوط
sha9ab	*people*	شَعَب
sha9bi / sha9biyya (M/F adj.)	*folkloric, popular*	شَعْبِي / شَعْبِيَّة
shakar	*sugar*	شَكَر
shakarchi / shakarchiyya (S/P)	*sweet seller/s* (see lesson 7)	شَكَرْچِي / شَكَرْچِيَّة
shaku?	*what is it?*	شَكو؟
shaku maaku?	*what is happening?* (see lesson 4)	شَكو ماكو؟
shahar / ashhur (S/P)	*month/s*	شَهَر / أَشْهُر
shawwaf, yshawwif	*to show*	شَوَّف. يُشَوِّف
sh-bii?	*what's wrong?* (see lesson 17)	شْبِي؟
shtira, yishtiri (WV)	*to buy* (see lesson 8)	شْتِرَا. يِشْتِري
sheekaat siyaahiyya	*traveler's checks*	شيكات سِياحِيَّة
shgadd?	*how much? how long?* (see lesson 15)	شْگَد؟
shgadd-ma	*no matter how much* (see lesson 20)	شْگَد مَ
shii / ashyaaʾ (S/P)	*thing/s, something/s*	شِي / أَشْياء
shirab, yishrab (RV)	*to drink* (see lesson 8)	شْرَب. يِشْرَب
shikar, yushkur (RV)	*to thank*	شِكَر. يُشْكُر
shloon?	*how?* (see lesson 15)	شْلون؟
shloon-ma	*however, any way that* (conjunction, see lesson 20)	شْلون مَ
shloon-ma thibb	*as you like* (idiom, see lesson 15)	شْلون مَ تْحِب
shloon-ma triid	*whatever you want* (idiom)	شْلون مَ تْريد
shoorba / shoorbaat (S/P)	*soup/s*	شورْبَة / شورْبات
shooka / shookaat (S/P)	*fork/s, thorn/s*	شوكَة / شوكات
shubbaach, / shabaabiich (S/P)	*window/s*	شُبّاج / شَبابيج
shukran	*thank you, thanks*	شُكْراً

shunu, sh-	*what?* (see lesson 15)	شُـنو، شْـ
shunu-ma, sh-ma	*whatever* (conjunction, see lesson 20)	شْـنو مَ، شْـ مَ
shwakit?	*when?* (see lesson 15)	شْـوَكِـت؟
shwakit-ma	*whenever* (conjunction, see lesson 20)	شْـوَكِـت مَ
shwayya	*little* (invariable)	شْـوَيّـة

ص S

saar, ysiir (HV)	*to become, to have been in place* (see lesson 8)	صار، يْصير
saayid (part.)	*hunting, having hunted*	صايـد
sabaah	*morning*	صَباح
sabaah il-kheer	*good morning*	صَباح الـخير
sabaah in-nuur (in reply)	*good morning*	صَباح النّـور
sabaahan, is-subuh	*in the morning* (adv.)	صَباحاً، الصُّبـُح
sabur	*patience*	صَبـُر
saabuun, saabuuna	*soap* (collective), *one piece of soap*	صابون، صابونـة
saabunchi / saabunchiyya (S/P)	*soap vender/s* (see lesson 7)	صابونْـچي / صابونْـچِيّـة
sahaafa	*press, journalism*	صَحافـة
sahafi / sahafiyya (M/F)	*journalist*	صَحَـفي / صَحَـفِـيّـة
sahiifa / suhuf (S/P)	*newspaper/s*	صَحيفَـة / صُحُـف
sahiih / sahiiha (M/F)	*true, correct* (adj.)	صَحيح / صَحيحَة
sarraaf / sarraafiin (M)	*teller/s, cashier/s*	صَرّاف / صَرّافـين
sarraafa / sarraafaat (F)	*teller/s, cashier/s*	صَرّافـة / صَرّافات
tasriif	*exchange, change (currency)*	تَـصْريف
sarraf, ysarruf (RV)	*exchange, to change*	صَرَّف، يْصَرُّف
sakk / sukuuk (S/P)	*check/s*	صَك / صُكوك
sakk shakhsi	*personal check*	صَك شَـخْـصي
sa9ub / sa9ba (M/F)	*difficult, hard* (adj.)	صَعـُب / صَعْـبـة
saghiir / saghiira/ s ghaar (M/F/P)	*small, little*	صَغـير / صَغـيرَة / صْغار
sammuun	*(French) bread* (collective)	صَمُّـون
sammuuna / sammuunaat (F)	*(French) bread/s*	صَمُّـونـة / صَمُّـونات
khubuz	*bread*	خُـبُـز

sanduuq / sanaadiiq (S/P), also	*box/es*	صَنْدوق / صَناديق
sanduug / sanaadiiq (S/P)	*boxe/s*	صَنْدوگ / صَناديگ
sanduuq bariid	*mail box*	صَنْدوق بَريـد
saydali	*pharmacist*	صَيْـدَلي
saydaliyya	*pharmacy*	صَيْـدَلِيَّة
siiniyya / swaani (S/P)	*tray/s*	صينِيَّـة / صُواني
sihha	*health*	صِحَّة
shloon is-sihha?	*how are you?* (lit., *how is the health?*)	شْـلون الصِّحَّـة
sihhi / sihhiya (M/F)	*healthy, hygienic*	صِحّي / صِحِّيَّة
si9ad, yis9ad (RV)	*to go up, to ascend*	صِعَد، يِصْعَد
sifa / sifaat (S/P)	*attribute/s, adjective/s*	صِفَة / صِفات
sifir / asfaar (S/P)	*zero/s*	صِفِـر / أَصْفار
skhuuna	*fever*	صُخونَـة

D ض

daabut / dubbaat (S/P)	*officer/s* (military)	ضابُط / ضُبّـاط
daabut jawaazaat	*passport officer*	ضابُط جَـوازات
daamm (part.)	*hiding*	ضامّ
dakhum / d khaam (M)	*huge, great*	ضَخُـم / ضُخام
dakhma / dakhmaat (F)	*huge, great*	ضَخْـمَة / ضَخْمات
damm, ydumm (DV)	*to hide*	ضَـمّ، يْـضُـمّ
dihak, yid hak (RV)	*to laugh*	ضِحَك، يِضْحَك

T ط

taabi9 / tawaabi9 (S/P)	*postal stamp/s* (also see **bariid**)	طابِـع / طَـوابِع
tawaabi9 bariidiyya	*stamps, postage*	طَـوابِـع بَريـدِيَّة
taar, ytiir (HV)	*to fly* (see lesson 8)	طار، يُـطير
taalib / tullaab (M)	*student/s*	طالِـب / طُلّاب
taaliba / taalibaat (F)	*student/s*	طالِـبَة / طالِـبات
tabiib / atibbaaᵓ (M)	*physician/s, doctor/s*	طَـبيـب / أَطِبّـاء
tabiiba / tabiibaat (F)	*physician/s, doctor/s*	طَـبيـبَة / طَـبيـبات
tab9an, bit-tabu9	*of course* (adv.)	طَبْـعاً، بِالطّـبُع
tamaata	*tomatoes*	طَـماطَـة
tayyaar / tayyaariin (M)	*pilot/s*	طَـيّـار / طَـيّـارين
tayyaara / tayyaaraat (F)	*airplane/s*	طَـيّـارة / طَـيّـارات
tayyib / tayyba (M/F)	*good, delicious, fine, okay* (depending on context)	طَـيِّـب / طَـيِّـبَة

ṭiiz / ṭyaaza (S/P)	*buttocks*	طِــيــز / طْيـازَة
ṭiḥiin	*flour*	طْحــيـن
ṭifil / aṭfaal (M)	*boy child/children*	طِفِــل / أطْفــال
ṭifla / ṭiflaat (F)	*girl child/children*	طِفْـلَـة / طِفْـلات
ṭili / ṭilyaan (S/P)	*sheep, lamb/s*	طِـلِي / طِلْيان
ṭooba / ṭoobaat (S/P)	*ball/s*	طوبَـة / طوبات

<h2 style="text-align:center">Z ظ</h2>

ẓaruf / ẓuruuf (S/P)	*envelope/s*	ظَــرُف / ظْـرُوف
ẓaruf ṭayyaraan	*airmail envelope*	ظَــرُف طَــيّـران
ẓaruf 9aadi	*regular envelope*	ظَــرُف عادي
ẓahar	*back*	ظَــهَـر
ẓuhur	*noon* (time)	ظُــهُـر
iẓ-ẓuhur	*at noon*	إلـظّـهُـر

<h2 style="text-align:center">9 ع</h2>

9aada / 9aadaat (S/P)	*custom/s, tradition/s*	عادَة / عادات
9aalam	*world, universe*	عالَــم
9aalami / 9aalamiyyiin (M)	*international/s*	عالَــمِـي / عالَـمِـيّـين
9aalamiyya / 9aalamiyyaat (F)	*international/s*	عالَـمِـيّـة / عالَـمِـيّـات
9aash min sima9 sootich	*nice to hear your voice* (see lesson 19)	عاش مِن سِمَع صُوتِـج
9aashat iid . . .	*well done* (see lesson 20)	عاشَـت إيــد . . .
9aamm	*public, general*	عــامّ
9aammiyya	*colloquial* (also see **lugha**)	عــامِّـيّـة
9addaad / 9addaadaat (S/P)	*meter/s, gauge/s*	عَـدّاد / عَـدّادات
9arabaana	*wagon*	عَـرَبانَـة
9arag	*arak* (the national Iraqi alcoholic drink)	عَـرَگ
9arraf, y9arruf (RV)	*to introduce*	عَـرَّف، يـعَـرُّف
9aziima / 9azaayim (S/P)	*food invitation/s, banquet/s*	عَزِمـة / عَزايِـم
9asha	*dinner*	عَــشـا
9ashra	*ten*	عَـشْـرَة
9ussi / 9ussiyya (M/F adj.)	*stingy, to be cheap*	عُـصّي / عُـصّـيّـة
9aṭ shaan / 9aṭ shaaniin (M)	*thirsty*	عَطْـشان / عَطْـشانـين
9aṭ shaana / 9aṭ shaanaat (F)	*thirsty*	عَطْـشانَـة / عَطْـشانات

9aẓiim / 9aẓiima (M/F)	*great*	عَظيـم / عَظيـمَة
9afwan, il-9afu	*excuse me, pardon me*	عَفْـواً، الْـعَـفـو
9ajala	*speed, quickness*	عَـجَـلَـة
bil-9ajal	*quickly*	بِـالْـعَجَل
9afya 9alee . . .	*Good for . . . , bravo* (see lesson 17)	عَفْـيَـه عَـلـي
9ala	*on, upon* (preposition, see lesson 15)	عَـلـى
9ala raasi	*with pleasure* (idiom, see lesson 6)	عَـلـى راسـي
9ala 9eeni	*with pleasure* (idiom, see lesson 6)	عَـلـى عـيـنـي
9ala kull ḥaal	*in any case, anyway* (idiom, see lesson 6)	عَـلـى كُل حـال
9ala fikra	*by the way* (idiom, see lesson 6)	عَـلـى فِـكْـرَة
9ala keefak	*as you like* (idiom, see lesson 3)	عَـلـى كـيـفَـك
9amm / a9maam (M)	*uncle/s* (paternal, also see **khaal**)	عَـم / أعْمام
9amma / 9ammaat (F)	*aunt/s* (paternal)	عَـمَّـة / عَـمّـات
9amaliyya / 9amaliyyaat	*operation/s, surgery/s*	عَـمَلِـيَّـة / عَـمَـلِـيّـات
9amiiq	*deep*	عَـمـيـق
9an	*about* (preposition)	عَـن
9an idhnak / 9an idhnich / 9an idhinkum (M/F/P)	*excuse me, with your permission*	عَـن إذنَـك / عَـن إذنِـج / عَـن إذنْـكُـم
9eeb / 9yuub (S/P)	*shame, defect/s*	عيـب / عُـيـوب
9eeb 9aleek	*shame on you* (idiom, see lesson 15)	عيـب عَـلـيـك
9eela / 9eelaat (S/P)	*family/ies* (also see **ahal**)	عيـلَـة / عـيـلات
9iid / 9yaad (S/P)	*feast/s, festival/s*	عـيـد / عُـيـاد
9ijab, yi9jib (RV)	*to interest, appeal to* (special verb, see lesson 7)	عِـجَـب، يِـعْـجِـب
9idda	*a number of, several*	عِـدَّة
9iraaq (il-9iraaq)	*Iraq*	عِـراق (الْـعِـراق)
9iraaqi/ 9iraaqiyyiin (M)	*Iraqi/s*	عِـراقـي / عِـراقِـيّـيـن
9iraaqiyya / 9iraaqiyyaat (F)	*Iraqi/s*	عِـراقِـيَّـة / عِـراقِـيّـات
9iraf, yu9ruf (RV)	*to know* (see lesson 8)	عِـرَف، يُـعْـرُف
9izam, yi9zim (RV)	*to invite* (see lesson 8)	عِـزَم، يِـعْـزِم

9ishriin	*twenty*	عِشْرين
9illa	*illness (also see **haruf**)*	عِلَّة
9ifa, yi9fi	*to forgive*	عِفَا، يِعْفي
9ind	*has, have, at the place of* (see lesson 14)	عِنْد
9iyaada / 9iyaadaat	*clinic/s*	عِيادة / عِيادات
9udhur / a9dhaar (S/P)	*excuse/s*	عُذر / أَعْذار
9umla / 9umlaat (S/P)	*currency/s*	عُمْلَة / عُمْلات
9umla sa9ba	*hard currency*	عُمْلَة صَعْبَة
9unwaan / 9anaawiin (S/P)	*address/es*	عُنْوان / عَناوين
9unwaan il-mursil	*address of sender*	عُنْوان الْمُرْسِل
9unwaan il-mustalim	*address of addressee*	عُنْوان الْمُسْتَلِم

GH غ

ghaali / ghaalyiin (M)	*expensive*	غالي / غالْيِين
ghaalya / ghaalyaat (F)	*expensive*	غالْيَة / غالْيات
rikhiis / rikhiisa / rkhaas (M/F/P)	*cheap, inexpensive*	رخيص / رخيصَة / رْخاص
ghada	*lunch*	غَدَا
ghalat	*wrong*	غَلَط
gheer	*other, different from, unlike, non-*	غِير
ghidab, yighdab	*to become angry*	غِضَب، يِغْضَب
ghurfa / ghuraf (S/P)	*room/s*	غُرْفَة / غُرَف

G گ

gaabal, ygaabul (RV)	*to meet, to face* (see lesson 3)	گابَل، يُگابُل
gaal, yguul (HV)	*to say* (see lesson 8)	گال، يُگول
gaam, yguum	*he stood up. he began to*	گام، يُگوم
gabul	*before, ago*	گَبُل
gabl iz-zuhur	*before noon, A.M.*	گَبُل الظَّهُر
ba9d iz-zuhur	*afternoon, P.M.* (also see **ba9ad**)	بَعْد الظَّهُر
gabul-ma	*before* (conjunction, see lesson 20)	گَبُل مَ
gahha	*a cough*	گَحَّة
gariib / garaayib (S/P)	*relative/s*	گَريب / گَرايِب
gass, yguss (DV)	*to cut* (see lesson 9)	گَصّ، يُگُصّ
gass, shaawirma	*grilled chopped meat*	گَصّ، شاوِرْمَة
gamaarig, gamaarik	*customs*	گَمارگ، گَمارك

gahwa / gahaawi (S/P)	*coffee/s, cafe/s*	گَـهْـوَة / گَـهاوي
gahawchi / gahawchiyya (S/P)	*coffee vendor/s (see lesson 7)*	گَـهَـوْچي / گَـهَـوْچِـيَّـة
giddaam	*in front, before, ahead*	گِـدّام
giras, yugrus (RV)	*to pinch*	گِـرَص، يُـگْـرُص
giriib / giriiba (M/F)	*close, near by*	گِـريـب / گِـريـبَة
gi9ad, yug9ud (RV)	*to sit down (see lesson 8)*	گِـعَـد، يُـگْـعُـد
gidar, yigdar (RV)	*to be able, can (see lesson 8)*	گِـدَر، يِـگْـدَر
glaas / glaasaat (S/P)	*glass/es*	گْـلاص / گْـلاصات
gumaz, yugmuz (RV)	*to jump*	گُـمَـز، يُـگْـمُـز

F ف

fahis	*check up, examination*	فَـحِـص
farr, yfurr (DV)	*to escape, run away*	فَـرّ، يْـفُـرّ
farwa / farwaat (S/P)	*fur/s*	فَـرْوَة / فَـرْوات
farhaan / farhaaniin (M)	*happy*	فَـرْحان / فَـرْحانـيـن
farhaana / farhaanaat (F)	*happy*	فَـرْحانَـة / فَـرْحانات
fasil / fusuul (S/P)	*season/s, segment/s, chapter/s*	فَـصِـل / فُـصـول
fakkar, yfakkir (RV)	*to think*	فَـكَّـر، يْـفَـكِّـر
faqat	*only*	فَـقَـط
bass	*only, but, enough*	بَـسّ
fann / funuun (S/P)	*art/s*	فَـنّ / فُـنـون
fanni / fanniyya (M/F adj.)	*artistic*	فَـنّـي / فَـنّـيَّـة
fawaakih	*fruits*	فَـواكِـه
fihas, yifhas (RV)	*to check up, to examine*	فِـحَـص، يِـفْـحَـص
fiiza / fiizaat (S/P)	*visa/s*	فيـزة / فيـزات
fiimaanillaa	*goodbye (lit., in God's safety, idiom see lesson 5)*	فيمانِـيْـلّا
fitah, yiftah (RV)	*to open (see lesson 8)*	فِـتَـح، يِـفْـتَـح
fi9il / af9aal (S/P)	*verb/s, action/s, doing/s*	فِـعِـل / أفْـعال
fi9il il-amur	*imperative verb (see lesson 7)*	فِـعِـل الأمُـر
fi9il il-haadir	*present tense verb (see lesson 11)*	فِـعِـل الـحـاضِـر
fi9il il-maadi	*past tense verb (see lessons 8–9)*	فِـعِـل الـمـاضي
fi9il il-mustaqbal	*future tense verb (see lesson 12)*	فِـعِـل الـمُـسْـتَـقْـبَـل
fikra / afkaar (S/P)	*idea/s*	فِـكْـرَة / أفْـكـار
filis / fluus (S/P)	*penny/money*	فِـلِـس / فْـلـوس
fluus 9iraaqiyya	*Iraqi money*	فْـلـوس عِـراقِـيَّـة
fluus Amriikiyya	*American money*	فْـلـوس أمْـريـكِـيَّـة

filim / aflaam (S/P)	*film/s*	فِلِم / أفْلام
filfil	*pepper*	فِلْفِل
filfil akhḏar	*green pepper*	فِلْفِل أخْضَر
filfil aswad	*black pepper*	فِلْفِل أسْوَد
findiq / fanaadiq (S/P)	*hotel/s, motel/s*	فِنْدِق / فَنادِق
foliklore	*folklore*	فولِكْلور
folikloori / foliklooriyya (adj.)	*folkloric*	فولِكْلوري / فولِكْلوريَّة
furṣa / furaṣ (S/P)	*occasion/s, opportunity/s*	فُرْصَة / فُرَص
fuṣ ha	*classical (Arabic, also see* **lugha***)*	فُصْحى
lugha fuṣ ha	*classical language (Arabic)*	لُغَـة فُصْحى

Q ق

qaabal, yqaabil (RV)	*to meet, to face, opposite*	قابَل، يُقابِل
gaabal, ygaabul (RV)	*to meet, to face, opposite*	گابَل، يُگابُل
qaa9a / qaa9aat (S/P)	*hall/s*	قاعَة / قاعات
qaamuus / qawaamiis (S/P)	*dictionary/s*	قاموس / قَوامِيس
qatil	*murder, killing*	قَـتِـل
qital, yuqtul	*to kill*	قِـتَـل، يُـقْـتِـل
qadiim / qadiima / qudamaaᵓ (M/F/P)	*old, ancient*	قَـديم / قَـديمَة / قُـدَماء
qariib / qariiba (M/F)	*near, close by, relative*	قَـريب / قَـريبَة
qariḏ / quruuḏ (S/P)	*loan/s*	قَـرض / قُـروض
qaṣir / quṣuur (S/P)	*palace/s*	قَـصِر / قُـصور
qalam / qlaam (S/P)	*pencil/s, pen/s*	قَـلَم / قْلام
qanaat / qanawaat	*(TV) channel/s*	قَـناة / قَـنَـوات
qira, yiqra (WV)	*to read (see lesson 9)*	قِـرا، يِقْرا
qisim / aqsaam (S/P)	*section/s, division/s, department/s*	قِـسِم / أقْـسام
qisim il-akhbaar	*news section*	قِسِم الأخْبار
qilaq, yiqlaq (RV)	*to worry, anxious*	قِـلَـق، يِـقْـلَـق
quṣṣa / quṣaṣ (S/P)	*novel/s, story/s*	قُـصَّة / قُـصَص
qundara / qanaadir (S/P)	*shoe/s*	قُـنْدَرَة / قَـنادِر
qundarchi / qundarchiyya (S/P)	*shoe repairman/s*	قُـنْدَرْچي / قُـنْدَرْچِيَّة
qunṣiliyya / qunṣiliyyaat (S/P)	*consulate/s*	قُـنْصِلِيَّة / قُـنْصِلِيّات
safaara / safaaraat (S/P)	*embassy/s*	سَـفارَة / سَـفارات

K ك

kaamira / kaamiraat (S/P)	*camera/s*	كامِرَة / كامِرات
kaan, ykuun	*was/were* (see **chaan**, lesson 13)	كان، يْكون
kaafi	*enough*	كافي
kabaab	*skewered meat*	كَباب
kababchi / kababchiyya (S/P)	*kabab maker/s, seller/s* (see lesson 7)	كَبابْچي / كَبابْچِيَّة
kabiir / kabiira / kbaar (M/F/P)	*big, large*	كَبير / كَبيرة / كُبار
chibiir / chibiira / kbaar (M/F/P)	*big, large*	چِبير / چِبيرة / كُبار
kathiir / kathiira / kthaar (M/F/P)	*many, much, plenty*	كَثير / كَثيرة / كْثار
kaslaan / kaslaaniin (M)	*lazy*	كَسْلان / كَسْلانين
kaslaana / kaslaanaat (F)	*lazy*	كَسْلانة / كَسْلانات
kalaam	*talk, speech*	كَلام
kalb / klaab, chalib / chlaab (S/P)	*dog/s*	كَلْب / كْلاب، چَلِب / چْلاب
chalba / chalbaat (F)	*dog/s*	چَلْبة / چَلْبات
kallaf, ykallif (RV)	*to cost, to assign* (see lesson 8)	كَلَّف، يُكَلِّف
kam, cham?	*How many?* (see lesson 15)	كَم، چَم؟
keef	*mood*	كيف
9ala keefak	*as you like, as you wish*	على كيفَك
keelomatir / keelomatraat (S/P)	*kilometer/s*	كيلومَتِر / كيلومَتْرات
ktaab, kitaab / kutub (S/P)	*book/s*	كْتاب، كِتاب / كُتُب
kitab, yiktib (RV)	*to write*	كِتَب، يِكْتِب
kidhab, yikdhib	*to lie*	كِذب، يِكْذِب
kisar, yiksir (RV)	*to break*	كِسَر، يِكْسِر
kilfa / kilfaat (S/P)	*cost/s*	كِلْفة / كِلْفات
kuub / kwaaba (S/P)	*cup/s*	كوب / كْوابة
kursi / karaasi (S/P)	*chair/s*	كُرْسي / كَراسي
kull	*every, all, whole*	كُل
kullish	*very*	كُلِّش
kullshi	*everything*	كُلْشي
kullshi b-makaana	*all right, everything in its place* (idiom, see lesson 16)	كُلْشي بْ مَكانَه

L ل

la- < laa	*no, not* (see lesson 4)	لـَ > لا
laa ghaali wala rkhiis	*neither expensive nor cheap* (idiom, see lesson 4)	لا غـالـي ولا رخـيـص
laa shiish wala kabaab	*not bad, so so, okay* (idiom, see lesson 4)	لا شـيـش ولا كَـبـاب
laazim	*must, ought to* (semi verb)	لازِم
luzuum	*need, must* (noun)	لـُزوم
laakin	*but* (conjunction, see lesson 20)	لاكِـن
laham	*meat* (collective)	لـَحَـم
latiif / latiifa / ltaaf (M/F/P)	*nice* (adj.)	لـَطيف / لـَطيفـَة / لـْطاف
la9ad	*then, so, in that case* (invariable transitional word, see lesson 12)	لـَعَـد
lamman	*when, at the time*	لـَمَّـن
laylan, bil-leel	*at night, nightly* (adv.)	لـَيْـلاً، بـالـلـيـل
leesh, ilweesh, luweesh?	*why?* (see lesson 15)	لـيـش، إلـْويـش، لـُويـش
leel, leela / layaali (S/P)	*night/s*	لـيـل، لـيـلـَة / لـَيالـي
li-, l-	*to* (preposition, see lesson 14)	لِـ، لْ
li'ann	*because* (conjunction, see lesson 20)	لأن
liban / albaan (S/P)	*yogurt/dairy products*	لِـبَـن / ألـْبان
lihusn il-hazz, min husn il-hazz	*fortunately, luckily* (idiom, see lesson 9)	لِـحُـسْـن الـْحَـظ، مِـن حُـسْـن الـْحَـظ
lizam, yilzam	*to catch, to hold*	لِـزَم، يِـلـْزَم
lisaan / alsina (S/P)	*tongue/s*	لِـسان / ألـْسِـنة
lisuu' il-hazz, min suu' il-hazz	*unfortunately* (idiom, see lesson 9)	لِـسوء الـْحَـظ، مِـن سوء الـْحَـظ
li9ab, yil9ab (RV)	*to play*	لِـعَـب، يِـلـْعَـب
loo, aw	*or, if* (see lesson 19)	لـو، أوْ
loo aani b-makaanak	*if I were you, if I were in your place* (idiom, see lesson 14)	لـو آنـي بْ مَـكانَـك
loon / alwaan	*color/s* (see lesson 18)	ألـْوان
lugha / lughaat (S/P)	*language/s*	لـُغـَة / لـُغات
il-lugha l-9arabiyya	*the Arabic language*	إلـْلـُغـَة الـْعَـرَبـيَّـة
il-lugha l-fus ha	*the classical language*	إلـْلـُغـَة الـْفـُصْـحى
il-lugha l-9aamiyya	*the colloquial language*	إلـْلـُغـَة الـْعـامـيَّـة
liga, yilga (WV)	*to find*	لِـگـا، يِـلـْگـي

M   م

ma- < maa	*not* (see lesson 4)	مَ > ما
maat, ymuut (HV)	*to die*	مات، يُـموت
maashaalla	*praise be to God* (idiom, see lesson 5)	ماشالله
maashi	(part.) (see **misha**)	ماشـي
maa9uun / mwaa9iin (S/P)	*plate/s, dish/s*	ماعون / مُواعين
maaku chaara	*no cure, no hope, no way out* (invariable, see lesson 18)	ماكو چارَة
maaku luzuum	*no need for . . .* (idiom, see lesson 16)	ماكو لُـزوم
maal	*wealth, money, have* (see lesson 14)	مال
maali / maaliyya (M/F)	*financial* (relative adj., see lesson 6)	مالي / مالِـيَّة
maalman?	*whose?* (see "**minu?**" lesson 15)	مالـْمَن
maani9	*objection, obstacle*	مانع
mathaf / mataahif (S/P)	*museum/s*	مَتْحَف / مَتاحِف
mathaf aathaar	*antiquity museum*	مَتْحَف آثار
il-mathaf il-9iraaqi	*the Iraqi Museum* (see lesson 11)	إلْـمَتْحَف الْـعِراقي
mahatta / mahattaat (S/P)	*station/s*	مَحَطَّة / مَحَطّـات
mahattat qitaar	*train station*	مَحَطَّة قِـطار
mahall / mahallaat (S/P) dukkaan / dakaakiin (S/P)	*place/s, store/s, shop/s* *store/s, shop/s*	مَحَل / مَحَلات دُكّـان / دَكاكـين
mahall-ma	*the place where* (conjunction, see lesson 20)	مَحَـل مَ
makhzan / makhaazin (S/P)	*store/s, shop/s*	مَخْـزَن / مَخازِن
madiina / mudun (S/P)	*city/ies, town/s*	مَديـنة / مُـدُن
madrasa / madaaris (S/P)	*school/s*	مَـدْرَسَة / مَـدارِس
mara / niswaan (S/P)	*woman/en* (notice the plural is another word)	مَرَة / نِـسْوان
mariid / mariida / mardaa (M/F/P)	*sick, ill* (adj.)	مَريض / مَريضَة / مَرْضى
marhaba / maraahub (S/P)	*hello, greeting/s*	مَرْحَبَة / مَـراحُب
marr, ymurr (DV)	*to go by, to pass*	مَـرّ، يْـمُرّ

marra / marraat (S/P)	*once, one time, instance/s*	مَرَّة / مَرَّات
kull marra	*each time, every time*	كُل مَرَّة
mazza / mazzaat (S/P)	*appetizer/s, hors d'oeuvres*	مَزَّة / مَزَّات
masaa°	*afternoon, evening*	مَساء
masaa° il-kheer	*good afternoon/evening*	مَساء الْخير
masaa° in-nuur (in reply)	*good afternoon/evening*	مَساء النُّور
masaa°an, bil-masaa° (adv.)	*in the afternoon/evening*	مَساءً, بِالْمَساء
mas°uul / mas°uuliin (S/P)	*authority/s, person/s in charge*	مَسْـؤول / مَسْـؤولين
mas°uul hukuuma	*government official*	مَسْـؤول حُـكـومَة
Masguuf	*Masguuf (popular fish dish)*	مَسْـگـوف
simach Masguuf	*Masguuf fish*	سِـمَـچ مَسْـگـوف
masluug	*boiled*	مَسْـلـوگ
beed masluug	*boiled egg*	بيض مَسْـلـوگ
mashruub / mashruubaat (S/P)	*drink/s (soft and alcoholic)*	مَشْـروب / مَشْـروبات
mash ghuul / mash ghuuliin (M)	*busy*	مَشْـغـول / مَشْـغـولين
mash ghuula / mash ghuulaat (F)	*busy*	مَشْـغـولة / مَشْـغـولات
mashhuur / mashhuuriin (M)	*famous, well known*	مَشْـهور / مَشْـهورين
mashhuura / mashhuuraat (F)	*famous, well known*	مَشْـهورَة / مَشْـهورات
mashwi / mashwiyyaat (S/P)	*broiled food*	مَشْـوي / مَشْـويـِّات
laham mashwi	*broiled meat*	لَحَم مَشْـوي
Masir	*Egypt*	مَصِر
Masri / Masriyyiin (M)	*Egyptian/s*	مَصْري / مَصْريِّـين
Masriyya / Masriyyaat (F)	*Egyptian/s*	مَصْريَّة / مَصْريّات
mataar / mataaraat (S/P)	*airport/s*	مَطار / مَطارات
mat9am / mataa9um (S/P)	*restaurant/s*	مَطْعَم / مَطاعُم
ma9a	*with (preposition)*	مَعَ
ma9a s-salaama	*goodbye (lit., with safety)*	مَعَ السَّلامَة
ma9bad / ma9aabid (S/P)	*temple/s*	مَعْبَد / مَعابِد
ma9luumaat	*information*	مَعْلـومات
magli	*fried*	مَگْلي
beed magli	*fried eggs*	بيض مَگْلي

makaan (ak) <u>kh</u>aali	*(You) were missed. (idiom, see, lesson 20)*	مَكانَـك خالي
maktab / makaatib (S/P)	*office/s*	مَكْتَب / مَكاتِب
maktaba / maktabaat (S/P)	*library/ies*	مَكْتَبَة / مَكْتَبات
malaabis	*clothes, clothing*	مَلابِس
malik / miluuk (M)	*king/s*	مَلِك / مِلوك
malika / malikaat (F)	*queen/s*	مَلِكَة / مَلِكات
malyoon / malyooneen / malaayiin	*one million/two millions/ millions (see lesson 17)*	مَلْيون / مَلْيونين / مَلايِـين
mamnuu9 / mamnuu9a (M/F)	*illegal, forbidden*	مَمْنوع / مَمْنوعَة
mamnuun	*to be indebted, grateful, pleased (idiom, see lesson 10)*	مَمْنون
man<u>d</u>ada / manaadid (S/P)	*table/s*	مَنْضَدة / مَناضِد
man<u>z</u>ar / manaa<u>z</u>ir (S/P)	*view/s, scene/s*	مَنْظَر / مَناظِر
manyo	*menu*	مَنْيو
mawjuud / mawjuudiin (M)	*present, located, to be found*	مَوْجود / مَوْجودين
mawjuuda / mawjuudaat (F)	*present, located, to be found*	مَوْجودة / مَوْجودات
mawkib / mawaakib (S/P)	*procession*	مَوْكِب / مَواكِب
<u>Sh</u>aari9 il-Mawkib	*Procession Street (in ancient Babylon)*	شارِع الْمَوْكِب
mawlaay	*my lord*	مَوْلاي
mawwat, ymawwit (HV)	*to kill*	مَوَّت، يُمَوِّت
may<u>kh</u>aalif	*it is okay, it is permitted, it doesn't matter (idiom, see lesson 13)*	مَيْخالِف
may<u>s</u>iir	*impossible, it can't be (idiom, see lesson 13)*	مَيْصير
mayy / miyaah (S/P)	*water/s*	مَيّ / مِياه
meez / myuuza (S/P)	*table/s*	ميز / مُيوزَة
mit°assif / mit°assfiin (M)	*to be sorry*	مِتْأسِّف / مِتْأسْفـين
mit°assfa / mit°assfaat (F)	*to be sorry*	مِتْأسْفة / مِتْأسْفات
mit9allig b-	*hanging on to*	مِتْعَلِّگ ب
mi<u>th</u>il	*like, similar, such as*	مِثِل
mi<u>th</u>il-ma	*as, the way that (conjunction, see lesson 20)*	مِثِل مَ
mirtaa<u>h</u> / mirtaa<u>h</u>iin (M)	*comfortable, rested*	مِرْتاح / مِرْتاحين
mirtaa<u>h</u>a / mirtaa<u>h</u>aat (F)	*comfortable, rested*	مِرْتاحَة / مِرْتاحات

mizzawwij / mizzawwjiin (M)	*married* (man)	مِـزَّوِّج / مِـزَّوِّجـيـن
mizzawwja / mizzawwjaat (F)	*married* (woman)	مِـزَّوِّجَـة / مِـزَّوِّجات
misha, yimshi (WV)	*to walk, to travel* (see lesson 9)	مِـشَـا، يِـمُـشـي
maashi / maashya (M/F, part.)	*walking, traveling*	ماشـي / ماشْـيَـة
maashi l-haal	*well, fine, okay* (common phrase)	ماشـي الـحـال
mghatti	*covering* (part.)	مُـغَـطّـي
mi9da / mi9ad	*stomach/s*	مِعْـدَة / مِـعَـد
miftaah / mafaatiih (S/P)	*key/s*	مِـفْـتاح / مَـفاتـيـح
mila, yimli (WV)	*to fill (in)*	مِـلَـا، يِـمْـلي
milih / amlaah (S/P)	*salt/s*	مِـلـح / أمْـلاح
mil9aqa / malaa9iq (S/P)	*spoon/s*	مِـلْـعَـقَـة / مَـلاعِـق
min	*when* (see lesson 20)	مِن
min > mni	*from* (preposition)	مِـن > مُـن
min fadlak / min fadlich (M/F)	*please* (expression used when requesting something, also see **tfaddal**)	مِن فَـضْـلَـك / مِن فَـضْـلِـج
min husn il-hazz	*fortunately, luckily* (idiom, see lesson 9)	مِن حُـسْـن الـحَـظ
min suu' il-hazz	*unfortunately* (idiom, see lesson 9)	مِن سـوء الـحَـظ
min hissa w jaay	*from now on* (idiom, see lesson 11)	مِن هِـسَّـة وجـايْ
min waqit li-waqit	*from time to time* (idiom, see lesson 11)	مِن وَقِـت لِـوَقِـت
min ween?	*Where from?* (see lesson 15)	مِن ويـن؟
minu?	*who?* (see lesson 15)	مِـنـو؟
minu-ma	*whoever* (see lesson 20)	مِـنـو مَ
minu abu baachir?	*who knows about tomorrow?* *life is too short.* (see lesson 19)	مِـنـو أبو باچِـر؟
miyya	*one hundred* (see lesson 17)	مِـيَّـة
mudda	*period of time, while*	مُـدَّة
mudiir / mudaraa' (S/P)	*director/s, manager/s*	مُـدير / مُـدَراء
mustashfa / mustashfayaat	*hospital/s*	مُـسْـتَـشْـفـى / مُـسْـتَـشْـفَـيات

muqaabala / muqaabalaat (S/P)	*meeting/s, interview/s*	مُقابَلة / مُقابَلات
muu	*not (see lesson 4)*	مُو
mu᾽min / mu᾽miniin (S/P)	*believer/s*	مُؤمِن / مُؤمِنين
Amiir il-Mu᾽miniin	*Prince of Believers (Caliph's title)*	أمير المُؤمِنين
muhaawara / muhaawaraat (S/P)	*dialogue/s, discussion/s*	مُحاوَرة / مَحاوَرات
mukhaabara / mukhaabaraat (S/P)	*telephone call/s (also see* **khaabar***)*	مُخابَرة / مُخابَرات
mukhaabara daakhiliyya	*domestic/national call*	مُخابرة داخِلِيّة
mukhaabara khaarijiyya	*international call*	مُخابرة خارجِيّة
musajjal / musajjala (M/F)	*registered*	مُسَجَّل / مُسَجَّلَة
mu9allim / mu9allima (M/F)	*teacher/s*	مُعَلِّم / مُعَلِّمَة
mufattish / mufattishiin (M)	*inspector/s, reviewer/s*	مُفَتِّش / مُفَتِّشين
mufattish gamaarig	*customs inspector*	مُفَتِّش گَمارگ
mulaahaza / mulaahazaat (S/P)	*note/s, remark/s*	مُلاحَظَة / مُلاحَظات
mumkin, yimkin	*possible, perhaps, may be*	مُمْكِن، يِمْكِن
mumtaaz / mumtaaziin (M)	*excellent*	مُمْتاز / مُمْتازين
mumtaaza / mumtaazaat (F)	*excellent*	مُمْتازَة / مُمْتازات
muwazzaf / muwazzafiin (M)	*employee/s, official/s*	مُوَظَّف / مُوَظَّفين
muwazzafa / muwazzafaat (F)	*employee/s, official/s*	مُوَظَّفَة / مُوَظَّفات
msaafir / msaafriin (M)	*traveling, traveler/s*	مُسافِر / مُسافِرين
msaafra / msaafraat (F)	*traveling, traveler/s*	مُسافِرَة / مُسافِرات
mshawwash / mshawwasha (M/F)	*static, disrupted by*	مُشَوَّش / مُشَوَّشَة
mneen, immeen?	*where from? (see lesson 15)*	مُنين، إمّين؟
min ween?	*where from?*	مِن وين؟
mneen-ma	*from wherever (conjunction, see lesson 20)*	مُنين مَ
mudhii9 / mudhii9a (M/F)	*broadcaster*	مُذيع / مُذيعَة
muraasil / muraasila (M/F)	*reporter, correspondent*	مُراسِل / مُراسِلة
muraasil ajnabi	*foreign reporter/ correspondent*	مُراسِل أجنَبي

mushtaaq / mushtaaqa/ mushtaaqiin (M/F/P)	*missing (someone)*	مُشْتـاق / مُشْتـاقـة / مُشْتـاقـيـن

N ن

naazil / naazliin (M, part.)	*staying*	نازِل / نازْلِـيـن
naazla / naazlaat (F)	*staying*	نازْلَـة / نازْلات
naam, ynaam (HV)	*to sleep* (see lesson 8)	نـام . يُـنـام
nabiidh	*wine*	نَـبِـيـذ
nazzal, ynazzil	*to lower*	نَـزَّل . يُـنَـزِّل
nasiib / nasiiba (M/F)	*relative-in-law*	نَـسِـيـب / نَسِـيـبَـة
nashra / nashraat (S/P)	*bulletin/s*	نَـشْـرة / نَـشْـرات
nashra akhbaariyya	*news bulletin*	نَـشْـرة أخْـبـارية
nashla	*cold* (illness)	نَـشْـلَـة
na9am, ii	*yes*	نَـعَـم، ئِـي
nafas	*breath*	نَـفَـس
nafis	*self, being, soul*	نَـفِـس
nahar / anhaar (S/P)	*river/s*	نَـهَـر / أنْـهار
Naynawa	*Nineveh* (the ancient Assyrian capital)	نَـيْـنَـوى
nija, yinja (WV)	*to be saved*	نْجَا، يِـنْـجَا
nisa, yinsa (WV)	*to forget*	نْـسَـا، يِـنْـسَا
nita, yinti (WV)	*to give*	نْـطَـا، يِـنْـطِي
nhizam, yinhizim (RV)	*to run away, to flee*	نْـهِـزَم، يِـنْـهِـزِم
nuur / anwaar (S/P)	*light/s*	نـور / أنْـوار
nushkur alla	*Thank God!*	نُـشْـكُر الله
nuss	*one-half*	نُـصّ
noo9 / anwaa9	*type/s, kind/s*	نوع / أنْـواع

H هـ

ha-	*this/these, that/those* (demonstrative prefix, see lesson 14)	هَـ
hal-ayyaam	*these/those days* (phrase, see lesson 12)	هَـل الأيّـام
haadha / haadhi / hadhoola (M/F/P)	*this/these* (see lesson 14)	هاذا / هاذي / هَـذولَـة
hadhaak / hadhiich / hadhoolaak (M/F/P)	*that/those* (see lesson 14)	هَـذاك / هّـذيـج / هَـذولاك
haak / haach / haakum (M/F/P)	*take* (imp. verb)	هاك / هاچ / هـاكُـم

haay (invariable)	*his/that* (see also lesson 14)	هـايْ
haay ween . . . ?	*where have . . . been?* (idiom, see lesson 3)	هـايْ ويـن؟
hadiyya / hadaayaa (S/P)	*gift/s, present/s*	هَـديَّـة / هَـدايـا
haddad, yhaddid	*to threaten*	هَـدَّد، يْـهَـدّد
hal?	*is/are . . . ?* (see lesson 15)	هَـلْ؟
ham	*also, too*	هَـمْ
hissa	*now, right this moment*	هِـسَّـه
hiyya	*she* (see lesson 2)	هِـيَّ
humma	*they* (see lesson 2)	هُـمَّـه
huwwa	*he* (see lesson 2)	هُـوَّ
hnaa	*here*	هُـنا
hnaak	*there, over there*	هُـناك
hwaaya	*much, plenty, a lot*	هُـوايَـه

W   و

w- < wa	*and*	و < وَ
waahid / wihda (M/F)	*one (1)*	واحِـد / وحْـدَة
walad waahid	*one boy*	وَلَـد واحِـد
binit wihda	*one girl*	بِـنِـت وِحْـدَة
waagi9 (part.)	*falling, having fallen*	واگِـع
wara	*behind, at the back of*	وَرا
wasat	*middle, medium*	وَسَـط
wasil / wusuulaat (S/P)	*receipt/s*	وَصِل / وُصولات
wasfa	*prescription*	وَصْفـة
watan / awtaan (S/P)	*nation/s*	وَطَـن / أوْطان
watani / wataniyyiin (M)	*nationalist/s* (relative adjective, see lesson 6)	وَطَـني / وَطَـنِـيِّـين
wataniyya / wataniyyaat (F)	*nationalist/s*	وَطَـنِـيَّـة / وَطَـنِـيّـات
waqit / awqaat (S/P)	*time/s*	وَقِت / أوْقات
waqqa9, ywaqqi9 (RV)	*to sign, to put a signature*	وَقَّـع، يْـوَقّـع
tawqii9 / tawaaqii9 (S/P)	*signature/s*	تَـوْقِـيـع / تَـواقِـيـع
wakiih / wakiiha (M/F)	*trouble maker, bold*	وَكِـيـح / وَكِـيـحَـة
wala	*and not, nor, or* (see lesson 4)	وَلا
walla	*by God, really, indeed, definitely* (swearing expression used for confirmation, see lesson 5)	وَاللّٰه
wallaahi	*by God* (variation form of the preceding word)	وَلّٰـاهـي

walad / wilid (S/P)	*boy/s, children*	وَلَد / وِلِد
walaw	*although, even though (see lesson 20)*	وَلَوْ
ween?	*where?*	وين
ween-ma	*wherever (see lesson 20)*	وين مَ
wija9 / awjaa9 (S/P)	*pain/s*	وَجَع ، أوْجاع
wi<u>s</u>al, yoo<u>s</u>al (RV)	*to arrive, to reach a point*	وِصَل، يوصَل
wilad, yoolad (RV)	*to be born*	وِلَد، يـولَد
wigaf, yoogaf (RV)	*to stand up*	وِگَف، يـوگَف
wiyya	*with (see lesson 10)*	وِيّه
ma9a	*with*	مَعَ

Υ ي

yaa a<u>ll</u>a	*oh God (idiom, see lesson 5)*	يـا الله
ya<u>ll</u>a	*hurry up (idiom, see lesson 5)*	يَـلْـلَـه
ya9ni	*well, oh*	يَـعْـني
yamm	*next to, adjacent, near*	يَـمّ
yooja9	*it causes pain, hurts*	يوجَـع
yoom / ayyaam (S/P)	*day/s*	يـوم / أيّـام
yoom-ma	*the day when (see lesson 20)*	يـوم مَ
yyaa	*(particle, see lesson 16)*	يّـا
tma<u>sh</u><u>sh</u>a, yitma<u>sh</u><u>sh</u>a	*to stroll, to walk*	تْـمَشّا، يِتْـمَشّا
yimkin, mumkin	*possible, perhaps*	يِـمْـكِـن، مُـمْكِـن

English–Arabic

In this section, only the basic equivalents of words are given in Arabic. For more detailed information or derivatives (e.g., feminine or plural forms, etc.) please see the same word in the Arabic–English section or cross-references.

A

abashed, ashamed, to be	khijal, yikhjal (RV)	خِـجَـل، يِـخْـجَل
able, to be; can	gidar, yigdar (RV)	گِـدَر، يِـگْـدَر
about	9an (preposition)	عَـن
accident	haaditha	حادِثـة
additional	idhaafi	إضافي
address	9unwaan	عُـنْـوان
adjacent, next to, near	yamm	يَـمّ
adjective, attribute	sifa	صِـفـة
afraid, to be	khaaf, ykhaaf (HV)	خاف، يْـخاف
after	ba9ad	بَـعَـد
afternoon, evening	masaaᵓ	مَـساء
ago, before	gabul	گَـبُـل
ahead, in front	giddaam	گِـدّام
air, atmosphere	jaww	جَـوّ
air, aerial	jawwi, tayyaraan	جَـوّي، طَـيَّـران
airmail	bariid jawwi (also see bariid)	بَـريد جَـوّي
airmail envelope	zaruf tayyaraan	ظَـرُف طَـيْـران
regular envelope	zaruf 9aadi	ظَـرُف عـادي
airplane	tayyaara	طَـيّـارة
airport	mataar	مَـطار
Akkad	Akad (ancient land and city in Iraq)	أكَـد
Akkadian	Akadiyyiin (ancient people)	أكَـدِيِّـين
all, every, whole	kull	كُـل
everything	kullshi	كُـلْـشـي
all right, okay, fine	tayyib, kullshi m-makaana	طَـيِّـب، كُـلْـشـي امْـكـانـة
alphabet	il-huruuf il-abjadiyya	إلْـحُـروف الأبْـجَـدِيّـة
alphabetical	abjadi	أبْـجَـدي
also, too	hamm	هَـمّ
A.M. (before noon)	gabl iz-zuhur	گَـبُـل الظّـهُـر
ambulance	sayyaarat is9aaf	سَـيّـارة إسـعاف
America	Amriika	أمْـريـكـا

American	Amriiki	أمْريكي
ancient, old	qadiim, athari	قَديم، أثَري
and	wa / w-	وَ / و
and not, nor, or	wala	وَلا
angry, to become	ghidab, yighdab	غِضَب، يِغْضَب
animal/s	haywaan / haywaanaat	حَيْوان / حَيْوانات
answer, to	jaawab, yjaawib	جاوَب، يُجاوِب
anyway, in any case	9ala kull haal (idiom, see lesson 6)	على كُل حال
appetizer, hors d'oeuvres	mazza	مَزَّة
approximately, about	hawaali	حَوالي
arak	9arag (popular Iraqi alcoholic drink)	عَرَگ
archaeological	athari	أثَري
archaeologist	aathaari	آثاري
archaeology, antiquities	aathaar	آثار
arrive, to	wisal, yoosal (RV)	وصَل، يوصَل
art/s	fann / funuun	فَنّ / فُنون
artistic	fanni / fanniyya	فَنّي / فَنِّيَّة
as, the way that	mithil-ma	مِثِل مَ
as soon as	awwal-ma (see lesson 20)	أوَّل ما
as you like	shloon-ma thibb (idiom, see lessons 15 and 20)	شْلون مَ تْحِب
as you wish	iddallal (idiom, see lesson 10)	إدَّلَلْ
ascend, to; to go up	si9ad, yis9ad (RV)	صِعَد، يِصْعَد
Ashur	Aashuur, (ancient land and god in Iraq)	آشور
ask, to	si'al, yis'al (RV)	سِأَل، يِسْأَل
assign, to; to cost	kallaf, ykallif (RV)	كَلَّف، يْكَلِّف
assist, to; to help	saa9ad, ysaa9id (RV)	ساعَد، يُساعِد
Assyrian	Aashuuri (ancient people)	آشوري
at night	laylan, bil-leel	لَيْلاً، بِالْلَيل
at noon	iz-zuhur	إلظُّهُر
attached pronouns	id-damaa'ir il-muttasila	إلضَّمائِر الْمُتَّصِلة
independent pronouns	id-damaa'ir il-munfasila	إلضَّمائِرالْمُنْفَصِلة
aunt	khaala (maternal), 9amma (paternal)	خالَة، عَمَّة
uncle	khaal (maternal), 9amm (paternal)	خال، عَمّ

authority/s, person/s in charge	mas°uul / mas°uuliin	مَسْؤُول / مَسْؤُولين

B

Babylon	Baabil (ancient city)	بابِل
Babylonian	Baabiliyyiin (ancient people)	بابِلِيِّين
back	ẕahar	ظَـهَـر
bad > worse	qabiiḥ > aqbaḥ (lit. ugly)	قَـبِيح > أقْـبَح
ball	ṭooba	طوبَة
bank	bank	بَـنْك
banquet, dinner invitation	9aziima	عَزِيـمَة
base, grammar	qaa9ida	قاعِـدَة
basic	asaasi	قاعِـدي
basis, foundation	asaas	أساس
bath, bathroom	ḥammaam	حَـمّـام
bath-house keeper	ḥammamchi (see lesson 7)	حَـمّـمْـچي
toilet	mirḥaad	مِـرْحاض
because	li°ann	لأن
become, to	saar, yṣiir (HV)	صار، يْـصِير
beer	biira	بِـيـرَة
before, ago	gabul	گَـبُـل
before	gabul-ma (see lesson 20)	گَـبُـل مَ
beg, to	twassal, yitwassal	تْـوَسَّـل، يِـتْـوَسَّـل
behind, at the back	wara	وَرا
believer/s	mu°min / mu°miniin (S/P)	مُـؤْمِـن / مُـؤْمِـنـين
Prince of Believers (Caliph's title)	Amiir il-Mu°miniin	أمـير المُـؤْمِـنـين
bellboy	booy (borrowed from English)	بُـوي
better	aḥsan	أحْـسَـن
big, large, old (person)	chibiir, kabiir	چِـبِـيـر، كَـبِـيـر
bill, invoice, account	ḥsaab	حُـساب
black	aswad	أسْـوَد
boat	balam	بَـلَـم
body/s	jisim / ajsaasm (S/P)	جِـسِـم / أجْـسام
boiled	masluug	مَـسْلوگ
boiled eggs	beeḏ masluug	بيض مَسْلوگ
book	ktaab, kitaab	كْـتاب، كِـتاب
bookstore	makhzan kutub	مَخْـزَن كُـتُـب
library	maktaba	مَكْـتَـبَة

born, to be	wilad, yoolad (RV)	وِلَـد. يولَـد
bottle/s	buṭil / bṭaala (S/P)	بُـطِل / بْـطالَـة
box	ṣanduug	صَنـدوگ
boy	walad	وَلَـد
boy child	ṭifil	طِـفِـل
girl child	ṭifla	طِـفْـلَـة
bravo, good for . . .	9afya 9alee	عَـفْـيَـه عَـلـي
bread	khubuz	خُـبُـز
(French) bread	ṣammuun	صَمُّـون
break, to	kisar, yiksir (RV)	كِـسَـر. يِـكْـسِـر
breakfast	rayyuug, fuṭuur	رَيّـوگ. فُـطور
breath	nafas	نَـفَـس
bring, to	jaab, yjiib (HV)	جاب. يْـجـيـب
broadcaster	mudhii9 / mudhii9a (M/F)	مُـذيع / مُـذيـعَـة
broiled	mashwi	مَـشْـوي
broiled meat	laham mashwi	لَـحَم مَـشْـوي
broken, not working	kharbaan	خَـرْبـان
brother	akh	أخ
brother-in-law	zooj ukhut	زوج اُخْـت
build, to	bina, yibni (WV)	بِـنـا. يِـبْـنـي
bulletin/s	nashra / nashraat (S/P)	نَـشْـرة / نَـشْـرات
news bulletin	nashra akhbaariyya	نَـشْـرة أخْـبارية
busy	mash ghuul / mash ghuula	مَـشْـغول / مَـشْـغولة
butter	zibid	زِبـد
but	bass	بَـس
buttocks	ṭiiz / ṭyaaza (S/P)	طيـز / طْـيـازَة
buy, to	shtira, yishtiri (WV)	شْـتِـرَا. يِـشْـتِـري
by	b- /bi (see lesson 5)	بْ / بِ
by God	walla, wallaahi (see lesson 5)	والله. ولّـاهي
by the way	9ala fikra (idiom, see lesson 6)	على فِـكْـرَة

C

cafe, coffee	gahwa	گَـهْـوَة
cafe keeper	gahawchi (see lesson 7)	گَـهَـوْچـي
caliph/s	khaliifa / khulafaaʾ (S/P)	خَـلـيفة / خُـلَـفاء
call, to	khaabar, ykhaabur	خـابَـر. يْـخابَـر
telephone call/s	mukhaabara / mukhaabaraat	مُـخابَـرَة / مُـخابَـرات
domestic/national call	mukhaabara daakhiliyya	مُـخابـرة داخِـلِـيَّـة
international call	mukhaabara khaarijiyya	مُـخابِـرة خارِجِـيَّـة

card	biṭaaqa, istimaara	بِـطاقَـة، إسْتِـمارَة
catch, hold, to	lizam, yilzam	لِزَم، يِـلْـزَم
certain	akiid	أكــيــد
certainly	bit-ta' kiid	بِـالتَّـأكــيــد
change, exchange (money)	taṣriif (fluus)	تَـصْريف
change, to (money)	ṣarraf, yṣarruf (RV)	صَـرَّف، يُـصَـرِّف
	ḥawwaal, yḥawwil (RV)	حَـوَّل، يُـحَـوِّل
channel/s (TV)	qanaat / qanawaat	قَـناة / قَـنَـوات
chart, table	jadwal	جَـدْوَل
check	chakk	چَـك
personal check	chakk khaaṣ	چَـك خـاص
check up, examination	faḥiṣ	فَـحِص
check up, to examine	fiḥaṣ, yifḥaṣ (RV)	فِـحَص، يِـفْـحَص
cheese	jibin	جِـبِـين
chicken	jaaj, dijaaj	جـاج، دِجـاج
chickpeas	ḥummuṣ	حُـمُّـص
chickpeas dip	ḥummuṣ bi-t ḥiina	حُـمُّـص بِـطْـحينة
chopped salad	tabbuula	تَـبّـولَـة
cigarette	jigaara	جِـگـارَة
climate, weather	jaww	جَـوّ
clinic/s	9iyaada / 9iyaadaat	عِـيادة / عِـيادات
cold (noun)	barid	بَـرِد
cold (adj.)	baarid	بـارِد
cold, to have a	nashla	نَـشْـلَـة
color/s	loon / alwaan	لُـون / ألْـوان
come (imp. V)	ta9aal	تَـعـال
come, to	ija, yiji (WV)	إجَـا، يِـجي
coming, arriving soon	jayya, 9ala jayya (see lesson 18)	جَـيَّـة، عَـلى جَـيَّـة
condition/s	shart / shuruut (S/P)	شَـرْطْ / شُـرُوط
consonant, letter	haruf	حَـرُف
consulate	qunṣiliyya	قُـنْـصِلِـيَّـة
cousin	ibin khaal (maternal)	إبِـن خـال
	ibin 9amm (paternal)	إبِـن عَـمّ
culture/s, civilization/s	ḥaḍaara / ḥaḍaaraat	حَـضارَة / حَـضارات
cultural	ḥaḍaari / ḥaḍaariyya	حَـضاري / حَـضارِيَّـة

D

dare, to	ijjarra' < itjarra'	إجَّـرَّأ > إتْـجَـرَّأ
daughter, girl	binit, bnayya	بِـنِـت، بُـنَـيَّـة

date (palm)	tamur	تَمُر
day	yoom	يـوم
deep	9amiiq	عَمـيـق
degree, level	daraja	دَرَجَـة
delicious	ṭayyib, ladhiidh	طَيِّب، لَذيـذ
demonstrative words	asmaa° il-ishaara	أَسْماء الإشارة
dialogue, discussion	muḥaawara	مُحاوَرة
dictionary	qaamuus	قـامـوس
difficult, hard	sa9ub	صَعـُب
dinar	diinaar (Iraqi currency)	ديـنـار
half-dinar	nuṣṣ diinaar	نُصْ ديـنار
quarter dinar	rubu9 diinaar	رُبُع ديـنار
dinner	9asha	عَشـا
director/s, manager/s	mudiir / mudaraa° (S/P)	مُدير / مُدَراء
dish, plate	maa9uun	مـاعون
doctor/s	diktoor / dakaatira (M.D. & Ph.D.)	دِكْتور / دَكاتِرَة
dog	chalib, kalb	چَـلِـب، كَـلْـب
dollar	duulaar	دولار
domino	doomna	دومْنَـة
door	baab	بـاب
double, husband	zooj, zawj	زُوج، زَوْج
drill, exercise	tamriin	تَمْـريـن
drink	mashruub	مَشْـروب
drink, to	shirab, yishrab (RV)	شِـرَب، يِـشْـرَب
drive, to	saaq, ysuuq (HV)	سـاق، يُـسـوق
driver	saayiq	سـايِـق
drum	dumbug	دُمْـبُـگ
drummer	dumbagchi (see lesson 6)	دُمْـبَـگْـچي

E

ear	idhin	إذن
east	sharq	شَـرْق
eastern	sharqi	شَـرْقي
eat, to	akal, yaakul (RV)	أكَـل، يـاكُـل
food dish	akla	أكْـلَـة
economics	iqtiṣaad	إقْتِـصاد
economical	iqtiṣaadi / iqtiṣaadiyya	إقْتِـصادي / إقْتِصاديّة
edge/s	ḥaaffa / ḥaaffaat (S/P)	حافّـة / حافّـات
editing	taḥriir	تَحْـريـر

editor	muḥarrir	مُحَرِّر
editor-in-chief	raʾiis qisim it-taḥriir	رَئيس قِسِم التَحْرير
egg	beeḍ	بيـض
eggplant	beetinjaan	بيـتِـنْجان
eggplant dip	baaba ghannuuj	بابا غَـنّـوج
Egypt	Maṣir	مَصِر
Egyptian	Maṣri	مَصْري
eight	thmaanya	ثـمانْيَـة
eleven	da9ash	دَعَـش
embassy	safaara	سَـفـارَة
emergency	is9aaf	إسْـعـاف
employee, official	muwazzaf	مُـوَظَّـف
enough	kaafi	كـافـي
enter, to	khashsh, ykhushsh (DV)	خَـشّ، يْـخُـشّ
	dikhal, yudkhul (RV)	دِخَـل، يُـدْخُـل
envelope	zaruf	ظَـرُف
escape (to)	farr, yfurr (DV)	فَـرّ، يُـفِـرّ
especially	khuṣuuṣan	خُصُـوصاً
Euphrates River (the)	nahar il-Furaat	نَـهَـر الـفُـرات
excellent	mumtaaz	مُـمْـتاز
exchange, change (money)	taṣriif (fluus)	تَـصريـف (فْـلـوس)
excuse/s	9udhur / a9dhaar (S/P)	عُـذر / أعْـذار
excuse me, pardon me	9an idhnak, 9afwan	عَـن إذنَـك، عَـفـواً
expensive	ghaali	غـالـي
inexpensive, cheap	rikhiis	رخـيـص
express mail	bariid sarii9	بَـريد سَـريع

F

falling, fallen (part.)	waagi9	واگِـع
family	ahal, 9eela	أهَـل، عيلَـة
famous, well-known	mashhuur	مَـشْـهور
far	bi9iid	بِـعِـيد
near, close by	giriib, qariib	گِـريب، قَـريب
fat, to make	samman, ysammin (RV)	سَـمَّـن، يُـسَـمِّـن
fat (adj.)	simiin/smaan	سِـمـين / سْـمان
father	ab, waalid	أبْ، والِـد
father of	abu (see Arabic–English section)	أبـو
feast/s, festival/s	9iid / 9yaad (S/P)	عـيد / عْـياد
fed up, to be	zihag	زِهَـگ

fee, rate	ujra	اُجْـرَة
fever	s̲k̲huuna	صُخـونَة
fifteen	k̲hmus-ta9as̲h̲	خْـمُـصْطـعَـشْ
fifty	k̲hamsiin	خَـمْـسـين
fill in, to	mila, yimli (WV)	مِـلا يِـمْـلـي
film	filim	فِـلِـم
financial	maali	مـالـي
find, to	liga, yilgi (WV)	لِـگـا، يِـلْـگـي
fine, okay	myk̲haalif (see Arabic–English section)	مَـيْـخـالِـف
fine, well, good	zeen	زيـن
first	awwal	أوّل
fish	simac̲h	سِـمَـچ
Masguuf fish	simac̲h Masguuf (popular food)	سِـمَـچ مَـسْگـوف
five	k̲hamsa	خَـمْـسَـة
fixing, repairing	tas̲liih	تَـصْـلـيـح
flee, ran away, to	nhizam, yinhizim (RV)	نْـهِـزَم. يِـنْـهِـزِم
flour	t̲ihiin	طِـحـيـن
fly, to	t̲aar, yt̲iir (HV)	طـار. يُـطـيـر
folklore	foliklore	فـولِـكْـلور
folkloric	folikloori / foliklooriyya, s̲h̲a9bi / s̲h̲a9biyya	فـولِـكْـلوري / فـولِـكْـلوريَّـة شَـعْـبي / شَـعْـبِـيَّـة
food	akil	أكِـل
eastern food	akil s̲h̲arqi	أكِـل شَـرْقي
western food	akil g̲harbi	أكِـل غَـرْبي
food dish	akla	أكْـلَـة
food invitation	9aziima	عَـزيـمَة
for, to	li / l- (see Arabic–English section)	لِـ / لْ
for your sake	ilk̲haat̲rak (idiom, see lesson 8)	إلْـخـاطْـرَك
forbidden, illegal	mamnuu9	مَـمْـنـوع
forget, to	nisa, yinsa (WV)	نِـسـا. يِـنْـسَـا
forgive, to	9ifa, yi9fi	عِـفـا. يِـعْـفـي
fork, thorn	s̲h̲ooka	شـوكَـة
form	istimaara	إسْـتِـمـارَة
formal, official	rasmi	رَسْـمي
fortunately, luckily	liḥusn il-ḥazz (idiom, see lesson 9)	لِـحُـسْـن الْـحَـظ

forty	arba9iin	أَرْبَـعـين
foundation, basis	asaas	أَساس
four	arba9a	أَرْبَـعَـة
freedom/s	ḥurriyya / ḥurriyyaat	حُـرِّيَّـة / حُـرِّيَّـات
fried	magli	مَـگْـلي
fried eggs	beeḍ magli	بـيض مَـگْـلي
from	min < mni (preposition)	مِـن > مُـن
from now on	min hissa w jaay (phrase, see lesson 11)	مِـن هِسَّـه وجـايْ
from time to time	min waqit li-waqit (phrase, see lesson 11)	مِـن وَقِـت لِـوَقِـت
fruits	fawaakih	فَـواكِـه
fun, to have	twannas, yitwannas	تْـوَنَّـس، يِـتْـوَنَّـس
fur/s	farwa / farwaat (S/P)	فَـرْوَة / فَـرْوات

G

garden/s	ḥadiiqa / ḥadaayiq (S/P)	حَـديقة / حَـدايِـق
gate	bawaaba	بَـوابَـة
gauge, meter	9addaad	عَـدّاد
general, public	9aam	عـام
gift, present	hadiyya	هَـدِيَّـة
girl, daughter	binit, bnayya	بِـنِـت، بْـنَـيَّـة
girl child	ṭifla	طِـفْـلَـة
give, to	niṭa, yinṭi (WV)	نِـطَـا، يِـنْـطي
glass	glaaṣ	گْـلاص
go, to	raaḥ, yruuḥ (HV)	راحْ، يْـروح
go up, to; to ascend	ṣi9ad, yiṣ9ad (RV)	صِـعَـد، يِـصْـعَـد
God	alla (see lesson 5)	أَللّه
going, going to	raayiḥ, raḥ- (see lesson 13)	رايِـح، رَحْ
good	khoosh (invariable)	خـوش
good, well, fine	zeen, ṭayyib, b-kheer	زين، طَـيِّـب، بْـخير
goodbye	ma9a s-salaama, fiimaanillaa	مَـعَ السَّـلامَـة، فِـيمانِـيلّا
good afternoon/evening	masaaʾ il-kheer	مَـساء الْـخير
good morning	ṣabaaḥ il-kheer	صَـبـاح الْـخير
government/s	ḥukuuma / ḥukuumaat (S/P)	حُـكـومة / حُـكـومات
government official	muwwazzaf ḥukuuma	مُـوَظَّـف حُـكـومَة
grammars	qawaa9id	قَـواعِـد
grandchild	ḥafiid	حَـفـيد

grandfather	jidd	جِدّ
grandmother	jidda	جِدَّة
great, huge	dakhum, 9aziim	ضَخُم، عَظيـم
greeting	tahiyya	تَحِيَّة

H

half	nuss	نُصّ
hall	qaa9a	ساعَة
Hanging Gardens of	ij-Janaaʾin il-Mu9allaqa	إلجَنائـن الْمُعَلَّـقـة
happy	farhaan, sa9iid	فَرْحان، سَـعيد
hard, difficult	sa9ub	صَعُب
has, have	9ind, maal, il- (see lesson 14)	عِنْد، مال، إلْ
have been, to; to become	saar, ysiir (HV)	صار، يُصير
he	huwwa	هُـوَّ
head/s	raas / ruus	راس / روس
health	sihha	صِحَّة
heat, temperature	haraara	حَرارَة
heavy	thigiil / thigiila (M/F)	ثِـگـيـل / ثِـگـيـلة
hello, hi	marhaba	مَرْحَبة
help, to; to assist	saa9ad, ysaa9id (RV)	ساعَد، يُـساعِد
here	hnaa	هُـنا
hide, to	damm, ydumm	ضَـمّ، يُـضُمّ
history	taariikh	تاريـخ
honor	sharaf	شَـرَف
honor, to	sharraf, ysharruf (RV)	شَـرَّف، يُـشَـرُّف
hors d'oeuvres, appetizer	mazza	مَـزّة
hot	haar	حـار
hotel, motel	findiq	فِـنْـدِق
hour, watch	saa9a	ساعَة
house, home	beet	بِـيت
How?	shloon?	شْـلـون؟
How are you?	shloonak?, shloon is-sihha?	شْـلـونَك؟، شْـلون الصّحَة
How do you know?	shmadriik? (idiom, see lesson 4)	شْـمَـدْريك؟
however, any way that	shloon-ma	شْـلـون مَ
How long?	shgadd? (see lesson 15)	شْـگَـدّ؟
no matter how much	shgadd-ma	شَـگَـدّ مَ
How many?	kam, cham? (see lesson 15)	كَـم، چَـم؟
How much?	beesh, ibbeesh?	بِـيـش، إبّـيـش؟

How nice!	a<u>ll</u>aah! (see lesson 5)	أَلـلاه!
huge, great	<u>d</u>a<u>kh</u>um	ضَخُـم
hundred	miyya	مِـيَّـة
hungry	juu9aan	جـوعـان
hunting, hunted	saayid	صـايـد
hurry up	ya<u>ll</u>a (idiom, see lesson 5)	يَـلـّـه
husband, double	zooj, zawj	زوج، زَوْج

I

I	aani (see lesson 2)	آنـي
ice	<u>th</u>alij	ثَـلِـج
idea	fikra	فِـكْـرَة
if	i<u>dh</u>aa, loo (see lesson 19)	إذا، لـو
if I were in your place	loo aani m-makaanak (idiom, see lesson 14)	لـو آنـي مُ مَـكـانك
illegal, forbidden	mamnuu9	مَـمْـنـوع
ill, sick	marii<u>d</u>	مَـريـض
illness, sickness	mara<u>d</u>	مَـرَض
impolite, rude	bala adab (idiom, see lesson 16)	بلا أَدَب
impossible, it can't be	may<u>s</u>iir (idiom, see lesson 13)	مَـيْـصير
it is permitted	may<u>kh</u>aalif (idiom, lesson 13)	مَـيْـخالِـف
in	b- /bi- (see lesson 5)	بْ / بِـ
in front, ahead	giddaam	گِـدّام
in general, generally	bi<u>s</u>uura 9aamma (idiom, see lesson 14)	بِـصورَة عـامَّـة
in particular, specially	bi<u>s</u>uura <u>kh</u>aa<u>ss</u>a (idiom, see lesson 14)	بِـصورَة خـاصَّـة
indebted, to be	mamnuun (idiom, see lesson 10)	مَـمْـنـون
independent pronouns	i<u>d</u>-<u>d</u>amaaʾir il-munfa<u>s</u>ila	إلـضَّـمـائِـر الـمُـنْـفَـصِـلَـة
inexpensive, cheap	ri<u>kh</u>iis	رِخـيـص
information	ma9luumaat	مَـعْـلـومات
inside, underneath	jawwa	جَـوَّه
inspector, reviewer	mufatti<u>sh</u>	مُـفَـتِّـش
interest, to, to please	9ijab, yi9jib (special verb)	عِـجَـب، يـعْـجِـب
international	9aalami	عـالَـمـي
interview/s	muqaabala / muqaabalaat (S/P)	مُـقـابَـلـة / مُـقابَـلات

introduce, to	9arraf, y9arruf (RV)	عَرَّف، يـَعَرُّف
introduction	ta9aaruf	تَعارُف
invite, to	9izam, yi9zim (RV)	عِزَم، يِعْزِم
invoice, bill, account	hsaab	حْساب
Iraq	il-9iraaq	إلْعِراق
Iraqi	9iraaqi	عِراقي
Islam	Islaam	إسْلام
Islamic	Islaami	إسْلامي
Muslim	Muslim	مُسْلِم

J

journalism, press	sahaafa	صَحافَة
journalist	sahafi / sahafiyya (M/F)	صَحَفي / صَحَفِيَة
juice	9asiir	عَصير
jump, to	gumaz, yugmuz (RV)	گُمَز، يُگْمُز

K

key	miftaah	مِفْتاح
kill, to	qital, yuqtul	قِتَل، يُقْتُل
kilometer	keelomatir	كيلومَتِر
knife	sich chiin	سِچّين
know, to	9iraf, yu9ruf (RV)	عِرَف، يُعْرُف
know, to	dira, yidri	دِرَا، يِدْري

L

lady, Mrs.	sayyida	سَيِّدَة
language	lugha	لُغَة
large, big, old	chibiir, kabiir	چِبير، كَبير
later on	ba9deen	بَعْدين
laugh, to	dihak, yid hak (RV)	ضِحَك، يِضْحَك
lazy	kaslaan	كَسْلان
learn, to	t9allam, yit9allam (RV)	تْعَلَّم، يِتْعَلَّم
leather/s, skin/s	jilid /jluud (S/P)	جِلِد / جْلود
leave behind, to	khalla, ykhalli (WV)	خَلّا، يْخَلّي
lesson	daris	دَرِس
let, to	khalla, ykhalli (WV)	خَلّا، يْخَلّي
let us	khaalliina	خَلّينا
letter	risaala	رِسالَة
letter, consonant	haruf	حَرُف
level, degree	daraja	دَرَجَة
library	maktaba	مَكْتَبَة

lie, to	kidhab, yikdhib	كِذَب، يِكْذِب
light	nuur	نـور
lift off, to; carry, to	shaal, yshiil (HV)	شـال، يُـشـيـل
like, similar, such as	mithil	مِـثِـل
like, to; to love	habb, yhibb (DV)	حَـبّ، يْـحِـبّ
line/s	khatt / khutuut (S/P)	خَـط / خُـطـوط
lion	asad, sabi9	أَسَـد، سَـبِـع
Lion of Babylon (ancient)	Asad Baabil	أَسَـد بـابِـل
literature/s	adab / aadaab (S/P)	أَدَبْ / آداب
little	shwayya	شْـوَيَّـة
much, plenty	hwaaya	هُـوايَـه
live, to	9aash, y9iish (HV)	عـاش، يُـعـيـش
live in, to	sikan, yiskun	سِـكَـن، يِـسْـكُـن
look, to; to see	shaaf, yshuuf (HV)	شـاف، يُـشـوف
look, to	baawa9, ybaawi9	بـاوَع، يُـبـاوِع
love	hubb	حُـبّ
love, to; like, to	habb, yhibb (DV)	حَـبّ، يْـحِـبّ
lower, to	nazzal, ynazzil	نَـزِّل، يُـنَـزِّل
lunch	ghada	غَـدَا

M

mail	bariid	بَـريـد
mailbox	sanduuq bariid	صَنْـدوق بَـريـد
mailman	abu l-bariid (see abu)	أبـو الْبَـريـد
make, to	sawwa, ysawwi (WV)	سَـوّا، يُـسـوّي
man	rijjaal, rajul	رِجّـال، رَجُـل
manager/s, director/s	mudiir / mudraaʾ	مَـديـر / مُـدَراء
many, much	hwaaya, kathiir	هُـوايَـه، كَـثيـر
market	suug, suuq	سُـوگ، سـوق
married	mizzawwij	مِـزَّوّج
meat	laham	لَـحَـم
media	i9laam	إعْـلام
medicine/s	diwa / adwiya (S/P)	دِوَا / أُدْوِيَـة
meet, to	gaabal, ygaabul (RV)	گـابَـل، يُـگـابُـل
meeting	ijtimaa9	إجْـتِـمـاع
meeting/s, interview/s	muqaabala / muqaabalaat (S/P)	مُـقـابَـلـة / مُـقـابَـلات
menu	manyo	مَـنْـيـو
military	harbi, 9askari	حَـرْبي، عَـسْكَـري
million	malyoon (see lesson 17)	مَـلْـيـون

minute/s	daqiiqa / daqaayiq	دَقِيقَة / دَقـايـق
misdeed/s, sin/s	<u>d</u>hanib / <u>d</u>hunuub (S/P)	ذَنـِب / ذُنـوب
miss, to; lonesome, to be	mu<u>sh</u>taaq	مُشْتـاق
missed, you were	makaan (ak) <u>kh</u>aali (see lesson 20)	مَكانـَك خالـي
modern	hadii<u>th</u>	حَـديـث
money	fluus, maal	فْلـوس. مـال
Iraqi money	fluus 9iraaqiyya	فْلـوس عِـراقـيـَّة
money orders	hawaala maaliyya	حَـوالـَة مالـيَّة
month	shahar	شَـهَـر
mosque	jaami9	جـامِـع
mother	umm, waalda	أُمّ. والـدَة
morning	sabaah	صَـبـاح
in the morning	sabaahan, is-subuh	صَـبـاحـاً. إلصّـبُـح
Mr./s	sayyid /saada	سَـيِّـد / سـادَة
Mrs., lady	sayyida /sayyidaat	سَـيِّـدَة / سَـيِّـدات
Miss	aanisa / aanisaat	آنِـسَة / آنِـسات
mouth	halig	حَـلِـگ
much, very	hwaaya, ka<u>th</u>iir, jaziilan	هْـوايَه. كَـثـير. جَـزيـلاً
museum	mat<u>h</u>af	مَـتْـحَـف
must, ought to	laazim (invariable)	لازِم

N

name	isim	إسِـم
nation	watan	وَطَـن
national, nationalist	watani	وَطَـنـي
national news	a<u>kh</u>baar mahalliyya	أخْبار مَحَـلّـيَّـة
international news	a<u>kh</u>baar 9aalamiyya	أخْبار عالَـمـيَّـة
near, relative	qariib	قَـريـب
need, to	<u>h</u>taaj, yi<u>h</u>taaj (WV)	حْتـاج. يِـحْتـاج
needle/s	ubra / ubar (S/P)	أُبْـرَة / أُبَـر
neither expensive nor cheap	laa <u>gh</u>aali wala ri<u>kh</u>iis (idiom, see lesson 4)	لا غـالـي ولا رِخـيـص
nephew	ibin a<u>kh</u> (brother's side)	إبـن أُخ
	ibin u<u>kh</u>ut (sister's side)	إبـن أُخُـت
new	jidiid	جـديـد
newspaper/s	<u>s</u>ahiifa / <u>s</u>uhuf (S/P)	صَحيفة / صُحَـف
	jariida / jaraayid	جَـريـدَة / جَـرايـد
next to, adjacent	yamm	يَـمّ
niece	binit a<u>kh</u> (brother's side)	بِـنِـت أُخ

	binit ukhut (sister's side)	بِنِت أُخُت
nice, pretty, sweet	hilu	حِلو
night	leel	لِيل
at night	bil-leel	بِالْلِيل
nine	tis9a	تِسْعَة
Nineveh	Naynawa (the Assyrian capital)	نَيْنَوى
no	laa / la- (see lesson 4)	لا / لَ
no hope, no cure	maaku chaara (see lesson 18)	ماكُو چارَة
no need for	maaku luzuum (idiom, see lesson 16)	ماكُو لُزوم
noon	zuhur	ظُهُر
at noon	iz-zuhur	إلظُّهُر
nor, and not	wala (see lesson 4)	ولا
normal, usual, regular	9aadi	عادي
not	maa, muu (see lesson 4)	ما، مو
not bad, so-so	laa shiish wala kabaab (idiom, lesson 4)	لا شِيش ولا كَباب
note, remark	mulaahaza	مُلاحَظَة
now, right this moment	hissa (invariable, see lesson 13)	هِسَّه
number/s, numeral/s	raqam /arqaam	رَقَم / أرْقام

O

occasion, opportunity	fursa	فُرْصَة
of course	tab9an, bit-tabu9	طَبْعاً، بِالطَّبُع
off, short of	illa (telling time)	إلّ
five to ten (time)	is-saa9a sitta illa 9ashra	إلسّاعَة سِتّة إلّ عَشْرَة
office	maktab	مَكْتَب
officer	daabut	ضابُط
official, employee	muwazzaf	مُوَظَّف
okay, all right, fine	tayiib, maykhaalif	طَيِّب، مَيْخالِف
okra	baamya	بامْيَة
old, ancient	qadiim, 9atiig	قَديم، عَتيگ
old (person), large, big	chibiir, kabiir	چِبير، كَبير
on, upon	9ala (see lesson 14)	عَلى
once, one time	marra	مَرَّة
one	waahid (number)	واحِد

one, someone	aḥḥad	أَحَّد
onion	buṣal	بُـصَل
one onion	raas buṣal	راس بُـصَل
only	faqat, bass	فَـقَـط. بَـسّ
open, to	fitaḥ, yiftaḥ (RV)	فِـتَـح. يِـفْـتَـح
operation/s, surgery/s	9amaliyya / 9amaliyyaat	عَـمَـلِـيَّة / عَـمَـلِـيَّات
or	loo, aw	لـو. أَوْ
orchard	bistaan	بِـسْـتَـان
orchard keeper	bistanchi (see lesson 7)	بِـسْـتَـنْـچي
order	amur	أَمُـر
origin	aṣil	أَصِل
original	aṣli	أَصْـلي

P

package	ruzma	رُزْمَـة
pain/s	alam / aalaam	أَلَـم / آلام
	wija9 / awjaa9	وِجَـع. أَوْجاع
palace	qaṣir	قَـصِر
passport	baasbort, jawaaz	بـاسْـبـورت. جَـواز
patience	ṣabur	صَـبُـر
Peace be upon you (greeting)	as-salaamu 9alaykum	ألسَّـلامُ عَـلَـيْـكُـم
And peace be upon you (in reply)	wa 9alaykum is-salaam	وعَـلَـيْـكُـم السَّـلام
pen, pencil	qalam	قَـلَـم
penny	filis	فِـلِـس
people	sha9ab	شَـعَـب
pepper	filfil	فِـلْـفِـل
perhaps, may	balkat, balki (see lesson 17)	بَـلْـكَـتْ. بَـلْـكي
period of time, while	mudda	مُـدَّة
person	shakhiṣ	شَـخِـص
person in charge	masᵓuul	مَـسْـئـول
personal, private	shakhṣi	شَـخْـصي
personality	shakhṣiyya	شَـخْـصِـيَّة
pharmacist	ṣaydali	صَـيْـدَلي
pharmacy	ṣaydaliyya	صَـيْـدَلِـيَّة
pilot (of a plane)	ṭayyaar	طَـيّـار
pinch, to	giraṣ, yugruṣ (RV)	گِـرَص. يُـگْـرُص
place	maḥall	مَـحَـل
plate, dish	maa9uun	ماعـون
play, to	li9ab, yil9ab (RV)	لِـعَـب. يِـلْـعَـب

please	rajaa°an (also see tfaddal, lesson 2)	رَجـاءً
pleasure	suruur	سُــرور
with pleasure	bikull suruurp	بِـكُـل سَـرور
plenty, much	hwaaya	هُـوايَـه
P.M. (afternoon)	ba9d iz-zuhur	بَـعْـد الظُّـهُر
pocket	jeeb	جِـيــب
political	siyaasi / siyaasiyya	سِـياسـي / سِـياسـيّة
politics	siyaasa	سِـياسَـة
postage	taabi9 bariid	طابِـع بَـريد
postcard	boskaart	بوسْـكـارْت
postman	boostachi (see lesson7)	بـوسْـطَـچـي
post office	bariid, maktab bariid	بَـريد، مَكْـتَب بَـريد
praise God	ilhamdu lillaa(h) (see lesson 5)	إلْـحَـمْـدُ لله
prescription	wasfa	وَصْـفَـة
present (adj.)	haadir, mawjuud	حـاضِـر، مَـوْجـود
present, gift	hadiyya	هَـدِيّـة
press, journalism	sahaafa	صَحـافَـة
journalist	sahafi / sahafiyya (M/F)	صَحَـفـي / صَحَـفِـيَـة
pretty, nice, sweet	hilu	حِـلـو
price, rate	si9ir	سِـعِـر
prince/s	amiir / umaraa° (S/P)	أمـير / أُمَـراء
private	khaas	خـاص
privately	khusuusi	خُـصُـوصي
procession	mawkib	مَـوْكِـب
Procession Street (in Babylon)	Shaari9 il-Mawkib	شـارِع الْـمَـوْكِـب
professor	ustaadh	أُسْـتــاذ
program/s	barnaamij / baraamij	بَـرْنامِج / بَـرامِج
pronoun, conscience	damiir	ضَـمـير
pull, to	sihab, yis hab	سِـحَـب، يِسْحَـب
purse, suitcase, luggage	junta	جُـنْـطَـة
put, to	hatt, yhutt (DV)	حَـط، يْـحُط

Q

quarter	rubu9	رُبُـع

R

radio	raadyo	رادْيـو
radio station/s	idhaa9a / idhaa9aat (S/P)	إذاعَـة / إذاعات

rate, price	ujra, si9ir	أُجـرَة، سِـعِـر
read, to	qira, yiqra (WV)	قِـرَا، يِـقـرَا
ready, present	haadir	حـاضِـر
really, definitely	walla (idiom, see lesson 5)	والله
reason/s	sabab / asbaab	سَـبَـب / أسْـبـاب
receipt	wasil	وَصِـل
red	ahmar	أحْـمَـر
registered	musajjal	مُـسَـجَّـل
registered letter	risaala musajjala	رسـالـة مَسَـجَّـلَـة
regular, usual	9aadi	عـادي
regular letter	risaala 9aadiyya	رسـالة عـادِيَّـة
relative, near	qariib	قَـريـب
relative (in-law)	nasiib	نَـسـيـب
religion/s	diin / adyaan (S/P)	ديـن / أدْيـان
religious	diini / diiniyya (M/F adj.)	ديـنـي / ديـنـيَّـة
remark, note	mulaahaza	مُـلاحَـظَـة
rent, to; to lease	ajjar, yᵓajjir (RV)	أجَّـر، يَـأجِّـر
repair, to	sallah, ysallih (RV)	صَلَّـح، يُـصَلِّـح
repairing, fixing	tasliih	تَـصْـلـيـح
reporter, correspondent	muraasil / muraasila (M/F)	مُـراسِـل / مُـراسِـلـة
reserve, to	hijaz, yihjiz (RV)	حِـجَـز، يِـحْـجِـز
reservation	hajiz	حَـجِـز
reside, to; to live	sikan, yiskun (RV)	سِـكَـن، يِـسْـكُـن
residing	saakin	سـاكِـن
rested, content	mirtaah	مِـرْتـاح
rest, sit down (imp. verb)	(i)stariih	إسْـتَـريـح
restaurant	mat9am	مَـطْـعَـم
rice	timman, ruzz	تِـمَّـن، رُزّ
right, everything in its place	kullshi b-makaana (idiom, see lesson 16)	كُـلْـشي بُ مَكـانَـة
river	nahar	نَـهَـر
room	ghurfa	غُـرْفَـة
rope/s	habil / hbaal (S/P)	حَـبِـل / حُـبـال
ruin	athar	أثَـر

S

salad	zalaata	زَلاطَـة
salesman	bayyaa9	بَـيّـاع
saleswoman	bayyaa9a	بَـيّـاعَـة
salt	milih	مِـلِـح

salty	maaliḥ	مـالِـح
saved, to be	nija, yinji (WV)	نْجَا، يِـنْجَا
search, to	dawwar, ydawwir (HV)	دَوَّر، يُـدَوِّر
season, chapter	faṣil	فَـصِـل
scene, view	manẓar	مَـنْـظَـر
school	madrasa	مَـدْرَسَـة
second	thaani	ثـاني
second (time)	thaanya	ثـانْـيَـة
section/s, division/s, department/s	qisim / aqsaam (S/P)	قِـسِـم / أقْـسـام
see, to; to look	shaaf, yshuuf (HV)	شـاف، يُـشـوف
self, being, soul	nafis	نَـفِـس
sell, to	baa9, ybii9 (HV)	بـاع، يُـبـيـع
sent, to	dazz, ydizz (DV)	دَزّ، يُـدِزّ
service	khidma	خِـدْمَـة
seven	sab9a	سَـبْـعَـة
shall, will, going to	raḥ- (prefix, see lesson 12)	رَحْ
shame on you	9eeb 9aleek (idiom, see lesson 15)	عيب عليك
she	hiyya	هِـيَّ
sheep, lamb/s	ṭili / ṭilyaan (S/P)	طِـلِـي / طِـلْـئِـيان
shoe	qundara	قُـنْـدَرَة
shoe repairman	qundarchi (see lesson 7)	قُـنْـدَرُچي
shop, store	dukkaan	دُكـان
show, to	shawwaf, yshawwif	شَـوَّف، يُـشَـوِّف
shut, to; to close	sadd, ysidd (DV)	سَـدّ، يُـسِـدّ
sick, ill	mariiḍ / mariiḍa / marḍaa	مَـريض / مَـريضة / مَـرْضى
sign, to	waqqa9, ywaqqi9 (RV)	وَقَّـع، يُـوَقّـع
signature	tawqii9	تَـوْقـيـع
sister	ukhut	أخُـت
similar, like, such as	mithil	مِـثِـل
sit!	(i)stariiḥ	إسْـتَـريح
please sit down	tfaḍḍal istariiḥ	تَـفَـضّـل إسْـتَـريح
sit down, to	gi9ad, yug9ud (RV)	گِـعَـد، يُـگْـعُـد
six	sitta	سِـتَّـة
skin/s, leather/s	jilid /jluud (S/P)	جِـلِـد / جُـلـود
sleep, to	naam, ynaam (HV)	نـام، يُـنـام
small	saghiir	صَـغـيـر
small change	khurda	خُـرْدَة
soap	saabuun (collective)	صابون

soap vender	saabun<u>ch</u>i (see lesson7)	صابُنْچي
something, thing	<u>sh</u>ii	شِي
son	ibin	إبِن
sorry (to be)	mit'assif, 9afwan	مِتْأسِف، عَفْواً
soup	<u>sh</u>oorba	شورْبَة
speak, to; to talk	<u>h</u>i<u>ch</u>a, yih <u>ch</u>i (WV)	حِجَا، يِحْچي
	tkallam, yitkallam (RV)	تْكَلَّم، يِتْكَلَّم
special, private	<u>kh</u>aa<u>s</u>, <u>kh</u>u<u>s</u>uu<u>s</u>i	خاص، خُصوصي
speech, talk	kalaam, <u>h</u>a<u>ch</u>i	كَلام، حَچي
spoon	<u>kh</u>aa<u>sh</u>uuga, mil9aqa	خاشوﮔَة، مِلْعَقَة
stand up, to; to stop	wigaf, yoogaf (RV)	وﮔَف، يوﮔَف
stand, to	gaam, yguum	ﮔام، يْﮔوم
stamp	<u>t</u>aabi9	طابِع
postal stamp	<u>t</u>aabi9 bariid	طابِع بَريد
station	ma<u>h</u>a<u>tt</u>a	مَحَطَّة
stay, to	buqa, yubqa (WV)	بُقا، يُبْقا
staying (part.)	baaqi, naazil (in a hotel)	باقي، نازِل
stomach/s	mi9da / mi9ad	مِعْدَة / مِعَد
story/s, tale/s	qu<u>ss</u>a / qu<u>s</u>a<u>s</u> (S/P)	قُصَّة / قُصَص
street	<u>sh</u>aari9	شارِع
student	<u>t</u>aalib	طالِب
study, to	diras, yudrus (RV)	دِرَس، يُدْرُس
sugar	<u>sh</u>akar	شَكَر
sugar vendor	<u>sh</u>akarchi (see lesson 7)	شَكَرْچي
suitcase, purse, luggage	jun<u>t</u>a	جُنْطَة
Sumer	Soomar (ancient land in Iraq)	سُومَر
Sumerians	Soomariyyiin (ancient people)	سُومَرِيِّين
surprised, to be	t9ajjab, yit9ajjab	تْعَجَّب، يِتْعَجَّب
sweet, nice, pretty	<u>h</u>ilu	حِلو
sweets (candy and pastry)	<u>h</u>alawiyyaat	حَلَوِيّات
Swiss	Swiisri	سْويسْري
Switzerland	Swiisra	سْويسْرا
symptom	a9raa<u>d</u>	أعْراض

T

table	meez, man<u>d</u>ada	ميز، مَنْضَدَة
table (list), chart	jadwal	جَدْوَل
take!	haak	هاك

take it easy	9ala keefak (idiom, see lesson 3)	على كـيـفـَك
take, to	akhadh, yaakhudh (RV)	أخَـذ، يـاخُـذ
take care, watch out	diir baalak (idiom, see lesson 7)	ديـر بـالـَك
talk, speech	kalaam	كـَلام
talk, to; to speak	tkallam yitkallam (RV, see above)	تْـكـَلـَّم، يِـتْـكـَلـَّم
taxi	taksi	تـَكـِسي
taxi driver	saayiq taksi, abu t-taksi	سايـِق تـَكـْسـي، أبو التـَّكـسي
tea	chaay	چـايْ
tea glass	(i)stikaan chaay	إسْـتـِكـان چـايْ
tea vender	chaaychi (see lesson 7)	چـايْـچـي
telephone, to	khaabar, ykhaabur (RV)	خـابـِر، يُـخابـُر
telephone/s	talifoon / talifoonaat (S/P)	تـَلِـفـون / تـَلِـفـونات
ground telephone	talifoon ardi	تـَلِـفـون ارْضـي
mobile/cell telephone	talifoon moobaayal	تـَلِـفـون موبـايَـل
telephone operator/s	baddaala / baddaalaat (S/P)	بَـدّالة / بَـدّالات
televisions	talfizyoon	تـَلـْفِـزْيـون
tell, mound	tall	تـَلّ
teller, cashier	sarraaf	صَـرّاف
temple	ma9bad	مَـعْـبَـد
ten	9ashra	عَـشْـرَة
thank you, thanks	shukran	شُـكـْراً
thank, to	shikar, yushkur (RV)	شِـكـَر، يُـشْـكـُر
thanks be to God	nushkur alla, ilhamdu lillaah (phrase, see lesson 5)	نُـشْـكـُر اللّه، إلْـحَـمْـدُ لله
then, in that case	la9ad (see lesson 12)	لَـعَـد
there	hnaak	هُـناك
there is/are	aku (see lesson 6)	أكـو
these	hadhoola	هَـذولـة
these days	hal-ayyaam (idiom, see lesson 12)	هَـلأيّـام
they	humma	هُـمـّه
thing, something	shii	شِـي
think, to	fakkar, yfakkir (RV)	فَـكـَّر، يُـفَـكـِّر
third	thaalith (ordinal)	ثـالـِث
third (one)	thilith	ثـِلـِث
thousand	alif	ألِـف

threaten, to	haddad, yhaddid	هَـدَّد، يُـهَـدّد
three	tlaatha	ثَلاثَة
throw, to	rima, yirmi	رمَا، يِـرْمي
ticket	tadhkara, biṭaaqa	تَـذكَـرَة، بِـطاقَـة
Tigris River	nahar Dijla	نَـهَر دِجْـلَـة
thirsty	9aṭshaan	عَـطْـشان
this	haadha (see lesson 14)	هاذا
time	waqit	وَقِت
tin	tanak	تَـنَك
tinsmith	tanakchi (see lesson 7)	تَـنَكْـچـي
tired	ta9baan	تَـعْـبان
tired, to be	ti9ab, yit9ab (RV)	تِـعَب، يِتْـعَب
to, for, in order to	li- / l- (see lesson 14)	لِـ / لُ
together	siwiyya	سِـوِيَّه
toilet (bathroom)	mirhaad	مِـرْحاض
tomatoes	ṭamaaṭa	طَـماطَة
tomorrow	baachir	باچِـر
tongue/s	lisaan	لِـسان
too, also	hamm	هَـمّ
tooth	sinn	سِـنّ
tour, tourism, touristic	siyaaha, siyaahi	سِـياحَة، سِـياحي
Tower of Babylon	Burij Baabil	بُـرج بـابـل
town, city	madiina	مَـدينَـة
translation/s	tarjama / tarjamaat (S/P)	تَـرْجَـمَة / تَـرْجَمات
translation section	qisim tarjama	قِـسِـم تَـرْجَمة
translator/s	mutarjim / mutarjimiin	مُـتَـرْجِـم / مُـتَـرْجِـمـين
travel, to	saafar, ysaafir (RV)	سـافَـر، يُـسافِـر
traveling, traveler	musaafir	مُـسافِـر
trip, travel	safra	سَـفْـرَة
good trip	safra sa9iida	سَـفْـرَة سَـعـيدة
true, correct	ṣahiih	صَحـيـح
turn around, to	indaar, yindaar	إنْـدار، يِـنْـدار
twelve	thna9ash	ثْـنـاعَـش
two	thneen	ثْـنـيـن
type/s, kind/s	noo9 / anwaa9	نوع / أنْـواع

U

uncle	khaal	خـال
unfortunately	lisuuʾ il-hazz (idiom, see lesson 9)	لِـسـوءُ الْـحَـظ
universe, world	9aalam	عالَـم

university	jaami9a	جـامَـعَـة
upon, on	9ala (see lesson 15)	عَـلـى
usual, regular, normal	9aadi	عـادي

V

vegetables	khudrawaat	خُـضْـرَوات
verb	fi9il	فِـعِـل
very	kullish (invariable)	كُـلِّـش
very much	jaziilan (invariable)	جَـزيـلاً
view, scene	manzar	مَـنْـظَـر
visa	fiiza	فِـيـزة
visit	ziyaara	زيـارَة
visit, to	zaar, yzuur (HV)	زار، يْـزور
vowel	haruf 9illa (also see haruf)	حَـرُف عِـلَّـة

W

walk, to; to travel	misha, yimshi (WV)	مِـشَـا، يِـمْـشي
take a walk, to; stroll, to	yitmashsha	يِـتْـمَـشَّـى
walking, traveling (part.)	maashi	مـاشـي
want, to; to wish	raad, yriid (HV)	راد، يْـريـد
war	harub	حَـرُب
warm	daafi	دافـي
was/were	chaan (see lesson 13)	چـان
watch, clock, hour	saa9a	سـاعَـة
water	mayy	مَـيّ
we	ihna	إحْـنـا
wealth	maal (see lesson 14)	مـال
weather, climate	jaww	جَـوّ
week	usbuu9	أُسْـبـوع
welcome	ahlan wa sahlan	أَهْـلاً وسَهْـلاً
well/s	biir / byaara (S/P)	بـيـر / بْـيـارَة
well, oh, so	ya9ni	يَـعْـنـي
well-being	zeen, b-kheer	زيـن، بْـخـيـر
well known, famous	mashhuur	مَـشْـهـور
western	gharbi	غَـرْبـي
what?	shunu? (see lesson 15)	شْـنـو؟
what did you think?	sh9abaalak? (idiom, see lesson 7)	شْـعَـبـالَـك؟
what is happening?	shaku maaku? (idiom, see lesson 2)	شَـكـو مـاكـو؟

whatever	shunu-ma, sh-ma (see lesson 20)	شُ مَ
when	min (see lesson 20)	مِــن
when?	shwakit? (see lesson 15)	شْـوَكِــت؟
when, at the time	lamman (see lesson 20)	لَــمَّــن
whenever	shwakit-ma (ee lesson 20)	شْـوَكِــت مَ
where?	ween?	وِيــن؟
where have you been ?	haay ween? (idiom, see lesson 3)	هـايْ ويــن؟
where from?	immeen, mneen?	إمْـمـيـن، مُـنـيـن؟
wherever	ween-ma (see lesson 20)	وين مَ
from wherever	mneen-ma (see lesson 20)	مُـنـيـن مَ
while	been-ma (see lesson 20)	بيــن مَ
who, whom, which, that	illi (relative clause, lesson 19)	إلْـلـي
who?	minu?	مِـنـو؟
whoever	minu-ma (see lesson 20)	مِـنـو مَ
whom?	ilman?	إلْـمَـن؟
whose?	maalman?	مـالْـمَـن؟
why?	leesh, ilweesh?	لـيـش، إلْـوِيـش؟
wife	zooja, zawja	زوجَـة، زَوْجَـة
will, shall, going to	rah-, ha- (see lesson 12)	رَحْ، حَـ
wine	nabiidh	نَـبـيـذ
window	shubbaach	شُـبّـاچ
with, have	ma9a	مَـعَ
with all	bikull	بِـكُـل
with pleasure	bikull suruur, 9ala 9eeni, 9ala raasi (see lesson 6)	بِـكُـل سُـرور، عَلى عيني، عَـلى راسي
with your permission	9an idhnak	عَـن إذنَـك
without	biduun	بِـدون
wolf/s	dhiib / dhyaaba (S/P)	ذيـب / ذيـابَـة
woman/women	mara/niswaan	مَـرَة / نِـسْـوان
world, universe	9aalam	عـالَـم
wrong	ghalat	غَـلَـط

X

Y

| year | sana | سَـنَـة |
| yellow | asfar | أصْـفَـر |

yes	na9am, ii	نَعَـم، يِـي
yogurt	liban	لِـبَـن
you	inta / inti / intu (M/F/P)	إنْت / إنْتي / إنْتو

Z

zero	ṣifir	صِفِـر
ziggurat	zaqquura	زقّـورَة